Coolie Ships of The Chinese Diaspora
1846 - 1874
John Asome
Proverse Hong Kong
2020

Proverse Hong Kong fully supports freedom of artistic expression. The statements, views and opinions expressed in this work as a whole are those of the author alone. The views and opinions expressed in the Foreword are those of the Foreword writer alone. In neither case, does the content represent the stand of Proverse Hong Kong, any person related to Proverse Hong Kong, or that of any other person named in this text.

Care has been taken to respect the rights of all. If there has been any omission, remedy will be made in any revised edition in due course if information is received.

JOHN ASOME was born in Hong Kong and educated in Hong Kong and Australia. His working life has been spent in the UK and Australia, with many years at sea. His first position—as a Radio Officer for the China Navigation Company—took him throughout East Asia, from China and Japan to Thailand and Indonesia, as well as to Papua New Guinea and Australia. Later, after some years spent in different positions in the UK, he had four years in the Royal Fleet Auxiliary Service (RFA)—the civilian arm of the Royal Navy—and served on ships based in Malta and Singapore as well as on patrol duties in the West Indies and both East and West Africa. When he retired, John pursued his interest in the Chinese diaspora—stirred first by finding Chinese people in many of the places he visited—and the related topic of the indentured trade to Cuba, Peru and the West Indies. This has taken him to various archival collections in the UK, and to many online encounters. He has communicated with many scholars in the field and been published on the subject in the *Journal of the Royal Asiatic Society Hong Kong*.

BETWEEN 1846 AND 1874, OVER 290,000 CHINESE were embarked as indentured labourers destined mainly for Peru, Cuba and the British, French and Dutch West Indies. Of these, 15.13% did not reach their destination.

The demand for labour was high. Among the poor, penniless and destitute of southern China, the search for remunerated work was also high. When demand outran the initial willing supply, trickery and misrepresentation, even kidnapping, came to be used in obtaining recruits. These were among the several factors contributing to onboard suicides, attempted insurrections and successful mutinies when captains and some crew were killed or tortured, ships set on fire and sometimes entirely destroyed. There were also occurrences when recruits signed on, intent on piracy, which was occasionally successful.

Authorities in the ports of departure introduced legislation to counter abuses. Receiving countries also introduced legislation related to imported labour.

In this study, John Asome provides data on 732 voyages and commentary on a good number of these. As an expert in the field, Walton Look Lai, says, John Asome has filled, "an enormous gap in our knowledge of the Chinese coolie trade....He has enabled readers and future scholars to distinguish fact from myth, reality from exaggeration, in the understanding of this vast and complex experience."

COOLIE SHIPS
of the
CHINESE DIASPORA
1846 - 1874

John Asome

A Proverse Prize Finalist 2019

Proverse Hong Kong

Coolie Ships of the Chinese Diaspora (1846 - 1874)
by John Asome
Alternate first edition published in paperback in Hong Kong
by Proverse Hong Kong, under sole and exclusive licence,
November 2020.
ISBN-13: 978-988-8491-99-5

First edition published in paperback in Hong Kong
by Proverse Hong Kong, under sole and exclusive licence,
November 2020.
ISBN-13: 978-988-8491-98-8
Copyright © John Asome 2020

Enquiries to:
Proverse Hong Kong, P.O. Box 259, Tung Chung Post Office,
Lantau, NT, Hong Kong SAR, China.
Email: proverse@netvigator.com;
Web: www.proversepublishing.com

The right of John Asome to be identified
as the author of this work
has been asserted by him in accordance with
the Copyright, Designs and Patents Act 1988.
Cover design by Artist Hong Kong.
Cover photo, American clipper ship, *Kate Hooper*,
courtesy the Dacre Smyth family.

All rights reserved. No part of this publication may be reproduced, stored in a retrieval system, or transmitted, in any form or by any means, electronic, mechanical, photocopying, recording or otherwise, without the prior written permission of the publisher or publisher and author. The book is sold subject to the condition that it shall not, by way of trade or otherwise, be lent, re-sold, hired out or otherwise circulated without the author's prior written consent in any form of binding or cover other than that in which it is published and without a similar condition including this condition being imposed on the subsequent owner or purchaser. Please contact Proverse Hong Kong (acting as agent for the author) in writing, to request any and all permissions (including but not restricted to republishing, inclusion in anthologies, translation, reading, performance and use as set pieces in examinations and festivals).

British Library Cataloguing in Publication Data
A catalogue record is available
from the British Library

Coolie Ships of the Chinese Diaspora (1846-1874)
John Asome

CONTENTS

List of Tables	7
Table of Illustrations and Figures	10
Acknowledgements	11
Foreword by Walton Look Lai	13
Preface	15
Introduction	19
In Search Of Labour	31
Peruvian Migration: The First Phase	59
Britain Enters The Trade	79
Cuban Allocations	109
Spanish Free Importation	151
Canton Becomes An Emigration Port	173
Ships For The West Indies	193
Peruvian Focus On Macao	221
Cuba Overwhelms Macao	253
The Final Years	273
Coolie Shipping In Review	319
Envoi	358

Appendices

I. The coolie master's log on the *Forest Eagle*	359
II. Summary of Macao Regulations	365
III. Departures for Peru	401
IV. Departures for Cuba	405
V. Departures for the West Indies	417
VI. Departures for Australia	420
VII. Departures for other Destinations	421
Glossary	422
Abbreviations	424

Editorial Practices 425
Bibliography 427
Notes 438
Index 447

Picture Acknowledgements

Gillian and Verner Bickley collection for 'Guano Bed Mining, Chincha Islands, 1875. By T Taylor. Fx Barbant, J.C.' and 'Loading lighters with guano from chutes'; both photographed by Gardner, Washington, D.C.; *Grace's Guide to British Industrial History* for 'Auxiliary steamer, *Glensannox*'; HSBC for 'General View of Hong Kong', photograph by William Pryor Floyd; Macao Museum of Art for 'Inner Harbour, Macau'; Martyn Gregory Gallery, London for photographs of the following paintings: 'Amoy c. 1865. Chinese artist'; 'Hong Kong, c. 1850. Chinese artist'; 'Macao: Praya Grande, early 1870s. Chinese artist'; 'Whampoa, c. 1850. Chinese artist'; National Library of Australia for the section from 'Chart of the World'; National Maritime Museum, Greenwich, London, for 'Callao harbour'; State Library of Victoria, Australia, for British ship, *Blenheim* (David Little Postcard Collection H27568/40); and British clipper ship, *Light Brigade* (Brodie Collection LaTrobe Picture Collection 92220 1982).

The following are in the public domain: 'Swatow Harbour', photograph by Lai Afong; *Challenge* (Library of Congress); Labourer's contract in Chinese and Labourer's contract in Spanish (both courtesy Kathleen López); 'Amoy Harbour', photograph by John Thomson; *Dolores Ugarte* (Wikicommons); 'Barracoons at Macao' and 'Coolies Embarking,' (*Harper's New Monthly Magazine*. v. 29 (June-Nov 1864)); 'Whampoa from Dane's Island', c. 1843, drawn by Thomas Allom, from a sketch by Lieut. White, Royal Marines. Engraved by William Pryor Floyd (https://commons.wikimedia.org/wiki/File:Whampoa_from_Danes_Island.jpg); Havana harbour, Cuba; Kingston harbour, Jamaica; Port of Callao, Peru.

Tables

10.1	Macao recruits (and brokers punished).	303
11.1	Shipments from various departure ports, together with the numbers embarked and landed.	319
11.2	Shipments from Amoy, 1846-1869, showing the number of shipments, numbers embarked and landed and the percentage who died.	320
11.3	Shipments from Swatow, 1852-1866, showing the number of shipments, numbers embarked and landed, the percentage who died and notes on mutinies and shipwrecks.	321
11.4	Shipments from Cumsingmoon, 1849-1854, showing the number of shipments, the numbers embarked and landed, the percentage who died, with notes on mutinies, etc.	322
11.5	Shipments from Whampoa, 1852-1873, showing the number of shipments, the numbers embarked and landed, the percentage who died, with notes on mutinies, etc.	323
11.6	Indentured coolie labour shipments from Hong Kong, 1848-1870, showing the number of shipments, the numbers embarked and landed, the percentage who died, with notes on mutinies, etc.	324
11.7	Shipments from Macao, 1851-1874, showing the number of shipments, the number of Agents involved, the numbers embarked and landed, the percentage who died, with notes on mutinies and shipwrecks.	325
11.8	Ship arrivals from various ports, the number embarked, number of agents used, number and percentage successfully landed.	327
11.9	Shipments to Cuba, 1847-1873, showing the number of shipments, the numbers embarked and landed, the percentage who died, the	329

	passengers per ton ratio and the average number of days per voyage.	
11.10	Active years of Cuban consignees and their principal agents, 1852-1873, the number of shipments undertaken, the numbers embarked and landed and the percentage who died.	331
11.11	Shipments to Peru, 1849-1874, showing the number of shipments, the numbers embarked and landed, the percentage who died, the passengers per ton ratio and the average number of days per voyage.	334
11.12	Active years of Peruvian consignees and their principal agents, 1849-1874, the number of shipments undertaken, the numbers embarked and landed and the percentage who died.	336
11.13	Shipments to the West Indies, 1852-1873, showing the number of shipments, the numbers embarked and landed, the percentage who died, the passengers per ton ratio and the average number of days per voyage.	339
11.14	Active years of West Indian principals and their agents and the numbers each recruited.	340
11.15	National flags used by ship type with minimum, maximum and average tonnages.	343
11.16	Dedicated coolie ships, their tonnages and number of voyages undertaken, the numbers embarked and landed and the percentage who died.	344
11.17	Successful mutinies, showing ships' flags, departure ports and dates, intended destinations and notes on the fate of captains and vessels.	347
11.18	Unsuccessful insurrections, showing ships' flags, departure ports and dates, intended destinations and notes on causes, results and times of occurrence.	348-9
11.19	Longest serving Captains, the number of voyages undertaken, their primary ship, the numbers they embarked and landed together	351

	with the average mortality rate over all voyages.	
11.20	National flags of vessels used for voyages to Cuba, Peru, the West Indies and other ports.	353
11.21	Mortality by national vessel flag, showing the number of voyages undertaken, average tonnages, total numbers embarked, passengers per ton ratio, average days per voyage and average mortality.	356

Illustrations and Figures

Hong Kong. Departure port, 1848-1870.	18
Departure ports of the Chinese coolie trade.	20
Swatow harbour. Departure port, 1852-1866.	30
Labourer's contract in Chinese.	58
Macao inner harbour. Departure port, 1851-1874.	78
Callao harbour. Destination port, 1852-1866.	78
Amoy harbour. Departure port, 1846-1869.	108
Blenheim	150
"Barracoons at Macao."	171
Labourer's contract in Spanish.	172
Whampoa. Departure port, 1852-1873.	192
Light Brigade	220
Dolores Ugarte	251
Guano bed mining, Chincha Islands.	252
Loading lighters with guano from chutes.	252
Challenge	272
Peru	318
"Coolies Embarking".	357
Glensannox	437

PLATES

Chart of the World. Section, showing Hong Kong, Macau, Callao, Cuba, the West Indies.	1
Hong Kong. Departure port, 1848-1870.	2
Macao Praya Grande. Departure port, 1851-1874.	3
Whampoa. Departure port, 1852-1873.	4
Amoy. Departure port, 1846-1869.	5
Havana harbour, Cuba. Destination port, 1847-1873.	6
Kingston harbour, Jamaica. Destination port, 1852-54; 1858-1884.	7
Port of Callao, Peru. Destination port 1852-1874.	8

Acknowledgements

The unsung heroes of researchers must be those anonymous people who laboriously transcribe illegible handwriting of original documents into clear typeset. Their contribution must be acknowledged with deep gratitude. I know how much time can be spent in trying to read hand-written script in the old style, especially on a dull microfilm reader with little or no desktop space to place your notes.

The National Library of Australia Manuscript Collection was a major source of valuable material. Anya Dettman so kindly waded through the massive Braga Collection on matters pertaining to Macao. Anya was responsible for the Library acquiring new copies of the Macao Government's official Boletim, and then ensuring that I had access to both the hard copy and microform collections by way of the wonderful Inter Library Loan system in Australia.

The National Archives at Kew expanded on the Colonial Office microform collections held by the Central Library in Hong Kong. How one could go through the Colonial Office files without Elizabeth Sinn's comprehensive Index of CO 129 is incomprehensible to me. Many thanks must be paid to her.

After Jardine Matheson gave permission to peruse their archives at Cambridge University, the Library Manuscript Collection provided interesting backgrounding into how shipping was conducted in early Hong Kong. My thanks go to Betty Schopmeyer of the Penobscot Marine Museum who kindly had the coolie master's Log of the *Forest Eagle* copied for me. Picture credits are also due to the Dacre Smyth family for use of the painting of the *Kate Hooper*.

In my many attempts to gather information on the internet, Andreas von Mach of Munich has been most generous in sharing his deep knowledge of, and web links to, merchant shipping of the 1850s. They have been invaluable in verifying details of the ships mentioned in this book. Thank you Andreas. Many thanks also to Tony Yip for his helpful advice on the texts in Spanish and Chinese of a Cuban indentured contract.

Of all the people who have encouraged me along the way, I especially thank Helen Atteck in St Catharines, Ontario. Her faith in my attempts to become an author has been my sustenance. Through her kind intervention, the preeminent authority on the Chinese in the West Indies, Walton Look Lai, has very kindly favoured me with his sage advice and patient guidance. I will always be indebted to Walton.

This book would still be languishing in a bottom drawer without the strong and continuous support of my publishers, Verner and Gillian Bickley, and the support also of the Ride Fund for accepting it into the Royal Asiatic Society Hong Kong Studies Series. My sincerest thanks to Gillian for her meticulous editorship.

Any and all errors which may remain are of course mine alone.

Foreword

Walton Look Lai
retired History Lecturer
University of the West Indies
St Augustine, Trinidad & Tobago

Scholars of the nineteenth century Chinese migrations have justifiably seen the "coolie trade" to Latin America and the Caribbean (1846-1874) as the dark side of the diaspora experience. Organised and operated mainly by Western plantation and shipping interests, its cruelties and contradictions at the embarkation and destination ends have been described and analysed by contemporary official reports as well as by diaspora scholars. From the 1874 Cuban Commission Report compiled by the Chinese delegation of Chen Lanpin and others, to modern studies by Yen Ching Hwang and Arnold Meagher, supplemented over the years by a variety of single country studies, we have learnt all about the mechanics and motivations of this ethnic version of the worldwide indentured labor experiment, as well as about official Chinese state responses to it while it was happening.

A missing ingredient of these studies until now has been the voyages themselves, the story of what actually transpired on these seven hundred plus vessels traversing the long journey from the China coast to the Western Hemisphere. Conventional doctoral research would normally shy away from this task, not only because of the difficulties involved in amassing this vast material, but also because of what many would consider its dubious value in helping us to understand the totality of the trade itself.

Unshackled by these academic inhibitions, John Asome, a retired seaman and Australian economics graduate with his ancestral and family roots in Trinidad-Tobago, England, Hong Kong and Australia, has spent the better part of twenty years going where others dared not go before, and in the process has succeeded in filling an enormous gap in our knowledge of the Chinese coolie trade, the "transportation" dimension to supplement the "recruitment" and "work experience" dimensions of this unique diaspora story. Here, described in great detail, is the story of what actually happened on a good many of these seven hundred or so voyages to Cuba, Peru, the British, French and Dutch West Indies over the almost thirty years of its lifespan. In the process of chronicling these voyages, John Asome has enabled readers and future scholars to distinguish fact from myth, reality from exaggeration, in the understanding of this vast and complex experience. The concluding chapter—'The Coolie Trade in Review'—is an especially valuable summation. Whatever minor inconsistencies may inevitably emerge in this vast assemblage of data, all will be inspired by this brave project, all the more so because it is the result of one man's single-minded devotion over the years, rather than the work of a collective body.

March 2020
Port of Spain, Trinidad & Tobago

Preface

I was born in Hong Kong and watched as hundreds of ships came in and out of that beautiful harbour each year. When I eventually went off to sea, I travelled the world. I was so surprised to find that there were Chinese just about everywhere I visited. In places such as Thailand, Indonesia, the Philippines, Malaysia, Singapore, Australia, New Guinea and even Trinidad as well as British Guiana, as it was known then, they spoke Chinese, but not in the Cantonese that I could understand. However, it was not until I retired that I succumbed to the niggling notion that I needed to know more about those overseas Chinese, and in particular, the controversial indentured labour trade.

Three books sparked my interest in the Chinese diaspora of the mid 1800s. The first was Walton Look Lai's *The Chinese in the West Indies 1806-1995*, and then it was Trev Sue-A-Quan's *Cane Reapers: Chinese Indentured Immigrants in Guyana*. Trev then introduced me to Helen and Philip Atteck who were completing their *Stress of Weather*, which documented the voyage which brought Philip's grandparents to Trinidad in 1862.

I initially followed the traditional path of perusing hard copy, but over time have found that many books are now available on-line and there is less need to visit a library. Many libraries have digitised their collections and made them available on the internet. Most are free, but unfortunately, some now require a subscription for access.

With patience and assiduous selection of key search words, almost anything can now be found on the World Wide Web. I commend this form of research to everyone, but with the caveat that some of the information not contained in accredited books and journals may not be authentic and should be verified by a second source, whenever possible. I only wish I could understand Spanish and Portuguese.

Exploring those websites will lead to far more information than I have included in this book.

I have found it very difficult to standardise Romanisation of names for Chinese towns and villages, not to mention identifying the Portuguese and Spanish variations for those places. I have used names as I came across them. When citing a place for the first time I endeavour to add the Pinyin spelling too.

Similarly, I have not always been able to determine the value of the various currencies cited.[1] The Mexican silver dollar was roughly equivalent to the Spanish dollar, but I am not sure why pesos were sometimes mentioned. Sterling was the accounting standard until the introduction of the Hong Kong dollar in 1862. The latter was on a par with the Mexican dollar and worth about four shillings and two pence. An American gold dollar was also in circulation, nominally also on a par with the Mexican silver dollar but often traded at a discount. Unless otherwise mentioned, or implied by the context of the topic, the national origin of the dollars mentioned is unknown. The local population would not have had any understanding of what a dollar was or what it was worth. The vast majority would have been happy if they had a few "cash". An agricultural worker could expect to earn 100 cash for a day's work. This was equivalent to sixpence. His assistant could earn 80 cash, or thruppence per diem.[2] The amount of four dollars a month all found could therefore have been readily touted as a very big inducement to emigrate.

Writers in the English language, contemporary with the period under study, generally use the term "coolie" to denote an indentured labourer who was taken to the destinations mentioned in this book. Other writers refer to them as "kulies" or similar variations. I understand it was first used by the British to describe the indentured Indian labourers they recruited for Mauritius and then for the British West Indies. The word, "coolie", is used in this book in the same sense; but in order to avoid over-use, or when sources indicate otherwise, I refer to "emigrants" in the context of their leaving China and "immigrants" when arriving at their destinations.

Cuban planters and entrepreneurs preferred to refer to them as "asiaticos" while the Peruvians usually spoke of "colonos". Portuguese authorities seem to have preferred the term, "settler". In this book, the usage of the primary sources is followed. As is well known, the word, "coolie" was also used as a derogatory term, liberally used when protesting against Chinese sojourners to other parts of the world.

To me, as a seafarer, a passenger is a person, other than a crew member, travelling from one port to another port. No distinction is made between a voyager paying his own fare or not. All the persons on the many ships described in this narrative were passengers. To avoid excessive use of that word when stating the number of persons on board a vessel I have mostly described them variously as Chinese, coolies, "asiaticos" or "chinos". Unless absolutely certain, I have tried to avoid using "men" as there may been women and children on some of those vessels who were not separately identified, or even counted.

It has taken me some fifteen years to complete my study, but I have enjoyed the journey immensely. I hope you will too.

John Asome
Melbourne
January 2020

**General View of Hong Kong, c. 1867-74.
Departure port, 1848-1870.
Photograph by William Pryor Floyd.**

Introduction

The early story of indentured emigration from China was fraught with danger for all concerned, due to the lack of proper legislation and controls. The need for unskilled labour to replace or supplement slave labour in various countries, especially the Spanish colonies of the New World, commenced in 1846 with much loss of life and loss of ships. It was not until the British government entered the arena and undertook to implement their Chinese Passengers' Act in 1855 that many of the abuses of the early days were corrected.

The coolie trades were stigmatised throughout the period of indentured migration by detailed stories of horror ships and cruel captains; of extremely high death rates due to opium deprivation, inappropriate food, and suicide. Cruelty accounted for most of the mutinies that occurred in the early stages of the Chinese diaspora.

Deception also was a reason for mutiny with many tricked into going on ships believing they were going to destinations in Australia or California. In the latter part of the migration, the mutinies were being more accurately classified as piracies. Many a captain faced well-planned attacks at inappropriate times.

Chinese indentured labour was mainly sourced from the southern provinces of Fukien (Fujian) and Kwangtung (Guangdong). Fukien is approximately 53,480 square miles with a population of about 14,777,410 people in 1850. There were 276 persons per square mile. Kwangtung is of approximately 79,446 square miles with a population of about 19,147,030 in 1850. The population density was 214 persons per square mile. Canton (Guangzhou) is the provincial capital of Kwangtung.

To the south of Canton the three counties of Nanhai, Panyu and Shunde, known as the Sam Yup, were at the centre of this migration. Further out to the south and west the four counties of Xinhui, Taishan, Kaiping and Enping, which constituted the Say Yup, were no less important.

In this study of the indentured labour coolie trades between 1846 and 1874, 732 voyages have been identified; 358 to Cuba, 274 to Peru, 63 to the main colonies of the West Indies—British, French and Dutch—and 37 shipments to various other destinations. Some 113,911 Chinese were despatched to Peru, 146,643 to Cuba, 21,845 to the West Indies, and 9,085 to other destinations, a total of 291,484. Arrivals amounted to 247,407, which represented 84.87% of the number placed onboard. The numbers shown are as complete as possible, but figures may not always be correct, with conflicting numbers sometimes reported in newspapers and even official documents. Five ports and a safe anchorage in the Pearl River Delta, just to the north of Macao, were seriously involved in the coolie trade.

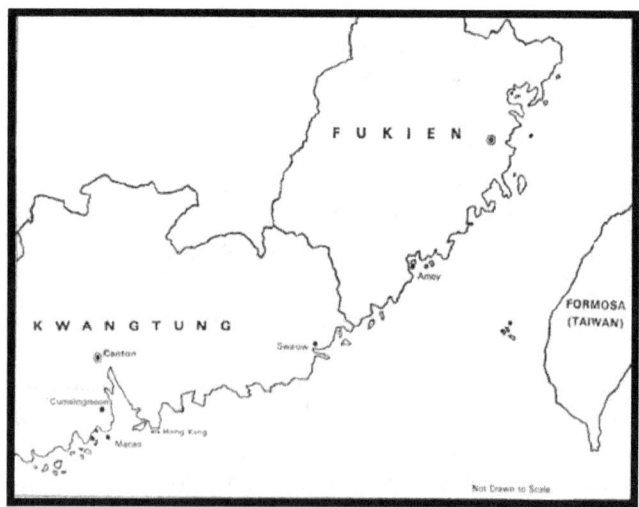

Departure ports of the Chinese coolie trade.

Amoy (Xiamen) in Fukien province was the traditional port of departure for sojourners to the Nanyang, the littoral states of the South China Sea—particularly Singapore, the Straits Settlements, and the Dutch East Indies. As one of the five original Treaty Ports it became the first to ship indentured labour further afield, with French Bourbon (Reunion) initiating the trade in 1846. Benefiting from their trading links between the Philippines and Amoy, Spanish interests undertook two experimental shipments to Cuba in 1847. Australian pastoralists first began taking Chinese in small numbers from Hong Kong in 1847 but then turned to Amoy, taking their first major shipment in 1848.

As the supply of willing emigrants in Amoy dwindled in 1852, Swatow (Shantou)—not a Treaty Port until 1858—became the centre of shipping. Swatow is in Kwangtung province close to the border with Fukien.

As Canton is on the shallow Pearl River, vessels could get only as far as Whampoa (Huangpu) some 12 miles downstream. It was a safe and commodious, picturesque anchorage surrounded by low wooded hills. The village on its banks was of dilapidated and decaying tenements erected on piles along the shore.[3]

Cumsingmoon (Junxingmen) in the Pearl River (Zhu Jiang) delta just north of Macao served as a safe anchorage for opium ships coming from India. Away from officialdom, it was Peru's preferred place of departure when the country entered the coolie trade in 1849.

Macao at the mouth of the Pearl River Delta became the major port of embarkation for indentured labour from 1857. Like Canton, it suffered from lack of water depth, and ships had to stand many miles off at an unsafe anchorage.

China ceded Hong Kong to the British in 1841. The strict provisions of the Chinese Passengers' Act of 1855 effectively stopped British shipping from participating in the indentured labour trade, but enabled Hong Kong to become the primary port for departing fare-paying emigration to America and Australia. As Hong Kong grew in prominence, the importance of Canton and Macao declined significantly. Macao would have ceased to be a trading port altogether had it not been for the coolie trade.

The demand for labour was not consistent. There were two distinct phases of Chinese departures to Peru, the first between 1849 and 1857, peaking in 1855. The second phase between 1860 and 1874 featured two pauses before rising to a final peak in 1872.

Cuba began trialling Chinese labour from Amoy in 1847, but regular shipments did not begin until 1852. In its first phase, shipments rose to a high in 1857 before falling to just two in 1862. Demand then climbed to a peak in 1866 before falling off with the advent of the 1868 Ten Years' War against Spain. A consequence of that war was the cessation of Chinese labour from 1873.

When compared with Cuba and Peru, the British West Indies demand for Chinese labour was never great. The British requirement for the West Indian colonies was also characterised by two waves. The first between 1852 and 1854 ended with the colonials complaining of the high costs involved. Inferior alternative labour from India, however, forced a recommencement of Chinese recruitment from 1858. It all but ceased when the commonly termed 1866 Kung Convention[4] banned contract labour without guaranteed return passages. There were four final voyages (two to British Guiana in 1874 and 1879, and one each to Antigua and Jamaica in 1882 and 1884). There were small shipments to Martinique and Guadaloupe in the French West Indies in the 1850s and to the Dutch colony of Surinam (Dutch Guiana) in 1858 and after 1865.

Four classes of indentured emigrants were soon distinguished.
- Firstly, there were those who willingly went abroad, having been ruined agriculturists, fugitive criminals or greatly burdened gamblers.
- Then there were those who were intimidated by lies warning them that unless they did as they were told they would be killed.
- The next class were probably the most unfortunate, being captured by actual physical violence.
- The fourth class were the connivers who embarked with the premeditated intent of plundering the

coolie ships, irrespective of what could happen to themselves or their fellow passengers

The Ships

The ships involved in the Chinese coolie trades varied considerably in type and size, from tiny brigs to fast clipper ships. Steamships were used early in the Cuban trade, but were about to be introduced to the Peruvian trade only when the trade was banned in 1874.

The ships first employed were small and ill equipped for the transportation of passengers on voyages sometimes in excess of four months. High mortality rates that exceeded 50% in some instances, were mainly from overcrowding, poor food and the frailty of the opium addicts. These factors improved over time, but high mortality was always a concern throughout the period.

A sailing ship is a vessel with three or more masts, square rigged on all. A square-rigged mast can be readily recognised by the horizontal booms extending out from it on both sides. Each mast carried four, five, six, or even seven booms that swivelled around it. They were perpendicular to the deck with sails tied securely to the yards as they are also called. The sides of the trapezoidal sail were dropped, or furled, to adjust the amount of sail required. The bottom ends of each sail were then secured to the ship's rail on deck. Furling of a sail was a laborious matter; with between six to eight seamen required to climb up the ratlines, then across the boom, before reaching down to secure the wrapped sail to the yard.

The number of crew on a sailing ship could vary from 16 to 44 or more. In this study of 732 vessels, 391 were classed as ships, with another 54 also known as clipper ships. The smallest ship used was of 342 tons, with the largest, of 2,078 tons.

A barque on the other hand is a vessel of three or more masts, square rigged on all except the aftermost mast, which is fore and aft rigged. The fore and aft rig was a much simpler sail. At the bottom was a single boom, which swivelled around the mast. A tapering sail was placed on this boom, the top of which was simply hoisted to the top of the mast. Where a greater sail area was required, a short spar extending outwards from the top of the sail could be added. When speed was not an important factor, the simpler sail plan of a barque, requiring a smaller crew, was preferred. The number of crew on a barque ranged from 15 to 33. Of the 240 barques identified here, their tonnage ranged from 191 to 1,278.

In the early years of the coolie trade smaller vessels, such as brigs and schooners, were also employed. A brig is a vessel with two masts, square rigged on both, while a schooner usually has two masts, fore and aft rigged on both. Larger schooners may have three or more masts. When regulations were introduced, limiting the number of passengers that could be carried based on the vessel's tonnage and available space, these smaller vessels fell into disfavour. Two schooners and 19 brigs were used to carry coolies. The brigs ranged from 168 tons to 391 tons.

Early steamships were sailing ships or barques with a small engine for use when the ship was becalmed. As these engines were not the primary means of propulsion, these ships were usually classified by their sailing rig. The first steamships were equipped with side paddles which were not very efficient in bad weather. It was not until the advent of the screw propeller that steamers began to surpass traditional sailing vessels. Of the 26 voyages undertaken by steamers, ten were ship rigged while two were barques. Tonnages ranged from 1,081 to 2,134.

The main criterion in determining the number of passengers that a ship could carry was its tonnage. The British benchmark as promulgated in their Passengers' Acts was of one person for every two tons burthen. This standard was generally adopted by other nations. For a short period, Macao accepted the initial Spanish standard of one person per every one and a half tons, but this was later replaced by a space allocation of up to three cubic metres per person depending on the ventilation of the vessel.

A ship mainly used in the emigrant trade would have more than the ordinary height in the between decks, together with good side and deck ventilation. There was usually a hospital in the forecastle and a large deckhouse divided into compartments, one with the ship's cooking equipment, while another contained the food preparation area. Water was kept in wooden casks before the advent of the fresh water condenser.

Most ships of the time were built with one upper deck and a deck part way up from the bottom of the hold, known as the between deck; more commonly referred to as the 'tween deck. On larger ships, an upper 'tween deck was sometimes added. Passengers could be carried on both these decks. The notional spacing between the decks was six feet, but this was not always so.

In the first ships employed in the coolie trade, the passengers simply slept on the deck. As the trade grew, ships began constructing bunks for the long voyage. The shelves were six feet wide with an eight inch footboard secured to the outside to prevent the men from slipping off. Each bedspace was then measured and marked off, allowing each person a breadth of from 20 to 24 inches; the average seldom exceeded 21 inches. There was no division between the sleepers, each shelf simply representing 150 bed spaces.[5]

The *Ticonderoga* was employed for one voyage as an emigrant ship from England to Australia in 1852. She had two 'tween decks, an upper and a lower. The heights were 7ft ten inches and 6ft eleven inches respectively. The accommodation plan shows bunks consisting of two rows of shelves running the whole length of the ship on both sides, as well as down the centre of the hold. The central tables and benches shown would have been replaced by bunks when she was employed as a Chinese coolie ship in 1857.

Fittings for the Chinese coolie ships were generally made in Hong Kong. In most cases three planks would be cut away at regular intervals along the whole length of the deck which were then reinforced with strong surroundings and a hinged cover eight inches above the deck. Through each of the poop and forecastle decks two enormous bell-mouthed ventilators would be mounted and two additional large pipes placed at each end to carry off the foul air below. These were additional to the original three large and two small hatches on the main deck.

As well, as many as 32 side-ports would be cut for additional ventilation. Over each hatch rain cloths were fitted, such that in rainy or wet weather they could be drawn over and laced down the sides, avoiding the necessity of having the heavy hatch covers put on.

In response to mounting insurgencies, special fittings were erected to protect the ship. Through the centre of each opening a strong iron bar would be placed to prevent coolie egress from the hold. Across each hatch were bars with opening just sufficient for single ingress or egress. The hatches leading to the provisions in the hold were encircled with trucks of strong iron bars secured to both decks so as to protect the provisions from being looted.

In case of an insurrection, an armed force could be positioned in them, firing on the masses if order could not be maintained. These fittings, made in Hong Kong, together with four pieces of strategically mounted artillery, a double stand of arms and boarding spikes placed in and around the pilot house on the poop could be fitted only in Macao as they were prohibited items in Hong Kong.

The crew was normally housed in the fore cabin behind an eight foot high barricade of strong iron bars with spike tops, running from rail to rail and securely placed forward of the poop front. On each side would be a gate, constantly manned, with another guarding the main hatch gratings and a third walking the forecastle.

As the trade matured, standard procedures were commonly adopted by masters, with separate sets of instructions for the chief mate, the doctors and interpreters and the guards, as well as for the coolies, and the coolie master. These included the requirement to ensure the sleeping spaces were cleaned out once a week and the 'tween decks fumigated and disinfected twice a week. The 'tween decks were to be dry-sanded each morning and swabbed and scraped each week. The coolies were to bathe at least once a day, weather and health permitting, and clothes were to be washed once a week.

The organisation on board a coolie ship depended on the number on board but was usually based on the capacity of the rice cookers, normally large enough to feed 50. To each, a cook with some experience would be appointed. They arose at 5.30 each morning to carry up the provisions for the day under the direction of the third mate. While this is was being done, a gang would be detailed by the Third or Fourth Mate to pump the day's water supply from below into the tanks on deck. When the meal was ready, the cooks and their assistants filled rice baskets and large plates which were then placed outside the cookhouse. When the bell sounded, the representative of each group of ten would gather a basket and plate, and take them to his mess. To assist in overall control, constables were appointed to assist in the supervision of the men. The scale was roughly one for each fifty men on board.

The person in command of a ship is the Master. The laws of all traditional maritime nations required Masters and Mates to undergo an examination and possess certificates of qualification before they were eligible to be in charge of a merchant vessel. The British government did not require this prerequisite until 23 March 1847 with a transitional period until it became compulsory from 1 January 1851.

The title of Captain is conferred only on one who has served a defined period at sea, passed the appropriate examinations and assumed command of a vessel. In the British Merchant Navy, promotion to Captain may be from the rank of seaman, or through a period of apprenticeship. The normal progression is from the attainment of a Second Mate's Certificate, to a Mate's Certificate and then a Master's Certificate.

There may be more than one captain on a ship, but only one master, who is in command. Where the master is not the owner of the vessel, he is responsible to the owner(s) for all matters pertaining to the ship under his command. This includes seeking cargo for his ship in ports where an agent has not been appointed. His authority on board is absolute, and his every command is to be obeyed without dissension. In the days of unruly seamen, many captains did not hesitate to use physical force to maintain discipline. His authority extended to all on board, including passengers, and when this caused discontent, he would treat them in the same manner as his crew. The callousness of some captains led to the many mutinies in the initial years of the Chinese diaspora.

On ships of traditional maritime nations, the captain would have been a national. Under the flags of emerging nations, nationals were not always available, and foreigners were often employed as Masters. Where laws did not allow this, a national with little or no seafaring experience would be appointed as the Master to sign and lodge official documents. A foreigner would then be engaged to command the ship. A less senior officer might also be engaged as Pilot to navigate the vessel should the Master not be familiar with the trade route.

A sailing ship would normally have a complement made up of a chief mate, second mate, third mate, carpenter, cook and steward, about nine able bodied seamen (AB) and seven or more ordinary seamen (OS) depending on how many sails the ship carried. On emigrant ships a Fourth Mate might be engaged, together with a coolie master and additional guards.

When ships of the traditional maritime nations left their home ports, they usually had a full complement of their own nationals. As voyages were normally in excess of one year, many of the men had to be replaced in the course of the voyage. Some would have become ill, others deserted their ships, usually because of a cruel captain, and some may have died. The captain or his agent then recruited new men as the need arose. In other circumstances, where a captain was unable to secure immediate employment for his ship, he would simply pay off as many of the crew as were surplus to the essential maintenance of a ship idle in port. Such men were thus stranded in strange ports, and left to their own devices to find their own way home. Waiting for new employment, they had to find accommodation in the seamen's boarding houses found in most of the main ports around the world.

An American ordinary seaman could be paid $6 or $7 a month, while an able bodied one would be paid $12. British rates would be lower than that, while locally recruited

Lascars or Manilamen could expect $5 a month. A carpenter or cook received $20, as did the third mate. The Steward received $25, the second mate was paid $30, and the chief mate $45. The Master would receive about $125, and on a coolie ship a bonus of about $10 for each passenger landed.[6]

The life of a seaman was not an easy one. The British Merchant Shipping Act of 1854 attempted to regulate conditions for seafarers, but unscrupulous owners easily circumvented such attempts. Conditions on board were atrocious. The accommodation allowance was 12 superficial feet with six feet from deck to deck giving a total of 72 cubic feet clear of stores and goods other than the property of the crew. In practice, this was seldom achieved, with some seamen even sleeping in hammocks slung over the tables where they had their meals.

While the forecastle was normally set aside for the seamen's accommodation, they could be displaced should that space be required for other purposes. There was no heating or cooling in those spaces. A sailor could be called out at any time of the day or night, in rain or in sunshine. He was often soaked to the skin and often went to sleep with damp clothing. He was offered very little sympathy when he took sick; and often made to continue working when hardly able to stand.

Each crew member had a daily allowance of three quarts of water for cooking, drinking, and washing his face. His body and clothes would have been washed in sea water. The food was inevitably bad, with the meat either pickled or salted. Seldom was there fresh meat, and a pint of peas per week was the only vegetable prescribed in the Merchant Shipping Act. Ships' biscuit, hard enough to break your teeth, was the main food when cooking was not possible due to weather conditions.

Swatow harbour (1860-1880).
Departure port, 1852-1866.
Photograph by Lai Afong (1839-1890).

1
In Search Of Labour

Voluntary free emigration to the Nanyang, the littoral states of the South China Sea, was an established practice long before China was opened to foreign trade. Traditional emigration was usually financed by sponsors from the home villages or by recruiters already based overseas. Hopeful emigrant sojourners had their passage paid by local brokers in Amoy or Swatow, or even in the Straits Settlements with the money advanced, then repaid with interest by an agreed period. Instalment monies were collected by the brokers or their representatives in the destination countries. These brokers accepted only men who were fit and healthy and when work was assured.

Each shipping season, brokers travelled to Amoy to engage men in China. Despite the higher cost, the greater reliability of square-rigged foreign vessels influenced a number of Chinese merchants in Singapore to begin chartering these ships rather than the traditional junk. In 1846, there were 27 Chinese recruiters from Malaya, most of whom held British passports.[7]

The Voyage of the *Sophia Fraser*
Nightfall was rapidly approaching. Captain Duncan McKellar was tired; and so was his crew. They had slaved away through the day, and all the previous night, desperately trying to keep their ship from sinking. All had gone well for the first few days, but then a severe typhoon caught the ship just as she was approaching the notorious Parcels. A position fix on 26 November 1846 put her at 15 13N 112 26E. The 1pm entry in the ship's log read that it was blowing a strong gale with every appearance of increasing with thick cloudy weather and the barometer falling. Captain McKellar first

furled the mainsail, then the topsails, but with the barometer still falling, hove to at midnight when it stood at 28 inches.

The gale continued to blow for the next 48 hours until about 9pm on the 29th when the clouds began to break, the barometer began to rise, and the wind to abate. In attempting to set a sail, the boom broke and a sailor was thrown overboard. Happily, he was saved. The mizzen sail was eventually set at 4am on the 30th, and then the fore and main sails at 8am.

The 292-ton *Sophia Fraser* had left Amoy on 23 November 1846, bound for Penang. She had $5,433 worth of sundry goods on board, but Captain McKellar had another reason for fighting so desperately. He also had 310 Chinese coolies crammed into the 'tween deck of the hold.

When the hatches were opened, about thirty badly bruised and mangled Chinese were found dead; with many more severely wounded. Seven casks, each containing 250 gallons of water were found stove in, and piles of firewood were strewn all over the deck. The Chinese supercargo threw the dead over the side while the captain attended to the wounded.

Whereas the crew had managed to survive on dry biscuits, there was no food for the passengers. The Chinese headman who was responsible for feeding them had made no provision for emergency food. In the turmoil of the typhoon, the hungry men turned on each other, first with words, but then with whatever implements they could find. In the ensuing mêlée, many were killed or seriously wounded.

The *Sophia Fraser* finally arrived at Singapore on 9 December 1846. At the Police Office in Singapore on the 10th, Captain McKellar testified that he had no doubt that many of the men died from seasickness and exhaustion. He declared that four had died on the voyage before the typhoon struck. As there were now only 275 left to answer the muster, 31 must have died during the storm.[8]

It also reported that Koo Hang Leng affirmed that he was the supercargo who had shipped 310 men from Amoy to Singapore and Penang. They were from 30 kampongs (villages), but were all friendly, and it was only from hunger during the gale that they were like drunken people through weakness and sickness. It was not disputed that some of the poor wretches died from positive inanition, which a supply of dry grain would have prevented.

Lee Shun Fah was a visiting broker from Singapore. A stranger to the area, he had been unable to find sufficient men to fulfil his contract. In his anxiety to fill the *Sophia Fraser* on her second voyage that year, Lee resorted to Francis Darby Syme for assistance. Syme was one of the first foreign (British) merchants to establish offices in Amoy after it had become an open port in 1842. As Syme had already rounded up all the beggars in the immediate neighbourhood of Amoy for French shipments to Bourbon, he needed to look further afield. Despite a warning of clan fighting around Amoy, Syme canvassed the nearby villages, and found enough men agreeing to migrate. They were from several rival villages, but Syme was not to understand the significance of that.

On hearing of the great tragedy, relatives of the dead men were adamant that the Chinese contractor Lee was to blame. They maintained that by mixing men from two rival villages, he caused the friction leading to their deaths. He was seized by the Chinese authorities and not released until after long negotiations with the British Consul. Lee, entitled to British protection, was eventually awarded $605 in compensation.

The plight of the *Sophia Fraser* brought the public's attention to what had been generally known in official and trading circles for some time. Emigration from China was banned, but had been quietly practiced with impunity for decades.

British investigation

For Britain, the serious search for labour began with the Act of Emancipation of 1833 following public demand for the right of African slaves to live in a free society. With the implementation of emancipation, the Government was to compensate West Indian planters for the economic losses they were to suffer. It introduced a six-year period of "apprenticeship" to train freed slaves in the responsibilities of freedom. The transition period was terminated in 1838 with all slaves freed, because the planters had continued to treat them as slaves,

Substitute labour from Madeira and elsewhere in Europe was tried with little success. In desperation, the British Government again turned to Africa in 1841, authorising the importation of labourers from the Kroo Coast. The scheme was doomed to failure, given the stringent safeguards against any hint of slavery.

In 1843, French sugar planters on the Indian Ocean island of Bourbon—known as Reunion since 1848—began sourcing Chinese labour from Penang for their plantations.

When the British planters in Mauritius heard of this initiative, they thought they should do the same. Early in 1843, Gignet & Co. arranged with Brown & Co. of Penang, for Chinese to be sent to Mauritius on the brig *Leswick*. When a member of the West India Committee (WIC) learned of this, he urged the Committee to lobby the British Government to allow similar shipments to the West Indies. This lobby group had been formed in the 18th Century by London merchants and absentee owners of West Indian estates. Not having succeeded in their opposition to the abolition of slavery, they then shifted their focus to the encouragement of substitute labour to the region.

The submission led to much discussion within the Government, which then gave the task of determining the feasibility of such a migration to the Colonial Land and Emigration Commission (CLEC). The Commission, within the Colonial Office, had been created in 1840; taking over functions of the Colonisation Commissioners for South Australia, and the Agent General for Emigration. Initially its duties were to manage the British emigration to North America and Australia, but following the abolition of slavery, it became responsible for the orderly migration of substitute labour, first from West Africa and the Atlantic basin, then India and now, possibly, Chinese labour.

In seeking further information, the Emigration Commissioners turned to John Crawfurd (1783-1868), an expert on Chinese matters in the Straits Settlements.[9]

Crawfurd was told that the Government had resolved that, should Chinese immigration into the West Indies be permitted, the people would, for the present, only be from the British settlements in the Straits of Malacca. It knew of the surplus of labour in China, but was also aware that Chinese law prohibited their nationals from emigrating. The questions posed reflected the Government's desire to appreciate the feasibility of transplanting Chinese into a strange environment halfway around the world and whether they would settle there. The Commissioners included an "Extract of Letters" to help him in his analysis.

Even though John Crawfurd had been away for nearly 20 years, he displayed his immense interest in the current Chinese migration. In his reply,[10] which was formulated within two days, he drew attention to the earlier, unsuccessful, experiment in 1806 when a shipment of Chinese was taken to Trinidad, and then remarked on current developments, including the Mauritius trial shipment, of which he was obviously well aware.

He estimated that there were then about 50,000 Chinese in the Straits Settlements of Singapore, Malacca and Penang as well as an unknown number, possibly about 20,000, in the Dutch settlements on the Rhio islands nearby. He quoted figures for the last two seasons, showing a significant increase in the number of junks with immigrants arriving from as many as 19 different ports in China. While many emigrants came from Amoy in the Province of Fukien, the greater majority came from the maritime ports of Canton, and even as far south as Hainan.

During his time in the East, about twelve junks only made the passage each year, and while European vessels occasionally brought Chinese immigrants, their numbers were not of great significance. However, in the shipping season from December 1842 to April 1843, 111 junks totalling 17,000 tons brought 6,391 immigrants to Singapore. In the previous season, 88 junks of 14,580 tons in total, had brought 6,156 Chinese. Crawfurd was able to say he knew of one junk alone carrying 800 passengers. He believed that the large numbers then being experienced were a direct result of the

British occupation of Kulangsu, in the bay of Amoy. (The occupation of Amoy in 1841 was effected during the Opium War of 1839-42.)

Crawfurd set the scene by claiming that there would be no difficulty in getting labourers in the prime of their life from the teeming population of China. In what was to become a contentious issue, Crawfurd stated that children and women never left China, and in fact not even their own localities. The Chinese settlers simply formed matrimonial connexions wherever they went in the Nanyang, but the resultant children were not considered as industrious as pure Chinese. While Chinese were very moneywise, they did not horde excessively, and were prepared to pay for a comfortable lifestyle. They expected to be paid the full value of their labour, and if not treated fairly could become "discontented, disorderly, and roguish".[11]

Crawfurd also expressed his doubts as to the expediency of hiring Chinese labourers on the basis of apprenticeship. His notion of Chinese people was that they were industrious and diligent only when working for themselves. If they found they could earn more that way they would readily forsake any form of contract labour.

Within days of its receipt, Lord Stanley wrote to the WIC agreeing that the Chinese would set a good example of continuous and industrious application, but that political considerations meant that they could be recruited only from Straits ports. Following consultations with the WIC, the Colonial Land and Emigration Commissioners then promulgated a set of Bounty Rules for Chinese emigration to the West Indies, together with Explanatory Notes. For the guidance of interested parties, additional information, substantially drawn from the Passengers' Act in force for the carriage of emigrants from Britain, was provided.

As soon as the Bounty Rules were promulgated, applications for licences were received from representatives of estates in Trinidad, British Guiana, and Jamaica. Further applications brought the total number of labourers sought to 2,850. But the WIC wanted changes to the Bounty Rules; and when further representations were rebuffed by Lord Stanley, no Chinese labourers were shipped to the British West Indies in the 1840s.

The British Government exacerbated the situation again when it passed the Sugar Duties Act of 1846 abolishing preferential tariffs for British sugar producers. The less efficient British planters in the West Indies faced ruin. Many estates simply closed, while the remaining ones amalgamated and dramatically reduced their recruiting from India. The British Guiana intake alone dropped from 11,519 in 1846 to 550 the next year. It recovered to 918 in 1848.

Once again, the WIC had to seek justice for its members. Despite the abundance of Indian coolies, greater productivity was needed if British plantations were to compete with slaveholding Cuban and Brazilian cane farmers; and the new sugar-beet producers in Europe. With a history of traditional migration to the Nanyang, China was beckoning.

French Initiatives

On 13 April 1844, the ship, *Suffren* landed in the harbour of Saint-Paul, and 54 Chinese got off. They would have been the first Chinese to set foot in Réunion and they would have come from Pulo-Pinang. That same year, the ships *Palladium* and *Nouveau Tropique* transported more Chinese to Réunion. They arrived without luggage, without money, some with a tin of sardines in their pocket.[12] When China signed commercial treaties with the United States of America and France in 1845, the French decided to recruit their labour directly from China. Among the first French callers at Amoy in 1846 was the 250-ton *Nouveau Tropique*, which arrived on 13 May with a cargo of rice from the Straits Settlements. There is no record of what she carried when she sailed for Bourbon on 1 June 1846.

In 1845, Marseilles merchants commissioned Captain Montfort to take the 304-ton French barque *Joseph et Claire* on a voyage to China.[13] A four-voyage veteran of the seas around China, Montfort was responsible for the mission, while his friend Captain Caillet sailed as Master on the vessel. Montfort was to proceed to Bourbon to receive instructions. He left St Denis, the capital of Bourbon, on 6

February 1846, bound for Amoy by way of Penang, Singapore and Macao. The British Consul recorded her arrival at Amoy on 12 June 1846 with a cargo of rice from Penang.

Captain Montfort's account of the voyage does not go into great detail, but he explains his prolonged stay in Amoy as necessary for the enlistment of voluntary workers who were to take the place of negro slaves in Bourbon. Again, Montfort does not elaborate on his contacts, but describes his recruiting agent as a Spanish-speaking Chinese Christian, named Vincent, who each night took thirty of his countrymen for examination on Kulangsu, an island directly opposite Amoy.

The pitiful appearance of those poor workers was miserable, with inveterate diseases, and devoured by scabies. Their poverty was extreme, most having had nothing to eat for days. Only the healthiest five or six could be chosen, and then held and fed in abandoned houses until departure. They were to be paid three dollars a month, and were given eight dollars as an advance. Montfort did not explain how that money was to be spent, as the men were then placed on board and constantly watched over in case they tried to abscond. No strangers were allowed on board in case of the unlikely event of a mandarin wishing to check on the men.

The British Consul listed the *Joseph et Claire* as having cleared Amoy on 6 July 1846 with an unspecified number of coolies for Bourbon. Captain Montfort says he left Amoy three months later, on 7 October 1846, having taken four months to enlist the 90 Chinese he had been charged with. Among them was a Chinese woman whom his crew-master, Sidore Vidal, had married in Canton. To keep her company, Montfort also took on a few other women. The *Joseph et Claire* did not arrive back at St Denis until mid January 1847.

The British Consul's returns report that the 290-ton *l'Avenir*, also under the French flag, departed from Amoy on 1 December 1846, with a second contingent of 200 coolies, again sailing for Bourbon. Francis Darby Syme took credit for the shipment of these coolies. The French shipments did not attract any significant interest from either the British

Consul or the local Chinese mandarins, but the shipping of Chinese emigrants was soon to come to the attention of the foreign community.

The Chinese trials were not continued as the local Bourbon Administration quickly banned further shipments of coolies, on the plea that they were unruly and uncontrollable. Apparently, the first settlers were too cunning, and most had abandoned their contracts as soon as they became familiar with conditions on the island.

Cuban trial shipments

While Spain did not officially abolish slavery until 1886, it was under considerable pressure to do so. Anti-slavery patrols by British and American vessels intercepted suspected slave ships heading for Cuba. With access to slaves severely restricted, Spain initially looked to the Indians of the Yucatan to supplement the slaves that still existed on the Cuban plantations. Spain found the Yucatan natives insufficient and unsuitable for plantation work. Driven by increased demand for sugar from the United States and the opening of the British market to Cuban sugar, the requirement for cheap labour increased considerably—not only for the plantations, but also for the building of the railways, which the plantation owners quickly realised were necessary in order to increase the amount of cultivatable land inland.

A Spanish Royal Order was passed on 3 July 1847 permitting Asian immigration in Cuba. The Real Junta de Fomento was entrusted with this task, which then commissioned Julian Zulueta y Cia to bring the first colonists to the island. He was to be paid 170 pesos per head.[14] The London office of the company was run by Zulueta's cousin Pedro, who then enlisted Matia Menchacatore in Manila and James Tait in London to carry out the task.—Tait was an Englishman whose company had traded in Spain.

The 350-ton Spanish brig *Oquendo* under Captain Osollo arrived in Amoy on 7 December 1846 carrying James Tait as a passenger. As Spain, like France, did not then have Consular representation in Amoy, Tait arrived bearing a commission from the Governor of the Philippines to become consular agent for Spain in Amoy. This was with the apparent approval of Lord Palmerston, the British Foreign Secretary.

The *Oquendo* created no great interest when she arrived on that occasion. But the British Consular staff, along with the rest of Amoy, could only look on in wonder as she sailed on 23 January 1847, loaded with 212 coolies bound for Havana. The *Oquendo* flew Spanish colours, and hence was not within the jurisdiction of the British Consul. It had taken James Tait, a forceful man, only a month to demonstrate his business skills in recruiting the required numbers.

The first contracts were hand-written, a laborious task as this 400-word document would have had to been produced over 642 times by a very conscientious clerk unfamiliar with Spanish. Matia, Menchacatore y Cia of Manila was named as the recruiting agent on behalf of the Junta. On arrival on 3 June 1847,[15] "many of the men were sick and skinny, covered with parasites, sullen, almost moribund".

They were taken to the barracks that were used to process African slaves, and there sold for the advertised price of 70 pesos. Buyers included Fevjo Sotomayor, and Pedro and Fernando Diago. Julian de Zulueta, Martin Pedroso and Ignacio de Arieta were among the planters buying for their plantation. Others were bought as servants. The Capitan-General (the Governor) was given a gift of two Chinese labourers.[16]

Following the success of the *Oquendo*, Tait went on to find another consignment of Chinese for Havana; this time on the *Duke of Argyll*, a British vessel. He then simply provided Captain Frank Bristow with a certificate allowing him to sail his ship with 430 Chinese coolies for Havana on 6 March 1847. British Consul Temple Hilliyard Layton considered it his duty to question the legality of the 629-ton vessel to carry Chinese passengers in excess of the 314 allowed under the British Passengers' Act. Tait simply retorted that the Act did not apply in Amoy.

Layton asked for advice from Hong Kong, but Governor Sir John Davis, unsure of himself, referred the request on to London. There it provoked alarm because it brought back the spectre of slave-trading. One hundred years earlier a British slave ship, also named *Duke of Argyll*, had been actively involved in the Middle Passage shipping of African slaves to the Caribbean.

The eventual response, long after the *Duke of Argyll* had sailed, was that it was not a breach of British law, and that there was no legitimate reason to detain the ship's papers. The Home Government had determined that the Passengers' Act did not apply to ships sailing from China.

Australian shepherds

Even as the French and Cuban coolie shipments were being undertaken from Amoy, an Australian adventurer was in China ascertaining the prospects of trade with that country. While in Amoy, he was taken in by the dense population of the city, and the great poverty of the inhabitants. Despite the poverty, he was impressed with their general demeanour and the tractability of their nature. On his return to Sydney, Adam Bogue wrote to the *Sydney Morning Herald* on 22 March 1847, offering his services to anyone wishing to learn more about importing Chinese labourers into the Colony.

The matter of shipments from Amoy arose again in 1848, when the 234-ton British barque *Nimrod* under Captain Espinasse arrived from Hong Kong on 12 June, ready to receive coolies. This was to be her second trip to Sydney, but the first with passengers. *Nimrod* created a lot of speculation in Amoy, causing a frustrated Layton to write a forceful, pleading, despatch on 17 July 1848 to the Superintendent of Trade in Hong Kong, the new Governor, Sir George Bonham.

Layton enclosed copies of the indenture agreement made between James Tait on the one hand and 100 Chinese coolies and 20 Chinese boys on the other hand, for the account of Captain J. Thomas Larkins.[17] The agreement was to serve Larkins or his assigns for five years in New South Wales, at a monthly rate of $2.50 for the men and $1.50 for the boys. They were to receive weekly provisions of 10 pounds of meat and wheat, a quarter of a pound of tea, and one pound of sugar, or such other provisions as might be mutually agreed. The $8 advanced was to be repaid through a deduction of 50 cents per month after arrival.

Layton warned that, with the coolies coming from the lowest and poorest, and in some cases from the most vicious classes in Amoy, the transaction had already become known as "buying men". The shipments were contrary to Chinese law but the mandarins showed no intention of interfering, with the Taontae[18] (Chief Mandarin) reportedly observing, "I cannot talk about emigration, for when that word is pronounced, my head assumes a very awkward position, and might chance to tumble off".

But what did the deeply concerned man receive in reply? Three months later, all Bonham could say was that he had referred the matter to Her Majesty's Government, and that in the meantime he was to adhere to previous instructions, and leave the matter to the Chinese. He voiced disapproval of Layton having permitted his Interpreter to explain the terms of their agreement to the coolies and what they were about to sign. He insisted Consulate staff were to desist from interfering in all questions of that description.

The 338-ton ship *London* under Captain Williamson first sailed from Hong Kong on 14 December 1847 with seven Chinese passengers and general cargo including matting, cigars, and almost 1,000 cases of tea. The *London* called at Manila on her way, where she loaded 4,654 bags of sugar and 30 cases of cigars. On her second voyage, again without any fuss or comment from the officials in Hong Kong, she loaded 149 coolies, and sailed on 25 November 1848 for Sydney, arriving on 22 February 1849. But as with the *Nimrod*, there was insufficient interest in employing the Chinese and on 28 February, she transferred 50 of those labourers to the *Elizabeth Jane*, which then sailed for Moreton Bay.

There were only two more Australian shipments from Amoy, and another waiting to load, when Layton died in 1850, after a long and intermittent illness that had lasted over two years. He left a distressed wife and young family to fend for themselves until their repatriation home.

The 465-ton barque *Cadet* was entered by the Amoy Consul as having loaded about 150 coolies on 4 November 1849 for Sydney. Like most other Australian ships, the *Cadet* called at Manila en route to load nearly 6,800 bags of sugar, as well as coffee, rope, and cigars.

Whereas the *Nimrod* and *London* did not suffer any loss of life, the *Cadet* was not so fortunate. She suffered 12 deaths during the voyage, which had been an unusually long one, taking four months from Manila. Battered by storms, she was forced to return to Manila for repairs. Again buffeted by further storms, the *Cadet* did not arrive off Moreton Bay, where she had hoped to put in for supplies, until 11 April. But she fell in with strong westerly gales and a current setting to the southward. She eventually arrived at Sydney on 23 April 1850.

With Adam Bogue's encouragement, Amoy became the centre for Australian shipments. The Amoy Consulate recorded the 241-ton British brig *Gazelle* as having sailed for Adelaide on 22 February 1850. Captain Ramsay sailed via Manila, where she loaded 3,695 bags of sugar. Of the 134 Chinese embarked at Amoy, 131 arrived at Sydney, not Adelaide, on 14 May 1850.

The 498-ton British barque *Duke of Roxburgh* was the next ship for Australia. She loaded 258 Chinese coolies, together with a cargo of sugar and sugar candy; and sailed on 8 November 1850, calling at Singapore where she loaded more sugar, coffee, tin, and coir rope on her way to Sydney. She arrived on 6 February 1851. Besides the chief officer who died from injuries suffered when he fell down the hold on an earlier voyage, 16 Chinese died on the voyage, ostensibly from cold and dysentery. The remaining 242 passengers were landed in Sydney, where 180 of them were subsequently transferred to the barque *Emma* as Captain Devlin prepared to sail for Moreton Bay on 18 February.

The *Duke of Roxburgh* undertook a second voyage the following year. On 16 August 1851 she left Amoy with 240 Chinese bound for Brisbane. This time Captain Kirsopp took the eastern route via Ascension Island (later known as Ponape, and now Pohnpei). He lost 13 men on her 85-day voyage.

The recruiting process

In 1851, some 1,478 men, in six ships, were recruited in Amoy for Australia alone. With criticism mounting against this migration, and the methods by which they were recruited, the *Sydney Morning Herald* began a series on Chinese Emigration. James Tait was more than happy to host their journalist, Paul Pax. In his feature on 13 March 1852, Pax described the process of recruiting Chinese for Australia in a detailed account. But he made no mention of how the men were enticed to sign up, and the increasingly aggressive methods required to coerce them.

Pax presented the Tait hong as being one of the greatest and most respectable English houses in China. He wrote that whenever Tait received an order from a ship's master, he would immediately apply to the headman among the Chinese brokers who invariably had many hundreds of men on his hands wishing to emigrate. The headman, in this instance named Bi-sente, would gather about double the number of the emigrants required, and feed and shelter them until the morning of a given day, when they were assembled in a large yard in front of his premises. There they would undergo an examination by the surgeon superintendent.

As they advanced to be examined, some would come up with amazing assurance, seeming to say "find a fault if you can". Others would come up with a degree of hesitation, having been previously rejected by other parties, but still hoping. Yet others, with disease having stamped them with outward marks, were quickly rejected by the medical examiner. With all hope gone, and with downcast eyes, they went off, waiting to die.

Then there was the instance of a reluctant man being brought up by two or three men who pushed him along unceremoniously. He was accepted by the surgeon knowing nothing of his objections. But then the man shook his head, indicating that he did not want to go in the ship. He was then seized by the tail (queue) and forced into the crowd of the accepted. On realising his mistake, the medical man immediately put a stop to that, telling the Chinese interpreter that on no account was any man to pass except of his own free will.

The work went on for three or four mornings, until the required number was made up, and a date nominated for receiving the emigrants on board the ship. On that day, they came, and with them an army of brokers and friends, cramming the ship to suffocation point: the Chinese clerks, the members of Messrs Tait's house, the commander of the vessel, the surgeon superintendent, and the leading Chinese brokers, all in their places on the poop. The emigrants on the main deck were again individually examined, and when finally accepted passed to the advances table.

There every man then signed the agreement if he could write. He then received $6.00, which nearly all of them handed over to the broker who had fed and clothed him. Sometimes three or four would turn restive and in the ensuing scuffle, escape into the ship's 'tween decks with their money. The broker seldom dared venture below to extract his fee.

Tait and the other recruiters always planned to ship all the men in one day, as the men, now having obtained perhaps two suits of clothes, tobacco, sweetmeats, and other little delicacies for the voyage, had been known to try to escape to the shore. Some of them may have had good reasons: their brothers were refused, or their friends were rejected: but vigilance was necessary to prevent the discontented from carrying out their intentions. But that was not to say that those tricks were not sometimes winked at by the brokers themselves, as even among the higher classes of the Chinese, trickery of every kind was not only encouraged, but also practiced.

Last shipments to Australia

Following the riots in Amoy (discussed in Chapter 3), the British 518-ton *Royal Saxon* managed to sail from Amoy on 25 November 1852 without incident. Captain C. Robinson took 327 Chinese on board and 72 days later landed 304 of them in Melbourne.

The 480-ton Brtish barque *Eleanor Lancaster* made her first voyage to Australia on 1 January 1852 with 240 Chinese without incident. On her second voyage, she arrived at Amoy on 10 October 1852, and was immediately redirected to Swatow due to increasing unrest at the port. She was to be the first to load at the quiet opium anchorage of Namoa, and sailed for Newcastle on 11 November 1852 with 255 men without incident. After a speedy passage, she arrived at that port on 8 February 1853. While approaching her berth a misunderstanding over water resulted in a skirmish with the crew. Captain M'Leod called for the police, who responded immediately without any further trouble.

The 364-ton British barque *Spartan* under Captain Thomas Marshall did not sail from Amoy until 8 January 1853 after arriving there on 8 October 1852. The 254 coolies had signed an agreement to go to Australia, whose terms were explained to them by the Chinese interpreter, and by the captain's agent, Robert Jackson, who spoke fluent Chinese. The men agreed to serve Captain Marshall or his assigns for a period of five years for four dollars a month as well as certain stipulated rations. Wages were to commence fourteen days after arrival at their destination. The $8 advance made was to be deducted by four quarterly instalments of two dollars each.

The men appeared to be content, and were allowed as much liberty as the size of the vessel would permit. They had more than a sufficient supply of rice, with the excess either fed to the fowls or thrown overboard after each meal.

On the morning of the 9th day, the captain and second mate were in the 'tween decks looking after the sick. Nearing Pulo Sepatu, a prearranged signal was given by the Chinese, when several of them rushed at the man at the wheel, and tried to throw him overboard, but he escaped by quitting the helm and taking to the mizzen rigging. At the same time, others rushed into the cuddy and the captain's cabin where they armed themselves with bayonets. They then proceeded to the pantry, where a large carving knife was taken from a Chinese lad who was cleaning it.

By this time the captain, the chief mate and the second mate had returned to the after-part of the ship. The second mate rushed towards the captain's cabin only to be met by the man with the carving knife, which was run through him. The second mate fell lifeless at the door of the captain's cabin. The captain and chief mate were also attacked, and both were severely wounded, the latter falling senseless at the cuddy door. The captain seized hold of a bayonet thrust at him and made his way out of the cuddy.

Armed with sticks etc., the crew managed to force their way aft. When the firearms were secured and discharged three or four times, the coolies were forced below, and the hatches closed over them. Ten of the coolies were either shot dead, or jumped overboard and were drowned. Three bodies were thrown overboard, and one man died the following day. When the American clipper *Witch of the Waves* appeared soon after, she kept company with the *Spartan* until they reached Singapore on 22 January 1853.

Nineteen of the Chinese were then taken into custody, and the Sitting Magistrate then committed them for trial at Penang on a charge of piracy and murder. The trial took place on 21 February. One of the accused was found guilty of murdering the second mate, and the others of aiding and abetting in the crime. From the evidence of the cruelties practiced on the coolies by the crew, the *Pinang Gazette* mounted a strong plea for mitigation for them. Of the eleven that were found guilty, nine were given five-week terms, and two only were transported for life. With the captain remaining to give evidence, the *Spartan* left Singapore on 6 February 1853 under Chief Mate Allen now promoted to captain, and arrived at Melbourne on 7 April with 180 Chinese on board.

The *Spartan* was the last ship to carry Chinese emigrants to Australia under an Agreement of Indenture. Henceforth emigration to Australia was conducted, mainly from Hong Kong, under what was to become known as the credit-ticket system[19] of voluntary emigration.

Peruvian interest

The first Peruvian ship to visit Canton was the *Lambayeque* under the command of Captain William Manoel Robinet in April 1847. He and his family stayed on to become the Consul for Peru. In 1852 there were at least two Peruvian-flagged vessels trading in China. One was the 350-ton *Carmen* under the Italian patriot Guiseppe Garibaldi. He held a Master's Certificate and while spending a period of exile in Peru was asked to undertake a voyage to China. There was much speculation that he participated in the coolie trade but there was no evidence of any Chinese on board when he returned to Callao.

The 290-ton Peruvian barque *Miceno,* under Captain B. Gonzales, was also in China in 1852. The Peruvian Consul listed her as having taken coolies on at Cumsingmoon, but as only five Chinese men were involved, it is debatable whether they had actually signed indentures or are more likely to have boarded at Whampoa.

Domingo Elias (1805-1867) was a slave owner. He bought and sold slaves to work on his Peruvian plantations as required. Peru did not abolish slavery until 1854 but by 1847 slaves were already becoming difficult to come by, and Elias began looking for other sources of labour. On hearing of surplus labourers in China, Elias sought to recruit some of them.

Elias approached Robinet for assistance. Wary of British superintendence in Amoy, Robinet looked to prominent Macao shipowner and agent José Vicente Jorge (1803-1857) to assist in recruiting the men. Jorge recommended a sheltered anchorage just 20 miles north of Macao. Cumsingmoon came into favour when Whampoa, the port for Canton, became too dangerous for ships coming from India laden with the controversial opium. Situated in a wide bay, it was sheltered from the strong easterly winds by Kee-ow Island, yet still allowed passage from both the north and the south.

Cumsingmoon was nothing more than a collection of makeshift buildings and a population of 3,000 to 4,000 petty traders who had established themselves there by 1846. Europeans spent the day ashore, but with few facilities apart from a billiard room, returned to their ships to pass the night. Opium was cheap and available in plentiful quantities. It became a pool of addicts and destitute men seeking solace with the drug.

The first trial shipment of Chinese was made when Elias chartered Captain N. Paulsen's 430-ton Danish barque *Frederick Wilhelm* for one voyage to Callao. She sailed from Cumsingmoon on 7 June 1849 with 75 Chinese and arrived at Callao on 24 October without incident and without any fatalities.

Even as his speculative shipment was arriving, Domingo Elias, together with a fellow planter, Juan Rodriguez, succeeded in having a law passed to promote immigration into Peru. When the legislation was passed on 17 November 1849, it decreed a payment of 30 pesos for each person between the ages of one and forty brought to Peru. This law was intended for European immigrants, but as it did not specifically exclude Asians, Elias was able to claim the payment for his coolies. With this concession, it soon became known as the "Chinese Law".[20]

That same year Elias and Rodriguez were given the exclusive right to import labour for four years into the Departments of Lima and La Libertad. Elias immediately returned to China for his labour.

Among the many British ships roaming the world seeking cargoes in the late 1840s was the 763-ton *Lady Montague*. On 22 April 1848, she left Southampton bound for Aden with coals for the P&O Steam Packet Co. While the ship was off Trinidad, Captain Wells took sick and died. The chief mate, James Robinson Smith, then took charge of the vessel. After discharging her cargo at Aden, the ship went to Bombay where she loaded cotton for Whampoa, the port for Canton. She then traded on the China coast for the next 18 months, a period very much longer than planned.

On announcing that the ship had just been chartered to take Chinese emigrants to Callao, her owner, John Vaux, declared that Captain Smith was keeping the ship in China without his permission. But he didn't complain too loudly. Captain Smith had negotiated a lucrative charter, said to be worth $60 or £12 a day, from the day the emigrants came on board until the vessel returned to Hong Kong.

The *Lady Montague* was to carry the first full shipment of Chinese. She left Cumsingmoon on 17 February 1850 with a crew of about 44, including Lascars and three of their wives. Amongst the crew were five apprentices. The 440 emigrant Chinese had signed indentures for four years, at four dollars a month, with three months' pay in advance. They believed they were going to the gold diggings in California, but it was with horror and fright when they learned it was for Callao that they were destined.

Three days after they left Cumsingmoon, dysentery set in, and deaths occurred daily. Some of the sickness amongst the Chinese was caused from withdrawal of their opium supply. The Chinese supercargo refused to provide the coolies with the drug, as he expected to receive a higher price for it on the Chinchas. The vessel touched at Sumatra in the beginning of March, where she took on water, but a few days after her departure the water proved sour and bad, and the fish became putrid. The death of the doctor did not help. It was reported that the coolies tried to revolt but this was stopped by the interference of the Chinese interpreter.

One day, one of the Chinese, in despair, slid into the water. When nearly drowned he was secured, and recovered after some difficulty. Another jumped overboard a few days later, and a boat was sent after him, but he kept diving, to prevent being saved, and at last re-appeared no more. Four others, in fits of madness and despair, successfully jumped overboard. The last they saw of another was as he was swimming away from the ship, making for land, which loomed a long way in the distance.

Before the *Lady Montague* reached Hobart on 13 April, 142 Chinese and two Lascar seamen had died. The second mate and steward had also succumbed to the fever just as the ship arrived. She was immediately placed in quarantine where a further five Chinese and two Lascars died.

It was alleged that this cruel, unfeeling Captain was drunk every morning and could be seen walking about the deck with a drawn sword. One day he flogged two of the wives of the Lascar seamen for some trifling offence. An apprentice had been made to hold a torch to enable the captain to see what he was doing.

In all, the voyage took four months, with the *Lady Montague* finally arriving at Callao on 26 June 1850. She was immediately placed in quarantine off the island of San Lorenzo directly opposite Callao until 9 July. There the Governor of Lima boarded the vessel when the number of deaths was stated as 245, with 201 remaining. The exact number of deaths is indeterminate as the ship's log was said to record that 171 Chinese, 17 Lascars, and seven of the crew had died on the voyage. The British Consul in Lima reported that the *Lady Montague* left with 440 men and landed 241, having lost 199 on the voyage from Cumsingmoon.

John Vaux, received a letter from Captain Smith, dated 13 July 1850, advising of the most awful passage—with dysentery and fever taking 274 souls, including 26 of his crew. He went on to say, "for weeks and weeks I had no more than four to six men to assist in navigating the ship in the cold stormy weather of the far South Pacific". The captain claimed he was also struck down, but recovered.

When the *Lady Montague* returned to Hong Kong on 15 February 1851, twelve months after she left Cumsingmoon, James Robinson Smith was replaced by Captain Le Shaw. When Smith attempted to take ashore a large box of money, he was prevented from doing so by the new captain, who proved to be just as cruel as Captain Smith.

The 446-ton Peruvian barque *Empresa* arrived at Hong Kong from San Francisco on 20 April 1850. Jesus Elias was a passenger, and on landing was accredited as the Vice Consul for Peru in Hong Kong. But his real purpose was to supervise the recruiting of coolies for the *Empresa*. Under the command of British Captain Thomas Blenkinsop White, she embarked 300 coolies at Cumsingmoon on 13 June 1850, but lost 48 on the voyage to Chincha. She arrived with 252 coolies to be placed in the service of his father Dom Elias. *Empresa* made a subsequent voyage from Amoy on 12 July 1852 with a loss of 27 lives, mainly from dysentery, and on a further voyage from Cumsingmoon the next year, the ship was wracked with fever, killing 96 men as well as Captain White.

Horror ships

The fourth vessel to load at Cumsingmoon, *Albert*, a 292-ton French barque, registered in Dieppe, under Captain Jean Paine, took on 180 coolies and departed on 24 September 1850. None of them reached Peru. These coolies had been shipped for Dom Elias through the firm of A.A. Ritchie & Co. They had each received a sum of $8, repayable out of a salary of $4 per month, commencing from their arrival at Lima. The contract was for general services as servants for a period of five years.

Whereas Captain Smith of the *Lady Montague* was castigated as being cruel to his crew, this French captain was said to have exercised his cruelty on the Chinese. He demanded that the Chinese keep themselves clean, but had difficulty in enforcing that requirement. It was claimed that he had cut off the pigtails of some of the men for insubordination. At around 6.30am on 7 September in position 32N 139E, Captain Pain was in the lower deck using his cane when he was set upon by the coolies. He managed to escape back up to the round-house on deck, but was then caught and had his throat cut, before being thrown overboard. The cook and third mate suffered the same fate, while the chief mate was chased up into the rigging. Seeing no escape, the chief mate descended and managed to kill one and seriously wound another before he too was killed and thrown overboard.

The second mate and the boatswain, Luis Argentine, were ordered down from the rigging where they were hiding, and directed to steer back to Canton. He accordingly altered course from NNE to S by W. Five days later, in position 28N 133.37E, a severe gale brought down the top-gallant masts. Approaching Canton, the Chinese hailed fishing boats and some 130 of them disembarked, but not before stealing the captain's barometer, chronometer, and compass. The coolies ransacked the cargo, scattering packages of silk shawls, tea, lacquered ware, medicines, etc., and sharing them among themselves. Forty more left the day before the ship arrived at Hong Kong on 28 September 1850.

The remainder decamped before news of her distress was known, but four of them were captured by the police as they were boarding a Macao-bound ferry. Amongst their baggage were items from the *Albert* as well as the agreements they had signed.

The *Albert* also had two cabin passengers—brothers—sailing as supercargoes. John Elias was killed at the same time as the cook, but Jesus Elias hid in his cabin. When he was discovered, he was severely beaten up, but his life was spared. They were the sons of Dom Elias, and revenge for this atrocity only added to the cruelty inflicted on any Chinese who landed on his little fiefdom. The Chinese were regarded as no better than slaves.

The 376-ton French barque *Chili* first sailed from Cumsingmoon on 12 September 1850, ostensibly bound for California. Within days, she had to put back to Hong Kong, having sprung leaks in her hull. Captain J. Vermial subsequently returned to Cumsingmoon, then sailed on 7 October 1850 with 300 coolies now bound for Callao, but was caught in a typhoon and lost her masts. She had to put back again, this time to Macao, arriving on 22 November. She was condemned and discharged her passengers, before being auctioned off on 10 February 1851.

A week later, on 14 October 1850, yet another French barque, the 150-ton *Manuelita*, left Cumsingmoon with another 180 Chinese for Callao. She too was severely damaged when she encountered the same typhoon soon after her departure. Captain Las Casas just managed to get to Manila, where the ship was condemned and the coolies had to be transhipped to the *Orixa*, another French vessel.

These five ships in 1850 were all for the account of Dom Elias. His expectations of cheap labour would not have materialised. Of the 1,400 Chinese he recruited, only 669 actually landed in Peru. The mortality rate on the *Lady Montague* amounted to 45.23%—on the *Empresa* it was 16.00%. However, 176 of the *Manuelita*'s original complement of 180 were landed from the *Orixa*—a mortality rate of 2.22%.

The tragedies continued in 1851. The 579-ton British barque *Victory*, under Captain William Lennox Mullens, left Cumsingmoon on 5 December 1851, bound for Callao with 350 coolies.—Captain Mullens was born in 1804 and held a Masters Class 2 Certificate issued in 1848.—Each coolie had been given a quilt, some clothes, and a dollar. There was no report of cruelty to the passengers, so it was with surprise that on the afternoon of 10 December, the coolies rushed the cabin and seized the ship's arms. The captain was on the poop at that time and another group tried to seize him. One of the crew went to his assistance, but he was cut down and his mutilated body thrown overboard. Captain Mullens then climbed up into the mizzen rigging, closely followed by a Chinese armed with a cutlass. The captain then slid down one of the topmost backstays. On reaching the deck, he was attacked with knives, cutlasses and iron bolts and then thrown overboard. The second mate, James Arauso, and the cook, Edward Bailey, were also killed.

When the Chinese spotted Chief Mate Vagg, who had been aloft on the foretopsail yard looking for land, they beckoned him down. When he did, he was led to the wheel, and directed to steer for land on pain of death. He shaped a course for Point Kamboja. On reaching the coast, some of the Chinese went ashore but returned when they discovered the area was uninhabited. They then endeavoured to beat up the coast to Cochin China.

The mutineers continually fought among themselves over their gambling debts. The ringleader, named Ah Meng, even had his hands and feet cut off before being thrown overboard. The crew lived in fear of their lives. One day they saw a large junk and the Chinese sent the Europeans, in two boats, to capture her, but they were too slow to catch up. The Europeans then attempted to land at several places, but each time they were repulsed by natives. Exhausted and without provisions, they returned to the vessel. Although the Chinese must have been aware of the crew's attempt to escape, they received them back on board without comment.

They then directed the chief mate to steer for Pulo Ubi on the coast of Cambodia. During this time, the Chinese destroyed the ship's papers and logbook. On finding a convenient place to anchor, they took ten days to unload the ship's cargo of tea, silver-plate, silk and jewellery. They continued to fight among themselves, but being unable to handle the ship, they allowed the crew to steer the *Victory* for Singapore, dropping most of the men along the Cambodian coast. She arrived on 26 January 1852.

Ho-aming and his brother had signed on to emigrate on the *Victory* after "being in distress" in Canton. The 17-year-old Ho and his brother had been promised $4 a month for work "in a foreign country" with the prospect of $30 a month after five years. The two brothers were left at Pulo Ubi with others to guard the treasure, but over the next two months some of the others were forcibly returned by the local authorities. On 21 February, several of them secured passage on a passing junk taking all the plunder with them, leaving only Ho-aming, his by-now dying brother, and three others to remain at Pulo Obi.[21]

Later that same day, HMS *Salamander* arrived at Pulo Ubi from Singapore with members of the *Victory*'s crew. Ho was identified by the crew as having taken part in the revolt. When his brother died, Ho became the sole coolie to stand trial in Hong Kong for revolt, assault, and piracy. He proclaimed his innocence, pointing out his willing assistance in searching for the escaped men. "If I had been one of the head men, I would not have been left destitute on the island, but would have escaped like them with money. I had my pigtail cut off by the Europeans; they might as well have cut off my head, for now I will be taken for a thief. Had I killed one person I deserve the same fate, but I am no thief, and had no hand in the matter." Against the sworn statements of two Englishmen, Ho didn't stand a chance, and was convicted and sentenced to 15 years transportation, and taken to Singapore.

Hawaiian servants

The first sugar plantation was established in Hawaii in 1835. It was only a small operation, but the owners had great difficulty in encouraging native labour to work the land. The islanders preferred to be self-sufficient with their own plots of land.

The Royal Hawaiian Agricultural Society was founded in August 1850. Among its list of correspondents was one John Bowring, the then British Consul in Canton. He undoubtedly advised the Society of the abundance of labour in China. With a dire need for labour, the Society looked to China.

Within a month of being formed, the Hawaiian Royal Agricultural Society entered into a contract with George F. Hubertson in September 1850, for the importation of two hundred Chinese coolies.[22] Captain Hubertson first arrived at Honolulu in 1849 in command of the British ship *Amazon*, but was then in command of the British brig *Corsair*, which had arrived in Honolulu from Shanghai on 22 August 1850. He had brought along his family to establish himself as a merchant in Hawaii. With his recent residence in China, Hubertson was considered the best person with whom to make the contract for Chinese servants.

The Society had understood Hubertson to be the owner of the *Amazon*. He did not seem to have told the Society he was not the owner, but would enter into a Charter Party to secure the vessel. The charge for the passage was fifty dollars per coolie, which together with two months' advances to the coolies and the purchase of rice supplies for a year, brought the sum to $71 for each coolie. To facilitate the voyage, between nine and ten thousand dollars—nearly two thirds of the total cost of the voyage—was advanced to Hubertson.

The 370-ton British ship *Amazon* was first reported by the British Consul in Shanghai as having left Shanghai on 22 July 1849 with 200 Chinese bound for San Francisco via Honolulu. The *Weekly Alta* reported the *Amazon* under Captain Hubertson as having arrived at San Francisco on 15 October 1849 with 101 passengers from China. It did not mention the possibility of this being the first large group of Chinese to arrive from China.

The *Amazon* then left San Francisco on 5 November for Singapore via Honolulu and Hong Kong. She was returning to San Francisco, now under Captain Vincent, in June 1850, when she had to call into Hong Kong in a leaky condition, before arriving in Honolulu on 14 August 1850.

The *Amazon* remained in Honolulu until November 1850 before returning to Amoy on 23 December 1850. She had begun loading her consignment of coolies but then they had to be taken off when the charter party terms could not be agreed with Captain Vincent.

Captain Vincent was still in command of the *Amazon* when she eventually sailed for Sydney on 12 December 1851 with 303 men. Three men were reported to have jumped overboard, in addition to the ten that died on that voyage. The *Amazon* continued to be involved in the coolie trades and was the first ship to sail for Callao from Swatow in February 1854. William Robinet, in the capacity of recruiting agent, had guaranteed that the 250 men he embarked would not go to the Chinchas. There were two deaths only on that 91-day voyage, still under Captain Vincent.

After waiting more than nine months without any sign of the *Amazon*, the Society turned to Captain John Cass of the *Thetis*. It is unclear whether Hubertson refunded any of the money advanced by the Society.

Like the *Amazon*, the 460-ton barque *Thetis* first called at Honolulu, on 27 April 1851, carrying Chinese passengers for San Francisco. On her way back to Hong Kong, members of the Royal Agricultural Society were successful in negotiating an agreement with Captain Cass to bring 200 Chinese to Hawaii. He was to receive $50 for each man landed.

The shrewd thirty-nine-year-old captain made a handsome profit when he landed 175 labourers and 23 houseboys in Honolulu on 3 January 1852. It was understood that he had paid $3 for each coolie. However, it had taken him a long time to collect his men; he had arrived in Amoy on 22 September and did not sail until 13 November 1851.

Even though Cass had initially intended sailing for Hong Kong, he headed instead for Amoy, knowing that that was where labour was readily obtainable. The only disappointment to the Hawaiians was that the men were from Amoy, and not Hong Kong as expected. But that did not prevent them from seeking a second shipment. This time Cass did head for Hong Kong, probably to take on additional provisions, then on to Amoy, arriving on 9 May 1852. Having established his credentials, the stay this time was much shorter, departing Amoy on 5 June 1852 with 101 men. Cass landed 99 men in Honolulu on 31 July. Two men had died on the first voyage, and two on the second.

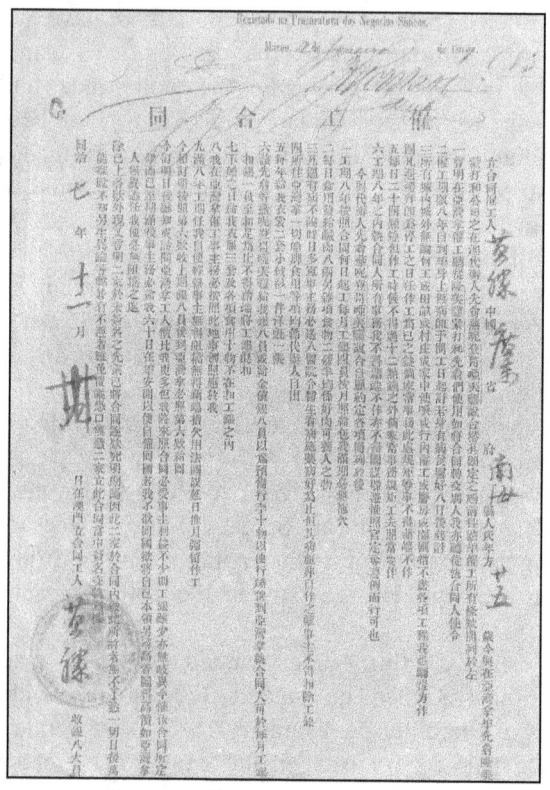

Labourer's contract in Chinese.[23]

2
Peruvian Migration
The First Phase

The first phase of the Peruvian recruitment of Chinese labour was disastrous. Of the 47 shipments undertaken, eight were marred by mutinies, three vessels were dismasted and two were shipwrecked. High mortality was a worrying factor, twelve shipments suffering casualties in excess of 20%.

José Sevilla
Dom Elias had a high profile as the instigator of Chinese labour. However, the main shipper to Peru in this period was José Sevilla. Starting life as a seaman, he quickly became a shipowner and entrepreneur. Even before he gained the right to import labour into other Departments (administrative regions) in February 1851, he had arranged with two Frenchmen, Messrs Guillon and Durand, to ship Chinese from Macao.

Situated at the mouth of the Pearl River about 40 miles west of Hong Kong, Macao was ideally located, close to the over-populated districts along the West Coast of Kwangtung. However, although Macao may have been a safe haven for ships when it was first occupied by the Portuguese, but by the 1850s alluvial silt had caused the inner harbour to become inaccessible to ships of any significance. Ships were therefore obliged to anchor at least three miles from shore, and most times even further. As they were not there sheltered from the prevailing easterlies, captains had to be continuously alert to any changes in the weather. When there was little prospect of an immediate cargo, most ships bided their time in the safer waters of Hong Kong, where they could dispense with most of their crews until sailing time.

Sevilla spoke English and utilised British ships whenever Peruvian ships were not available. On 31 January 1851, Captain Harland of the 685-ton British ship *Mariner* took 121 days to reach Callao, where he landed 400 of his 409 passengers, while Captain T. Brown left three weeks later, on 21 February 1851, on the 663-ton British barque *Coromandel*. Brown required 127 days to land 400 of the 404 he had embarked. In sharp contrast to the disastrous Elias shipments from Cumsingmoon, both ships arrived without incident. Sevilla subsequently employed the 797-ton *Eliza Morrison* and the 1,006-ton *Nepaul* in 1853, without any problems.

The Peruvian ships that Sevilla used all had British captains. Thomas White was still in command when he took the *Empresa* for two further voyages in 1852 and 1853. When Captain Thomas Beazley was transferred to the newly bought 866-ton *Catalina*, he took 500 Chinese from Swatow on 6 April 1855 and successfully disembarked 492 of them in Callao 110 days later. *Catalina* made a second voyage the following year with Captain C.J.H. Wilson in command. There were 13 deaths only among the 500 taken onboard.

The 514-ton British vessel *Susannah* attracted the attention of the Lords of the Privy Council after she arrived at Arica, on the border with Chile, on 27 May 1852. The Chargé d'Affaires in Bolivia claimed that the *Susannah* cleared from Hong Kong in ballast and sailed, not for South America, but for Cumsingmoon, where she took on board 325 coolies. On her arrival at Arica, her passengers had been openly offered for sale, and Captain Lukey and his agent had sold some of them for $112 each, with a promise to pay the men $4 monthly. The *Susannah* sailed on to Callao where the Peruvian Foreign Ministry recorded her arrival on 15 June with 319 Chinese still on board. They were bought by Dom Elias for use on his mainland estates as well as on the Chinchas.

It would appear that after obtaining his Port Clearance from Hong Kong Captain Lukey set sail for Cumsingmoon where he took on board Chinese coolies for Peru. Robinet, the then Consul for Peru, stated that she sailed on 2 February

1852 with 325 coolies contracted for five or eight years. Contract No. 286 between a 15-year-old boy named Cow-hoy and J. Sevilla, as agent for Don Domingo Elias, was witnessed by Richard Pollard.

Mutinies

The *Susannah* was then bought by José Sevilla and renamed *Isabel Quintana*. (Dom Elias's wife was Isabel de Quintana y Pedemonte.) She undertook her first voyage from Cumsingmoon under this name on 26 January 1853, losing nine of her complement out of the 325 who had embarked. British Captain Thomas Beazley was in command.[24] Beazley undertook a second voyage on 20 February 1854 with another 325 men, landing 278 of them after a 190-day voyage. She was the last ship to load at Cumsingmoon.

E. Gurney Wooldridge was in Hong Kong in 1853 looking for a berth as chief mate after working in the opium trade for three years.[25] He was accosted by an elderly man crippled by paralytic stroke, who asked if he would undertake the duties of sailing master on a 500-ton ship, then lying in the Boca Tigris in the Pearl River Delta bound for Callao. He was met by a sentry with a drawn sword, and noticed that the ship did not seem very loaded and that the hatches were off but with closely crossed iron bars secured to the coamings. The next morning 20 Chinese were embarked and he was asked to question each man as to their willingness to go to South America. They all eagerly answered that they did, but he found out later that the Chinese interpreter did not ask that question, but rather one that elicited the positive responses.

When some 500 miles down the China Sea, they rose against the crew, intending to kill them all except him. He was to be spared and forced to return before being killed too. There were six Englishmen on board and 25 Lascars. Many lives were lost with the Chinese jumping overboard on being overpowered. The *Isabel Quintana* put into Anjer, but the Dutch Governor refused to take the ringleaders, fearing the presence of so many Chinese in the settlement.

They then sailed on with the intention of leaving them on Christmas Island, but the captain realised that he was to receive $500 for each Chinaman landed and the owner would be at a great loss on the voyage. The ringleaders were then put in irons while the rest had free range of the 'tween decks, but under barred hatches. When off Swan River in Western Australia, the Chinese began to die off, the captain treating them for yellow jaundice, but later it was confirmed that the ship had had yellow fever. The *Isabel Quintana* made calls at various Chilian and Peruvian ports to try to sell the men.

Wooldridge left the ship at Coquimbo, Chile, and took command of an English vessel going to the Chinchas for a cargo of guano. There he saw about 70 of the poor wretches who had been on the *Isabel Quintana*.

He said that the captain was given a larger ship and the second mate was made Master. He did not identify the captain, who would have been Captain Beazley, who indeed was given the 866-ton Peruvian ship *Catalina* for his next voyage. The second mate (who was possibly named Smith) was made Master and was in command when the *Isabel Quintana* called at Honolulu on 23 September 1854 on her way back to China. However, she did not undertake another voyage and was offered for sale in January 1855.

In John Bowring's 1851 Annual Report on Trade, the Canton British Consul reported that some men were so desperate to leave China, that, "the letter C painted on his breast, designating him for California, P for Peru, or S for the Sandwich Islands, is really a matter of indifference to him". Bowring did not say if he personally saw those men, or where.

The *Chili* had initially sailed from Cumsingmoon supposedly for California, but after putting back, set sail again, this time openly for Callao. There was no report on whether the Chinese knew their true destination. However, the *Robert Bowne* mutiny did not appear to substantiate Bowring's assertion that the men would have been indifferent as to where they were going.

The 504-ton *Robert Bowne*, an American ship of New York, under Captain Leslie Bryson, left Amoy on 21 March 1852, with a crew of 14 and 410 coolies ostensibly for San Francisco but strongly believed to be for Callao and the

Chincha Islands. The vessel was wholly owned by the captain. She was fitted up in the most compact manner for an emigrant ship, but the sanitary conditions were grossly inadequate. Coolies began to die almost immediately after leaving port, from opium withdrawal and cholera.

Some of the crew gave an account of this gruesome incident.[26] Approaching the Loochoos, when only the captain, the man at the wheel, and a lad were on deck, about thirty of the coolies rushed on the captain, stabbing him with a bayonet. He was cut to pieces and thrown overboard. A guard was placed over the helmsman, while others went to the Mate's cabin and literally beat him to pieces. The thirty ringleaders, joined by many others, then marched forward driving and murdering the watch on deck.

When the second mate, who had been out on the jib boom, found the captain murdered along with some of the crew, he rushed down the forecastle to warn the watch below. With three muskets, they went back on deck, shooting one coolie in the leg. The second mate fought desperately, killing five coolies with an axe, but was eventually overpowered, and thrown overboard. The remaining men then took refuge in the forepeak.

The ringleader was an Amoy man, who had recently left the *Flying Cloud* and acted as the interpreter. He stood on one of the deckhouses, with a six-barrel revolver in one hand and a flag in the other, giving orders. He had lieutenants and quartermasters; one standing over the American at the wheel with a long knife in his hand. It was later found that the thirty who rose first all belonged to one society or one village, seventy to another, and so on.

After anchoring the ship at Ishigaki to the north of Formosa (Taiwan), 380 of the mutineers went on shore making the remainder of the crew take them in the ship's boats. Just as the sailors rowed back to the ship, a breeze sprang up, and the crew shipped the anchor, and stood out to sea. The *Robert Bowne* struck on a coral reef, but the sailors managed to jump the ship over it. With patient negotiation, the crew succeeded in winning over the 21 Chinese guards still on board. The remaining crew, consisting only of six

Americans and three Kanakas (Pacific islanders), then brought the ship back to Amoy.

The *China Mail* went on to comment that they were not satisfied that there was no more to be told, or that it was altogether without provocation that the captain and his officers were murdered. "If it be true that they wantonly cut off the men's pigtails, the provocation was equivalent to cropping the ears or slitting the noses of so many Europeans; and were the experiment tried upon a shipload of Irish emigrants, for example, who would be surprised at the outrage being similarly avenged?"

The *China Mail* was yet to be convinced that, in the frightful tragedies on the *Albert*, the *Victory*, and now the *Robert Bowne*, the outrages had been unprovoked; or that they would have occurred, even had the treatment been different. It was necessary to show a probability that under different management they would have made the voyage without a murmur and without crimes, "at which civilized humanity shudders".

José Sevilla continued his relationship with Elias when he bought another British ship, the 233-ton *Sarah*, and named her *Rosa Elias*—after the daughter of Dom Elias. She left Cumsingmoon on 8 March 1853, bound for Callao. The *Rosa Elias* had 200 coolies on board, including 45 boys under the age of 12, and a Chinese doctor. Most of them had been kidnapped and then forcibly carried on board, or were enticed by Chinese coolie brokers on various pretexts to see the vessel, from which they were then not allowed to leave.

At first all was well, but within a month of departure, the water ration was cut by nearly half, with the resultant dissatisfaction starting a riot. This was suppressed by the crew, but the strong antagonistic feeling that was displayed meant that firearms were kept in constant readiness. On 6 April, the vessel passed Anjer, where supplies of water and supplies could have been obtained, but no water was procured.

Santos Roymundi, a servant on the *Rosa Elias*, was quoted as saying, "all had gone well until the vessel was abreast of Anjer when the coolies made a rush for the round house while the Captain and crew were at dinner".[27] On the alarm being given, the captain and the chief mate fired pistols, shooting two of the assailants. They then retreated to their cabins, but when the coolies began pouring boiling water into the cabins, they escaped through the ports into the sea. Several of the Chinese, having armed themselves with cutlasses, lowered a boat, pursued the Master and Mate, and butchered them in the water. Some of the crew, most of whom were Manilamen, jumped over the side and held on by ropes, while others mounted the rigging. The carpenter succeeded in swimming to shore, a distance of between three and five miles, and reached Batavia.

The coolies, now in control of the ship, then compelled one of the crew to navigate to China. He steered in the direction of Singapore instead, and this was discovered by the Chinese only when about 40 miles from port. During the night, most of the crew escaped and reached Singapore. On hearing of the mutiny, the brig, *Rival*, under Captain Franklyn, sailed with a large party of Europeans, quickly falling in with the *Rosa Elias*, and succeeded in bringing her in. Ten of the ringleaders were taken into custody to await instructions from the Peruvian Consul at Canton.

In September 1855, James Tait & Co. of Amoy chartered the 749-ton American ship *Waverly* from her owner, Thomas Curtis of Boston, for worldwide trading for a period not exceeding 30 months. In turn, Tait chartered her to Robinet & Co. of Canton for a voyage from Amoy and Swatow to Callao. Extracts from the log kept by Chief Mate French show she took on board 353 coolies in the outer roadstead of Amoy on 27 September 1855 and sailed for Swatow on 2 October, arriving on the 4th. On 8 October, the *Waverly* took on another 97 coolies but one immediately escaped by swimming ashore during the night. Even before the ship sailed on 12 October, two more had jumped overboard and drowned.[28]

Within a day of departure, a fight lasting half an hour had broken out between the Amoy and the Swatow coolies. Then two coolies jumped overboard and drowned before a boat could be lowered. On 15 October, Captain Wellman took sick and died two days later. In the ship's log, Chief Mate French recorded that many of the coolies were sick and the "remainder nothing else than a set of pirates and thieves".[29]

Chief Mate French decided to head for Manila. As they passed Corregidor on 24 October and as provisions were being served, a great number of the coolies made a rush towards the barricade, demanding opium. Not able to control the coolies, French conceded. That evening they again rushed the barricade. On 25 October, the cooks refused to cook, demanding wages to be paid every month. The others continued fighting among themselves, almost killing one of the Swatow cooks. They also demanded to be fed three times a day and paid a dollar before they went back to sea.

On arrival at Manila, the Mate alerted the health authorities about the sanitary condition of the ship, which he considered caused the death of the captain, and one of the coolies. The next morning the coolies again demanded more opium and French once again obliged and also provided bread as requested.

When ordered to proceed down the bay to Cavite the crew refused, claiming they were not safe. The *Waverly* eventually proceeded to Cavite on 27 October, but on arrival, the coolies once again rushed the barricade. This time the crew resisted and shot four of the men before driving them below. Venturing below for water at 3pm, the crew found that the lock to the provisions area had been broken. Before returning on deck, Chief Mate French shot one of them for being impudent. Several of them tried breaking off the hatch but were repulsed.

After attending the captain's funeral, French then spent the rest of the day ashore. After midnight of the 28th, the hatches were removed only to discover that the coolies had murdered one another. They had broken the bar off the hatches, and broken up two or three of the bunks to use as weapons. "Some were hanging by the neck, some had been shoved down into the tanks; some had their throats cut, many were strangled to death." Of the 150 survivors, 16 were classed as sick.

The mate and crew were imprisoned on board by the Spanish authorities. On 17 December, at Manila, lighters were brought alongside and the captain of the Port offered to take the Chinese ashore, but they refused, indicating they would die first. They had armed themselves with capstan bars and knives, refused food, and took only water.

By 20 December, the Spanish Government still had done nothing further, so the crew of the *Waverly* took it upon themselves to remove the 138 remaining Chinese. The coolies had bars, knives etc. for their defence, but the crew acted so fast that they were useless. By noon all were delivered to the barque *Louise*. This 284-ton German barque, identified by Mario Castro de Mendoza[30] as the 216-ton *Lamsa*, arrived in Callao in April 1856 from Manila with 110 Chinese, 34 of the original 144 having died on the voyage. The mortality rate was 75.56%, the highest rate of this Chinese diaspora.

Robinet sued Tait for the loss of the voyage, provisions and advances to the coolies, alleging that it was the fault of the ship and officers. Tait paid $17,000 in damages, and the ship was released and sent on another voyage. When Curtis pursued Tait for the charter money, Tait counter-claimed alleging that the loss of the voyage was due to the incapacity and misconduct of Acting Master French, and to there being no second navigator on board. The owners were thus to be held responsible for those breaches.

Another mutiny involving an American vessel at Namoa occurred on the clipper *Winged Racer* which left on 24 December 1855 with 900 men. After a speedy voyage of 68 days, 730 were able to land, a loss of 170. The coolies mutinied even before the ship had left, but Captain Gorman simply flogged sixty of them, putting down the insurrection, and the ship sailed on without further mishap. Among the 450 Chinese on board were seven girls.

The 414-ton Peruvian barque *Carmen* left Swatow on 1 March 1857 with seven cabin passengers and 260 men. On 5 March, when off the Great Natamas, the interpreter warned the captain that the coolies were intending to take the ship. He immediately confined the coolies below, and all was quiet until the next morning, when the coolies were permitted to come on deck. Whilst the crew were at breakfast the Chinese went forward and set fire to some straw, upon which the officers and crew armed themselves, and forcibly drove the coolies below again, and fastened down the hatches. The explosives were thrown overboard as the crew fought the flames, but in vain, as they spread over the whole ship in a few minutes, so quickly that they hardly had time to lower the boats. Without water or provisions, and without a chart or compass, the captain returned to the *Carmen* to retrieve these and a sail which could not be found in the boat. He was not seen again. The Chinese had forced open the hatches, and climbed the rigging, but not for long, as the masts soon fell over. It is supposed that the captain's boat went down with the ship, which soon sank. Most of the Chinese were suffocated by the smoke. All of them perished except the interpreter, from whom it was ascertained that it was the intention of the Chinese to murder the officers and crew, and to beach and plunder the vessel.

In addition to the six mutinies there were three others which did not reach their destination.

William Robinet continued using Cumsingmoon for Sevilla when Elias lost his Chincha concession. But his first venture on his own account was not a success. The Peruvian ship *Beatrice,* of 376 tons, sailed from Cumsingmoon on 2 February 1852 bound for Callao. The ship became leaky, and the captain bore up for Singapore. While at anchor in the roads, riots broke out with affrays marked by instances of stabbing, and even an attempt to wound the captain. Small parties escaped from the vessel almost nightly, and two days before the Chinese New Year, the coolies seized the lifeboats and went ashore. With no coolies left, the voyage was aborted.

The 650-ton *Grimaneza* was a Peruvian-flagged ship under the command of British Captain M.H. Penny. She left Namoa on 25 April 1854 with 648 coolies consigned to Sevilla & Co. in Callao. Following one of the several routes used by ships destined for South America, the *Grimaneza* headed to the north of the Philippines then south towards New Guinea. She went aground on Brampton shoal in the

Coral Sea on 4 July. The loss of the *Grimaneza* provided an insight into the indifference and callousness of ship captains to the lives of their charges, and their sometimes contempt for fellow seafarers.

The second mate and carpenter deposed that when the ship struck, the captain, doctor, and four of the crew put a case of wine and other things into the gig and left the ship. They believed that they ultimately took the chief mate with them. But before this, they secured all the Chinese men under hatches and left them so. There were some 648 Chinese, and 50 crew on board at the time.

The Chinese had been left battened down to perish, but they managed to burst open the hatch. About an hour after they got on deck, the ship floated off the reef. The ship made water very fast, but they baled and pumped. After scudding to the west for three days, the ship foundered when some of the Chinese would not continue to bale the ship. Before she went down, many made small rafts, and some embarked on single planks, clinging to them till exhaustion and the sharks put an end to their frightful existence.

Twenty-three of the crew and coolies escaped from the wreck. Some of the crew took to the long boat, and the second mate, along with 11 others, then took to a small boat, the only one left, after trying to back the ship off the weather shore. They sailed with their blankets before the wind to the eastward before being picked up by the *Scotia*. That day they had agreed to kill a little Calcutta boy, who was about twelve years old, for food. That was fortunately prevented. The *Eliza Warrick* of Boston had also picked up 17 men, six of whom Captain Thomas Strickland subsequently took on board the *Scotia,* as the *Eliza Warrick* was short of water and provisions.

After Captain Penny abandoned the *Grimaneza* in one of the quarter-boats, he landed on New Ireland after 25 days, and met up with a friendly tribe who took them to the whaler *Australia*. Captain Wiles was totally unsympathetic and uncouth, swearing that he was not bound to take them on, and wondered how he was to feed them. After three hours in his soaking clothes, Penny asked for a change of clothing, which was grudgingly thrown at him. He went on to say he was refused a glass of wine on the excuse there was none. In refuting the subsequent allegations, Captain Wiles said he took them onboard, clothed and fed them, as well as he could.

Captain Lewin Wiles returned to Sydney on 7 March and gave an account of the wreck of the *Grimanesa* to the *Sydney Morning Herald* the next day. Captain Strickland, who had returned to Sydney earlier, followed with his account on 10 March 1855. At the same time Captain Penny wrote to the Melbourne newspaper, *Argus*, accusing Captain Wiles of being a heartless man.[31] Captain Wiles's immediate rebuttal, countersigned by some former members of his crew, then appeared in the *Sydney Morning Herald*. This in turn provoked a letter to the Editor of the *Sydney Morning Herald* from someone using the penname of "Neptune", very critical of Captain Penney whom he declared had abandoned his charges.[32] He called on Wiles to defend himself, and praised Captain Strickland for his humanitarian actions.

On 1 June 1854 the 482-ton British ship *Topaz* under Captain Sevinton left on a voyage from Hong Kong to Callao with 408 Chinese bound for Callao. When news reached Hong Kong that she had been wrecked on the Pratas reef, a small schooner, the *Victoria,* set off on 13 June 1854 to look for survivors. On arriving at the reef, the *Victoria* was able to take on board only 147 men, leaving some 300 others to lie in the burning sun with no food or water. On returning to Hong Kong, the authorities tried to get a steamer to pick up the remaining survivors, but no offers were forthcoming unless an amount of £1000 was paid. However, Captain Lukey of the British barque *Cassiterides* did eventually bring 261 of those stranded on the Pratas reef to Hong Kong.

High mortality

In the testing years between 1852 and 1857 there were eleven sailings for Peru which resulted in mortality rates above 20%.

There was only one sailing from Amoy for Callao in this period. The 560-ton American ship *Dalmatia* suffered a loss of 24.77% after taking on 331 Chinese on 31 August 1855. Captain Hunter was able to produce only 249 of them 154 days later. Of the two sailings from Cumsingmoon, the *Empresa* on her third voyage suffered a mortality loss of 22.59%. There were 425 coolies placed on board on 19 March 1853 with 329 able to disembark.

An American ship to be involved in the coolie trades was the barque *Ohio* which arrived at Whampoa on 7 November 1852. She was reported by the US Consul at Canton as having been cleared for San Francisco on 2 December 1852. However the *Ohio* had actually been chartered by Macao Emigration Agent Alson for a voyage from Cumsingmoon to Callao. The Danish Captain Raupach loaded 300 men on his 373-ton vessel and sailed from the anchorage for Arica in Chile on 24 November 1852. She arrived after a 174-day voyage with 228 of them. After landing some of the men she then went on to Callao and landed the remaining 195 of them there.

There were four sailings from Swatow with high rates of mortality. The *Buenaventura* suffered a loss of 24.30% in 1855. When the American 272-ton brig *Ernani,* flying the Chilean flag, took on board 202 Chinese on 1 February 1856, only 155 of them disembarked, reflecting in part a disregard of the tonnage rules.

The 489-ton Chilean barque *Francisco* left Swatow on 1 May 1855, with 350 Chinese. Captain Haas took 123 days to reach Callao, but only 201 men were left to go ashore. The mortality rate was 42.57%, one of the highest recorded. No cause was identified.

The 415-ton Peruvian ship *Amalia* was another vessel to cause concern. Sailing from Swatow on 1 August 1855, she took more than 153 days to arrive at Callao, losing 130 of her 415 complement, a loss of 31.33%. There was serious overcrowding on this ship, with a ratio of one person for each registered ton of the vessel. The notional number for the time was one person for two, but seldom enforced.

Macao was only slightly better. In 1855 William Robinet secured the charter of the Peruvian *Cora* for at least two voyages. This 1,297-ton ship, previously the American *Gazelle*, left Macao on 14 October 1855 under British Captain E. Vincent with 710 coolies bound for Callao. She passed Anjer on 9 November, and after a 109-day voyage, landed only 480 of those men. The loss of 230 was attributed to foul ballast. The mortality rate was 32.39%.

The 1,110-ton American clipper *Indiaman* sailed from Swatow on 14 June 1855 with 565 Chinese, including the first known shipment of women, 93 in all. She arrived at Callao on 24 September 1855 after a voyage of 102 days. The disturbing factor was that 129 coolies had died before reaching land. The mortality rate for this Lomer & Co. charter was 22.83%.

Apart from the *Carmen*, mentioned earlier, the only other shipment in 1857 was by the 730-ton Peruvian ship *JCU*, with another severe loss of life as 278 men only were disembarked out of 450 taken on in Macao on 21 March 1857. The mortality rate was 38.22%. This was the last ship to bring coolies under the "Chinese Law".

The Chincha Islands

The Chinchas are a group of three islands some 13 miles south of Lima near the town of Pisco. The two main islands are about one mile square and steeply rise to a plateau about 100 feet above sea level. These plateaux provide nesting sites for thousands of birds, whose droppings form guano, a rich form of fertilizer.

The "Chinese Law" of 1849 had been introduced to satisfy the demands of planters, but many Chinese were employed by the owners of haciendas as house servants, cooks, bakers, and gardeners. They had also been employed as porters and general handymen in mercantile houses.

The many abuses perpetuated on the Chinese, particularly on the guano fields of the Chincha islands, were becoming a cause of concern, and this led to calls for the repeal of the "Chinese Law". The multiple abuses gave rise to sharp criticism, forcing the Government to issue decrees, dated 3 March 1853 and 9 July 1854, designed to improve the condition of coolies, but with little effect.[33]

To forestall any attempt to abrogate this law, Elias had a pamphlet published in which 100 employers gave their opinions of their Chinese labourers. Those employed in factories were said to work well, but those in the fields were weak and lacked intelligence. Nevertheless, they performed their tasks with exactitude.

Surprisingly, Elias allowed the publication to report the state of the Chinese, working guano on the Chinchas, as being particularly bad. He was said to have employed 600 coolies on the islands, along with 50 slaves and 200 natives of Chile and Peru. The coolies were made to dig the dusty guano, then wheel the fertiliser to a holding depot as much as a mile away. Their quota was five tons per day, seven days a week.

On 27 June 1854, the captains of nine British ships which had recently returned from the Chinchas sent a Memorial to the Lords of the Privy Council for Trade. The masters drew their Lordships' attention to the murderous cruelty practised on the Chinese labourers brought to those islands, mostly, if not solely, in British vessels.

In a vivid description of the atrocities being practiced on the Middle island, they named Don Elias and his negro foreman Kossuth as the perpetrators. Floggings "by a lash of four plaits of cowhide laid in the form of what seamen call 'round sennet', five feet in length, an inch and a half in diameter, tapering to a point, and such as we, who have never been in slave countries without witnessing flogging, could not have thought could be applied to human beings without causing death, and can only compare to the Australian stockwhip".

This *cri de coeur* touched the Lords who asked Lord Clarendon to intervene. He immediately ordered Consul Sulivan in Lima to request that some person accompany a Peruvian officer to ascertain how the orders of the Government were executed.

The Earl of Clarendon then wrote to Governor Bowring in Hong Kong instructing him to prevent fresh shipments of Chinese emigrants to the Chincha Islands. Bowring issued a Proclamation prohibiting British subjects from engaging in that trade on 11 September 1854. That proclamation brought a strong response from the Consul for Peru in Canton. But Consul Robinet was already well aware of the atrocities at

Chincha. On 11 February 1854, he had written to his Foreign Minister saying the Guano Islands were seen to be prisons where Chinese were maltreated. He said that it would be difficult to deny this, as the captains of Peruvian vessels themselves gave such information. The captain of the *Victoria* had told him, in presence of another person, that the Chinese in the Chincha Islands were treated worse than slaves.

Despite frequent promptings from British Consul Sulivan, Gomez Sanchez, the Peruvian Foreign Minister, did not reply until 12 December 1854. He admitted that the Peruvian Government had known of the accusations, and had instigated an inquiry. On receipt of that despatch from Lima, Clarendon instructed Bowring that it was unnecessary to continue the prohibition against the conveyance of Chinese emigrants to the Chincha Islands in British vessels.

The stigma of the Chinchas remained long after the last Chinese had left the islands. Whenever a Chinese coolie ship to Peru was mentioned, it was inevitably referred to as a slave ship bound for the guano pits on the Chinchas.

Peruvian Decrees of 1854

On 15 September 1854, President Ramon Castilla of Peru issued a Decree declaring that the Chinese were to receive 8 dollars a month, that they not be ill treated and that good provisions were to be supplied. In a later statement, the Peruvian Government had resolved that any person who embarked in Asia for Peru should be young, moral, healthy, and industrious. Care had to be taken to ship them in good, sound vessels, in condition to perform the voyage, and provided with sufficient wholesome food. The number to be received on board was no more than that allowed according to the tonnage of the vessel. Thirdly, that at the foot of every contract with emigrants, there must be appended the certificate and seal of the Peruvian agent or Consul, who was to certify to the free and voluntary agreement made between the emigrants and contractor, and witnessed by two persons.

Then, on 3 December 1854, Castilla decreed that all slaves were forever free. As this was appreciated to cause a shortage of labour, special licences were available to those who could show they needed Chinese workers.

Lomer & Co. were quick to take advantage of these special licences, advertising extensively that they were going to use only fast American clipper ships which would make the journey faster than steamships, thereby allowing for healthy and happy labourers. He sought only robust and healthy people with strong constitutions.

The first and third charters, both previously mentioned, were the *Indiaman* with high casualties and the *Winged Racer* which suffered a mutiny. The second Lomer charter was incident free. The *Westward Ho,* a 1,633-ton American clipper built in 1852, sailed from Whampoa on 27 October 1855 with 830 Chinese. After a 100-day voyage Captain S.B. Hussey landed 728 of them. The *Westward Ho* was subsequently bought by the Compania Maritima del Peru which utilised her for seven coolie voyages before she was wrecked in Callao.

The 1,283-ton British ship *Zetland* supposedly cleared from Amoy on 28 April 1855. Her 400 Chinese coolies had actually been taken on at Camboy near Swatow. After a 156-day voyage, Captain Flavin was able to see only 336 of them go ashore in Callao. The 643-ton Dutch barque *Delfshaven* left Whampoa for Callao on 22 May 1855. Captain P. Van Calcar had a good voyage delivering 340 of the 342 he had taken onboard.

The 1,704-ton clipper ship *Bald Eagle* of Boston made the 15,662 mile voyage from Swatow to Callao in 83 days. She averaged 188 miles a day, with the last 37 days averaging 203. Carrying royal sails, her longest run was 346 miles.[34] She left on 6 September 1855 with 650 men under Captain Treadwell but landed only 550 of them. The mortality rate was 15.38%.

The 581-ton Peruvian ship *Maria Natividad* under Captain Sullivan made her second voyage in the coolie trades on 28 January 1856, sailing from Whampoa to Callao wih 350 men, 330 of whom were landed. The *Maria Natividad*'s first voyage had been with free emigrants from Hong Kong to Melbourne in 1855.

In October 1855, Captain E.M. Jefferson left Callao as Master of the Peruvian 198-ton brig *Theresa Terry* on a voyage to China via Manila. Jefferson had sailed for 16 years on American ships mainly out of New Orleans. The chief mate was Francisco Duble whom Jefferson soon considered incompetent and stood down, but with freedom to roam the ship. Duble incited the crew to refuse to take orders from the captain, and eventually held him captive, first in his own cabin, then chained and manacled in the ship's hold. The owner, John Terry, joined the ship on 15 March 1856 in Manila when she sailed for Ningpo and Hong Kong. Terry did not release Jefferson from captivity in the hold and appointed Duble master of the *Theresa Terry*. In April, while the ship was at Whampoa, Jefferson was able to have a letter smuggled off the ship and taken to the British Consul at Whampoa. On receipt of the message, Vice Consul Sampson alerted Captain Jenkins of HMS *Comus* who boarded the ship and released Jefferson into the care of the British Consul.

The *Theresa Terry* and her sister ship, the 1,069-ton Peruvian *Antonia Terry*, caused great speculation in local circles as the two ships shuffled about the China coast, seemingly without purpose. On 28 May 1856, both the *Theresa Terry* and the *Antonia Terry* arrived at Macao from Whampoa, then sailed the next day for Peru.

The *Antonia Terry* was off the north coast of Formosa when she was dismasted in a typhoon. She was struggling to make Shanghai when she was caught in another storm. She eventually did arrive at Shanghai and sailed on 28 July 1856, still with her original complement of 550 who had boarded in Whampoa. When she eventually arrived at Callao in November 1856, Captain Geycour was able to disembark 486 of those men.

Meanwhile, the *Theresa Terry* may have escaped the storms but had to call at San Francisco for water on 5 August 1856. Many years later, Captain J.M. Shotwell recalled the visit.[35] He had been consigned the vessel (which he described as a barque) and had to go out to her in the middle of a gale. He found that the seamen were deserting one by one and the Chinese clamouring to be put ashore. He had the Chinese battened below deck. The captain was helpless and the crew openly laughed at him.

Back on shore he told the agents of the situation who in turn informed him that the Chinese merchants of San Francisco were getting out writs of habeas corpus for all the coolies onboard. That would ruin the owners and he had to get the vessel back to sea again. The only tug in the bay was being overhauled, but Shotwell managed to persuade Captain Charles Goodall of the urgency. With the promise of no expense to be spared he got an extra gang and the tug was ready to sail by nightfall. The stevedore Bill Nye promised to have all the water casks filled by 3 o'clock and the boarding master agreed to ship a new crew on time. Boarding the *Theresa Terry* at daybreak, Shotwell found the captain hiding among the casks to avoid arrest should any Revenue Officer go onboard.

The Revenue cutter *Martin L. White* had a harrowing time beating down to the vessel. The officer however could not board as he was met by 20 men armed with cutlasses. He left and when he returned the next morning the ship had gone. The *Teresa Terry* eventually arrived at Callao in October with only 145 Chinese on board.

Peruvian "Chinese Law" abrogated

The Peruvian "Chinese Law" was abrogated on 5 March 1856, on the ground that it had not fulfilled its purpose. and was degenerating into a kind of slave trade. The proclamation also highlighted the crowded conditions on board the emigrant ships, and the poor quality of the food which at times accounted for one third of those embarked dying, and the remainder arriving with dangerous diseases. The abrogation was to come into effect four months from that date. However, the traffic did not cease completely with the publication of this decree.

"On October 1 of the same year, the government made a contract with an English company for the short railway linking Lima with Chorrillos, a coastal residential town, and inserted a clause which permitted the introduction of 700 Chinese under the former system of contracts".[36] This shipment was identified as being on the *Westward Ho*, which sailed from Whampoa on 17 March 1857 with 770 Chinese. The 723 who landed were consigned to J. Ugarte.[37]

**Macao: The Inner Harbour, c. 1840. Chinese artist.
Departure port 1851-1874.
Macao Museum of Art.**

**Callao harbour.
Destination port, 1852 -1874.
© National Maritime Museum, Greenwich, London.**

3

Britain Enters The Trade

Following representations from the West India Committee in 1850, the Colonial Secretary, Lord Grey, agreed to consider again the possibility of Chinese labour. He wrote to Governor Bonham of Hong Kong, "to ascertain and report on the practicability of inducing Chinese labourers to proceed from China". His reply was in the form of a Memorandum, dated 3 October, from James D. Muir, the Hong Kong partner in Syme, Muir & Co., a merchant house engaged in recruiting emigrants from Amoy, where the other partner, Francis D. Syme was based.

Muir gave a general overview of the emigration scene and listed the destinations to which labourers had been sent to date. He considered the French Bourbon emigration to have been successful, but the British Mauritius experiment not so, from Penang. He did not know much about the Havana recruitment, but thought that it had been a financial failure, as was the *Nimrod* shipment to Australia.

Impatient at the slow progress of agreement, the Court of Policy of British Guiana decided to take things into their own hands. They induced Governor Barkly to recommend to the Home Government that James Thomas White should be nominated for the post of Emigration Agent in India. White had been the proprietor of three sugar plantations recently placed in receivership, and was in the process of returning to England. They considered his practical experience would be ideal in selecting the proper type of coolie.

Earl Grey agreed in September 1850; but as the incumbent Emigration Agent Caird had only just been re-appointed, White would be given the opportunity only of seeing for himself the conditions in India; and to assist in the selection of migrants. But James White was free to go to

China at the end of the season, to gather information on the means of procuring labour from that source. With that approval, White embarked on the P&O mail liner *Erin,* on her maiden voyage from Calcutta, arriving in Hong Kong on 26 May 1851. He carried letters of introduction from the Colonial Secretary, Earl Grey, and the Foreign Secretary, Lord Palmerston.

One of his first contacts in Hong Kong was the James Muir who had supplied Governor Bonham with his evaluation of the prospects of Chinese emigration in 1849. Muir offered his firm, Syme, Muir & Co. as the supplier of Chinese emigrants from Amoy. Syme Muir was experienced in the business and knew exactly what was required.

They would land the migrants for £18 a head, or £7 shipped on board. The Chinese contracts would be for five years, for two to four dollars a month, with two suits of clothing each year. Their passage would be found, as also their provisions, medical expenses, and housing. While a return passage had not previously been included in earlier contracts, he suggested that a bonus for renewal of contract after the initial term would be preferable. He thought the Chinese would prefer to be paid by the task rather than on a daily basis of nine hours work, if it grossed a higher figure than that originally agreed to.

White went on to Canton, where he met the colourful John Bowring (1792-1872). A one-time Member for Bolton, his membership of the Select Committee on Commercial Relations with China led, in 1847, to his appointment as British Consul at Canton. Bowring had settled in quickly, adding Chinese to his list of languages. He was interested in his surroundings and was very eager to enlighten White on the characteristics of the Chinese people. Bowring's enthusiasm was so infectious that after a single visit to the countryside observing men toiling away in the fields, White was moved to describe one Chinese as equal to five Bengalis.

In his first letter to Governor Barkly of British Guiana, dated 21 June 1851, White proposed four possible courses of recruitment. First was the use of houses of high character and established repute such as Dent & Co. and Russell & Co. His second option was to utilise agents already procuring recruits for Manila and Peru, paying a commission for placing them on board, with the British West Indian colonies (in this instance, British Guiana and Trinidad) taking the risk of transportation. He then suggested the free market approach, whereby a bounty would be paid for every migrant landed, and his fourth course was to appoint an emigration agent to undertake the whole task. He did not indicate his preferred option.[38]

In his second letter, of 19 July 1851, White went to great length describing the difficulty of recruiting women, and suggested that boys could be more readily obtained. Given the greater shipping distance involved, he estimated the cost from China would be £2 more than from India.

Four days later, James White's third letter contained propositions from an elder from the sugar-growing district of Tung Wan, and from Teo Cheo (from where many Chinese had already emigrated to Singapore and the Straits Settlements). The propositions were very clearly laid out. Hawa, from Teo Cheo, promised only strong and hale men who did not smoke opium, headmen who were conversant with English, and who would also have Chinese medical qualifications. But these points were not to be appreciated by White until he himself became involved with the recruiting process.

While James White's despatches were full of promise, it was John Bowring who convinced the West Indian plantation owners. In his Annual Report on Trade, as already mentioned, Bowring wrote of the abundance of suitable labour available in China, and the apparent eagerness of the men to migrate irrespective of destination.

Without waiting for any further reports from James White, the Court of Policy of British Guiana resolved, on 25 August 1851, to bring Chinese immigrants to the colony as soon as possible. The Court resolved to provide a $100 bounty for each effective Chinese immigrant engaged to labour for five years, and allocated £50,000 as a guaranteed loan for the importation of Chinese.

So great was the excitement in Georgetown, following this resolution, that George Booker,[39] a prominent plantation owner on the Court of Policy, continued to discuss it with his fellow members and planters. This led to a letter to J. Gardiner Austin, the Acting Government Secretary, on 2 September, offering his ship, the *Lord Elgin*, to sail for Hong Kong to begin the recruitment programme as early as possible.

Governor Barkly was more circumspect, but not wishing to go against the influential planters, sought clarification as to what exactly they wanted. He then wrote to Earl Grey on 31 October 1851 explaining how this proposal came about. In defending his granting of licences for both the outward and return voyages for the *Lord Elgin*, Barkly mentioned only that the vessel had been approved, and that Dr David Shier, the brother and assistant to the Agricultural Chemist, had been engaged as surgeon. The licences had been based on the requirements imposed on ships already under contract for the carriage of Indians. He concluded by hoping that he did not exceed his authority, but considered that the undertaking could prove beneficial to the colony, with little prospect of profit to Mr Booker.

This British Guiana resolution led to Hyde, Hodge & Co. announcing that they would be sending two or three ships to China in order to claim the bounty from the Government. James Hyde came from a long-established family with mahogany plantations in British Honduras. Hodge was a London merchant. Their company employed their own vessels to carry their mahogany to Britain, then to ship liberated Africans from Sierra Leone and St Helena to the West Indies.

The Trinidad planters were not nearly as enthusiastic. With a smaller crop, their needs were not nearly as acute, but they did not want to be left out of this possible migration programme. As the British Guiana Government had already taken steps to satisfy their immediate needs, the CLEC called on Hyde, Hodge & Co. to divert one of their bounty ships to Trinidad instead of British Guiana, and as a reward offered them a charter for two additional ships.

On White's return from China, the Court of Policy pressed the government for him to be appointed as the Government agent in China. When White accepted the position, he returned to China in August 1852, spending less than two months in England.

Meanwhile, on 12 June 1852, new Foreign Secretary Malmesbury directed Acting Superintendent of Trade John Bowring to enquire of the British Consuls their opinions on the prospects of Chinese emigration.[40] Adam Wallis Elmslie was Bowring's replacement as Canton Consul, and the first to reply to Malmsbury's questions on 25 August 1852. He provided statistics on the number of emigrants from Whampoa, Cumsingmoon, Macao, and Hong Kong. He stated that placards were openly distributed all over the country notifying the departure of vessels for California, with the Chinese authorities not interfering in any way with the emigration. Elmslie was the first to alert the Government to the misery and suffering endured by the Chinese sent to dig guano on the Chincha islands of Peru but added that the traffic appeared to be at an end with no ships prepared to accept charters for what could be a dangerous voyage marred by insurrections.

Harry Smith Parkes (1828-1885) was Interpreter, then Vice-Consul at Canton. Greatly impressed with the young man, Bowring asked Parkes to comment on the Malmesbury questionnaire. In describing the Chinese character, Parkes generally concurred with John Crawfurd's views. "The absorbing aim of the Chinese emigrant is to better his condition. Of this object he never loses sight; and as he often continues to retain it, even after he has gained the competency for which he first commenced to strive, it frequently follows that he finally adopts as his permanent home the locality in which he has reaped his profits, if adapted, by climate and the presence of others of his countrymen, to his native habits and mode of life."

Parkes argued, "China sanctions by law the emigration of its subjects for purposes of trade, or as hired labourers; but it is necessary that each person should be furnished with a pass on leaving his country, as without one he is liable to heavy punishment, graduated according to the extent of the intercourse he may have held with the foreigners whom he visited without permission. But the law in this respect, involving as it does even capital punishment, is far too severe for a weak government to carry into execution; and thus a pass from the authorities is the last thing that a Chinese emigrant ever thinks of procuring; not because it would be refused him, but on account of the cost of the application, perhaps ten or twenty dollars, by which sum may be estimated the extent of the risk incurred by the omission."[41]

Parkes had noted that emigration from Canton, both in junks and foreign vessels, continued to increase each year. For deck-passages in foreign vessels, which they preferred to their own junks, they paid from five to ten dollars, and always provided their own food. The great majority of the emigrants were relations or friends of planters or tradesmen, and were proceeding under contract to join them. They generally travelled in small parties of twenty or thirty, sometimes in charge of a man of respectability, who had perhaps come from the south specifically to engage them. Terms differed considerably. That was the traditional emigration pattern.

Parkes then identified a different form of emigration that was emerging. In the hope of finding gold, or participating in the high remuneration paid for labour of any kind, Chinese who flocked to California went merely as sojourners for one or two years. Many started with the expectation of returning as soon as they had amassed two or three hundred dollars, exclusive of expenses. The dispatch of those men was largely undertaken by moneyed parties purely as a matter of speculation. They paid the passage of the coolies, which rose as high as $50, and other expenses amounting to about $20 more, on condition of receiving the sum of $200 upon their return. Parkes surmised that emigration to the gold fields of Australia would probably be conducted in a similar manner.

Parkes ventured the view that a wholly different system would have to be pursued in obtaining coolies for the West Indies. He thought that passengers, rather than coolies, would be the better term for any Chinese emigrating under these circumstances—the former being reserved to denote labourers who are engaged to serve for a number of years at a uniform rate of pay. Chinese of this class contracted by Europeans had been shipped to Callao. That they were men of bad character, and others in most indigent circumstances, was evident from the harshness of the terms on which they consented to engage, as well as the frequent tragedies which occurred on board the vessels transporting them.

Charles Alexander Winchester was another "old China hand" who impressed Bowring with his understanding of the Chinese character. Winchester was the doctor in the Amoy Consulate and was convinced, "that it was a fiction that no child of the Great Emperor could withdraw himself from the parental rule", but he was unable to be as specific as Parkes.[42] While prohibition of emigration flowed from the common law, no mandarin would interfere when they knew that emigration relieved the pressure of surplus population on food supplies, and wild and lawless vagabonds were better out of the country. It was also true however that only the poorest and refuse of the population had so far volunteered to emigrate. Winchester was adamant that the Chinese never emigrated with their families, and one reason for their frequent return to the homeland was their anxiety to form matrimonial connexions and to leave descendants in their native villages to maintain an unbroken chain of reverential honours paid to the ancestral tombs. No Chinese ever left without the hope of eventually returning.

Winchester drew attention to the employment of crimps, politely called coolie brokers, used by the English merchants of Amoy. He said that no respectable Chinese would engage in a trade in what was regarded as, "the selling of men to an English merchant". The reputation of those coolie brokers was very low. They distributed printed bills containing the terms of the contract and acted as general touters, offering food and lodgings to anyone willing to be mustered. While they undoubtedly practised all the arts of recruiting, the men were not ill treated as the crimps received 50 cash daily for each man mustered, and a dollar for each coolie ultimately shipped. Competition was strong with rival brokers given to frequent quarrels. Kidnapping had so far not been practised.

In conclusion, Winchester quoted the late Consul Layton as estimating that 10,000 coolies could be recruited. A merchant of great experience had put the figure at 12,000, with Winchester declaring that neither figure was exaggerated. He however thought that such numbers would eventually require spacious roomy barracks to accommodate the coolies awaiting shipment. Present facilities were adequate for 6,000 labourers.

British Bounty Ships

James White arrived back in Hong Kong on 10 October 1852. With no new instructions, he sailed that same evening for Canton in order to learn from Turner & Co., the agents for Hyde, Hodge & Co., what progress was being made. He learned that two ships, the *Lord Elgin* and the *Glentanner* had already loaded at Amoy and departed for British Guiana before his arrival.

The first ship to sail for the British West Indies with Chinese passengers was the *Lord Elgin*, owned by the Booker family of British Guiana. Built in 1847 in Hampton, New Brunswick, she was 111ft long and had a breadth of 25ft. From her upper deck to the bottom of her keel, her measurement was 18ft. Under the new measurement rules that came into effect in 1846, her new registered tonnage of 351 tons allowed her to carry 110 passengers under the British Passengers' Act of 1852.

The *Lord Elgin* arrived at Hong Kong on 1 June 1852, and departed for Amoy ten days later. With no specific orders, Captain M'Clelland decided to place his ship in Tait's hands to arrange a complement of coolies. James Tait's interpretation of the Passengers' Act of 1849, then in force, was that it allowed one passenger per two tons of the ship's burthen. By this calculation, the *Lord Elgin* was permitted to carry 170 coolies, but Tait was able to place only 154 emigrants on board when she sailed for Demerara.

Demarara was one of three districts which were merged to form the colony of British Guiana and was the name most frequently used when referring to the colony. Georgetown was the capital and main port of the colony, but again ships were invariably cleared for Demerara rather than Georgetown.

The Passengers' Act would not have given Tait any guidance as to the appropriate stores for the voyage to the West Indies. In what would have been a sincere effort to provision the ship, he supplied the *Lord Elgin* with the following items.

Invoice of Stores for the voyage to Demerara

350 bamboo pillows	350 sleeping mats	100 razors
10 choppers	500 rice bowls	250 tea cups
200 brooms	250 combs	100 fireplace bricks
33 cooking places	10 iron pans	4 baskets soup pickles
100 rice ladles	50 baskets	50 mess lids
12 rice measures	50 large plates	6 gongs
14 guitars	12 flutes	500 bales chop sticks
2 bundles playing cards	6 bottles mustard	20 piculs pumpkins
8 large water tubs	50 catties tobacco	50 catties sulphur
90 jars sour pickles	15 piculs biscuits	10 piculs dried fish
20 piculs salt fish	20 piculs potatoes	10 piculs salt
2 tubs vinegar	2 piculs tea	10 piculs sugar
50 tubs cabbage	22 tubs, salt beef	12 piculs tea oil
5 piculs garlic	320 sheets	295 pairs of shoes
160 white waistcoats	160 yellow trousers	200 wooden shoes
160 yellow jackets	160 black jackets	160 black trousers

Note: A picul was equivalent to 100 catties, or 60.5 kg, 133 1/3 lbs.

By the time the *Lord Elgin* sailed on 23 July 1852, it was already well into the season of the southwest monsoon, and with adverse winds she took 62 days to reach Singapore where she took on provisions and firewood along with 45 tons of water. Four Chinese died on that first passage. The *Lord Elgin* left Singapore two days later, and as was the custom of sailing vessels, headed southeast to the Straits of Sunda. It took 23 days for her to reach Anjer on the western tip of Java, a distance of about 500 miles. It was a useful port of call for provisions or emergency assistance. Captain M'Clelland had not intended to call there, but because of the already extended length of the voyage, he decided to stop for more supplies.

Three days after leaving Anjer, she sprang a leak, probably caused by her grounding on a shoal known as Brower's Bank just two days before Anjer. She refloated without taking water then, and the captain thought all was well, but the ship had a cargo of rice in the lower hold which began to ferment. The ship was enveloped in a cloud of sulphurated hydrogen gas, which persisted for many days. Lingering smells persisted for most of the 46 days it took the ship to arrive at Cape Town with a loss of a further 41 Chinese.

More fresh food, including eight sheep and a carcass of mutton, as well as more medicines were taken on board before the *Lord Elgin* set sail for the 39-day voyage to Demerara. A further 19 Chinese died, making 69 deaths out of the 154 emigrants shipped at Amoy. After a voyage totalling 177 days, the ship arrived at Demerara on 17 January 1853 with 57 adults and 28 boys. The mortality rate was a horrendous 44.81%.

This sorry outcome from a brave attempt at importing new labour from China invoked the inevitable inquiry, which was chaired by Adriaan van der Gon Netscher, with members R.G. Butts, and Daniel Blair, the Surgeon-General. They found that poor water quality was partly to blame, but also the poor ventilation from the small hatches, and the closeness between decks did not help. The fact that 154 Chinese had been embarked meant that fewer than 11 superficial feet had been provided for each person.

Their conclusions were that the long confinement in foul air was the primary cause of the deaths; that the crankiness of the vessel did not allow for sufficient exercise, and the lack of fresh food did not help. They recommended that the Passengers' Act be the basis on which immigrants should be carried, and that no vessel of fewer than 1,000 tons be used. Despite the great mortality on his vessel, George Booker put in his claim for the bounty on the 85 immigrants landed. Despite some reservations, the bounty was eventually paid.

The 615-ton *Glentanner* was the first Hyde, Hodge & Co. bounty ship. She sailed from Amoy on 1 September 1852. As with the *Lord Elgin*, Tait calculated that she could carry 307 passengers. He accordingly provided her with 305 Chinese emigrants who had signed his form of agreement. The *Glentanner* arrived at Demerara on 12 January 1853, five days before the *Lord Elgin*. She arrived with 262 Chinese, suffering a loss of 43 emigrants. These first two ships for Demerara were completed without any form of government supervision, and without any recruiting problems.

White returned to Hong Kong on 14 October and had a long meeting with John Bowring, now Acting Governor. Warned of potential trouble, James White went on to Amoy on 17 October to find that Syme, Muir & Co., together with Tait & Co., held the Spanish contracts for Cuba, while Robert Jackson held two of the three contracts for Australia. Hyde, Hodge & Co. in London had appointed Turner & Co. of Canton as their agents, but as Turner's did not have an office in Amoy, they appointed Tait & Co. as their sub-agents there. White considered this an exceedingly objectionable position as Tait & Co. were already working for the Spaniards.

At this critical time, Tait had to find an additional 1,800 men in order to honour his contracts. Amoy and the surrounding countryside had already been scoured for willing, and not so willing recruits, and desperate measures were being taken by his Chinese brokers and their crimps to gather the required numbers. Tait himself went to Swatow seeking to organise a recruiting base in that quiet opium out-station.

Riots in Amoy

A peanut seller in a village some two days away from Amoy was accosted by a coolie broker who promised the man more rewarding work if he joined him in Amoy. Having agreed, he was taken to the Syme Muir receiving station. When he was not allowed out again, the coolie escaped through an opening in the water closet on 18 November 1852. The man took refuge in the servants' quarters of the Rev. Elihu Doty, an American missionary, when he was pursued by Syme's employees.

This incident was the spark that ignited the growing agitation of the local population against the unsavoury methods utilised by the coolie brokers. In the afternoon of Sunday the 21st, they cornered the broker, Lin Hwan, proceeded to beat him up, and then handed him over to the local police where the beating continued. On hearing this, Francis Syme took his assistant William Cornabe with him to the police station to demand his release. They left on being told the man was not the person they wanted. However, they returned when they learned that their man was indeed at the station. Securing his release, they were returning to their hong when the mob pounced on them. They were able to escape to their premises, together with Lin Hwan. But the crowd was not to be appeased and turned on three Europeans who were walking nearby. Arthur Walthew, a passenger on the ship *Australia*, resembled Syme, and was, together with Richard Vallancey, the mate of the *Australia*, returning to their ship. The third man was Aeneas Mackay of Tait & Co. In the ensuing scuffle, Vallancey was severely hurt.

The shops in Amoy remained closed the next day, and there was a feeling of great tension. The Acting Sub-Prefect at Amoy issued an Official Notice, warning that, "Kih-Tows (brokers), who deluded poor people to exploit them, committed a serious breach of the law. Strict orders had been given to the police for the apprehension of those guilty persons".

On Wednesday the 24th, the crowd gathered in front of the Syme hong demanding the broker. Syme immediately summoned the mandarins who took him away. But when the crowd was not to be pacified, Syme called for assistance from HMS *Salamander*, which was stationed at Amoy. As the sailors and marines dispersed along the street to protect British properties, the crowd began to throw brickbats, injuring several persons. After their commanding officer had twice been knocked down, the sailors opened fire, killing twelve, including a baby, and wounding about sixteen others.

The next day, Sub-Prefect Wang issued another Proclamation, "to reassure the native population, to calm all foreign merchants, and rigorously to prohibit ill-disposed persons from seeking occasion to foment disturbances". He advised that the broker Lin Hwan had now provided a deposition in which he confessed, "I am a broker; I have deceived and entrapped people. Because that day I had entrapped a man in Chuh-tsae Street, I was seized by the people who took and gave me over to the Chung-ting. Foreigners from the Ho-ke and Tih-ke hongs with their clerks came to claim me. A riot then took place on this account; I took this opportunity to escape into the Ho-ke hong; on the 24th of November I was removed from the hong to the magistracy".

But there was still disquiet, and placards appeared, some anonymous, and some attributed to scholars and merchants, exciting the multitudes, causing Wang to issue a further Proclamation dated 27 November calling on the populace to report such matters to him, and he would punish the parties concerned with the "utmost penalty of the law, and without a particle of mercy".

In a despatch, dated 26 November 1852, Bowring said that Commander Fishbourne of Her Majesty's steamer *Hermes* had just returned from Amoy and told him that coolies were penned up, ten to twelve, in a wooden shed, like a slave barracoon. In a space 120 by 24 feet, about 500 nearly naked and very filthy men had sufficient room only to lie on the bamboo floor. Many of the men had been induced to come into the town by Chinese crimps and then confined. While some escaped when they could, and others objected to the treatment, many stated that anything was better than starvation. A few who refused to embark were allowed to leave, but those who were not allowed to do so, had begun to take things into their own hands. Bowring also said that Amoy could no longer offer an adequate supply of labour to match the immense demand. It was reported that the captain of one of the opium ships at Namoa provided 1,000 coolies to the account of the Demerara contract.

Acting Consul John Backhouse, in poor health, had not been able to send his despatches until the 27th. When Bowring received them, he immediately sent Frederick Harvey, the Secretary to the Superintendency of Trade, to Amoy on HMS *Hermes* to investigate and report further. Harvey, together with Commander Fishbourne of HMS

Hermes, determined that a formal investigation would be appropriate. The Court of Inquiry commenced on Monday 13 December 1852.

With the great numbers that Tait controlled, an ordinary barracoon was not big enough to accommodate his gathered coolies. An expensive ship was his solution. It was also a very useful method of imprisonment, as the coolies could not easily escape from a ship several miles from shore. The 569-ton British barque *Emigrant* arrived at Amoy on 28 July 1852 where she was chartered by James Tait to become a coolie receiving ship.

Richard di Bois-Agett, the chief mate of the *Emigrant*, testified that he was not aware of any coolie on board his vessel being detained against his will, and had been instructed to release any who asked to do so. Seven coolies from the *Emigrant* were also interrogated. Each testified that they had been offered work in Amoy, taken to the ship on various pretences, and confined against their will. They declared they did not wish to emigrate.

Robert Jackson, originally a partner in the firm, Mitchell & Co. of Hong Kong, now engaged in recruiting coolies, was next to give evidence. Able to speak Chinese, Jackson produced a Notice expressing his desire to recruit labour for foreign lands at rates far higher than obtainable in Amoy. In Jackson's second Notice, he appealed to any person who did not have any relations dependent on him to come forward, and again promised that any victim of abduction should call on him, and he would be returned to his home.

Francis Syme then testified that he did attend the police station with the intention of freeing his broker Lin Hwan, while Cornabe would not admit to the practice of sending cards to the mandarins demanding certain things. John Connolly of Tait & Co. admitted to sending such cards; but only after having approval from the previous Consul, George Sullivan.

During the hearings, the broker Lin Hwan was produced, but he was in such a terrible state that he could only nod his head, acknowledging that he was the broker. He did not have much longer to live.

The result of the Inquiry was that Syme was fined $200, and Cornabe $20 for unlawfully visiting a police court and subsequently causing a riot. The gravely injured Vallancey made an extravagant claim for $5,000 compensation, which Backhouse arbitrarily dismissed as excessive. Pending an appeal, he put the claim aside and it was never followed up. But Bowring did question the existence of the claim.

But even as this was being finalised, relatives of the Chinese killed in the riots were petitioning the British Government to bring the Chinese brokers to trial and thus effect compensation. This of course was not within the British bailiwick, and the upshot of this was that the fines were given to the families of those innocently killed.

Perhaps it was due to the mild proclamation by the Scholars and Merchants of Amoy, and the Proclamation by the Inhabitants of the Eighteen Wards (of Amoy) threatening brokers with death, should they be found working for Syme or Tait, that no more coolies could be found. Backhouse then confirmed that the traditional Chinese migration to Singapore was still active with one ship sailing for that destination with cargo as well as 100 passengers.

The 669-ton British vessel *Samuel Boddington* arrived at Amoy on 12 September 1852 to load for British Guiana. She lay at anchor for 59 days before she received her first batch of 95 coolies. The weather had turned cold and some wished to go ashore, saying that they were deceived by Tait's brokers. Two men endeavoured to swim ashore on some small boards, a distance of two miles, but the gig was lowered, and they were picked up exhausted. Two days later another 104 coolies, were sent on board, more than half of them unfit for the purpose they were intended.

On 22 November, Tait & Co. said that in consequence of the city and country being "much disturbed"' they could get no more coolies, and that those collected must either be taken, or they would throw up the charter. The next day 147 coolies were brought alongside. Those already on board commenced heaving wood, pieces of iron bolts, belaying pins, etc. at the Europeans and coolie brokers, because they had been "kept so long without clothes or proper food".

When things quietened down and the coolies allowed to board, Dr Ely examined the men rejecting six of every ten men as not of the kind to make good labourers.

Captain Hurst and Dr Ely were told in plain terms that they had but one of two things to do; either take the complement, or lose any recompense for a short shipment. With that ultimatum, they could do nothing but accede to the 352 coolies already on board; 150 of whom had previously been rejected.

On 24 November, Amoy was in a state of great confusion and alarm. Captain Hurst was given a clearance certificate for 352 adults signed by Tait & Co. There was no demur from the British Consul even though the *Samuel Boddington* had been measured as having 4,144 superficial feet, which would have equated to 276 passengers at 15ft per person, or 345 at 12ft per person. She sailed from Amoy the next day, bound for British Guiana, without all of their supplies.

The first few days were uneventful, with many seasick. After a fight on 7 December over the theft of opium, there were signs of a mutiny among the coolies. This was highlighted when Captain John Hurst wrote to the *Shipping & Mercantile Gazette* from St Helena on 6 February 1853.

"On 9 December 1852, while persevering to get the ship through the narrows of Gaspar Strait during rain squalls, I received information that the coolies were making arrangements to murder myself and crew, and run the ship on the isle of Pulo Leat this afternoon. I at once gave directions to let run sheets and halliards, down helm, and down bower anchor, 20 fathoms water; ship took 90 fathoms of chain. I then put all hands under arms and went to work to pick out the ringleaders of this diabolical plot, and without shooting a man, I secured the ringleaders on the poop, with an exception of six who jumped overboard and perished. We then searched for arms, and found enough to arm 200 men, consisting of sharp ground axes, Malay cresses, dirks, knives and a variety of other murderous weapons. We have secured all, and no question this prompt stop has saved the ship."

The British Guiana Health Officer, John M. Johnstone, reported the ship's arrival after the 98-day voyage, during which 52 Chinese had died; another 27 being sent immediately to hospital. He conveyed the Captain's and Dr Edward Ely's remarks on the troublesome voyage which was chiefly due to the "quarrelsome disposition and vile habits" of the Chinese. Governor Barkly reported to the Secretary of State for War and the Colonies, the Duke of Newcastle, on the number of deaths, and then referred to certain delicate matters in Dr Ely's diary, which confirmed the urgent necessity of procuring a certain proportion of Chinese women for the Colony.[43]

The 1,170-ton ship *Australia* was chartered by Hyde Hodge & Co. in China. British Emigration Agent White had no direct responsibility for the ship, but with the turmoil in Amoy, he agreed to have her load at Namoa, the opium anchorage off Swatow. She left on 15 December 1852 with 445 coolies for Trinidad. White reported that the *Australia* loaded a, "very fine set, the best who have yet emigrated", without any bother. According to White, the *Australia* was admirably adapted for the service, having a great height between decks.

The *Australia* arrived at Port of Spain on 4 March 1853 after a voyage of 78 days with 432 adults on board and 31 crewmembers. Thirteen had died on the voyage and eight were sent to hospital. Thos Anderson, Inspector of Health of Shipping, reporting to the Acting Colonial Secretary, said the accommodations of the ship were good, with the exception of deficient aeration between decks. Additional ventilating tubes and side ports were wanting. Nevertheless, with the comparatively small mortality among the immigrants, and their satisfactory condition, he considered it a credit to the officers of the ship.

But Trinidad's Governor Lord Harris, not nearly as enthusiastic, chose to find fault. In his despatch to the Duke of Newcastle on 22 March 1853, he believed the cost of shipping was too high, and drew attention to the form of contract used, which though altered in one place was left incorrect in another. He observed that the English Consul in

Amoy refused to sign the ship's papers because he had no authority to do so from his own Government.—Harris did not understand that Swatow was a non-Treaty Port over which the Amoy consul had no authority.

Despite the Governor's negative feelings, the Trinidad Legislative Council resolved that a further 300 Chinese should be imported during the next year. They also wished that at least half that number should be women.

Emigration Agent White had agreed to have the 550-ton British barque *Clarendon* also load at Namoa, but this veteran of the East India Co. had already spent 56 days getting to Hong Kong from Singapore, and would have been excessively delayed beating up to Namoa. She accordingly was directed to load at Whampoa. Turner & Co. was confident of finding sufficient labourers for this new venture. They utilised a Mr Hunt at Whampoa, who in turn used Chinese brokers.

In his report of 8 January 1853 to Secretary Stephen Walcott at the Emigration Commission, White advised that the *Clarendon* left Whampoa on 2 January 1853 with a full complement of 257 adults. He said that the people were so eager to go that they remained in boats alongside for three or four days rather than stay ashore. Another 40 others had to be rejected to remain within the legal limit. They had been given a $10 advance and two suits of clothing. They were a cheerful lot and perfectly happy to board the *Clarendon* in the same manner as the ships taking migrants to California. He had explained through an interpreter how long it would take to Trinidad, and the type of work they would be expected to do, the wages they could earn, and a list of daily provisions they could expect. He was disappointed that he was unable to find any interpreters at either Amoy or Namoa, but hoped that some could possibly be found in Hong Kong. He also mentioned that it would have been possible to procure a few women, but the captain objected on the grounds of possible disturbances during the voyage.

The *Clarendon* arrived at Port of Spain on 23 April 1853. Captain George Bilton declared he departed Whampoa on 29 December 1852, which was four days earlier than reported by White. There were 254 emigrants at the commencement of the 114-day voyage, with only three deaths on passage, one being from dysentery, which also took the life of the chief mate.

White was aware that the unscrupulous coolie brokers at Amoy originally came from Canton. In order to overcome any strong public feeling against emigration, White had notices and instructions printed in English, and Chinese, for distribution throughout the region. In this endeavour, White enlisted the services of William Scott who had been the Secretary of the Chamber of Commerce in Canton, and well versed in the habits of the Chinese. The Notices advertised for healthy able-bodied Chinese coolies to work in the English settlements in the West Indies. It described how far away the islands were and the expected suitability of the climate. The terms of the contract were carefully set out and explained.

American Fears

It is not known if the Notices had any bearing on the only shipment from Whampoa in 1853, but it drew the attention of Humphry Marshall, the first United States Commissioner with the Legation based in Canton. A southerner concerned with the question of slaves, he worried about Chinese competition. When a Chinese version of White's notice found its way to the Legation and the re-translated version brought to Marshall's attention, he immediately became alarmed. He wrote to Edward Everett, his Secretary of State on 8 March 1853.[44]

He drew attention to the British Government's pursuit of Chinese emigration and the effect it would have on the United States. He contended that a strong British colony in the geographical position of British Guiana would command the Amazon valley and the entrance to the Caribbean Sea, and all the trade from the south with the Windward Islands. He wanted to know if the President contemplated a stop to prevent the use of American shipping in the furtherance of this emigration. He suggested the President send an order to the American consuls to refuse clearances to any ship under

American papers and colours when carrying coolies from China.

It was only after the *Australia* had loaded and left on 15 December 1852 that James White learned that Swatow was not a Treaty Port and that trade conducted there was illegal. White had also agreed to have the *Lady Flora Hastings* load at Namoa, but on learning of the breach of Treaty terms asked for the ship to revert to Amoy. Tait refused claiming it was too late to change arrangements. The ship was to complete the season's complement for Trinidad and had been chartered at £10 5s for every adult landed in the West Indies. She had taken on an English surgeon for £200 for the voyage.

The 674-ton *Lady Flora Hastings* departed from Namoa on 11 March 1853 with 314 Chinese emigrants under Captain W. Wild. When she arrived at Port of Spain on 28 June after a 108-day voyage, 9 men had died. On her arrival, 13 men had to be sent to hospital suffering from scurvy, complicated with rheumatic pains. The passengers, all aged between 14 and 40 were tended by two Chinese doctors, in addition to G.W. Nichols, the Surgeon.

Just as it appeared that no further shipping would become available, and White was preparing to return home, Turner & Co. was able to charter the *Emigrant*. This British vessel of 753 tons was rigged as a ship, and was not to be confused with the 594-ton barque *Emigrant*, also of British registry, had been used by Tait as his receiving ship at Amoy the previous year. William Pedder (1801-1854), the Hong Kong Harbour Master, surveyed the ship on 23 March and provided a certificate showing that the number of passengers allowed was 320. There were two stern ports, and twelve scuttles on each side; three hatchways, two large deck ventilators, and windsails. She had sound water casks, and four boats.

White left Hong Kong before the *Emigrant* sailed from Whampoa on 24 April 1853 bound for Demerara with 350 coolies, some 70 to 80 of whom were opium addicts. The next morning, the doctor found that one of the passengers had died of fever, and that there were several cases of typhoid. By the time the ship arrived at Hong Kong on 27 April, 30 cases had been recorded, and two more died soon after arrival.

A Commission of Enquiry, made up of the Chief Magistrate, the Harbour Master, the Colonial Surgeon, and two other medical men, was appointed on 5 May. The Commissioners reported within four days that the last captain had been sacked for drunkenness, and this was the first command for the new captain, James Elder, who had a Second Class Master's certificate. The Surgeon, John Livingston, RCS Edinburgh, had admitted to being drunk since Whampoa, and had died of the delirium tremens within days of the voyage being abandoned.

They found that the medicine chest was poorly stocked, and no medical checks had been conducted on the coolies. While they found that the provisions on board were of good quality, they would have been insufficient, especially the water supply, for the probable length of the voyage, which the master estimated could be of five months.

The coolies themselves attributed much of their predisposition to sickness due to cold water. Each man had to cook his own allowance, but there was insufficient fuel. There was sufficient room for 350 coolies at 12 feet per person, with three men allocated to a bunk. However, there was insufficient ventilation. Water closets were at the waist of the ship, abaft the forecastle. They were cleaned several times a day, but the waste did not flow out properly.

The Commissioners believed healthy coolies had boarded initially, but were swapped off before the ship sailed. They repeated the oft-mentioned warning that such a system of collection, which was probably the only practicable one, required very great watchfulness, a strict examination of every candidate for emigration; a full identification of him, and a perfect understanding on his part of the agreement by which he has consented to become bound.

This Commission of Enquiry confirmed all that had been generally acknowledged as conditions on board emigrant vessels, and more importantly, documented the profiles of the coolies and the reasons they chose to emigrate. The Commissioners had asked Daniel Caldwell, the acting

Superintendent of Police, and General Interpreter, to enquire of the passengers their circumstances. He drew up an extensive questionnaire, tabulating the responses. This first analysis of the composition of a shipment of Chinese coolies provided the benchmark from which later shipments can be compared.

The ages of the coolies ranged from 19 to 39, and they came mainly from Poon Yu in the Department of Kwang Chow, and Kwei Sheen in the Department of Weichow. The occupations listed included being a boatman, barber, in agriculture, a vegetable seller, a weaver, as well as candle maker, distiller, bricklayer, lacquer worker, rice pounder, chandler, carver, hawker, carpenter, paper maker. One claimed to be an accountant in a rice shop, but only one admitted to not having a job.

Caldwell noted that when he asked if they were quite willing to go to Demerara as coolies, most of the men stated that they were willing, but he felt that they said so only because they believed that having once come on board and signed the agreement, it would be useless to say that they were unwilling. Here are some of their replies:

- I was told by a man named Alok that he would give me $5.
- When I got on board, he told me that he had bought clothes for me, but I did not get them, and he left me and ran away with the money.
- If I am really to be sent back in 5 years, I won't mind going.
- I want to save money to support my mother.
- The agreement says 5 years, so I must work that time.
- I was told that if I went I should receive $5 a month and $2 would be passed to my family. I found this is false and I don't want to go.
- I am sorry I engaged to go. I can get no opium.
- If I don't get opium, I shall die.
- I was told I could return when I pleased. The agreement says 5 years but I only want to go for 2 years.

- I am too sick to go. I think I shall die.

Most were not married, and did not have family other than mother or father. Many admitted to smoking opium, for varying amounts and periods. These first remarks are indicative of the early reasons why such men volunteered to leave home.

In concluding their report, the Commissioners recommended that messes should be matched to the 16 cooks appointed, with the cook and headman to be given a gratuity. Men should be given special duties such as to get provisions, check beds rolled up, deck cleaned. The men should be made to wash daily, with a special wash day, and barbers to shave each week. Then they suggested that more rice and provisions be supplied, and two suits be issued per man. Surprisingly, they thought a promise to mail letters was an important factor, and finally that the master was to be humane. On receiving the Medical Officer's report, Turner & Co. agreed that the voyage be aborted and the remaining coolies sent back to their villages. The *Emigrant* remained in Hong Kong until she was sold to Portuguese interests in Macao in 1854.

Female dilemma

White arrived back in England while Bowring and Winchester were on home leave. The Emigration Commissioners convened a series of meetings in June 1853 where the question of Chinese emigration was discussed. Governor Barkly had also completed his term in British Guiana and was then also on home leave awaiting re-assignment to Jamaica. He was asked to attend some of the meetings in order to provide his assessment of the programme.

The meetings in London were at times acrimonious. White espoused the view that female emigration was a possibility, but both Bowring and Winchester strongly opposed this idea. While they did not object to the emigration of females as wives by some special bounty, they did not think that any attempt would lead to much result, as female emigration (except of the least creditable kind) was unprecedented. They maintained that it could result only in the wholesale purchase and shipment of prostitutes, and that it would be in violent opposition to Chinese law and custom.

But White was not without hope that such an emigration could be gradually set on foot through Hong Kong. He recalled his report of 23 July 1851, where the proposal of Hawa of Teo Cheo included the offer to provide females, and on this, the Commissioners thought that White should be authorised to try, even though a considerable increase in the customary advance to male emigrants would be necessary. Bowring was especially appalled and from then on offered no further assistance to White.

White was re-appointed for another year after strong representations from the WIC. He arrived back in Hong Kong on 11 November 1853, only to find that there were no vessels open for charter anywhere along the coast. He reported to the CLEC on 10 December that, with the fierce competition for ships, Tait & Co. would only contract to take up any shipping on the condition that the ship load at Namoa. This was to allow Tait to obtain a commission. Although this was contrary to his express wish that the emigration should be conducted from Hong Kong, White acceded, fearing that if he rejected the proposal he would lose the chance of any vessels that might arrive at Amoy.

White also came to the conclusion that if emigration was to be carried on from Hong Kong, it was absolutely necessary to have a depot there. This would enable emigrants to be collected and prepared for embarkation without delay when a vessel was ready to receive them. He suggested a hulk that would cost from £3,000 to £4,000, could serve as a depot afloat. He also advised that some disused lots could be had for £300 a year, but that they could not be made available until the Governor, who was residing in a house adjoining the lot, had moved into the new Government House.

On Boxing Day 1853 White reported that only a few vessels had arrived, and all under previous engagements. On 10 December, an unscrupulous Captain Hubbert had written saying he was informed that James White was ready to pay very liberally, and was offering his ship, the *Jamestown*. She was already marked out for Manila, but he was prepared to abandon the latter on receipt of the best offer from White. The offer had to be very clear; so much per head for 500, or as many more as the ship could take in her 'tween decks. Freight was to be paid on the number shipped, less two percent, in the event of any mortality amounting to more than that percentage.

White then raised the contentious issue of procuring women by purchase, directly or indirectly. Girls of ten to fifteen years of age, of respectable connexion, could be obtained for about forty dollars, and he proposed to pay this amount to a few of the more respectable emigrants, leaving them to make their own arrangements, as long as they were married before the departure of the vessel. The information he was given was that there was no probability of obtaining women without purchase, for that was the universal custom of the country.

The Commissioners approved of the White proposal to obtain women, on the understanding that the intention was that, as wives were in fact obtained by purchase in China, he would furnish the means of effecting marriages in this, the usual manner, to some of the emigrants procured by him. He was to take care that the connection was as legitimate and obligatory as the law and usage of China rendered possible.

But the Commissioners would not sanction the expenditure of money for a depot. Emigration from Hong Kong was experimental. The Commissioners then drew White's attention to his instructions which authorised him to despatch emigrants only from Hong Kong, or from Amoy. The Commissioners reminded White that emigration from Namoa was in direct violation of their treaties with China, and when emigration was set on foot from that port in 1852, it elicited an immediate remonstrance from the Foreign Office.

The only ship to sail in 1854 was also the first ship to load indentured labour for Jamaica. It was the 619-ton British ship *Epsom* which departed from Hong Kong on 1 April 1854 with 310 emigrants. White enthusiastically reported that the vessel got under way amid the firing of crackers and the uproar of gongs and drums. The emigrants were all fine able-bodied agricultural labourers with a few who had a slight knowledge of English.

White did not explain how he had recruited the men, merely saying that being unsure of the vessel's readiness, measures to procure emigrants did not commence until 10 March, when they had come forward in considerable numbers, and were sent straight out to the ship. He did not have a depot ashore to accommodate them. When it was discovered that they would not receive any money until the ship was ready to sail, the contractors claimed that the ship was going to take them away as slaves without paying advances. In the confusion that followed, many of them went away in the boats that had come alongside, taking articles that had been put on board for their use.

When the vessel moved further offshore, the people remaining on board were paid, and a bumboat sent alongside with articles they were likely to require. For several days no emigrants came forward, but with the favourable account given by the people on board, men came to the office to make inquiries, and finally to offer themselves as emigrants. After this, matters went on smoothly, and the number required was completed without difficulty.

Learning from the experience of previous departures, White appointed twelve cooks, six headmen, and two barbers, amongst the coolies. If they conducted themselves to the satisfaction of the captain, they were to be entitled to $2, $3, and $2 per month respectively, payable in Jamaica.

Frustrated with his inability to procure ships, and the rebuke over Namoa, White had written personally to Commissioner Rogers advising that he was leaving Hong Kong in April; and that he had no expectation of returning. The heated debates with Bowring and Winchester over female emigration still rankled, and now John Bowring was going to become Governor of Hong Kong.

An unidentified passenger on that voyage wrote as follows.

> "Dear Grandpa, Uncle, Grandma, Dad, Mum and my friends,
> "I am leaving for a period of time. I am sorry that I cannot fulfil my filial duties. As a rover, I have to leave my siblings and

friends, and being separated from parents. I introspect myself every night, feeling contrite for my unfilial behaviour.

"The journey began on 4 March from Hong Kong and will be arriving Jamaica by 6 July. That is a completely different country from where I lived. Hopefully I can adapt to the place. I have had a hard time on the ship. There are always huge waves that surge like mountains, not to mention the other difficulties. Fortunately thanks to the blessings, I am safe throughout the ship. I always pray to keep my family safe. That is my only wish in my life.

"After arriving Jamaica, a local officer will provide guarantee for me. A five year contract will be made. The salary is $8 each month. Once the contract is ended that company will send me back to Hong Kong. I dare not stay in Jamaica and will definitely come back at that time.

"I have much more to say, but words cannot express all my feelings.

"Best wishes"[45]

The *Epsom* arrived 118 days after leaving Hong Kong.[46] It was an uneventful voyage until 14 days before arrival when more than 40 died from scurvy and beriberi. Another 12 died after her arrival in Kingston on 30 July 1854.

Shipments to Panama

The 1,600-ton American clipper *Sea Witch* departed Namoa on 27 January 1854 with 719 coolies consigned to the Panama Railroad Company. She had been chartered in New York after a Director and agent, Samuel W. Comstock, tried unsuccessfully to arrange a charter for the similar sized *Williamsburgh* which proceeded to San Francisco instead.

The *Sea Witch*, owned by Howland and Aspinwall, was 192 feet long with a 140-foot mainmast so tall it was able to carry five tiers of sails. Captain Fraser had her upper deck housed over from the mizzen (aftermost mast) forward, so that she could carry nearly as many passengers on that deck as on her 'tween deck. After a 65-day passage in which some 14 Chinese died, the *Sea Witch* arrived in Panama on 29 March 1854 with 705 coolies. From a 1861 speech by the President of Manhattan Life Insurance Company, he related how the ship's owners had sought to take insurance on the lives of the coolies which they valued at $120 each. In one of the first Group policies written by an American Life

Insurance Company, the owners had been able to convince Manhattan Life to take one quarter of the total risk. On 29 April 1854, Manhattan Life paid $408, a quarter of the total loss, and made a profit of $432 on the transaction.

The *Sea Witch* was followed by the slower 480-ton Spanish ship, *Bella Vascongada*, which had left Swatow on 10 February 1854 with 325 Chinese. Her arrival complement of 305 brought the total to 1,009 Chinese labourers who had been imported. They were the first shipments of what was proposed to be 2,000 Chinese workers recruited for $25 per month. Comstock was free to make whatever arrangements he wanted with the coolies, with the expectation that the coolies would be paid a few dollars per month, with the balance considered as passage money, and food provided prior to shipment. The contracts were to be between three and four years, but it was hoped that they would be extended to eight years if possible.

From the start, the Chinese shipments were a disaster. Deprived of their opium, the addicts could not cope with the weather. Soon after their arrival, many were seen roaming the streets worn out and emaciated, heartbroken and miserable. Destitute and homeless, they were reduced to begging, and suicide. About 125 Chinese coolies were found hanging from trees, and over 300 from drowning and other forms of self-inflicted death. Hardly one of the 800 men could have been considered fit to labour.

Jamaican opportunism

News of the Panama Railroad recruitment disaster reached Jamaica through expatriate negro and Indian coolies who had earlier been recruited to Panama. Governor Barkly, now of Jamaica, seeing an opportunity to import labour cheaply, requested sanction from the Home Government to proclaim a bounty of £6 or £7 on each Chinese immigrant brought from Panama. Sir George Grey, the British Colonial Secretary, approved the bounty, but stipulated that females had to be included in the shipments. He did not elaborate on how this was to be achieved as no Chinese women had been shipped to Panama.

Just as in British Guiana in 1851, the Jamaican Board of Immigration Correspondence pre-empted the home government's approval, and resolved that Dr Falconer, and Wang-te-Chang (the interpreter who had arrived on the *Epsom*) should accompany Samuel S. Wortley of Kingston to go to Panama to assess the suitability of the men. On their return, they reported on the poor condition of the Chinese, with the particularly moving diary of Wang circulated for emphasis. Nevertheless, they were authorised to return and negotiate with the Panama Railway Co. for their shipment to Jamaica. They came back with 197 emaciated men on the brigantine *Vampire* on 1 November 1854. The *Theresa Jane* brought the remaining ten on 18 November. Only 50 or 60 were left behind, too ill to travel; this from the original number of 1,009 Chinese who had landed at Colon.

On 8 November, Barkly wrote to Sir George Grey advising of the arrival of the *Vampire* at Jamaica and that the conduct of the majority of the men off the *Epsom* was favourable. Of the 25 who had proven retractable, it was explained by interpreter Wang that it was because they were not paid when wet weather prevented them working. He was of the opinion that the White Agreement was the root of the evil, and that a new contract should be written.97

Even before the *Epsom* had sailed from Hong Kong, the Jamaican Board of Immigration Correspondence advised Governor Barkly on 20 March 1854 that they could not sanction further shipments of Chinese labour, as recently quoted freight rates would have brought the cost above the $100 originally fixed.

While this correspondence was being conducted, Trinidad and British Guiana independently determined that the cost of transporting Chinese to the West Indies was too high to sustain. On learning of this, Newcastle replied that as the Emigration Commissioners considered it hopeless to proceed on the original terms, they would not be taking any further steps to send Chinese to any of the West Indian colonies.

**Amoy harbour, 1870-71.
Departure port, 1846-1869.
Photograph by John Thompson.**

4

Cuban Allocations

The first shipments of Chinese coolies to Cuba in 1847 do not appear to meet expectations. Nevertheless, the Chinese were deemed to be useful labour by the Real Junta de Formento.

First Cuban contracts

On 10 April 1849, the Governor and Capitan-General of Cuba published "Government Regulations for the Management and Treatment of Asiatic and Indian Colonists". The Royal Decree allowed anybody to import Chinese, but it was not until February 1851 that a contract was awarded by the Real Junta de Formento to Villoldo, Wardrop y Cia for the importation of Chinese labourers to be paid at a rate of $4 a month. The quota was initially for 8,000, but subsequently reduced to 3,000, with another 3,000 being awarded to Pereda, Machado y Cia.

Villoldo Wardrop

With the awarding of the contracts, Robert Wardrop, the Scottish partner of Villoldo Wardrop, went to China to supervise the shipment of the coolies. In Amoy he contracted with Tait & Co., in conjunction with Syme, Muir & Co., to provide his recruits. The speculation was that he would receive a bounty of $125 for every emigrant landed in Havana.

In the two years between 1852 and 1853, Tait was able to provide Villildo Wardrop with 3,153 Chinese coolies on nine shipments. However, the first Wardrop Villoldo ship did not arrive at Havana at all.

The 450-ton British ship *British Sovereign* left Amoy on 18 August 1852 with 321 coolies for Havana. Approaching the island of Palawan in the Philippines, she ran aground three times, on the north and south Pensilvanian Rocks, and the third time on the half-moon rock close to Palawan. There she lost two of the mates, along with the three men who were in the long boat trying to refloat the ship. Captain C. Harris brought the vessel to Kema in Celebes on 20 October, where he died. On 22 December Chief Mate Martin took the vessel away but he died on 9 January 1853. The bosun and Doctor then tried to take her to Singapore but were not competent enough to do so. They managed to take the vessel to Zamboanga desperately short of provisions. The Governor of Zamboanga provided all assistance and a pilot to take her to Manila where she arrived on 1 March 1853 with 138 of her coolies. The 75 who were sick remained at Zamboanga, with the rest of them having run away in Kema.

Soon after the 522-ton British barque *Panama* left Amoy on 26 September 1852 with 351 Chinese on board, the coolies made several unsuccessful attempts to take her. She eventually put into Singapore on 17 October where Captain Fisher landed 16 of the worst offenders. The original crew however could not be persuaded to continue the voyage.

The *Panama* called at Jamaica before arriving in Havana on 7 February 1853 the day before another British ship, the *Blenheim,* which had sailed from Amoy 16 days later with coolies. The close arrival of the two ships caused confusion in the waterfront holding area with some uncertainty as to which coolies came off which ship. The *Boletin de Colonizacion* recorded the combined arrivals as 480, but the *Diario de la Marina* reported 261 as having arrived on the *Panama* on 7 February 1853 and 412 on the *Blenheim* on 8 February.

The 808-ton ship *Blenheim* was the fourth consigned to Villoldo Wardrop. With all the turmoil in Amoy, she eventually sailed from Amoy on 23 October 1852 after waiting 56 days to complete her complement of 453 coolies for Cuba. She arrived a day after the *Panama* which had sailed on 12 August but had suffered a mutiny on the voyage.

The contracts were signed by Aeneas Mackay (of Tait & Co.) committing the recruits to the orders of the Junta de Formento, or whomever the contract was transferred, to for a period of eight years. Each coolie was to be paid four pesos a month commencing 48 hours after arrival in Havana and would be given eight ounces of salted meat, one and a half pounds of bananas, sweet potatoes or other root food. He would also be given two changes of clothing, including a woollen shirt and a blanket each year, as well as medical assistance and supervision. If his illness lasted more than 15 days, nursing care would continue but his pay would be suspended. Mackay was to provide transportation and advance nine pesos in addition to suits of new clothes for the voyage. Villoldo Wardrop & Cia or their assigns would deduct a peso a month until the advance was repaid in full.

Contract No. 331 indicated that 19 year old Tan Lim of Chang Chu in Fukien signed his printed Spanish and Chinese contract in Amoy on 21 October 1852, two days before sailing. The contract had an additional name written in. It is not known when the Christian name Vicente was added but it would appear that it was inserted in his contract on his arrival and before his transfer to the new holder of the contract. This practice became commonplace in subsequent ship arrivals.

The 605-ton British barque *Gertrude*, under Captain John Campbell, left Amoy on 12 October 1852 with 299 coolies bound for Havana. She was the third of Wardrop's ships. For the first three days, the weather was so boisterous that the coolies were all sea-sick, and could not eat anything. On the fourth day, the men were each given one biscuit and a half as their nourishment for the day. When the weather improved, they were allowed rice, salt fish, and vegetables, but not enough to sate the hunger of four days.

On the fifth day, they managed to make the crew understand they wanted more rice. Two bags were then delivered to them, each containing upwards of a picul, but the rice was very dirty, and had a great deal of paddy in it. On the sixth day, four bags of rice were served, two in the morning and two in the evening; each bag contained from 110 to 120 catties, but about one quarter of the quantity was inedible paddy. For some reason, the only two galleys they had were not capable of cooking it all, and they were still hungry. They made signs that they wanted more galleys, but the Europeans could not understand them.

It was on the next day that the affray took place. It started between the 80 men of the Tang clan and the 100 from Chuan Chue, all from Hokien. They began to fight and throw basins, etc., at each other. An apprentice had been placed on the main deck to assist the carpenter and to keep the men away. He stated that the carpenter was making a studdingsail boom. He was surrounded by a good many coolies around him who kept stepping on the boom, and rubbing out the lines he had drawn on it. He did not know whether they were doing so in fun, or else to annoy the man. In the ensuing scuffle, they so badly wounded the carpenter that he died from his wounds.

The captain's deposition provided a different point of view. On the 20th, at about half past ten, he was asked by some of the coolies to go below to see a sick man. As he did so, he was immediately surrounded by a number of coolies. When he heard a yell on deck, he realised that something was wrong, and jumped on the ladder to go up, but was held by the foot. He succeeded in reaching the deck, but was struck on the forehead with what he thought was an iron belaying pin. He estimated that there must have been 150 men about, but was not positive. He fought his way through them.

When he reached the poop, he was attacked by another coolie with a boarding pike. He grappled with him, and threw him down on the main deck. Joined by his men, the captain then drove back the coolies, who were attempting to reach the poop, using belaying pins, pieces of wood, iron bolts, and stones.

The ship's steward and the captain's wife then supplied the party on the poop with loaded muskets through the cabin skylight. Captain Campbell fired about six shots without hitting anyone; but a seaman, Atkinson, who proved to be somewhat of a marksman, shot, and killed two, while wounding another two with just four rounds. The Chinese then began to disappear below; and when the mate and three seamen who had been on the forecastle, finally succeeded in joining their shipmates aft by means of the rigging, about a dozen of the Chinese went forward, falling on their knees, seemingly to beg for mercy. The captain made signs to bring the ringleaders aft. The Chinese brought forward four men, who were placed in irons. From the commencement until something like order was restored, the insurrection lasted two hours. The *Gertrude* put into Singapore on the 28 October 1852.

At the subsequent inquiry, one of the Chinese stated that the captain paid $11½ to each of them and they signed a paper to that effect. But when they went below, the Chinese man who had brought them to the ship then took the money away from them, saying that it was for their provisions for the voyage. He did not know whether the captain knew this or not. They also each received a suit of clothes, a shirt, and waistcoat.

There was no one on board who could interpret between the Europeans and Chinese. They made themselves understood by signs. Captain Campbell, "unaccustomed to the Chinese face", was unable to identify any one of the coolies engaged in the attack. During the gale, 1lb of biscuit was ordered for each man, but it and the provisions were served to the different groups, not individually to each man. He went on to say he "never heard any complaints, nor did the Chinese make signs that they did not have enough to eat".

The testimony of the Chief and second mates and three of the seamen was in accord with that of the Master's. The chief mate, Robert Campbell, said that the ship earned £9.10 for each coolie landed in Havana, and that it was in the captain's interest that the coolies be well-fed and kept in good health. He declared that the captain's orders had always been "to treat the coolies well, to speak kindly to them, and to avoid giving offence". The *Gertrude* eventually continued on her voyage to Havana, arriving there on 14 March 1853. Only 198 Chinese were landed, a mortality rate of 33.78%.

The 440-ton British ship, *Lady Amherst*, departed from Amoy on 29 November 1852 with 275 coolies for Havana. The men appeared happy and contented until 13 December when it was learned they were contemplating murdering the captain. They resisted when told to return below deck and did so only when confronted with arms. As the *Lady Amherst* was near the Natunas, Captain David Reid headed for Singapore, arriving on 15 December. On arrival, the crew refused to sail and a new crew signed on. She arrived at Havana on 18 April 1853 with 225 Chinese still on board.

The next three ships were much more successful for Villoldo Wardrop. The *Columbus* eventually sailed from Amoy after waiting 90 days and the *Inchiman* and *Sir Thomas Gresham* sailed quietly from Namoa also without incident. Their last shipment however was somewhat delayed.

On 17 January 1853, the British ship, *Medina*, received her papers from the Amoy Consulate, and cleared for Namoa, to ship coolies for Havana. But the majority of the crew refused to heave up the anchor; claiming that the ship was short-handed.

On obtaining additional numbers, the crew of the *Medina* still refused to obey, and a complaint was laid against them at the Consulate. Acting Consul Backhouse convened a Court at which the crew said they believed their lives to be in danger, as the ship was taking coolies to Havana. Captain Joshua Sandford admitted that proceeding to Namoa for the purpose of shipping coolies was an illegal act, in contravention of the Treaties. He further admitted that in some instances he neglected to comply with regulations, endeavouring to carry the ship to sea without a proper complement of men. The case was dismissed, with the men being warned to return to their duty.

The agents undertook to provide them with a passage to Hong Kong, after they had worked the vessel to Namoa. They persisted, saying they had no confidence in the Master, but they were ordered back on board. However, that same evening, seventeen of them re-appeared at the Consulate, seeking shelter. On the Monday morning Backhouse requested Commander Ellman to help take them back to the *Medina*. They once again returned to the Consulate, and said they would take the vessel to Namoa as long as they were guaranteed their wages and a passage to Hong Kong. The captain agreed with each man being furnished with an account showing the balance of wages due to him. The *Medina* sailed from Amoy for Namoa then loaded 450 men there for Havana, also without incident. Leaving on 1 March 1853 she arrived on 1 September with 380 on board. The *Medina* was the ninth and last ship to carry coolies for Villoldo Wardrop. They had all been British vessels. In total 3,153 Chinese coolies were embarked for Cuba, but only 2,397 arrived. With one non-arrival and three mutinies, the success rate amounted to only 76.02%, which prompted Commissary Judge George Canning Backhouse in Havana (the brother of Amoy Acting British Consul Backhouse) to remark that the undertaking did not seem to have turned out well, and that he had been informed by the firm that it "had no intention of further engaging in Chinese importations".

Pereda Machado

When the Spanish Junta in Cuba granted permission to Villodo to import Chinese, they also granted a similar quota to Manuel Bernabe de Pereda in partnership with Machado. Pereda was a Portuguese with relatives in Macao. Nevertheless, with the awarding of the contract, they appointed Ignacio Fernandez de Castro, to be their Emigration Agent in China. Aware of the problems in Amoy, Castro based himself in Macao and turned to José Vicente Jorge to help with the recruitment of Chinese labourers there. Jorge obliged with three ships in which he had a financial interest.

The first to load for Pereda was the Portuguese brig *Sophia* under Captain Rozario. 250 coolies were crammed into the small 240-ton vessel which sailed on 31 December 1852, arriving at Havana 125 days later on 17 April 1853. Despite the gross overloading of the vessel, only 17 died on the voyage, representing a mortality rate of 6.8%.

Another Portuguese ship, the 376-ton *Viajante*, left Macao on 14 January 1853 with 300 Chinese under Captain Francisco Passos. Scurvy killed most of those 51 coolies who did not survive. The third Jorge vessel was the 894-ton Spanish *Victoria* which sailed on 8 March 1853. She too suffered a loss of 13.49% of her original 393 complement.

Pereda suffered only one mutiny in the nine years he was in the trade, during which he conducted 33 shipments. It was the first mutiny on a sailing from Macao. The 400-ton Portuguese ship *Adamastor* left on 24 October 1853 but did not arrive in Havana. Few details are known, but under the threat of losing his life, Captain da Souza was compelled to take his vessel to Singapore where all the Chinese deserted the ship immediately after her arrival.

The American 713-ton ship, *Hound*, had been chartered on 16 September 1854 by James Tait for a voyage from New York to Manila and thence to Macao. Using the Spanish calculation of 1.5 tons for each colonist, José Vicente Jorge arranged to put 470 Chinese on her. Captain Amos Peck would take on 230 only, claiming that he had taken the maximum number allowed under American regulations. He had been warned by Peter Parker (1804-1888), the Acting Commissioner of the United States, that if he took more on board and put into a port in the United States, his vessel would be liable to forfeiture. The *Hound* lost only two of her 230-man complement.

Pereda was then granted a further allocation of 10,000 in direct continuation of their previous allocation even though his permit was not issued until 19 October 1855. Pereda had three shipments from Swatow in 1857 before taking three shipments from Macao in 1858. The Dutch *Soolo* had a mortality rate of 0.50% and the Spanish *Bella Vascongada* 9.35%, but the 567-ton German barque *Kepler* was not as successful, suffering a loss of 72 of the 364 men whom Captain Hasselhoff had taken on in Macao on 19 February 1858, a mortality rate of 19.78%.

Emigrante was the unfortunate British-flagged *Emigrant*, which had originally been chartered to carry emigrants to British Guiana in 1853. She became a Portuguese vessel following the hurried cancellation of her charter. The 753-ton ship *Emigrante* took 550 Chinese from Swatow to Havana on 26 January 1854. Captain Guterres lost 11 men on this 117-day voyage, arriving on 23 May 1854 still with 539 men on board.

The *Emigrante* took 230 days on her second coolie voyage. This now Spanish ship left Macao on 15 April 1856 and did not arrive in Havana until 2 December 1856 after a voyage via Manila and St Helena. Captain J.F. San Juan took on board 504 Chinese in Macao but was able to discharge only 316 of them in Havana. The mortality rate was 37.30%.

Emigrante's third voyage was much better, with Captain San Juan managing to land 378 of her original 400 complement. Her fourth voyage in the coolie trades was Pereda's final shipment, which was from Manila. The number boarding at this unusual port was not reported, but the *Boletin de Colonizacion* in Havana listed her as having arrived on 26 September 1860 with 178 "asiatico" labourers.

Pereda did not abandon Amoy altogether. His first shipment from Amoy was on the *Bella Gallega*, a 499-ton Spanish ship under Captain E. Benavides, which left on 20 January 1853 with a large contingent of 403 coolies for Havana. She lost a mast on the voyage and took 158 days to reach her destination. This was also the first non-British ship to be utilised from Amoy. His second shipment from Amoy was on the 446-ton British barque *Sappho* which sailed with 250 men without incident. The third and final shipment from Amoy was made on the 1,210-ton American ship *Sky Lark* in 1855 taking on 593 men, again without incident.

Swatow was undoubtedly the favoured port for Pereda. No fewer than 15 shipments were made from that port, the first being on the British *Menzies* on 26 December 1853. Their three shipments from Swatow in 1855 were on British ships. The 1,121-ton *Roxburgh Castle*, the 1,241-ton *Martin Luther* and the 1,460-ton *Carpentaria* all had speedy voyages with the latter taking only 64 days. They arrived in Havana with mortality rates of around 4.5%. As Swatow was not then a Treaty Port, the captains of those ships risked being fined by the British authorities. Pereda's three sailings from Swatow in 1856 were on the American ships, *Golden Eagle*, 1,121 tons, the 1,067-ton *War Hawk*, and the 688-ton *Florida*. This was followed in 1857 by the American *Waverly*, the Peruvian *Architect*, and the British, *Robert Small*, all with mortality rates below 5.83%. The last ship to sail from Swatow in 1858 was the *Alavesa* which entered the coolie trade as a 502-ton Spanish ship. She left on 1 April 1858 with a cargo of 360 Chinese consigned to Pereda,

Machado y Cia. By then high losses were being sustained in Swatow with Captain M. Dobaran losing 142 on the voyage, a mortality rate of 39.44%.

In December 1857, Captain G.H. Carlton of the 1,650-ton American ship *Wandering Jew* entered into a charter agreement with Andrew Conolly, a British subject, to transport coolies from Shanghai to Havana. Captain Carlton had supposedly given a guarantee to American Consul Knapp which he would forfeit if she loaded coolies for Cuba. Just before leaving his post, Knapp's assurances caused the Chinese authorities to grant clearance to the *Wandering Jew*, and handed the captain his papers. When acting American Consul Alfred L. Freeman checked with Captain Carlton, he denied having given such a guarantee, and immediately left Shanghai to anchor downstream at Woosung to await his cargo of coolies. Freeman asked for assistance from the Chinese authorities who immediately ordered district magistrates to arrest anyone trying to send men on board. One official claimed Captain Carlton asserted he was merely taking a few passengers to Fukien Province. When British Consul Daniel Brooke Robertson became involved, he promptly charged Conolly with breaching the Treaty of Nanking, as it was illegal for Chinese to emigrate. He was found guilty and fined $500 for the offence.

Consul Freeman boarded the *Wandering Jew* on 28 January 1858 and examined the 236 coolies then on the ship. Many claimed they were given $3 to work for a few days on the ship, while others were lured to Shanghai to serve as soldiers or servants for the mandarin. None had any idea that they were being transported overseas. When told of their plight, 117 of them were found to be there against their will, and were handed over to the Chinese authorities. The remainder, mainly beggars, preferred to emigrate rather than starve to death. Captain Carleton was given a written warning but he defiantly proceeded on to Amoy on 31 January to complete his contract with the Spanish Agent Lorenzo Soto.

The *Wandering Jew* arrived at Amoy on 3 February 1858 with 130 coolies, and Captain Carleton had no trouble in charming the Acting American Consul, the Rev. Elihu

Doty, into declaring him, "a gentlemanly person of correct feelings and bearing", and therefore unwilling to stop the *Wandering Jew* from proceeding to Havana. The ship sailed from Amoy for Swatow on 5 February 1858, without taking on any men. There she took on 220 coolies, and sailed on 11 February with 350 coolies, arriving on 15 May after a 99-day voyage with 259 able to walk ashore, a 26% mortality rate.

The last Pereda Chinese charter was the 1,228-ton Spanish ship *Concepcion* on her first voyage as a coolie ship. It also introduced Captain Juan A. Tuton to the trade. On 17 April 1859 he took 480 coolies from Macao to Havana, delivering 423 of them after a 115-day voyage.

Pereda conducted 33 shipments between 1852 and 1860. Apart from the unknown number taken on board in Manila, he recruited 13,146 Chinese coolies of which 11,834 were able to land. The average mortality rate was 9.98% with only four shipments incurring losses in excess of 20%.

There was one shipment that did not seem to get prior Government approval. On 10 December 1855 Emigration Agent José Jorge loaded 250 Chinese on the 348-ton Spanish-flagged *Paquita* at Macao bound for Havana. Three days earlier they had signed a de Castro worded contract that consigned them to Julian Zulueta. On arrival, 246 Chinese were able to walk ashore, suffering only four deaths on that 103-day voyage. She was the last of three sailings from Macao that year.

Spanish-born Julian Zulueta was a slave-trader, merchant, and multiple-plantation owner, the most noteworthy being "Alava", a modern and efficient estate. This "prince of slave owners" and "acknowledged political boss" was considered the representative of the great planters. As a member of the Havana City Council between 1860 and 1876, he was Deputy Mayor three times and once, Mayor.

New Cuban Allocations

A Spanish Royal Decree of 22 March 1854 allowed private persons in Cuba to introduce colonists on their own account, subject to permission from the Government. Drake y Compania was given permission to import 6,000 asiaticos on

25 January 1855, while Torices, Puente y Cia was given permission to import 10,000 Chinese on 6 June 1855.

Drake y Cia

Santiago Drake and his brothers were principals in the company, but shipments were usually made in conjunction with Pedrosos and J.M. Morales. Drake employed Nicolas Tanco Armero as his Emigration Agent and commenced his participation in the coolie trades with one shipment in 1855 and five in 1856. Another 12 shipments were undertaken in 1857 and a final one in 1858. Although Amoy was no longer a significant recruiting port following the riots of 1852, it was the port chosen by Drake for five shipments, including the first American ship to be chartered by them.

This 1,600-ton American clipper ship *Sea Witch* under Captain W. Lang with 581 men on board was on her second voyage with coolies, this time from Amoy for Cuba, when on 29 March 1856, she lost the breeze as she was approaching Havana with a pilot on board. She began drifting inshore then ran aground about 12 miles west of the port and began taking in water. Captain Lang managed to walk to the Drake offices where he arranged with the Harbour Master to have two naval steamships and an armada of launches and boats to take his passengers and crew ashore. The Government tally sheet recorded 485 men were landed on 29 March, but with the confusion following the rescue it was not until 9 June 1857 that the *Boletin de Colonizacion* listed 460 men as arriving on the *Sea Witch*.

The three departures from Swatow in 1856 were on British ships. By then the Chinese Passengers' Act had come into force. It required all British ships carrying Chinese passengers to call at Hong Kong in order to obtain a proper clearance from the Emigration Officer there. Only Captain Robert Putt of the *Henry Miller* did so, and he was praised for disembarking his over-supply of passengers when he arrived in Hong Kong. He had the extra men sent ashore, and provided them with board and lodging before finding passage for them back to Swatow. The 433-ton *Henry Miller* had left on 19 July with 191, losing only six on the 124-day voyage.

The 819-ton *Hope* left on 14 March with 504 coolies, of whom 452 were able to land.

Edwin Fox arrived at Hong Kong on 17 August 1857 after almost a full year of frustration seeking cargoes in China. She was then chartered by a local agent to carry coolies from Swatow to Cuba. Much time was spent getting the ship ready for some 300 people, particularly with regard to fresh water. Many barrels had to be loaded in Hong Kong before departure for Swatow. Regulations required that 3.6 metres of space and 4.5 litres of water per head be available for each passenger, for 100 days.[47]

On sailing on 15 September for Swatow, she met a typhoon, but the ship eventually arrived a few weeks later. Preparations at Swatow were slow and the passengers did not board until late October. She finally sailed for Hong Kong on 1 November to complete documentation and top up with fresh water.

The *Edwin Fox* departed for Cuba on 9 November 1857 with 310 passengers aboard. The barque proceeded through the Gaspar and Sunda Straits and thence across the Indian Ocean, arriving at Cape Town on 14 January, 65 days out of Hong Kong. Six days later, she departed after replenishing at Table Bay. On 19 March 1858, the *Edwin Fox* arrived at Havana with 269 passengers, a loss rate of 13.23%.

Mutinies

Two vessels not only suffered high casualties but were also victims of mutinies. A third vessel subjected to mutiny resulted in the voyage being abandoned.

The 1,002-ton British ship *Gulnare* arrived at Hong Kong on 13 March 1857, Captain John Wardrop claiming that she had left Swatow on 11 March with a crew of 32 men and 432 Chinese consigned to Drake in Havana. On the following morning, a desperate and well-combined attack was made by the emigrants to obtain possession of the ship. When they failed through the determined conduct of the officers and crew, they attempted to set her on fire. They were finally put down, after severely wounding the third mate and one of the crew. Nine of the Chinese were shot, many more wounded, and three jumped overboard to avoid capture. The next day, the most prominent twenty of the Chinese were placed in the custody of the police when the ship put in at Hong Kong.

The Emigration Officer was directed to inquire into the state of the provisions, etc., on board the *Gulnare*. He reported that she was provided in every way in a complete and satisfactory manner. Following investigation by the Chief Magistrate, eighteen were committed to trial at the Supreme Court for piracy. To facilitate the despatch of the ship, the Chief Justice held an extra criminal session of the Supreme Court on the 27th March. All eighteen were pronounced guilty, with three—Ng-king-seang, Cheem-koong-sew, and Chun-amoon—sentenced to execution, and a sentence of "Death recorded" to be entered up against the remaining fifteen.[48]

At a meeting of the Executive Council on 6 April 1857, Bowring, despite objections by the Lieutenant-Governor and the Colonial Secretary, decided that justice would be sufficiently answered if the extreme penalty was carried out in the case of Ng-king-seang only. This man had clearly acted as a ringleader; was apparently of a different, if not of a superior, station in life from the other prisoners. He was executed on Thursday, April 9th, and the other 17 prisoners were transported for life. Labouchere replied that he had no doubt that Bowring used, to the best of his discretion, the prerogative of mercy with which he was invested. This was to be the only official execution of a mutineer in the history of the Chinese diaspora.

The *Gulnare* sailed again on 1 April 1857 with 326 emigrants, and arrived at Havana on 19 August. On that voyage of some 20 weeks, 58 Chinese died, 21 of fever, eight of dysentery, 12 (including nine opium smokers) of debility, three by suicide and 14 of other various diseases. The number landed was 268 resulting in a mortality rate of 37.96%.

The third Drake mutiny for 1857 was on the 2,006-ton American clipper ship *Challenge*. She departed on 18 October 1857, and took 115 days against the monsoon from Swatow to Havana. Soon after departure, the coolies rose over a dispute relating to the amount of water being issued. The mutiny was suppressed, but only 620 of the 915 that boarded were able to walk ashore on 10 February 1858. The mortality rate of 32.24% did not distinguish those who died as result of the mutiny from other causes.

When Captain Bakker of the Dutch barque *Henrietta Maria* left Macao on 9 February 1857, she had a cargo of 350 Chinese coolies bound for Havana. They were being consigned to Drake Morales. About two weeks later, in the Palawan Straits, the coolies set upon the crew who took to the boats. The remaining boats were taken over by 240 of the Chinese, setting off for the land they could see in the distance. Four crew members, left behind in the mad scramble to get away, together with 60 coolies, were left to drift about until they were come across by the American *Coeur de Lion*. When the captain learned of the revolt, he ordered his chief mate, Crawford, to take the ship to Singapore.

When the *Henrietta Maria* arrived in Singapore, the Dutch authorities were informed, and they quickly sent a contingent from the warship *de Haai* to take over the ship, and sail her to Batavia. The American Consul was advised of the proceedings, but even as this was being done, the American Vice Consul unilaterally authorised Captain Crawford to raise the American flag on the *Henrietta Maria*. When the British Assistant Resident Councillor Vaughn went on board to hand the ship over to the Dutch, Crawford refused to lower the American flag.

The next day, Vaughn again requested that the American flag be lowered, when, on being rebuffed, he went to the British frigate *Spartan* for assistance. With an armed guard behind him, Vaughn forcibly took the halyard from Crawford, and lowered the American flag, while signalling the Dutch *de Haai* to come alongside. Next day the *Henrietta Maria*, in company with the *de Haai*, left for Batavia. Captain Crawford and two of his men remained on board, being assured that their claims on the vessel would be fully heard in Batavia. Months later, the Governor of Singapore wrote to the American Consul acknowledging he was wrong in his direction, and offered to pay reparation for damages that may have been sustained.

In the four years between 1855 and 1858 the Drake brothers recruited a total of 7,838 Chinese coolies over 19 shipments, but were able to land only 5,606 of them in Cuba. The overall mortality rate of 28.48% came about from two of the three mutinies suffering casualties in excess of 30%, in addition to eight other shipments with mortality rates above 24%. This was the highest rate of all the importers in the Cuban trade.

Torices Puente y Cia

Rafael Rodrigues Torices and his partner Puente gained entry to the coolie trade with an initial allocation of 10,000 Chinese in 1855. On being awarded the allocation, he formed the Compania Asiatica de la Habana together with Dr Marcial Dupieris, the physician who examined the first Chinese arrivals, and sugar *refaccionista*[49] Antonio Ramon Ferran. A fourth partner was plantation owner Juan Atilano Colome. Ferran was to be their emigration agent in China where he opened his own barracoon.

Unlike Villoldo Wardrop and Drake, who had strong British associations, Torices's connections were with American interests. The partnership made 20 American shipments out of the eventual total of 55. Ferran however had also developed a close relationship with the British firm of Lyall, Still & Co. in Hong Kong, and would have employed more British ships had it not been for the Chinese Passengers' Act. Two of the three shipments he made from Hong Kong were affected by that Act, which came into effect in 1856.

The first Torices shipment was on the British 1,170-ton *Australia* which left Swatow on 30 October 1855 bound for Havana, with 450 labourers including the first recorded shipment of seven girls. With 364 disembarking, the mortality rate was a discouraging 19.11%. Ferran however persisted with three departures from Swatow in 1856. With a very high load factor of 0.85, the 459-ton Spanish ship *Teresita* took on 390 coolies on 6 February 1856. Captain Cardona was able to discharge only 327 of them, experiencing a mortality rate of 16.15%. Captain F. Buis of the 707-ton Dutch *Vriendschap* left on 19 November 1856 with 399 coolies on a voyage to Havana. He handed 352 of them to Cuban importer Rafael Torices 140 days later. The mortality rate was 11.78%. Only one shipment from Swatow, the 560-ton German *Felix*, had a mortality rate below 10%.

There had been only one shipment of indentured labour from Hong Kong in 1848 (for Sydney) and two in 1853-54, to Melbourne and Jamaica, before Ferran entered into a contract with the prominent British shipowner and manager Lyall, Still and Co. for three shipments from Hong Kong. The first was the 1,036-ton American clipper ship *Swordfish*, which loaded 375 men on 27 December 1855. Captain Osgood took only 80 days to reach Havana, and did not lose a single man. However Ferran was not to be as fortunate with his subsequent shipments from Hong Kong. The Chinese Passengers' Act had just been enacted.

Chinese Passengers' Act

When British ships began taking passengers from China in 1847, captains simply took as many as could physically fit on board, sometimes as tightly packed as on the slave ships that plied the Middle Passage from Africa to America and the West Indies. When the British Passengers' Act of 1849—the twelfth since the first attempt in 1803 to ensure passengers were not abused on ships—was passed, it was not generally regarded as applying outside British ports and parts of the Mediterranean. But Clause 4 also said that the Act extended "in every colonial voyage".

When Consul Layton in Amoy sought advice in 1847, the Home Government had determined that the Passengers' Act did not apply to ships sailing from China. But it immediately set about once again to amend the Passengers' Act. A Passengers' Act of 1852 had just been passed, but by then, the British Government had already decided that the 1852 Act was inadequate and not suited for Chinese emigrants. Along with a wide-ranging amendment to the Act of 1852, it began drafting a new Act specifically to cover the movement of ships engaged in the transportation of Chinese passengers. Neither the Hong Kong authorities, nor any officials at the British Consulates were consulted, but general comments in earlier despatches on the conditions on the vessels used were taken into account.

The Chinese Passengers' Act, 1855 and the Passengers' Act 1855 were each passed on 14 August 1855. The Chinese Act contained only 17 Clauses and six Regulations in three Schedules; compared to 102 Clauses in the new Passengers' Act.

The Chinese Passengers' Act defined a Chinese passenger ship as any ship carrying from any port in Hong Kong, and every British ship carrying from any port in China or within one hundred miles of the coast thereof, more than twenty passengers, being natives of Asia. Clause IV deemed no Chinese Passenger Ship should clear out or proceed to sea on any voyage of more than seven days, until the Master had received a Certificate from the Emigration Officer.

Unlike in the main Act, the requirement for bunks was not mentioned, nor was the tonnage check included. The Harbour Master was determined to be the one who would provide the certificates of survey as to the seaworthiness of the vessel and the number of passengers it would be allowed to carry under the Passengers' Act.

The Chinese Passengers' Act was to come into force on 1 January 1856. Colonial Secretary Labouchere emphasised to Governor Bowring in Hong Kong that the duties prescribed devolved on the Emigration Officer, and it was this officer alone who controlled the amount of protection the emigrants would receive.

In Schedule A, no Chinese Passenger Ship could proceed to sea without a Certificate from the Emigration Officer. That officer was not bound to provide a certificate within seven days; and until evidence of an approved surgeon and interpreter were on board. The Emigration Officer was free to inspect the ship at any time to ensure that she was seaworthy, properly manned, equipped, fitted, and ventilated, as well as not carrying any cargo that could prejudice the health or safety of the passengers. The space appropriated to the passengers was to be at least twelve superficial feet and seventy-two cubic feet for every adult, with two children aged between one and twelve years counted as one adult. An area of five superficial feet was also to be allocated on the upper deck for exercise purposes.

Schedule A also prescribed the Dietary Scale and Medical Comforts applicable for every 100 passengers, and warned that provisions, water and fuel was to be of good quality and sufficient for the duration of the voyage as proclaimed by the Governor. The sixth regulation prohibited the Emigration Officer from issuing his Certificate until he had mustered the passengers to ascertain that they understood whither they were going and understood the nature of the Contract of Service they had signed. He could detain the ship if he thought that fraud or violence had been used in the collection of the passengers.

The Chinese Passengers' Act was not generally welcomed in Hong Kong, both in commercial circles and within Government. Newly arrived Attorney General Thomas Chisholm Anstey openly criticised the many shortcomings of the Act.

One of the first ships to load under the new Chinese Passengers' Act was the *John Calvin*. By early March 1856, Lyall, Still, & Co. her Hong Kong owners, had gathered 301 coolies on board and applied for a clearance for 302 passengers (the ship had capacity for 301 and a portion). When the passengers were mustered and the contracts explained by Emigration Officer Hillier,[50] all but eighty-one declined to go.

Hillier was not convinced that the dissidents were genuinely unwilling, but evidence of consent in each case was necessary. George Lyall was told that a certificate could only be granted for the passengers who had come on board willingly; and had signed their contracts with full knowledge of its contents. Lyall could not produce this evidence, as the contracts had for the most part been witnessed before the Procurador of Macao. He preferred, therefore, to receive a clearance for the eighty-one who had consented, and offered to have any who did not want to go to Havana taken to Macao and there disembarked. He restated that intention to the

Colonial Secretary, William T. Mercer, who, together with Hillier, said it was a matter for Lyall to decide.

Hillier signed the certificate, but for 81 men only, and he did not order the men to be taken off. He had been a seafarer himself, and would have had a good idea as to how Captain Thornhill would react to the order to disembark the surplus men. Captain Alfonso Thornhill, born in 1826 with only a Class 2 Masters Certificate issued in 1849, took the certificate, and without seeking further instructions from the owners, sailed directly for Havana on 8 March 1856.

Thornhill would have escaped any recrimination if only he had not suffered the consequences of having lost 111 coolies and eleven of his crew by death from fever, dysentery, anasarca and the effects of opium. After leaving Anjer, he was forced to anchor in the Straits of Sunda until 15 April, as the wind was coming from the south-west, with a three-knot current setting to the eastward. It was during that time that typhus fever broke out with ten deaths.

According to the crew, an English super-cargo took charge of the passengers and issued the provisions in accordance with the dietary scale, which was ample, and there were no complaints. Water and firewood were not provided according to scale, but were sufficient. They had blankets, and slept in good and comfortable fitted-up berths in the 'tween deck. There was no overcrowding. On fine days, all the passengers, including the sick, were allowed on deck. The sick were attended by a Chinese surgeon.

Between clearing the Straits on the 17th April, and arriving at St Helena on the 28th June, he lost another 55 coolies. He arrived at Havana on 2 September after a long and tedious passage of 173 days. He received pratique on the 9th after eight days in quarantine, during which time he lost another eleven coolies. The number landed was 175, a 41.86% mortality rate.

An immediate outcome of the problem with the *John Calvin* was the recognition of the difficulty Hillier faced in confirming the status of each emigrant in a timely manner. As a consequence, within two days of Hillier signing the Emigration Certificate, a Government Notification was issued, advising persons engaging emigrants to present each labourer before the Emigration Officer or Magistrate, who would then fill in a form which contained the person's name in Chinese and English, his age, his province, district and place, and distinguishing marks if any. Then, as a Justice of the Peace for Hong Kong, he would certify that, on that date, the contract was fully, distinctly and intelligibly explained to the labourer in a dialect he understood, and he had agreed to be bound by the terms. The emigrant also acknowledged the receipt of any advance wages handed to him in the presence of the JP.

Lyall, Still & Co. were the Hong Kong agents for the *Duke of Portland* which had also been chartered by Ferran residing in Macao. She had been surveyed by J.V. Watkins, the Harbour Master on 28 February and certified to carry 334 passengers.

The first 25 coolies came on board immediately. A week later, 225 came aboard from a steamer from Macao, and then another batch of 86 from the same steamer, after a very rough passage from Macao. By 31 March, some 332 coolies had been placed on the *Duke of Portland*. Except for the cuddy, the emigrants had the whole of the lower deck. She was fitted with scuttles, and had previously carried emigrants. Two days before the ship was to sail, Emigration Officer Hillier went on board and addressed the men in Chinese. Some 38 men were in their bunks, too ill or still seasick, to go on deck to hear what Hillier had to say. With no objections from the men, Hillier issued the appropriate documentation on 1 April.

This was to be Hillier's last certificate as Emigration Officer. Following a serious altercation with Attorney-General Anstey, he had been appointed British Consul at Bangkok. He sailed for Siam (Thailand) on 10 May on what was to be a short assignment. Soon after his arrival there, he contracted dysentery and died on 14 October 1854. With Hillier's departure for Bangkok, William H. Mitchell was appointed Acting Chief Magistrate and Emigration Officer.

The *Duke of Portland* was about to sail on 2 April when the Chinese passengers crowded aft, taking belaying pins from the rails and pieces of firewood, yelling and shouting, and throwing things overboard. The interpreter later explained that they were rioting because their advance had not been paid. Captain George F. Seymour had been ashore at that time, but on returning and hearing of the riot, returned ashore. He came back with Hillier, in his capacity as the Stipendiary Magistrate, together with a troop of policemen. George Lyall arrived soon after. When the coolies were pacified, several policemen were left on board to act as sentries. They stayed until daybreak when the ship sailed off towards Havana.

The first suicide occurred on the third day and for each day after that, an average of three jumped overboard until they reached the Straits of Sunda. On 15 April, the captain was warned that a plan to take the ship was brewing. When it came about later that day, he was prepared, with canon placed facing the crowd and cutlasses at the ready. The attempt failed, and more than a dozen of the more unruly men were placed in irons. On the evening of the 28th, an attempt was made to rescue one of their ringleaders who had been placed in irons. When one of them threw a large bone at the captain, he thought it time to clear the decks, and in the ensuing struggle, one crewman was wounded in the side.

The general opinion on leaving China was that the coolies appeared in good health. The emigrants were not on short allowance during the voyage. There was plenty of water, rice, and meat. The provisions were served out to the ten cooks twice a day, and they then shared them among the men. The doctor went round twice every day to visit the sick men, and of a night, when called upon.

The water closets were not built for the way in which the Chinese used them. There was always a great stench in the ship. The urine not carried off was left to run along the deck. One water closet was within five feet of the ship's galley. The men slept on mats, which were very lousy. As no soap was provided by the ship, except to the sick, they were very filthy, and were covered with vermin.

The ship lost 136 Chinese (40.72%) on the 151-day passage to Havana, chiefly from congestive fever, similar to the Hong Kong fever. When they could not eat, the crew tried to force food down their throats. The captain and Doctor could see the difference between those who died from congestive fever, and those who suffered from the want of opium. The opium required by law was put on board in China, but it was all consumed before the ship arrived at St Helena. The captain gave the doctor full authority to get all the opium and medicines he required at St Helena.

The *Duke of Portland* had called at the Cocos Islands in the hope of getting vegetables, fresh meat, and fish for the invalids, but to no avail. It was 100 days to St Helena, where, after remaining three days taking on provisions, they had vegetables to within a few days of Havana. No reason was given as to why the ship did not stop at Cape Town.

High mortality concerns

The high mortality suffered by the two British ships from Hong Kong caused great concern in London. The *John Calvin* had sailed three weeks before, but arrived after the *Duke of Portland*, the first ship to arrive at Havana without scurvy on board.[51]

The losses of the Chinese was reported in the Havana press, which was repeated in a New York newspaper. The *British Shipping and Mercantile Gazette*, in turn printed the report stating that the *John Calvin* had lost 110 men on a 185-day passage, while the *Duke of Portland*, it was claimed, had lost 130 on her voyage from Hong Kong.

This article was seen by the President of the "Strangers' Home for Asiatics, Africans and South Sea Islanders" in London. This institution was founded in 1855 by the Church Missionary Society to provide for destitute foreign seamen, who had been abandoned when their ships arrived in England, after being recruited from overseas ports. In what must have seemed an unusual request from a party not directly involved in such matters, President Edward Buxton wrote to the Earl of Clarendon, the Foreign Minister, asking for the facts to be established; not about any Lascar seamen on board, but about the fate of the coolies. As they had boarded in a British colony, Mr Buxton then wrote to Henry

Labouchere, the Colonial Secretary, also asking about the coolies.

While Clarendon very quickly wrote to John Bowring seeking clarification, Labouchere initially sought information from the CLEC. The Commissioners had no information on the *John Calvin*, but the owners of the *Duke of Portland* were able to confirm that 130 coolies had died on that voyage, and that the number engaged was 330, not 500 as reported.[52] The CLEC suggested that the Consul at Havana be asked for further information.

Consul-General J.T. Crawford, in Havana, was able to reply that he had already instituted investigations, and it was found that neither Master was to blame for the high mortality rates on their vessels. Despite both vessels being well suited for the carriage of emigrants, the deaths could be attributed to the poor quality of the men embarked, and while the water taken on in Hong Kong was good, the voyages were probably too long for the quality to be maintained. He enclosed a translation of the detailed Cuban medical report.

But that was not the end of the matter. On 5 December, the *Times* printed a police report on proceedings relating to the *Duke of Portland*. The Committee of Privy Council for Trade saw that report, and immediately requested the Local Marine Board of London to inquire into the case.

Not satisfied with directing the Marine Board to inquire into the *Duke of Portland*, the Privy Council for Trade also requested the Lord Advocate for Scotland to inquire into the case of the *John Calvin*, which was then in Greenock.

The investigation team took depositions from several of the crew, but not the Master, who had by then left the ship for London. As the ship was still in port, Edwin Hanley, the measuring surveyor of the Customs at Greenock, was directed to measure her in accordance with the Chinese Passengers Act, 1855, Schedule A s.4.

Hanley's measurements showed that the 1,823 superficial feet in the 'tween decks, gave twelve superficial feet to each of 152 adult passengers. The cubic feet in the same space amounted to 12,152, which also gave 80 cubic feet to each of those passengers. The height of the 'tween decks was six feet eight inches; and it was this extraordinary height which allowed 80 cubic feet to each passenger. Had the 'tween decks been the usual height of six feet, the cubic space would have been only 72 feet, being the space prescribed in the said Act. The measurement showed that there was, on the upper deck of the *John Calvin*, 1,329 superficial feet, which give a space of five superficial feet per adult left clear on the upper deck for 266 passengers.

It was determined that there was no reason to attribute the sickness on board both vessels to overcrowding. However, it was found that the Emigration Officer in Hong Kong included all those parts of the upper deck which were housed over in his measurement, which were not the intention of the Act.

High mortality rates suffered by all four shipments for Drake from Amoy. Two British ships, the 783-ton *Admiral* in 1857 and the 1,190-ton *Tasmania* in 1858 had losses of 24.73% and 29.16% respectively. This was in spite of Captain James Nourse (1828-1897)[53] taking only 92 days for the voyage. The passenger/ton ratio on the *Tasmania* was only 0.31 which led to some doubt as to the effectiveness of that control formula.

Bellona was the 885-ton Dutch ship used for Drake's second shipment from Amoy. Captain Tentam needed 226 days to deliver 319 men after taking on 500 on 10 May 1856. The mortality rate amounted to 36.20%. That was followed by the Robinet-chartered *Cora*, which departed on her second coolie voyage on 20 October 1856. On that voyage only 315 men landed out of a total complement of 600, a mortality rate of 47.50%. The rest had died of dysentery along with the Mate, doctor and nine of the crew. This was the highest mortality rate since the inception of the indentured labour trades.

Drake shipments continued to suffer high mortality rates. The one sailing from Hong Kong undertaken by the 342-ton American ship *Tuskina* had a loss of 24.53%. Captain Broadbent lost 55 of the 227 men he loaded there. This loss was matched by the British 1,327-ton *Catherine Glen* which left Swatow on 5 December with 597 men. She suffered a mortality rate of 26.80%. This loss rate was equalled by another British ship, the 892-ton *Earl of Eglinton* with the last of twelve Drake shipments from Swatow in 1856-57.

After a long period of shuffling between ports seeking a cargo, the 279-ton Chilean brig *Alianza* finally departed from Swatow on 1 April 1857 with 256 Chinese consigned to Drake. When she arrived in Havana on 26 October, Captain A. Wilson was able to land only 155 of them. This large mortality rate of 39.45% was put down to the extended 208-day passage and the serious overcrowding on the vessel. The passenger/ton ratio was 0.92.

Macao Regulations for Chinese Emigration

By 1855, it became clear that Macao was the most suitable port for shipping coolies. The Portuguese authorities were well aware of the abuses, which characterised the traffic in coolies at Amoy, Swatow, Cumsingmoon, and Whampoa, and adopted measures which should have satisfied the most cautious of legislators and humanitarians around the world. Ordinances in 1853 and 1855 allowed the Macao government to assume control of the coolie houses, the registering of contracts and for the coolies to be inspected by the Procurador on shore and by the Port Capitan on board ship.

Taking the lead from the Chinese Passengers' Act, on 5 June 1856, the Portuguese authorities immediately issued "Regulations for Chinese Emigration at Macao", which detailed the processes to be followed by brokers, emigration agents and their registered depots, and the vessels on which the colonists (emigrants) were shipped.[54]

Mutinies

A low point for Ferran was the number of mutinies his captains had to endure. Of the eight vessels he was responsible for, four of them resulted in the vessels not reaching their destination. There were four other Torices mutinies, three undertaken by his successor Vargas, and the final one from Whampoa.

The 395-ton British barque *Samuel Enderby* sailed from Macao on 24 November 1855 with 200 Chinese for Havana.

In a letter from St Helena, Captain Henderson said the coolies rose two days after clearing the Straits of Sunda Strait, "making a rush aft, yelling and howling hideously, and armed with everything they could lay their hands on, viz., the axes used for cutting their firewood, the choppers, knives and cleavers used for cooking etc". The crew got out muskets and overpowered them and they retreated to the 'tween decks. Two of the ringleaders were put in irons. There had been no indication of subordination, and all had appeared to be remarkably contented and happy.

They had been fed beef, pork and salt fish on alternate days, with pickles and all the rice and bread they wished for. One gallon of water was provided each per day. After that a continuous guard was kept with loaded muskets as the captain dared not close the hatchways for fear of suffocation. He was strongly of the opinion that, "Every vessel in the trade ought to have iron bars across all the hatchways so as to have only one passage up and down to the 'tween decks".[55] The ship continued on her voyage of 101 days, delivering 196 persons to Torices on 4 March 1856.

The 492-ton Portuguese ship *Resolucao* left Macao on 19 February 1856 for Havana with 450 men on board. There were two versions of what happened then. Singapore and Hong Kong newspapers reported that, three days out, the *Resolucao* ran into heavy weather and sprung a leak. Over the next few days the leak got worse and Captain Fernandes attempted to make course for Singapore, but as the leak got worse, he then headed for Cape St Jacques. On arrival in the bay, Captain Fernandes ran her aground as there was no hope of saving her. The Chinese passengers overloaded the first boat and many were drowned. The crew then abandoned ship, leaving one boat for the Chinese. Only the captain and ten of the crew managed to reach the shore, and were eventually sent on to Singapore by the local authorities. Two of the passengers who reached the shore reported that all the Chinese, except for about 40 or 50 of them, had reached the shore.

The other version was an account from the *Boletim do Governo*.[56] On the sixth day out, when they saw land the coolies embarked on a predetermined plan to murder the crew and run the ship ashore. They stole knives from the galley and assaulted the boatswain before heading for the cabin. There they were met by the captain and mate who drove them back into the hold. Doubting his ability to contain the conflict Captain Fernandes decided to desert the ship, taking the wounded boatswain and the rest of the crew in the boats. They made for Cape St Jacques, where to his surprise he found the *Resolucao* stranded in the bay. They did not reboard the ship but proceeded ashore where they were harshly treated by the natives. Captain Fernandes eventually reached Singapore where he successfully obtained insurance for the vessel for his owners.

Against the prevailing monsoon, the 760-ton Dutch ship *Banca* under Captain Heymans left Macao on 12 July 1856 for Havana with 350 passengers. She had been only a few days out when she encountered a severe typhoon. The cargo shifted, and her water casks broke loose, requiring her to put back to Macao, where she anchored in the outer roads. While she was under repair, her officers exercised strict vigilance to prevent the coolies from escaping ashore. All went well for three weeks, until the Chinese doctor warned the captain that mischief was brewing. In preparation for any rising, small arms were placed on the poop, and two guns were loaded with grape and pointed forward.

About 9 o'clock on the night of 8 August, the disturbance commenced, and the crew took refuge on the poop. The captain at first fired a shot or two overhead, but that had no effect. Armed with belaying pins, and bricks from the cooking places, the coolies advanced towards them, yelling frightfully. The captain then gave orders to fire, and immediately a volley was poured into the infuriated mass from the two guns and from the small arms. This put down the riot, and the coolies were driven below. But they sought revenge by setting fire to the ship. Within a few minutes, the captain was appalled to see flames issuing up from the fore hatch.

A frightful scene of carnage followed, as the coolies rushed up on deck, and murdered all the officers. None of them, including the captain, were seen again. The ship was soon in a blaze, fore and aft. In about an hour the mainmast fell with a crash, then the fore and mizzen, and about midnight, the magazine blew up with a tremendous explosion. The ship was hurled into fragments, and a vast number of poor creatures, who had climbed on to the two chains, perished with her. Of the approximately 400 passengers and crew who were on board, only 150 escaped with their lives, the remainder were either burnt in the ship or drowned.

A ship not to arrive was the 675-ton French ship *Port de Bordeaux* under Captain Minandes, which left Macao on 11 January 1857 with 450 on board. One day out, a fire broke out in the 'tween decks. As the crew fought the fire, a large number of the passengers went aft and took possession of the arms. The interpreter told the captain that some fifty or sixty of them had taken passage for the Straits, and not for Havana. With no choice, Captain Mirandes returned to Macao and threw up his charter. The other emigrants were then put on a Dutch vessel soon after.

In yet another tragedy, the 632-ton French ship *Anais*, under Captain J. Carignac, departed Swatow on 29 January 1857 with 420 passengers for Havana. The day after departure, the Chinese revolted, killing the captain, officers, supercargo and his son, and took possession of the vessel. They then ran her ashore on Tonglea, five miles distant from Breaker's Point.

The Dutch schooner *Boreas*, on passage from Singapore to Macao, came across the French vessel *Fernandez*, flying signals of distress on 16 April 1857 when off Pulo Sepatu. On boarding, the Dutch captain was informed that the coolies had twice risen on the crew and thirteen of them had been killed. They tried to set fire to the ship, but when forced back below they put the fire out themselves. Captain Penney suppressed the insurrection then continued on the 162-day voyage to Havana, losing only a further six men on the way.

Kate Hooper was a 1,489-ton American clipper built in 1853. She was 205ft long, with a 30ft 6in beam, and 20ft of depth, with two passenger decks. On 18 August 1857,

Captain John J. Jackson entered into a contract with Lyall, Still & Co., agents for A.R. Ferran of Macao, to transport Chinese to Cuba. She was consigned to Don Rafael Rodriguez Torices.[57] The *Kate Hooper* undertook modifications in Hong Kong. In the 'tween decks, the whole space, fore, aft, and amidships, was completely lined with bunks. On main deck, four large cookhouses were constructed, three with six large in-built pots, similar to furnaces, and fit to cook for six or seven hundred men. In the lower hold, there were two tiers of casks for water. At each of the fore, main and after hatches, coamings for gratings were prepared. The hatches were encircled with iron bars securely fastened to the deck, creating impregnable cages in which the crew could watch over their passengers in time of trouble. These iron gratings were then put in place after the ship left Hong Kong.

She left Hong Kong on 3 October 1857 for Macao, arriving 16 hours later. Two days before leaving, the Chinese labourers boarded. They came in small junks, each with approximately fifty men, and well guarded by policemen. The *Kate Hooper* then left Macao on 15 October 1857 with 652 Chinese labourers. The Chinese realised that they were heading to Cuba when they noticed the ship was sailing on a southerly course, toward the Indian Ocean and Cape of Good Hope, rather than north-east to North America, their expected destination. On 19 October, some of the labourers threatened the crew with an insurrection. Well over three hundred were on deck at the time, but the crew on watch was able to force them below deck and fasten the hatches. With this uprising, Captain Jackson had four men put in irons, and three flogged.

On 6 November, the *Kate Hooper* was preparing to enter the Gaspar Straits separating Java and Sumatra. On sighting land, the Chinese again rose in revolt, but the crew forced the men below and fastened the hatches. The agitators then took straw stuffing out of the sleeping mattresses, added straw hats to the piles, and set them afire. The crew immediately placed tarpaulins over the hatches which cut the air flow and put out their fires. Three more times the coolies set fire to straw and each time the fires were extinguished with tarpaulins placed over the covers.

Captain Jackson had taken ill soon after they left Macao, and his condition worsened as the journey proceeded. He felt that if these disturbances continued, the ship and crew would be in danger. Flying the American flag upside down as a signal of distress, he ordered two lifeboats to be prepared for abandoning ship. One lifeboat was loaded with food supplies, charts, and a compass and lowered into the water. A second lifeboat was kept hanging from the davits.

Another American vessel, the *Flying Childers* spotted the distress signal, and sent the chief mate across to the *Kate Hooper*. Captain Jackson stated that the *Kate Hooper* should be abandoned or even blown up. Chief Mate Bowden argued that if the crew stuck with the ship, they could restore order if they had more arms, which the *Flying Childers* provided. She accompanied the *Kate Hooper* into Anjer on 13 November.

Chief Mate Bowden then asked the Chinese to identify the ringleaders. No mercy was given to the five ringleaders. One was bound head and foot and thrown overboard. While he was floundering at sea, he was shot by the coolie master, as were two others on the poop deck. Another was shot between decks, and the last one was hanged by the spanker gaff. Four more were flogged, and eighteen others were picked out and put in double irons until just before landing in Havana.

Then the Chinese were allowed to come up on deck, but only twenty-four at a time. The fearful crew decided not to return to their quarters but to sleep on deck. Captain Jackson appealed to the Harbour Master at Anjer for a guard of soldiers to help him. He was advised to seek assistance from the American consulate in Batavia (now Jakarta), some sixty miles away. Vice Consul Henry Anthon, Jr was unsure what to do but found eleven men who were prepared to sign the shipping articles in the consul's office. After returning to Anjer, another four sailors were found.

The *Kate Hooper* resumed her voyage on 25 November. On 15 December, while off the coast of Madagascar, Captain Jackson died. After rounding the Cape of Good Hope, she arrived at St Helena on 5 January 1858, where she took on fresh provisions and stores. The remainder of the trip was uneventful, with no more trouble from the Chinese. The *Kate Hooper* anchored in Havana on 12 February 1858. Of the 652 men who boarded in Macao, 612 survived the voyage.

Mutiny or Piracy?

Occasionally, an emigration agent would remark that it appeared that some intending emigrants had actually presented themselves with the sole purpose of gaining temporary entry to a ship. Once on board these men plotted to overcome the captain and crew, and if possible sack the ship along the China coast. Such plots would therefore not be considered acts of mutiny but rather acts of piracy.

The 1,915-ton American clipper, *Flora Temple*, made her first voyage in the coolie trade on 1 February 1857 when she took 900 coolies from Macao to Havana. After a 100-day voyage, 852 of them were landed.

Her second voyage commenced on 8 October 1859, when Captain Charles R. Johnson, sailed from Macao, with some 850 coolie labourers bound for Havana. Her crew, including officers, numbered about 50 men. On the Monday after they left all seemed comfortable and cheerful. The coolies' food was plentiful and good, and their state was well cared for, the necessary order and discipline among them being enforced by their own headmen. An outbreak was the last thing anticipated.

Three days after leaving Macao, the morning watch on deck were scattered about the ship. While the guard at the port gate of the barricade was away from his post, the coolies suddenly fell upon the guard at the starboard gate, struck him on the head with an iron belaying pin as he was stooping down. They then drew out his sword, cut him with cruel ferocity, and dispatched him with a hatchet. They then made a rush through the barricade towards the cabin. While this was going on aft, other coolies were calling "fire, fire" to induce the watch, who were forward, to go down below.

The captain had come to the poop in time to see the rush aft. He ran to his cabin, seized his revolver, and called the surgeon up. The captain's brother armed himself too, and with half a dozen shots put them to the rout, as one of the crew was hacked to pieces and others wounded. The coolies were armed with the cook's axes, chain-hooks, iron belaying pins, spikes, and every weapon they could lay their hands upon.

The next day they encountered a heavy gale from the south-west. Captain Johnson declined to put on more sail, worried that a current might set the ship to the eastward where reefs were marked on the chart. The captain directed a good lookout to be kept, with orders to maintain their course until 8pm. The sights obtained at noon were good. The cry of "hard up" was heard when the ship was within a short distance of the breakers, which could now be distinctly seen and heard. The *Flora Temple* struck slightly and then several times with very heavy bumps. With water rapidly increasing until it reached between the decks, she developed a heavy list to port. The ship was 300 miles from land.

Captain Johnson had no intention of abandoning his ship, but had the two quarter boats lowered, and placed an officer and five men in each, with orders to remain close to the ship so that refuge and assistance might be at hand. At 12 o'clock, the other boats were got out, only leaving the longboat, which the panic-stricken men had declared impossible to get out. It was finally got over the side, and its crew including Captain Johnson, his brother, and A.P. Childs, the surgeon, passed safely through the breakers. The coolies, who had remained below all night, were now up and clustered on the upper decks.

Throughout the seven days while the gale lasted, the longboat was hove to under a close-reefed mainsail. On the 22nd the wind and sea abated. Captain Johnson had saved his sextant and chart, and as they found their longboat had been driven by the gale as far as 13N, he decided to make for Touron, the French settlement in Cochin China.

They reached Touron on the evening of the 28th, where they were received on board His Imperial Majesty's steamer *Gironde*. Captain Johnson begged French Admiral M. Page, to search for the missing boats, as well as to rescue the coolies. On 2 November, they sighted the ship, on her port side, but floating. Of the 860 coolies, no trace remained.

Captain Johnson was said to be very humane and a courageous man, but the crew were so terrified that it was only by the exertions of the captain, his brother, and a few others, that the crew were saved. The boats were no more than sufficient to save the crew. No attempt was made to save the coolies.

British Consular Agent Cleverly at Macao reported that he had had a conversation with the surgeon of the *Flora Temple* on his return to Macao. Dr Childs had said that after the suppression of the attack it was discovered that among the rebels was one sufficiently educated in foreign vessels to take entire charge of one. The business-like manner in which the coolies furled sails and took judicious precautions clearly showed that he was supported by many trained Chinese seamen. Cleverly suggested that the attempt to seize the ship was planned, with the supposed emigrants intending to seize and plunder the ship. However there was only one other mutiny in 1859.

A similar mutiny occurred on the American ship, *Norway*. Captain Hugo B. Major left Macao on 26 November 1859 bound for Havana with 1,038 coolies. Five days out, a mutiny broke out among the coolies who set fire to the ship in two places, and endeavoured to force the hatches. Mr Stimpson, one of the mates, had charge of the deck. The watch, with the exception of the man at the wheel, was aloft taking in sail. As Stimpson rushed to the hatch to repulse the coolies, the crew from aloft and below tried to seize the boats and leave the ship. The surgeon, an Englishman, drew his pistol and threatened to shoot the first man who dared to make that attempt. The crew then rallied and went to the assistance of the officers, and a fight ensued, which continued until after daylight the next morning.

Thirty of the coolies were killed, and more than ninety wounded before the mutiny was quelled. The captain then gave the coolies one hour to deliver up their arms. If they did not, he threatened to cut away the masts, set fire to the ship, take away the boats and provisions, and leave them to their fate. The mutineers soon came to terms.

Ironically Cleverly had commented that the *Norway* had been fitted up with great care and expense, and no pains had been spared to render the passengers comfortable and the ship secure from outbreak or attack. He said he had visited the principal barracoon then in operation in Macao and saw some 500 men and boys destined for the *Norway*. They appeared contented, happy and healthy. They were for the most part young and undersized, and from their appearance, could have little to hope for in their own country, but for the precarious subsistence that might be afforded elsewhere. The men were clean and well dressed and the food plentiful and good. Each man was given a few cash daily to buy on the premises whatever luxury they wanted. The barracoon was well secured and watched, but in every other respect, excellent in its arrangements.

The receiving ship *Messenger* arrived at Macao from Whampoa on 16 February 1860, where she took a cargo of 380 coolies to Havana, consigned to Torices. According to Gideon Nye, the American Vice Consul at Macao, Captain Manton had requested clearance on the evening of 22 February. He was extremely rude and insulting on arrival at the Consulate.

It was not until 23 July 1883 that the *New York Times* published an account from Captain James Keene on what happened on the voyage of the *Messenger*. He had sailed on her as Quartermaster at that time. His recollections did not entirely coincide with documented events, but included the unsuccessful attempt by what was claimed to be a group of twenty-five Ladrone pirates who had joined the ship with the specific intention of capturing her, plundering her cargo and converting her boats into pirate ships.

Keene told how the men came on board in Macao in the middle of the night from four lorchas, and the ship was well at sea by morning. The men were all numbered by a tin medal hung around the neck, Chinese on one side, and the English equivalent on the other. They were fed on rice and fish. Bread made from rice and flour was also provided, but it was so hard it could be thrown the length of the ship without breaking it. Ten days out, and close to Hainan, Sing Hi and his cohorts stormed the high picket barricade after securing most of the crew below. They were subdued with cutlasses and revolvers. Sing Hi did not survive the attack. Keene then vividly described the punishment doled out to the ringleaders. They were whipped with bamboos such that the cross cuts would rip off pieces of flesh, and, with blood flowing freely, they were doused with sea water. They were stripped naked before being trussed up in small cages kept on deck and not allowed out except for a wash once a week. They were also made to ensure the greatest humiliation of having their pigtails cut off. They were given their clothes back on arrival at Havana where the coolies were sold at auction for between $600 and $1,100 each.

Despite his displeasure at the treatment he had received from the Chinese and American authorities, Captain Manton still found employment in the trade profitable. He returned to Macao, and took another consignment of 555 coolies on 20 March 1861. There were no reports of any problems on that voyage which was arranged by new Emigration Agent C.J. Yturraide. That was also the last voyage by an American ship in the coolie trade to Cuba.

On 3 November 1860, Mr Thorndike of the Anglo American Cuban Emigration Agency was advised that an outbreak had occurred on the Chilean ship *Greyhound* anchored half way between Shameen and the Macao Passage Fort. During the night, as they were being allowed on deck, two of the coolies attacked the crew. In the ensuing struggle, 30 of the 138 men on board managed to reach the deck. Nine jumped overboard, one had his skull clove and another was shot.

On the day following the investigation, some Customs officers pointed out to the Chinese that under the new Royal Decree, unless they left Cuba within two months of the conclusion of their contract they would be liable to serve another term of eight years, or a shorter term to earn enough to pay for their return passages. This had a remarkable effect on the coolies and they asked for a mandarin to explain it to them. This was promised but not fulfilled. After the coolies embarked on a hunger-strike, the Emigrant Inspectors boarded and the resulting inquiry resulted in seventy-eight of the men refusing to leave. The Inspectors determined that, as they had accepted their advance payment, they were bound to depart. The *Greyhound* eventually sailed for Havana on 20 November 1860 with 230 men.

High mortality

Five of the ten Ferran departures from Swatow had mortality rates above 21%. Captain Henderson of the 683-ton British ship *Ellen Oliver* risked losing his ship by not calling at Hong Kong after loading 336 coolies for Havana on 11 May 1856. After an exceedingly long voyage of 198 days, he was able to land only 261 of them. This equates to a mortality rate of 22.32%.

The American clipper, *Kitty Simpson*, left Swatow on 28 November 1857, for Havana. When she arrived in Havana on 19 March 1858, Dr Thomas H. Somerville, surgeon of the *Kitty Simpson*, reported as follows: "The high mortality of 93 Chinese coolies is attributable to the vast amount of disease on board, and the broken-down debilitated condition of the patients, which rendered them not only prone to disease but unfitted them for contending with it when attacked. Of the coolies, only about 50 were in good health, the remainder feeble, sickly, emaciated wretches, whom hardship, disease, and hunger had reduced to the lowest ebb of vitality. Almost all trace of muscular substance had disappeared. Most of them were covered with spots from recent skin disease, some covered with blotches from head to foot.

"The number of cases averaged 50 per day, never below 30, with deaths averaging one per day. The diseases were from intestinal worms, opium, and tubercles. Worms are not fatal to Europeans, but the size and number in the Chinese were intense, as shown when the intestine of a dead man was opened, the worms gushed out as under considerable pressure. The accommodation was ample, well ventilated and kept scrupulously clean. The provisions were of good quality and abundant; and minimal discipline was required."[58]

Dr Somerville's report had been seconded by Dr. E.B. Pellew of the *Tasmania* and Dr Thomas Gwynne of the *Edwin Fox*. They had arrived at Havana within days of each other; the *Tasmania* had lost 107 of her passengers from Swatow, a mortality rate of 29.16%.

The *Julian de Unzueta* was the fourth vessel in 1857 to suffer a high loss at 25.71%. This was followed in 1858 with the 1,007-ton Danish ship *Freya* suffering a 35.74% loss on her voyage from Swatow on 20 February. Captain J.P. Sorenson landed 302 of the 470 he had taken on board.

The highest rate suffered that year however was on the Norwegian barque, *Norma*. Captain Johan Normann chartered his 440-ton vessel to take Chinese to Havana at $75 for each man landed. The ship was not surveyed in either Hong Kong or Swatow. The hold was 100 feet long and there was seven feet between decks. Two tiers of bunks were built to sleep the men three, four, or five to a berth.

Captain Normann sailed from Swatow on 30 March 1858 with 276 men. Only 139 of them landed in Havana after a 146-day voyage. The Chinese doctor Chuy Foy claimed that the 137 who died (a mortality rate of 49.64%) had done so from sudden deprivation of opium, pestilence, heart disease, and insufficient water. Captain Normann had taken Chuy on as a doctor but he was useless. He had two boxes full of opium and despite being told not to, he was seen to sell it to the men. At St Helena, he bought more even though he did not go ashore. The captain maintained that he was so incompetent he once declared a man dead and asked permission to throw him overboard. In the process of doing so, the bosun noticed that the man was breathing. He subsequently fully recovered.

Chuy sued Captain Normann in Hong Kong on 1 June 1860, for $500 in back-wages. He had received only $208. In defence, Normann said that Chuy had been hired at $25 per month and had been paid $60 in Hong Kong, $20 in Swatow, $100 in Havana and $16 in Charleston after leaving Havana. Chuy did not win his case.

High mortality plagued Ferran with his only shipment from Amoy on 8 May 1857. Captain Pouyallet of the 538-ton

French ship *Giscours* was not able to explain why only 171 of the original 334 coolies embarked were able to walk ashore after the 161-day voyage. The mortality rate was 48.80%. There were also two Ferran shipments from Macao with high mortalities. Captain L. Poszetto on the 657-ton Peruvian ship *Tinita Torices* left on 6 May 1857 with 370 coolies but could declare only 167 on arrival 185 days later. The mortality rate was 54.86%. The other was on the 1,145-ton Dutch ship *Admiraal Van Heemskerk* on 31 March 1858. That voyage incurred a mortality rate of 20.98%. This was Antonio Ferran's last vessel for Torices. Ferran then returned home in 1858 after a short handover period to a Peruvian national, S.R. Vargas. Over the next two years Vargas employed three vessels with mortality rates in excess of 23%. They were the two French ships *Malabar* in 1858 and *Succes* in 1859 and the 1,319-ton Spanish *Primera de Espana* also in 1858.

The 1,435-ton American clipper, *Swallow*, under Captain J.H. Morton, had 750 coolies on board and was waiting for only a few more before departing for Havana. She was jointly managed by Ferran and Vargas and sailed from Whampoa on 3 July 1859 with 650 men consigned to Torices but only 552 managed to land. In reporting the vessel, Vice Consul Frederick Howe Hale wrote to Acting Consul Winchester telling of a new ploy now being used to lure unsuspecting persons. A woman with a child on her back would drop her bonnet, and when it was picked up and returned, the victim would be sincerely thanked and offered drugged cakes as a reward. When the drugged targets sat down to rest, they would be accosted by two accomplices who on the pretext of helping the men home would take them to the receiving ships instead.

Vargas's first American vessel was the 1,637-ton clipper ship, *Live Yankee*, delivering 778 coolies out of 800 that were taken on in Macao on 4 March 1859. Dr Gerald Potts wrote to the *Friend of China* from Anjer to say that all the coolies were alive and well. No sickness, and as quiet as could be. He said he was far happier with the Chinese than he had been when he looked after English Government emigrants to the colonies who were fifty times more trouble. He had the full support of Captain Eben A. Thorndike and Captain Holmes who was the coolie master. Dr Potts and the captain had good reason to look after the Chinese. He was to be paid $10 for every coolie landed, but down to 50c if greater than 50% of the 700 taken on board did not reach Cuba. *Live Yankee* returned to complete another equally good voyage in 1860.

The aggressive recruitment methods of Torices's Agents, brokers and crimps in the Canton area led to the eventual acceptance by Chinese officials that emigration had to be condoned. The cynical way in which his Emigrant Agent Vargas utilised American ships would have been instrumental in the United States banning the participation of American ships in this controversial trade.

Vargas gained notoriety for himself with his use of American vessels as receiving ships in Whampoa. In conjunction with Lyall, Still & Co. of Hong Kong, Vargas chartered six American vessels in early 1859 for an estimated half a million dollars.[59] After serving as receiving ships, the 1,849-ton *Pioneer* and *Kitty Simpson* eventually sailed from Whampoa without passengers. The 1,429-ton clipper ship *Governor Morton* succeeded in taking 557 coolies away from Whampoa on 5 May 1859, leaving the 1,350-ton *Messenger* and 1,637-ton *Live Yankee* to revert to Macao to embark their complements in 1860. The 1,225-ton, *J Wakefield*, and 619-ton, *May Queen*,were the two other American vessels to sail from Macao to Havana in 1860. The last ship that Vargas despatched was the *Francis P Sage*, which left Macao on 17 January 1861 with 550 Chinese for Havana. Captain Thos. R. Ingersoll took 103 days to deliver the 520 that were still on board.

Two American ships departed from Whampoa for Havana in 1861. The *Alice Thorndike* and the *Independence* were filled by the Thorndike house and left without incident and experienced very low mortality rates.

The *New York Times* of 31 May 1861 reported the suspension of payments by its principal R.R. Torices. It added that it was a singular fact that most of the houses that had been engaged in the coolie trade had "gone to the bad".

The losses associated with three American receiving ships at Whampoa may have been a factor in this enterprise.

The Torices involvement in the coolie trade lasted for seven years from 1855 to 1861. In all, fifty-five shipments were made. Macao was the centre of their operations, with only one shipment from Amoy, and ten from Swatow. Torices agents recruited 25,497 Chinese coolies of whom 20,149 duly arrived in Cuba. Overall the mortality rate was 20.98%, with five shipments exceeding 40%. There were eleven mutinies, four of which resulted in the vessel not completing its voyage. Four of the mutinies were on American vessels.

In the five years to 1859 that Ferran was based in Macao he recruited 15,975 Chinese for the 39 shipments he conducted. With eight mutinies and ten voyages with high mortality, 12,270 coolies were landed in Havana. The mortality for those five years amounted to 23.19%. Between 1858 and 1861 Vargas handled 15 shipments for Torices, three of which had casualties in excess of 22% and three mutinies, one of which resulted in the ship being wrecked. The mortality rate of 19.02% was achieved from embarking 8,880 men while leaving 7,191 to disembark in Havana.

Blenheim
**Sailed from Amoy for Cuba on 23 October 1852
with 453 coolies.**

5

Spanish Free Importation

Capitan-General José Gutierrez de la Concha had been critical of the licences granted to Villodo, Pereda, Torices and Pedroso, and wanted a freer market. Acting on advice from planters such as Zulueta, Concha, in Cuba, recommended to the authorities in Spain on 12 February 1857 that the introduction of free Chinese settlers should be without limit, possibly as many as 60,000. With this encouragement seven companies entered the trade.

Colonizadora

Torices was a very astute man. Knowing that Capitan-general Concha wanted to see a freer market, it appears that Torices persuaded his Asiatico de Habana partners—Antonio Ferran, Marcial Dupierris, and Juan A. Colome—to accept the Earl of Lombillo into a new partnership to be known as "Colonizadora". Concha subsequently allowed the formation of this consortium. This could be regarded as tokenism as Torices continued to be the named consignee for all but three of the shipments which were made after this arrangement was put in place.

These three shipments were made in 1858, the only year when shipments were made under the name of Colonizadora. The 533-ton Peruvian *Don Julian* left Macao on 22 January 1858. She arrived in Havana 110 days later where Captain Cortina delivered all of the 326 men he had embarked. The second voyage was by the now veteran of the coolie trades, the *Westward Ho*. On 10 July 1858 Captain A. de Araucoa was able to land in Havana only 611 of the 700 he had embarked in Macao. This mortality rate of 12.71% was surpassed when Colonizadora's third vessel arrived in Havana on 31 August 1858. Captain N. Koens of the 997-ton Dutch ship *Pieter Cornelis zn Hooft* could show only 368 of the 570 coolies he had taken on in Macao. The mortality rate was 35.44%.

The first vessel of the three was handled on arrival by Escauriza y Serpa and the captains of the other two were responsible for their own vessels. The *Boletin de Colonizacion* listed Colonizadora as the consignee for all three arrivals.

Campbell and Caro

The Campbell brothers were planters who had also applied to introduce colonists on their own account in accordance with the Royal Decree of 1854. However it was not until 1856 that they made their first shipment in conjunction with a fellow planter, Charles Caro.

The 687-ton Dutch ship *Doggersbank* arrived in Macao late in October 1856 and left after 30 days on 28 November 1856. As Campbell and Caro had no agent in Macao, contracts were exchanged directly between Captain A.P. Achenbach and each of the 380 recruits he had managed to procure. He arrived in Havana 141 days later with 373 of them landing safely.

To the north of Amoy, Foochow (Fuzhou) is the capital of the Province of Fukien, and the principal port for the export of tea from China. It was a Treaty Port but was not generally regarded as being within the main recruiting districts of China. However, on 23 February 1857, Vice Consul Frederick Howe Hale reported to Governor Bowring, that the firm of Campbell and Caro of Havana had appointed Mr Flotard of Hong Kong and Macao as agent, together with Messrs Vaucher Freres & Co. of Hong Kong and the Swiss firm Borel in Foochow, to act as sub-agents for the recruitment of Chinese emigrants.

Borel met with strong resistance from the local authorities and population, and it was only after a prolonged period that he was able to find sufficient men to fill his chartered 589-ton French vessel *Etoile* for a voyage to Havana. However as the 320 men were about to embark, local opposition was so great that the charter had to be aborted. Carlo Flotard was not to be put off however, and went on to arrange the next two shipments for Campbell and Caro.

It was in 1857 that the first ship, fitted with an auxiliary steam engine, was used in the coolie trades. The French shipping company Bazin & Léon Gay[60] of Marseilles entered the trade with the 1,583-ton *Francois 1*. The *Friend of China* described her as of 72 metres (237ft) and a beam of 11 metres (36ft) with a depth of hold from upper deck to top of keel of 21ft. The height between decks was seven ft with a further 8ft to the orlop deck. Her 60hp engine and screw propeller enabled her to make six knots in calms and light airs. She also had a condensing machine which converted the escaping steam to make 75 gallons of water each day. For ventilation, she had ports of between 2ft and 3ft square every 15ft, and large hatchways with cupola iron gratings. That charter had been arranged by Pereda Machado in conjunction with Campbell and Caro in Havana.

British Consul-General Jos. T. Crawford was particularly impressed with this French steamer. Even though Captain H. Closmadeau and his crew of 51 had had to suppress a mutiny prior to arriving on 25 November 1857, they had been able to land 842 men out of the 900 who had boarded in Macao on 4 August 1857. However, he gave no details of the mutiny.

The *Francois 1* made two more voyages from Macao in 1858 and 1860. With a complement of 1,000, the mortality rate on the second voyage was 16.50%, compared with 6.44% on the first voyage. On her third voyage, Captain Conil took on only 790 Chinese and was able to discharge 773 of them at a mortality rate of just 2.15%.

Had Crawford delayed his report on the first voyage by a few days, he might have modified his admiration for steamers. Another French-flagged steamer, the *Charles Martell*, was of a similar size to the *Francois 1*. Also owned by Bazin & Léon Gay, she left Macao on 17 October 1857 with 830 Chinese on board. Whereas *Francois 1* took 115 days on the voyage, the *Charles Martell* needed 143 to reach Havana. Those additional 23 days may have accounted for the 154 deaths which represented a mortality rate of 18.55%.

Charles Martell was to suffer a worse tragedy on her next voyage on 11 September 1959. Captain A. David lost 560 of the 900 men taken on board in Macao. The mortality rate of 62.22% after 148 days again raised concerns over steamers undertaking long voyages. She was not employed again.

The Chinese Passengers' Act still required British ships with passengers to declare them in Hong Kong in 1857. Captain Alexander Wilson of the 1,106-ton *Dream* however thought he would circumvent the Act by simply applying for clearance at Hong Kong for Macao, claiming it was a ballast voyage. Once at Macao, he then commenced taking on 503 coolies and sailed on 14 November 1857, without returning to Hong Kong. When Emigration Officer Mitchell learned of this breach of the Act, he advised the Harbour Master, who in turn alerted John Bowring. In his despatch to Labouchere, Bowring expressed the hope that the *Dream* would be captured before she could discharge her cargo. That did not come about, and the *Dream* arrived at Havana on 24 March 1858 discharging her 438 coolies without intervention from the British Consul there. The mortality rate had been 12.92 percent.

Charles Caro introduced two emigrant agents to China, Lorenzo Pereira and French emigrant agent, L. Boye, recently-arrived in Macao. The former recruited 356 Chinese for the 566-ton *Daguerre*, which left Macao on 2 April 1859 with 356 coolies. The latter, in conjunction with French shipowner Bazin & Léon Gay, chartered the 849-ton barque *Emile Pereire* for a 108-day voyage from Macao, which sailed on 23 January 1860. There were only three deaths among the 460 who were taken onboard.

Boye continued with the 1,015-ton ship *Sigisbert Cezard* leaving Macao on 4 April 1860 together with Campbell's 534-ton French barque *Brave Lourmel* which was loaded by H. de Closmadeau who had been Captain on the *Francois 1*. The former had eleven deaths out of 410 embarked while the latter lost two from a total of 302.

The 1,151-ton American ship *Forest Eagle* under first-time Captain Thomas Pillsbury was chartered to take 500

Chinese emigrants under the age of 30, men and boys, from Macao to Havana. They were all described as being in very good health when placed on board by Emigration Agent L. Boye on 8 February 1861. As an incentive, Captain Pillsbury was to receive $5 a head if the mortality rate did not exceed 5% and $3 if it did not exceed 10%. As was usual with coolie ships by then, she had a barricade built across the after deck to protect the crew, a qualified doctor, and a coolie master to manage the emigrants. There was also an interpreter, Mr Souza, whose name suggests that he was born in Macao of Portuguese and possibly Chinese extraction. Each coolie was given a numbered card, which he had to keep with him for identification purposes. *Forest Eagle* sailed on 8 February 1861, and arrived at Havana on 20 May after a largely uneventful voyage of 101 days during which 42 Chinese died. She was placed in quarantine until 4 July where another 69 died from causes undetermined by the local doctors.

The coolie master's log[61] faithfully records the routine doling-out of food rations, and the frequent cleaning of the living spaces. It also records some of the causes of death and the unnatural practices first recorded by Dr Ely on the *Samuel Boddington* to Demerara. The number of deaths recorded in the log differs from that published by Zulueta's publication *Boletin de Colonizacion* which indicated that 458 asiaticos had arrived on the ship

In December 1860, Captain John Wood of the 690-ton American ship *Leonidas* entered into a charter party with H. Closmadeau on behalf of J. Campbell of Havana. She was to proceed to Macao for at least 300 passengers and provisions. The sum of $65 was to be paid for every passenger delivered alive at Havana. The 70 lay-days had a 15-day grace period after which the demurrage rate was $75 per day. The ship was to provide berths, privies and cooking places and water for 100 days at 6 gallons per day[62] and firewood. The Charterer was to provide food. At least half the passengers at a time would be allowed on deck for exercise and to smoke, except in bad weather. The captain was to receive $5 per head if losses did not exceed 5%, and $3 per head if losses were in excess of 10%. $10 per head was to be advanced to Captain Wood to defray expenses at Havana.[63]

The *Leonidas* was dispatched from Canton on 25 February 1861, by the French Maritime Agency in connection with Credit Mobiller for Caro & Co. While she was at anchor two or three miles below the Macao Passage Fort, waiting for a breeze to carry her over the bar, a disturbance broke out in the 'tween decks. This was simply a ruse to attract the officers to the spot. The chief mate and third mate immediately went below to ascertain the cause, when they were savagely set upon by the coolies. The chief mate managed to get back on deck, though severely cut about the head and neck. He then found that a large batch of the coolies, whom he had left on deck at breakfast, had rushed into the cabin and were assaulting the captain, on whom they had inflicted two desperate cuts. The captain's wife was assailed with basins, etc. and severely cut on the head. The captain managed to seize a musket with which he shot and killed one of the coolies, felling another with the butt.

By this time, the crew had come aft, loaded arms, and driven the coolies below, shooting some twenty-nine of them. The coolies then collected a heap of wood and set fire to it. The captain battened them down, until the coolies put out the fire themselves. The hatches were then removed and the third mate extricated. He was so badly wounded that he was not expected to live. As this was happening some eighty or ninety coolies jumped overboard, but only about half of them reached the shore. The coolie master chased them with a cutlass and re-captured thirteen of them. He lost a finger from the bursting of a musket he was firing and the steward received a severe cut to the back of his head.

The captain then sent his wife away to Canton in the pilot boat. In passing the Macao fort, she gave the alarm. The officer in charge sent thirty soldiers down, with orders to put down all resistance with arms. Captain Wood who had received two severe cuts across his nose was taken ashore together with the third mate. HM gunboat *Weasel* then towed the *Leonidas* back to the anchorage. Out of 289 coolies, only 210 could be accounted for, and of these 195 appeared in no condition to continue the voyage. The *Leonidas* eventually sailed for Havana on 18 March 1861 with 290 men. They were consigned to Caro.

In a letter dated 21 March 1861 to the Editor of the *Friend of China* "A Lover of Liberality" drew attention to the injustice handed to Captain Wood. According to this letter, instead of condoling with the captain, the French Emigration Company had demanded that he take on new coolies to make up for those who had jumped overboard. It had also insisted on a reduced rate of $10 for each of them. The loss to the ship amounted to $900 which, in addition to $600 in demurrage, meant it suffered a loss of $1500. The French company had also promised to pay $100 to the coolie master for his gallantry, but reneged on that too.

The *Leonidas* was the third vessel to suffer a mutiny in Whampoa, after the *Greyhound* (as described above), and the *Sebastopol* (described below). Attacks on three of the five vessels loading coolies at Whampoa led to speculation as to the true motive behind them. The *Friend of China* of 2 March 1861 suggested that they could have been planned by the mandarins themselves, who were determined to stop all emigration from Canton after the armies of the Allied Commission[64] left the city later that year.

Caro y Cia
Caro left the trade in 1861 but returned in 1866 with two shipments by French vessels from Whampoa. The first was the 374-ton French barque *Ville de St Lo*, which left Whampoa on 22 January 1866 with 260 men bound for Havana. Several days out Captain F. Dubois had to quell a mutiny, killing 12 men in suppressing it. The *Ville de St Lo* then made for Saigon before continuing on to Havana. The second was the 479-ton barque *Gaulois*, which departed on 3 April 1866. Captain Lavignac was able to disembark 290 of the 300 Chinese he had taken on board.

Caro made eight other shipments from Macao in the same period, utilising various flags. Three of them were marred by high mortality rates. The 381-ton Austrian barque, *Barone Kellner*, under Captain J.M. Corich, had 268 men come on board on 1 February 1866, but after 116 days was able to see only 177 of them walk off. The mortality rate was 33.96%. The next was on the 329-ton French barque, *Sagittaire*, which lost 42 of her 165 passengers, a mortality rate of 25.45%. Captain M. Cardonnet was in command for the 155-day voyage, which left Macao on 15 November 1866. In 1867, the 1,025-ton Spanish *Cervantes* suffered a loss of 31.24% of the 541 men taken on in Macao.

Over the 17 shipments Charles Caro made in the coolie trade, he recruited 6,130 men and landed 5,475of them. The mortality rate averaged 10.69%.

Morales y Cia

José Maria Morales was originally a partner in Drake y Cia. As the Drakes gradually withdrew from the trade, Morales took over their allocation and continued trading in his own right. Morales continued to use Nicolas Tanco Armero as his agent, as Drake had done, and made eight shipments in 1858 then only one each in 1859 and 1860.

Still showing the preference for British ships indicated above, Morales made four shipments, including, for the first time, three by auxiliary steamers. The first was by the 2,134-ton *Mauritius* under Captain D. Cruikshank, which left Macao on 18 May 1858 with 741 Chinese for Havana. The mortality rate was 11.07%. However mortality rates were generally higher than this, with three shipments exceeding 24%. Another high loss was on the 1,195-ton auxiliary steamer *Scotia*, which had arrived at Amoy to load, but, experiencing difficulty in collecting coolies, proceeded to Macao, leaving port on 24 June 1858. Captain John Bell recorded a mortality rate of 24.39% when only 431 of his original 570 passengers disembarked. These high mortality rates sparked an urgent enquiry by British authorities.

On 31 May 1858, *Cleopatra,* a 300hp, 1,089-ton British steamer, left Amoy for Havana by way of Manila, Singapore, Cape Town and Barbados. British Consul M.C. Morrison reported on 16 June 1858 that he had personally ascertained from each individual that he proceeded of his own free will. In the presence of the Spanish Consul he re-landed 15 who did not wish to proceed. The *Cleopatra* experienced strong winds throughout her passage down the South China Sea, and had to call at Manila and at Singapore on 25 June for coals, water, and a crew change. While there, twenty coolies absconded from the vessel. It took Captain Peregrine 144 days to deliver the remaining 364 men out of the 464 taken on board in Amoy. The mortality rate on that voyage was 19.40%. The *Cleopatra* had been several weeks in Amoy awaiting her complement and eventually sailed, about 100 men short.

Morales's first American ship was the 978-ton *Mary Whitridge*, which had an uneventful voyage from Swatow to Havana. His second ship from Swatow, however, was not as fortunate. The 871-ton *Competitor* took only 98 days for the voyage under Captain White, but still lost 157 of her initial complement of 382, 41.10% of the coolies who had embarked.

When the small 168-ton Chilean brig *Diana* arrived in Havana from Swatow on 12 July 1858 with 74 from an original complement of 113, British Captain Mortimer O. Sullivan could not even say the 134-day voyage was excessively long. The eight shipments made by Morales in 1858 took on board 3,640 coolies. The mortality rate for 1858 was a discouraging 20.11%.

After the disastrous voyage in 1857 (described above), the 698-ton *Kitty Simpson* went on to New York where she took on passengers for Melbourne, Australia. She then continued carrying passengers whenever she could, eventually returning to Macao on 22 December 1859. On 20 February 1860, she left Macao with 350 coolies for Havana.

On 3 March 1860, the coolies attempted to take the *Kitty Simpson*. One was shot dead and several wounded. The ringleaders subsequently received 50 to 100 lashes each, and were then secured in irons. She put into Table Bay on 3 May for water and refreshments before continuing on to Havana without further incident. This was the last shipment for Morales who shipped 4,490 Chinese and landed 3,648 of them in three years. The overall mortality rate came to 18.7%.

Fernandez Schimper

A new entrant to the trade in 1859 made three shipments only in the two years he participated. Fernandez Schimper's first shipment was on the 678-ton ship *Alexandre Ralli*, when Captain J. Ferras took on 424 coolies in Macao on 16 January 1859. After a 131-day voyage he delivered 398 of them safely in Havana. Schimper was even more successful with his second ship. The 1,016-ton French ship *Ville de Dieppe* sailed from Whampoa on 5 March 1859 with Captain C. Rousseau taking on 530 men and landing 521 of them after a 113-day voyage. The ships were chartered, respectively, from the French shipowners Bazin & Léon Gay, based in Marseilles, and another French shipowner, Sellier, based in Dieppe. In contrast, Schimper's third and last ship was an American one.

On 13 February 1860, the *Hong Kong Daily Press* reported that it had received a letter from Swatow telling of 26 kidnapped coolies who jumped off the American ship *Staghound* while loading at Double Point for Havana. Eighteen of the men drowned in attempting to swim ashore. Of the eight remaining, four managed to reach home where they described their ordeal, greatly discrediting the fame and credit of foreigners. The *Daily Press* correspondent related that a few days earlier he had met a woman whose husband had been kidnapped for the *Staghound*. On enquiry, she learned that a ransom of six dollars could free him. To pay the ransom she sold her daughter for four dollars, and was then begging in the streets for the other two dollars.

The atrocities associated with the coolie trade had resulted in foreigners being held in great odium, and coolies could be procured only with great difficulty. The *Staghound* had been months in loading, whereas a Siamese ship of 900 tons had more than 1500 Chinese on board, each paying $6 for the privilege. So crowded were the decks that lying down was out of the question. The crew had to work the ship on the rail,[65] and cooking for the captain and Officers had to be done in the cabin.

The crew of the *Staghound* comprised three mates and 32 men before the mast. There was a carpenter, two ship's cooks and a cabin steward, as well as six quartermasters, whose main duty was that of keeping guard over the coolies.

The *Staghound* eventually sailed for Havana on 23 March 1860 with 612 passengers. Captain Samuel B. Hussey was reported by Henry Anthon Jr, US Consul in Batavia on 1 May 1860 as saying all the Chinese on board understood perfectly what they signed on for. He had rejected 250 of them who did not appear to be leaving of their own free will.

After suppressing a mutiny in the Sunda Strait, she arrived at Anjer on 30 March. While at anchor the next day, some of the crew refused to obey orders, and in the ensuing struggle the second mate, Captain Hussey's son, was stabbed in the abdomen. He later died in hospital. The mutiny was quelled with the assistance of HMS *Odin* which was at Anjer at that time.[66] The ringleaders were sent to Singapore for eventual return to America.

Staghound finally arrived at Havana on 10 August 1860 with only 343 left on board. The 269 coolies who did not complete the 140-day voyage represented a mortality rate of 43.95%. Captain Hussey died on arrival in Havana.

Zangronis

Another newcomer to the trade in 1859 was Y.M. Zangronis. The Zangronis brothers first became interested in shipping when they started a steamship service between Cuba and Europe in 1854 with a shipping office in Paris. Their French connections were well represented in the ten years they participated in the coolie trade. Of the 26 shipments they undertook, only three were not on French ships.

Zangronis entered the trade with the chartered 780-ton French ship *Formose* owned by Louis O'Lanyer of Bordeaux. O'Lanyer had previously become involved in coolie shipping to the French West Indies. On this voyage, 465 Chinese embarked at Macao for Havana on 2 April 1859. The mortality rate for this first Zangronis shipment recruited by Emigration Agent E. Chabert came to 13.98%.

In 1860 Zangronis employed Bauran as his Emigration Agent and entered into an arrangement with Sellier of Dieppe. The 935-ton *Ville de Lima* sailed on 14 January

1860, taking 500 emigrants to Havana. Captain G. David delivered 476 of them safely after a 110-day voyage. Two smaller ships completed Zangonis's first foray into the Chinese trade. The 299-ton barque *Solide*, departing on 16 February 1860, took 184 without loss, and the 456-ton *Alexandre Delphine* followed on 4 April 1860 with 201 Chinese. Captain Ravult landed 196 of them after a 152-day voyage.

Like Caro, Zangronis then withdrew from the trade only to return in 1864 with three uneventful voyages in conjunction with yet another French shipowner, St Ange Richon, Bernado Solares being the emigration agent in Macao. There were also three shipments in 1865. Their only non-French ship in 1865 was the 1,169-ton Italian ship, *Queen of England*, with a mortality rate of 6.51%. The 360-ton German barque, *Ammerland*, had a loss rate of 10.67% in 1866 while the 1,206-ton Italian *Luisa Canevaro* lost 11.17% of her passengers.

Sama, Sotolongo y Cia were one-time importers of Chinese coolies in 1859. Captain Castillo of the 246-ton Spanish barque *Gravina* embarked 120 men at Macao on 26 July. After a 145-day voyage, eighty-two only were able to walk off. The mortality rate was 31.67%.

Galdiz y Nenninger were also one-time importers. On 31 January 1860, Captain J. de Galdiz of the Spanish ship *Serafina* took on board 430 coolies in Amoy. Built in Bilboa, Spain, in 1849, her dimensions were 123ft long with a beam of 29ft and a depth of 14ft. If either the American edition of *Lloyd's Register*, which listed her as of 491 tons, or the French *Bureau Veritas Register*, which listed her at 416 tons, was correct, the fact that 400 of the coolies were able to land in Havana 117 days later would make it very difficult to show that tonnage was necessarily a critical factor in determining passenger capacity. However the Cuban newspaper *Diario de la Marina* reported her on arrival as of 700 tons, thus making it difficult to determine the true situation.

Mutinies

Many mutinies were reported but often without sufficient detail as to the cause. The French Maritime Agency in Whampoa reopened its doors in 1865 in response to Cuban demand. Three French vessels sailed from Whampoa in 1865, all for Zangronis. The *Côte d'Or* did not encounter any problems, with only two casualties on her voyage to Havana. The two others however suffered insurrections. Of the seven departures from Whampoa in 1866, three were for Caro and four were for Zangronis. One Caro ship, as mentioned above, and two Zangronis ships were each subjected to mutinies; tangible evidence of the problems British emigration agent Sampson was having recruiting for the West Indies around Canton at that time.

The first mutiny was on the 535-ton barque *Louis*, which left Whampoa on 5 May 1865. A few days out, the ship experienced a mutiny and Captain Auguste Aubril took his ship to Hong Kong. Despite speculation that the ship was then subject to the Chinese Passengers' Act, she was allowed to return to Whampoa with her passengers. *Louis* resumed her voyage to Havana on 6 June, but suffered a mortality rate of 30.34% on the passage. The next sailing was by the 666-ton *Caroline* which left Canton for Havana on 12 October 1865 with 360 Chinese coolies. The insurrection was subdued only by shooting twelve of the Chinese. The ship then made for Saigon.

The 470-ton French barque *Hong Kong* did not start her career in the coolie trades on a good note. She left Whampoa for Havana on 23 January 1866 with 260 Chinese consigned to Zangronis. Within four days, the coolies mutinied, and the vessel had to return to Hong Kong. After a nine month refit, she returned to the trade as a Spanish vessel under Captain Ignacio Yriberri.

Over the next 5 years, Captain Yriberri commanded the *Hong Kong* for five voyages. On the two voyages to Havana for Troncoso, each of 107 days, only one man died on the first and on the second there were no deaths. In 1870 the *Hong Kong* changed her flag to that of Peru in anticipation of calling at Callao only. Her last voyage to that port was in 1873 under Captain Domingos Borainca. With a career total of 1,885 men embarked and 1,819 landed, her average mortality was 3.5%.

The 389-ton French barque *Flore* was about to set out from Whampoa on a second voyage, this time to Havana, when a disturbance broke out. It was quelled only by severe measures, which resulted in the death of at least one coolie. The *China Mail* was not able to provide details, complaining that secrecy was a matter of course prevalent in such matters. The *Flore* sailed on 10 February 1866 with 310 men. No further incidents were reported even after a 182-day voyage. Captain LaFontaine delivered all but one man on arrival.

The last ship to sail from Swatow with Chinese coolies was the 754-ton French barque *Ste. Croix* which sailed on 18 June 1866. The 130-day voyage by Captain J. Robert was uneventful, with 432 of the 444 men embarked landing safely. Emigration Agent Solares in Macao had arranged that shipment on behalf of Zangronis.

Zangrois did not return to China in 1867 and only made one final shipment with Chinese coolies in 1868. The 448-ton French barque *Pactole* left Macao on 8 November 1868 with 245 coolies. Captain J. Olivaud delivered 220 of them after a prolonged 153-day voyage. In the ten years Zangronis was in the trade he undertook 26 shipments taking 8,593 Chinese to Cuba. With 7,793 disembarking, the average mortality rate was 9.31%.

Spanish Royal Decree of 1860

On 10 February 1860, Governor Captain-General Francisco Serrano issued a decree based on several Royal Orders saying that the importation of Chinese coolies would be tolerated from 10 February to 31 December 1860 only. It would be strictly forbidden from 1 January 1861. The discontinuance of this emigration had been recommended on 28 December 1859, citing considerations of humanity to the colonists.

However, a Royal Decree, dated 6 July 1860, issued by the Spanish Government in Madrid, permitted the free importation of Chinese coolies under certain regulations. The

Friend of China summarised the 82 points of the decree on 24 November 1860. Among the enormous amount of detail, it described the information required in each contract with four copies to be made together with three copies of the Chinese translation. They were to be legalised by the Spanish Consul at the port of embarkation, who was to keep one copy and return the rest for distribution. Passenger lists were also to be completed with quadruple copies.

The maximum number of passengers whom ships would be allowed to carry would be restricted to one person per two tons, with the space calculated on the remaining room available after allowance for cargo. Sufficient food and water was to be proportioned to the numbers carried and length of voyage, but no quantities were mandated. Cleanliness and ventilation were indispensible, but again this was not defined. A physician and medicine chest were to be provided if the number carried exceeded forty. Whenever examination of the papers showed that the mortality rate exceeded 6% on arrival at Havana (the only Cuban port permitted), a special inquiry would be required, with the Governor or tribunal determining the fine to be imposed.

Clause 7 stipulated that the immigrant was to leave Cuba on expiry of his contract at his own expense if not re-contracted. Clause 18 emphasized that the Chinese had to renew their contracts within two months of expiry or leave. If unable to do so they would be made a public works labourer until sufficient funds had been raised for them to be repatriated.

Cost of Cuban labour

On 5 February 1861 Jos. T. Crawford, now British Commissary Judge in Havana, wrote to Lord John Russell ruefully reporting that the slave trade was still rampant in Cuba, with corrupt officials colluding with estate owners to avoid detection.[67] In his long despatch, Crawford included calculations of the cost of a negro per day compared to that of a Chinese. That for a negro came to $57.50 a month or £11.10.0 per month or 8s 10d for each of 313 working days a year. As slaves worked 365 days in the year the daily cost to their masters was reduced to 7s 6d. For a Chinese coolie the cost came to $21.41, or £4.5.9 per month, 3s 3d a day of 313 working days.

This compared very unfavourably with the price of labour in the British West Indies. He submitted that no agricultural produce could sustain such wages, and therefore would result in ruin for all those who engaged in such enterprises. Crawford then observed that a proposal could be made to Her Catholic Majesty for the introduction of Africans as free labourers under contract, but it would still be a farce. In conclusion, Crawford estimated that upwards of 58,000 Chinese had been brought to Cuba since 1847, with the majority of them not desirous of returning home.

Concern at the cost of labour had already led to a tightening of credit. Crawford would have been quoting from the Cuban press which saw the number of shipments drop from 16 in 1859 and 21 in 1860, then to ten in 1861 and down to just two in 1862. But the need for labour was too great and shipments once again began to rise in 1863.

Troncoso, Castro, Bustamente
Narciso Troncoso entered the coolie trade in an unconventional manner. On 19 March 1860 the 236-ton Spanish brig *Carmencita* left Manila with an unknown number of Chinese under unstated terms. Captain J. Villeta delivered 126 of them to Troncoso after completing a 132-day voyage. It is unclear why he chose Manila for his first shipment, but it was a success.

With the withdrawal of Pereda from the trade, Emigration Agent I.F. de Castro began recruiting for Troncoso with the 913-ton *Guadaloupe* taking 400 Chinese from Macao to Havana on 1 April 1860. This Spanish ship went about her business with no fuss during the early years of the 1860s. First commanded by Captain Ramon Nunez in 1860, he took her on three voyages to Havana without incident.

Antonio G. Bustamente was a land owner. His first involvement in the coolie trade was with the Colonizadora when he took their first whole consignment of 326 men off the *Don Julian* in 1858. There was not a single mortality on that voyage. He then entered the trade directly, with the *Maria Clotilde*, in conjunction with both Troncoso and Castro the latter having just returned from China (in 1861). There were only two lives lost on a 106-day voyage commencing on 7 February 1861.

The only two shipments to Cuba in 1862 were both for the loose partnership of Troncoso, Castro and Bustamente in Havana and Joao Garcia in Macao—the 832-ton Belgian ship *Leopold Cateaux* and the *Guadaloupe* on her second voyage. *Leopold Cateaux* was ordered as the *Bengale* but was renamed on 1 March 1857 before being launched on 24 June that year. After a 118-day voyage, Captain A. Nicaise was able to produce all of the 416 men he had taken on board in Macao on 5 November 1862. Bustamente then undertook a second shipment in 1863 with the 597-ton Spanish barque *Arizona* which departed from Macao on 20 December 1863 with 298 coolies. The voyage under Captain A. de Valparda took 126 days and the lives of eighteen men.

Bustamente made a second sortie into the coolie trade in conjunction with Troncoso and Castro in 1866. Troncoso paid a visit to Macao in 1866, and supervised two shipments with Virana Garcia as his agent. Troncoso relied on the *Emigrante* to make her sixth voyage to Havana with 359 coolies on board. Captain D. Tramoja was able to deliver only 319 of them 124 days later. He then called on Captain J.A. Gardoqui of the *Guadaloupe* to make a third voyage on 14 February 1866. This trip took 125 days with a much better result, 438 men landing of the 454 taken on board.

The 618-ton Spanish barque *Altagracia* under Captain N. Landa sailed from Macao on 16 March 1866 with 361 passengers. On this, the first of five voyages she was to make, she arrived at Havana after a 115-day passage with 350 Chinese able to walk off the ship. On her second voyage the following year, Captain Landa was able to deliver only 303 of the 360 men he had taken on in Macao. *Altagracia* made a third voyage for Troncoso in 1868.

In the nine years Troncoso was in the trade, he and his associates made 25 voyages, all but three in Spanish ships. The *Altagracia* was used for three voyages, *Encarnacion* for four, *Guadaloupe* for two and the *Hong Kong* for two. There were two voyages with no casualties at all. The only voyage with a mortality rate above 25% was on the 673-ton *Bilbaina* which sailed on 18 October 1866. Overall, 93.64% of the 8,630 Chinese embarked were delivered safely.

Emigration Agents

On 21 September 1861, *O Boletim* published three tables showing the ships which had sailed from Macao between May 1860 and March 1861, and identified the eight barracoons that were then being operated by the six Emigration Agents licensed in Macao. A third Table showed the numbers of recruits registered at each address and the numbers that were actually embarked during that period.

The Peruvian J.M. de Ugarte and Spaniard Ignacio F. de Castro worked together to gather recruits for both Peru and Cuba. According to one source, Ugarte had 2,618 men awaiting shipment from his barracoon at Tarrafeiro, but only 1,534 were taken on the four ships he supplied. Castro, on the other hand, had 602 coolies in his barracoon on the Largo da Santo Antonio, which exactly matched his first two shipments to Cuba. For his other two shipments, he had to rely on Ugarte to make up his shortfall.

The numbers above have been extracted from the *O Boletim* list. However, there is a discrepancy in the number actually shipped on one of the four ships, the *Reina del Oceano*. The *O Boletim* list shows only 294 men were placed on this 1,011-ton vessel, which was capable of carrying at least 505 passengers. As the Cuban authorities reported 497 as having landed the more likely departure figure would have been 529 on a 0.52 passengers/ton ratio. The difference, if any, would have been amply accommodated from the Ugarte surplus. But as the *Friend of China* also reported that two other of the four ships, the *Reina del Oceano* and *Francois 1*, had taken on unspecified numbers at Whampoa before going to Macao, the actual number is indeterminate.

With just one shipment, Camino y Cia housed their 330 recruits to Peru at Ponyta da Redo. Of the three Agents recruiting for Cuba, Vargas had two "establishments", one at Gamboa and the other at Rua de Sm Lourenço, and H. de Closmadeau, ex-Captain of the *Francois 1,* also had two addresses, one on the Praia Grande and one on Travessa da Palanchica. Frenchman L. Boye, with only one location on the Rua do Hospital, had 838 men to ship but was able to provide only 571 from his premises. Vargas would have provided him with the shortfall.

During the period, 10,690 men were initially registered in the eight establishments. Because of subsequent refusals to proceed, only 8,499 were eventually placed on ships. For example, for his single shipment, Camino admitted 545 coolies, but was able to place only 330. The success rate (the percentage of coolies shipped from among the number initially registered) was 60%. Closmadeau also had a poor record with success rates of 65% and 73% at his barracoons. Vargas's record was 76% and 82%, with the latter figure also for Castro. Despite his large recruitment pool Ugarte had a good return of 84%. In contrast to Camino, Boye was able to keep 571 of the 580 he admitted into his barracoon. That was a success rate of 98%.

In 1866 there were at least fifteen emigration agents in Macao. The most active at that time was Calderon who filled eight ships. Calderon sent 3,198 Chinese to Cuba on behalf of the Alianza in 1866. Solares was another active agent with 1,736 coolies in six ships consigned to Zangronis in Havana. At least 45 other foreigners have been identified as emigration agents in Macao in the 23 years of emigration. Prominent general traders, Caro as well as Troncoso in Havana and Canevaro in Lima, sent their principals to Macao to supervise recruitment. But most importing houses employed agents resident in Macao.

For example, Sagues was the main agent for the wealthy plantation owner Domingo. When Rafael Torices closed his doors, Antonio Ferran worked for the Empresa de Colonization consortium from 1856 until 1865 after arranging at least 29 shipments to Havana. Following his return to start his own importing house in Havana, he had F.P. Noronha handle five shipments from Macao.

Henrique W. Pearce arrived on the *Uncowah* on 22 November 1866 along with sixteen Chinese expatriates from Callao. Until his departure in December 1873, Pearce arranged for sixteen shipments to Callao and one to Havana. These seventeen shipments were matched by Francisco Landabaso between 1870 and 1872 when he too completed seventeen shipments, all for Canevaro of Lima.

When Troncoso returned to Cuba, he appointed José A. Tuton as his agent in Macao. Tuton was to become by far the most active Emigration Agent in Macao. He opened his office in Macao in 1866 and filled his first ship, the *Bilbaina*, with 492 Chinese consigned to Troncoso in Havana. She arrived with 367 Chinese, the 25.41% loss being the only Troncoso shipment with a mortality above 20%. Tuton provided recruits for three of the six shipments Troncoso made on his own account in 1867.

José then brought his son Fernando into the firm. They assiduously cultivated the Spanish Consul Munoz del Cano and his staff, but did not win favour with the Portuguese Governor over a new regulation changing the space allocation for passengers boarding in Macao. However, he did win back some esteem when he inaugurated a fund to assist in the welfare of destitute children and orphans in Macao. He advised the Governor that he would be contributing 10 cents for each emigrant he shipped from Macao, and would be asking fellow agents to do the same. His initial contribution of $52.70 was payment for the 527 Chinese he had placed on the *Italia*. The amounts received were published in the weekly *Boletim*.

When Lombillo began operations in China, he appointed Nicholas Tanco Armero as his agent. A native of Colombia, he had first arrived in Hong Kong on 23 June 1855 following his appointment as agent for the Cuban planters Morales and Pedroso. Between 1855 and 1858, he arranged nine shipments to Havana before travelling the world. Armero returned to Macao in 1866 where he recruited enough men to fill twenty-two ships for Lombillo in Havana and one for

Peru. He left Macao again in 1869, only to return in 1872 to conduct another nine shipments, this time for Canevaro, in Lima as well as the only shipment of Chinese coolies to Costa Rica.

Another Havana agent was Francisco Abella. He first acted as assistant to Armero, then, between 1869 and 1873, in conjunction with Ybanes. It seems that Abella did not go out of his way to please Consul del Cano, for he was accused of shipping minors without permission, while Tuton was excused for the same indiscretion.

"Barracoons at Macao."
Harper's New Monthly Magazine, **June 1864.**

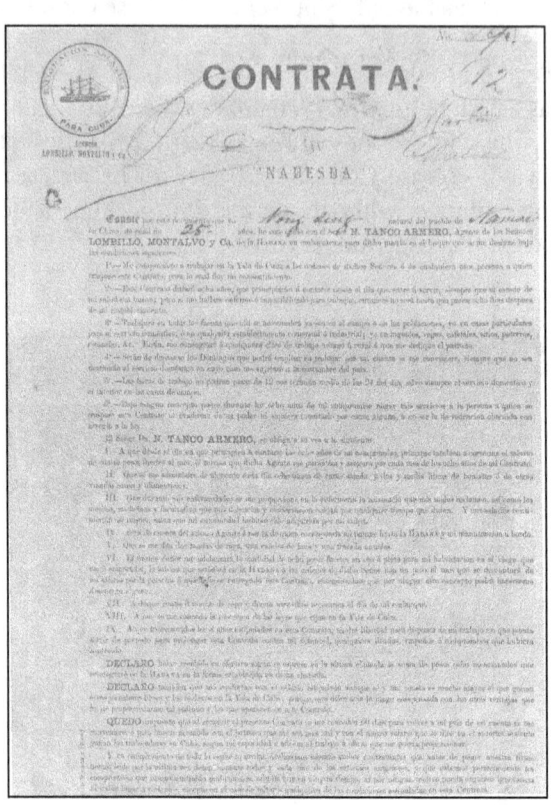

Labourer's contract in Spanish.[68]

6

Canton Becomes An Emigration Port

Under the 1842 Treaty of Nanking, Canton was one of five ports open to foreign trade. However, the local Governor refused to accept this and the British were still confined to their original factories and unable to secure the right of entry into Canton proper. Despite repeated attempts, British Consul Parkes was unable to persuade Governor Ye Ming Chen to accept the treaty. In total frustration, Parkes then used the seizure in 1856 of the Chinese-owned, but British-flagged, *Arrow* as the basis for demanding redress. With the active backing of Governor Bowring in Hong Kong, he persisted in demanding an apology. When none was forthcoming, a naval force was used to storm the city. After a brief occupation of the town, the European settlement was set on fire, forcing Parkes to retreat to Hong Kong for a year.

Then in December 1857, British forces once again attacked Canton, this time in conjunction with the French. During a lull in the battle, a party of sailors led by Parkes succeeded in entering Governor Ye's *yamen* (compound). There Parkes discovered the original Treaty documents relating to the opening of Canton to foreign trade. Ye had refused to accept the treaty and had hidden the documents. He was taken prisoner and transported to Calcutta where he died two years later. He was unrepentant to the end.

The occupying armies led by British Sir Charles van Straubenzee and the French commander, M. d'Abouville, appointed a mixed commission of military and consular officials to supervise the city's administration. Pih Kwei, the Governor of Canton was reinstated, but the real government was exercised by three Allied Commissioners, a British officer, Colonel Holloway, a French soldier, Captain Martineau de Chesnez, and a British consular official, Harry Parkes. They were ostensibly equal, but in actuality were led by Parkes, as he was the only one able to speak Chinese.[69]

The demand from Cuba continued apace with annual shipments rising from over 8,000 in 1856 to more than 12,000 in the next two years, before falling back to 9,000 in 1859. With contracts amounting to more than half a million dollars, foreign agents, mainly Spanish, began recruiting Chinese labour on a massive scale throughout Kwangtung. Between 1859 and 1860, no fewer than 37 vessels were used to take on 17,637 Chinese coolies. In the following two years, however, shipments fell back to an all-time low of two in 1862, due in part to rising costs and to the uncertain political situation at that time.

As the supply of labour diminished in the northern hinterlands around Amoy and Swatow, Spanish attention turned south. As the pool of mendicants and layabouts dwindled in the population centres surrounding Canton, the Chinese brokers, earning between twenty and thirty dollars or more for each coolie presented, did not hesitate to employ any means to meet the required numbers. Common methods were to offer to help unsuspecting youths to find work, to pay for a meal, or to advance a few coins to gamble with. When thus trapped, pressure was put on the luckless man to agree to emigrate.

When such methods failed, kidnapping was resorted to. It had become so rampant, that the local population ventured from their homes only when necessary. In desperation, they began taking things into their own hands, killing several kidnappers early in April 1859. Twenty-three traders of the Chinese mercantile community petitioned Consul Rutherford Alcock[70] for the British authorities to put an end to the atrocities.[71]

Kwangtung Emigration Proclamations

The Chief Magistrates of the Districts of Nanhai and Panyu had become so concerned about the rampant kidnapping that they issued a proclamation, advising all persons who wished to emigrate that there would be no objection to them going with the foreign emigration agents. Two days later, Governor Pih Kwei belatedly confirmed the magistrates' proclamation, with one of his own, with far-reaching consequences. He acknowledged that because of the crowded population some people were compelled to accept employment overseas for various reasons. He then decreed, "Permission to them doing so should not, it is clear, be withheld in any of these cases, provided the parties themselves really consented to the arrangement".

Pih Kwei then warned of villains kidnapping men under the pretence of providing them with employment. He said that the traffic had now become known as the "sale of pigs". Pih said he had directed all civil and military authorities to arrest such villains, offered rewards for information leading to the arrest of kidnappers, and warned that the houses in which kidnapped persons were found would be pulled down.

In the course of the year, Governor Pih died and was succeeded by Governor Laou. With the freeing up of emigration by the Chinese mandarins confirmed, the problem facing Laou was the need to establish a system of emigration free of the abuses now endemic in the province.

Whampoa Kidnappings

In reality, the Proclamations of April 1859 did not serve to lessen the extent of kidnapping that still flourished. Laou ordered a crackdown on the kidnappers. Chinese officials boarded several junks at the Whampoa anchorage on 1 November 1859 and arrested 77 men, of whom 41 claimed to have been kidnapped and the remaining 36 were identified as kidnappers.

The kidnappers themselves seemed to be opportunists. Ho yew stated, "I am 29 years of age, and belong to Shwuy kiao village in Tung kwan district. My father is dead. My mother, Hwang she, is 56 years of age. I have no brothers. My wife is dead; she died childless. I have in general been employed on board Ho a ching's cargo boat. On the 31st October, when in Tung kwan district, the idea came into my head of kidnapping an acquaintance of mine, Chang ah sai, belonging to Hwang village, in that district, and I offered him work on board a fishing boat, engaging to give him thirteen dollars a year for seven years, at the expiration of which time he should return home. Chang ah sai expressed his willingness to go with me, and I gave him two dollars. On the same day, we embarked in a Shih lung passage boat for Canton. As we were passing Chang chow, I hailed a sampan, which took us to the coolie boat of Yung ah tsin, where I sold Chang ah sai for thirteen dollars, telling him at the time that he was to be taken to the fishing boat. I was just about to return home, when I was arrested. This is the first time I have kidnapped and sold a man as a coolie. I have never been brought up before for any crime".

Sing woo also knew of the coolie boats. "I am 28 years of age, and belong to Kwei shen district. I live at home, and practise surgery to gain my living. I was acquainted with Chang ah urh; and through his telling me that twenty or thirty dollars could easily be gained by kidnapping, and that he knew a Tung kwan man called 'Pockmarked Yao' who kept a sugar boat at Chang chow, and who was intimate with the coolie brokers, I was persuaded to join him, on the 4th of the 8th moon, in kidnapping, at the town of Po lo, a man named, Chang ah che. Pockmarked Yao took and sold him to the coolie brokers, and gave us twelve dollars, which Chang ah urh and myself divided. Again, on the 27th of the 9th moon, I by myself, in the town of Po lo, kidnapped Chin ah yao, and gave him to Pockmarked Yao, from whom I received twenty dollars. I had gone to the sugar boat to live at ease for awhile, when, on the 2nd November, the soldiers arrested me and brought me hither".

As had been proclaimed, Laou had originally intended to execute twenty-three of the kidnappers, but on mitigation from the Allied Commissioners, beheaded eighteen of them only. Seven of their heads were later displayed at Whampoa as a warning to potential kidnappers. Laou also ordered the stationing of three war junks at Whampoa to watch for kidnappers.

Victim Depositions

From the depositions of some of the kidnapped persons, it would appear that many were simply naive. Li fu deposed, "Am from the Hai feng district aged 38, a labourer; have a younger brother named Li a ming, a shopkeeper at Macao. On the 1st of the 10th month being at San to chu, in the Hai feng district, I crossed over in the ferry to Hwei chow, and met an acquaintance, named A kwei, on the road. This man said that he also knew my brother, and persuaded me to go to him in his boat. I followed him without suspicion on board, and was taken to Chang chow, to be sold against my will as a coolie. I was confined in the hold of a vessel, until released and sent up for examination by a military officer who came to institute a search".[72]

No force was used then but another victim Yu leang stated, "I am 25, and belong to the Tung kwan district. On the 4th of the 5th moon I was in the Ching kwang meao when I first met Tai ah shing, the man who kidnapped me. I went with him on board a boat to get a meal, little thinking, as I entered the boat, that he would, as he did, unmoor the boat and go to Chang chow. At Chang chow, he took me to sell to the foreigners. On my resisting, he took a club and struck me at random. I then, finding I had no recourse, went with him to the foreigners; but when they saw the marks of the blows on my body, they refused to take me, and I remained on board the boat until the soldiers who were charged to examine came."

That statement showed that the recruiters actually examined the men as they boarded. Liang chi yeng also deposed, "Was formerly a resident in the Nan hai district, but removed with my father to Lio chow fu in Kwangsi; I am 33 years old. In the third month of the current year, became one of the guards of a mandarin named Tou, went in the seventh month to Te ching, where I was discharged; later I served as a brave at Shao ching fu but was thrown out of employ together with more than twenty others, on being attacked with ulcers, and on the 12th of the 9th month, I went to Te ching chow to seek medical assistance. I had never been to Canton, and on the 25th of the 9th month, a man named Hwang a siu, of the

Po lo district, imposed upon me with the statement that he was about to return to Canton to serve as a soldier under the above-mentioned Tou. I was on board Hwang A Siu's boat until the 29th of the 9th month, being quite ignorant of the locality; when I witnessed him offering me for sale to foreigners, who, however, on seeing that I was suffering from ulcers would not purchase. Later I was released by soldiers, who took me up for examination."

Receiving ships in Whampoa

In early 1859, recruiting houses, depots or barracoons as they were more commonly known, were not to be found in Canton. Instead, the Tait practice of using a ship at Amoy was employed.

One of the first receiving ships to arrive in Whampoa was the Vargas-controlled 1,429-ton American *Governor Morton*. Captain J.C. Berry arrived on 15 March 1859, while the 1,350-ton American-flagged *Messenger* arrived at Whampoa under Captain Ben Manton on 15 May 1859. Vargas had also arranged for Lyall, Still & Co. of Hong Kong to charter two other American ships, the 1,849-ton *Pioneer*, Captain Montgomery, which arrived on 8 August 1859, while the American ship *Swallow* was also anchored at Whampoa in June 1859.

Transfers to Macao were then regularly made but the first reported incident was when the *Messenger* had accumulated eighty-seven coolies and transferred them to the Portuguese lorcha *Louisa No 10*, for transportation to Macao on 12 August 1859. The lorcha was found washed ashore between the two ports with her masts and rigging cut away. She was deserted with all her guns removed. It was presumed that the coolies had revolted and that the crew had escaped only by jumping overboard.

In addition to the American ships at Whampoa, there was the 633-ton Dutch barque, *Soolo*, which was expecting to undertake a second voyage to Cuba. Captain Van der Moulen had already taken a shipment of 400 men to Havana for Pereda Machado early in 1858. With different recruiting agents, the 1,409 Peruvian ship *Westward Ho* under Captain

Araucoa had been chartered for Callao, but because of the increased surveillance, headed for Macao instead, as did the 935-ton French ship *Ville de Lima,* and the 385-ton Spanish *Santa Lucia.*

Alarmed at news of the happenings at Whampoa, Governor Laou wrote to the Allied Commissioners on 8 November 1859, asking them to communicate to the various Consuls in Canton the necessity for their nationals to lodge with his office the regulations under which they would hire coolies. If the regulations were not satisfactory, they would be prohibited from hiring Chinese, and kidnapping would be prevented. In response to this request, the *Soolo* was compelled by the Dutch Consul to revoke her charter.

On receipt of the Allied Commissioners' communication, the American Consul, Oliver H. Perry, wrote to Laou, asking for an officer to be appointed at Whampoa to assist in procuring labourers and in following the rules for the prevention of kidnapping. Laou was adamant that the request was at variance with what had been agreed by the French and British for establishments at Canton, where recruitment would be under constant Chinese supervision. Laou rejected having an officer at Whampoa, "which was too far away", and where the officer would find it difficult to work.

In rejecting Perry's request, Laou also wrote to the Allied Commissioners enclosing a copy of his reply to Perry. He stressed that procuring labourers was to be at the provincial city only and not at different places away from the city.

Eight petitions had been lodged with the Allied Commissioners, seeking kidnapped relatives thought to be on board the ships. They were forwarded to Laou, who requested the American Consul to allow a Chinese officer to accompany him to search for the men. Consul Perry agreed and found the men on board, but in doing so was assailed by scores of others begging to be liberated.

With this evidence, Laou then requested Perry to have all the American vessels inspected. As the ships were too large to reach Canton, Perry in return asked Laou for permission to have the coolies inspected at Whampoa, but the request was rejected. It was then agreed that a Chinese delegation would proceed with Perry to Whampoa. A British interpreter, William S. Frederick Mayers,[73] was to assist, purely to interpret for Perry, whose own interpreter could speak only the local dialect.[74]

They were also to inspect the 477-ton Oldenburgh (German) barque *Fanny Kirchner*. She had arrived early in December 1859 under Captain Bluck and was anchored at Whampoa. She had been chartered by Emigration Agent Bidau, on behalf of Morales, to take 350 coolies to Havana at $55 a head. On 7 December, she transferred 150 coolies to Macao for onward shipment. On 31 December 1859, the party left for Whampoa, but as, by then, Perry had gone to Hong Kong, Vice Consul Blanchard agreed to attend, but expressed reservation over the presence of Mayers, whom he thought could be prejudiced against the Americans. Accordingly, Blanchard and one official visited the American ships, while Mayers went on board the Oldenburg vessel. Fifty men were released from the American ships. Another fifty were removed from the *Fanny Kirchner*.

Laou refused to accept the result and demanded that 578 men be brought to Canton and that clearance for the *Messenger* would not be granted. In two despatches to Perry, he warned that the *Messenger* was about to leave with unauthorised passengers and demanded she not be given her papers. Perry agreed; then, together with Mayers, he visited the *Messenger* on 2 January. Captain Manton was most belligerent and threatened to have the Chinese taken off. When Manton saw Mayers, he physically threatened him, such that Perry, after a ten-minute heated argument advised Mayers to leave. Whilst waiting in the small boat alongside, Mayers witnessed the arrival of the captains from the other American vessels. As it was then late, it was agreed that the inspections would be carried out the next day. This was despite Mayers warning the officials that the coolies had to be taken to Canton.

On 3 January Perry and some Chinese officials went on board the American vessels. Perry was able to identify 28 coolies from the *Messenger*, seven from the *Governor*

Morton, and fifteen from the *Pioneer*, who did not want to leave China. Both sets of Chinese officials appeared to be more interested in partaking of the refreshments provided by the various captains than interviewing the men. Meanwhile Mayers and the other officials again visited the *Fanny Kirchner*. It took the whole day before 59 coolies indicated their unwillingness to go abroad. However, they were not allowed to leave the ship.

Perry returned to Canton the next day, while Mayers went back to the *Fanny Kirchner*. Once again, the officials were provided with champagne and sweetmeats, and it took all day before Bidau the recruiter and Richard von Carlowitz the Spanish Consul, agreed that the men who did not want to emigrate could be taken ashore to Canton for processing. But before they were taken off, they were made to strip naked, their new clothes taken from them; and they were then told to select from the rags they had originally come on board in. The remaining ones were transferred to the American *Kitty Simpson* on 5 January.

The following day, Perry called upon Laou, who was fuming because his (Laou's) officials were not following instructions. (They had been too-well entertained the previous day!) Laou had demanded that all coolies be brought to Canton for examination. Perry replied that he was not aware of this instruction, but if that was what was desired, he would arrange for boats to bring the men up. On return to his office, Perry found Captain Manton waiting for him. Manton was told to bring his ship to Canton, but when Perry was told she was too deep to cross the bar, he advised Manton to charter steamers to bring the men up. Manton complained bitterly of the injustice being done to him, and pleaded for his papers.

Captain Manton returned to the Consulate the following evening to advise Perry that while he (Manton) was in Canton, all the men on the *Messenger* had been taken off, on the order of Vargas. He did not know what had happened to them. On being told that, unless he produced them, he would not receive his papers, Manton complained that he could not produce what he had no control over. He had never given a receipt for the men.

It was later learned that the previous night, most of the passengers from the other two American ships had been transferred to the *Messenger*, which then weighed anchor and went down river where in the dead of night she transferred most of the 578 men to a small American steamer, the *Meilie*, which immediately left for Macao. The remainder were placed on native junks, and were later recovered by the Custom house chartered steamer *Cum-fa*. Ironically, she was also an American vessel. The *Messenger* then, in all innocence, returned to her original anchorage.

On 7 January 1860, Captain Manton applied to the Customs house at Whampoa for a clearance. Despite paying the tonnage dues, and having the ship devoid of coolies, this was not granted on the grounds that he had not paid duty on the rice he had on board. Later it was acknowledged that this was done on the express orders of the Governor General. Manton then wrote to Perry demanding his intervention. Perry refused.

An exasperated Laou wrote six letters to Perry over this incident, then in total frustration wrote to John Elliott Ward (1814-1902), the American Envoy Extraordinary and Minister Plenipotentiary in Hong Kong, deploring the disregard of his requests. When Ward met with Laou on 1 February 1860, Ward stated that, of the 475 coolies who had been taken off the *Messenger*, twenty-five had absconded at Macao, twenty-six had been handed to Chinese officers by the Portuguese authorities, and over 200 had already been returned; the remainder were expected back within the next two days.

Like the Spanish and Peruvians, the Americans were keen to be assured that the Allied Commissioners would not be involved. They were very suspicious of Harry Parkes, believing that he was trying to establish a recruiting monopoly through the establishment of an English emigration depot. Ward was not prepared to submit the Chinese for examination by the Allied Commissioners. However, when he was given an assurance by Parkes, Ward told Laou the men would be brought to Canton for examination whenever the Governor desired. Ward then had the men retrieved from Macao.

Samuel Wells Williams (1812-1884)—a long time China resident and fluent Chinese speaker—with Oliver Perry, sat on the bench, together with the district magistrates of Nanhai and Panyu. Each of the 215 men questioned unhesitatingly answered that they did not go on board willingly, nor did they voluntarily sign contracts, some even declaring they would rather die than go in the ship. The men were aged between 16 and 25, generally in good health, and belonged to the lowest order of society—field labourers, boatmen, artisans and porters, with only a few able to read. Nearly all of them complained of harsh treatment, some having been beaten with sticks or thongs. Others had knives drawn across their throats, or had been strapped on boards, with their toes and wrists bound. One man produced a tooth that had been knocked out of his mouth. Others displayed creases left by cords, or weals made by sticks.

When made to sign the contracts, they knew only that they were going to a Spanish country for eight years at four dollars a month. They did not think they had any option but to sign, and did so with the tip of a finger dipped in ink and stamping the paper. Often their hands were seized by one man, and the stamp made by another, but in every case without their consent. Most of the men were from Kwangtung, from nearly every district, with only a few from adjoining provinces. In total 432 men were lodged in quarters before being presented to the Governor General and sent home.

In Ward's 24 January 1860 report to Secretary of State Cass, he sincerely hoped that the attention of Congress would be called to the coolie trade, and that some law be passed regulating it and putting it more under the control of the American Minister or Chief Diplomatic agent in China. It was two years before the "Prohibition of Coolie Trade Act" was passed by Congress.

On 24 February 1860, Ward described the method in which the coolies were induced to express their willingness to emigrate. He described how Vargas, the recruiting agent in

Macao, simultaneously chartered four ships to arrive at staggered intervals. When a Chinese man was kidnapped or stolen, he would be taken to the first ship and asked if he wished to emigrate. If he declined, the captain, with apparent honesty, would then declare he could not be received on board. His captors would then leave the ship with him, and he would be held in the water, or tied by his thumbs, or cold water would be poured down his back, or some other torture, until he consented to go. He would then be taken to the next ship, and the same question repeated. If he still declined, he would be taken off, and the process repeated until consent was wrung from him, and he would then be received as a "willing emigrant". When the Consul came on board, he would be questioned under the painful recollection of what he had already endured, and would continue to endure until he consented.

Ward said that all the captains of the American ships at Whampoa were connected with the coolie trade, and thus seriously affecting American relations with China. He praised Perry for his untiring labours; but with no law to sustain him, he was not able to achieve much.

Shipping to the British West Indies resumes
In October 1855, the Governor of British Guiana, P.E. Wodehouse, advised Lord Grey, the British Colonial Secretary, that the planters wanted more Chinese labourers. On 8 April 1856, Governor Charles Elliot of Trinidad also wrote to Lord Grey requesting that 300 Chinese immigrants be immediately introduced. It was not until 31 July 1856, however that incoming Colonial Secretary Labouchere replied, declining the request for Chinese labour. He claimed the resident British authority in China considered it undesirable at present, and also mentioned that the impossibility of obtaining the requisite proportion of female emigrants would not make the emigration successful.

On 22 January 1858, Governor Wodehouse again advised Labouchere that the planters of that Colony had reconsidered their position, and wanted more Chinese labourers. With that renewed request from Governor

Wodehouse, the Emigration Commissioners agreed that private emigration, with some women, was desirable and proposed a draft Ordinance for the Legislatures of British Guiana and Trinidad, allowing proprietors to introduce Chinese immigrants at their own expense, within the general provisions of the Chinese Passengers' Act.

On learning of the proposed Ordinance, the WIC lost no time in canvassing members' requirements and appointed an agent of their own to go to China. Thomas Gerard was to proceed to China to procure 2,990 immigrants, including women, at no more than £25 per head. His salary was to be £1,500 per annum, to commence on his departure from England, and to include clerical assistance and all personal expenses. The agreement was for two years, terminable at the end of the first year, at the option of either party. In his instructions, dated 3 June 1858, he was fully authorised to engage shipping as required, and to affect charter-parties. Only able-bodied agricultural labourers should be allowed to embark, and special care was to be taken to exclude all who were addicted to opium. The Committee had no objection to a small proportion of boys under 15, and girls under 13, equal to 10 percent of the total of males and females, being recruited. His instructions permitted him to recruit anywhere in China where he considered suitable emigrants could be procured.

Gerard was said to have had some experience in China. It was probably as the mate of the opium-receiving ship *Hong Kong*, which was stationed in Swatow at the time of the riots in Amoy. He set off in time to effect recruitment for the 1858-59 shipping season. On arrival in Hong Kong, he introduced himself to Governor Bowring, who provided him with introductions to each of the Consuls in China.

Gerard had intended heading directly to Canton, but as he was warned that the city was in a state of turmoil, Gerard went to Macao instead. During November 1858, he was able to find enough coolies to fill a ship, simply by visiting a single barracoon.

On 22 November 1858, Gerard applied to have the 545-ton *Royal George* cleared at Macao. The reason he gave was that it would save six to eight days by not calling at Hong Kong. Gerard's application was supported by Andrew Lysaught Inglis[75] in his capacity as Emigration Officer in Hong Kong.

Gerard's application was also supported by the Acting Colonial Secretary, Frederick H.A. Forth, who was of the opinion that it was within the Governor's power to approve the application. Governor Bowring however, thought otherwise, and on 27 November, instructed the Hong Kong Colonial Secretary, William T. Mercer, to deny Gerard's request to leave directly from Macao.

The *Royal George* accordingly left Macao on 3 December 1858 and was cleared to sail from Hong Kong for Demerara on 7 December 1858, with 292 coolies on the passenger-list, a delay of at most four days.

The *Royal George* had been measured at Liverpool by an officer of the Emigration Commissioners which allowed 280.4 adults to be legally carried.[76] In Hong Kong, the Government Surveyor's measurements were based on a different interpretation, which allowed for 293 adults. Neither set of measurements was correct, as the proper calculation would have allowed for 260 adults only. Somewhat unfairly, only Mr G.H. Heaton in Hong Kong was severely censured by the Duke of Newcastle. The unnamed surveyor in Liverpool escaped censure.

Gerard had actually placed 300 Chinese on board her in Macao, following advice from Inglis that additional cooks would be required for the number of men embarked. Even though the six additional men would be landed in Demerara, they had cunningly been signed on as ship's cooks, hence part of the crew, and not passengers. No reason was given as to why Inglis permitted this flagrant breach of the Government Notification of 9 April 1856, which expressly prohibited such a practice; and there was no inquiry as to how this was permitted.

Gerard then prepared another shipment from Macao, this time on the *General Wyndham*. She had been idle at Macao for many months, waiting while the *Royal George* was being loaded. Gerard had 461 Chinese to ship, and the 865-ton vessel would have allowed for only 433 adults. By including some dubious spaces in his calculation, Inglis once again pointedly allowed the ship to sail with 440 adults and six boys on 14 February 1859. As with the *Royal George*, no women were embarked. The ages of the children on the *General Wyndham* were not stated, but she would have been liable to detention had those passengers whose ages exceeded 12 years been entered on the list as children. Once again, the extra Chinese were classed as ship's crew.

The *Royal George* arrived at Demerara on 29 March 1859 after a voyage of 112 days, which saw the deaths of 49 Chinese. The subsequent inquiry found the major causes were the small size of the vessel, the difficult ventilation, and insufficient room for exercise, especially as the excessive supply of food caused many to become fat and dropsical in the feet. An unexpected recommendation was the disuse of berths, as was the case with East Indian ships. The Emigration Commissioners agreed, but took the view that, as much depended on the habits of the people, a decision on this would be best ascertained by the agent in China. The *General Wyndham*, a roomy clipper ship, arrived at Georgetown on 13 May after a rather shorter voyage of 91 days during which eleven lives were lost.

Gerard returned to England soon after despatching the *Royal George*. With the controversy over his method of recruitment in Macao, his use of superseded contracts left behind by White, and the confirmed appointment of a government officer, the option to renew his contract was not taken up.

British Emigration Depot established

The WIC had commissioned its own emigration agent at the very same time as John Gardiner Austin[77] was offered the position of emigration agent in China by the Combined Court in British Guiana. Surprisingly, the long time proponent of Chinese immigration, the Hon. Peter Rose, was the only dissenter when Austin was offered the position on 25 May 1858. His salary was to be £1,500 per annum from 1 July 1858, exclusive of travelling expenses. As his employment was not expected to be of a long duration, he would be entitled to resume his former office on its termination.

The Government had no wish to engage in abusive behaviour in securing these migrants, and considered, above all, that it was desirable to secure a large proportion of females. It was emphasized that every emigrant was to leave China of his own free will, and with a full knowledge of the terms of his undertaking. Austin was to submit proposals for the establishment of a permanent system of immigration. Trinidad agreed to the appointment of Austin.

Austin did not arrive in China until August 1859 after some negotiations over his entitlement to passage at the Government rate.[78] There he was informed that the Governor of Canton had placed the emigration of Chinese men and women on a legal footing that April. On learning of this, he immediately went to Canton to ascertain the possibility of establishing a depot in that city, and sought permission from the Colonial Office to commence recruiting from Canton while maintaining Hong Kong as his base.

With Government approval received on 12 October, he wrote to Harry Parkes, seeking confirmation on the legality of Chinese emigration, and assistance in establishing such an operation.[79] Parkes was only too pleased to establish a well-regulated emigration programme free of coercion and unscrupulous recruiting practices. Relieved that a well-administered system was at last a possibility, he convinced his fellow Commissioners to write to the replacement Acting Governor-General of the southern Chinese provinces, backing the Austin proposal. They were not sure how Governor Laou would react.

On 26 October 1859, Austin was able to provide Parkes with the Regulations under which the proposed emigration programme to the British West Indies would be conducted. Much to the relief of the Commissioners, Laou's reply, the next day, confirmed his recognition of voluntary emigration and acceptance of these regulations. This was communicated to Austin. On Parkes' instigation, Laou issued a Proclamation on 28 October, making known that Austin's emigration plan had the fullest sanction of the local government.

Within a week, Austin had found waterfront premises suitable for a depot. It was at the rear of the western extremity of the Shameen site, within the city limits, and thus easily accessible by the authorities who had been nominated to monitor conditions at the depot. To regulate the depot, Austin drew up another set of regulations. This time it was to define how the depot would be administered.

He appointed Theophilus Sampson as his deputy, who would be resident at the Emigration House. Sampson had been a seafarer who became stranded without a ship in Whampoa in 1856. Befriended by Parkes, he became the cashier and chief clerk to the Allied Commission in 1858.

Next, Austin had public notices printed, setting out the objectives of the British emigration programme. The Emigration House was opened on 10 November 1859, with one prospective labourer already waiting at the door. Despite some tampering by Whampoa crimps, 170 Chinese had registered to emigrate by the end of the month, not all being able to be accommodated in the unfinished building. The success of the British emigration programme was welcomed by the Chinese authorities.

With the enthusiastic urging of Parkes, the Admiral of Kwangtung undertook to distribute 100 copies of Austin's Notice in the maritime districts, and Governor Laou ordered that the Notices be posted at every village or market town throughout the province. Three sub-districts in Nam Hoi, to the west of Canton, were chosen, the most populous being Shing An. A two-man team visited the eight townships and many of the 170 villages in this sub-district.

Allied Commissioners' Depot Rules

Following the approval of the British Emigration Depot, the Allied Commissioners took Chinese emigration from Canton under their control and paid the inspectors' salaries, Mr Mackay on behalf of the English, and Mr Jekyll on behalf of the French agents.

They then set about establishing procedures for the office and promulgated rules for the inspection of depots. Permission to open an emigration house required written particulars of the applicant, of the nature and extent of the operation and the rules for the establishment. Proprietors had to provide suitable offices for the Allied Inspecting Officers, who would visit each day together with Chinese officers. At each visit the inspectors would match the register with any new applicants, who were to be allowed free egress and ingress within certain hours each day.

Inspections were to take place each afternoon, and contracts signed every alternate morning. The contracts were not to be signed until four days had elapsed since registration. Each applicant would be asked if he accepted the terms of the contract and whether he was willing to sign. If so, the contract was then read to the applicant, and his advance paid over. After this was paid over, he was no longer be allowed to leave the premises. The contract reading and signing was normally done by Mr Mackay, who could speak fluent Chinese, in conjunction with the Chinese officials.

The applicant's name would then be entered in the "Shipping List", which the Inspectors closed when the Agent signified that the ship's complement had been completed. Permission to depart would only be granted when the Agent provided a Certificate from a competent authority to say the ship was fit for purpose, and the number of emigrants it could accommodate.

When Vargas found his business greatly disrupted at Whampoa, he applied to open a depot in Canton in December 1859, but his application was rejected because the Macao contract he presented was considered inadmissible.—These contracts expressly took away the right of the labourer to appeal to the laws which the Government of Cuba had made, for the protection of immigrants.

Vargas then arranged to have an American citizen, E.A. Thorndike, establish a depot in a joint agency with the Cuban house of Torices, Ferran, and Dupierris, to operate from Canton and Whampoa. With the recommendation of Consul Perry in March 1860, the Allied Commissioners reluctantly accepted his application after several objectionable clauses were removed, but Thorndike was warned that as the Chinese translation was so imperfectly made, the application could be rejected by the Inspecting Officers. This was to become known as the Anglo-American house.

The application differed widely in several significant points from the version approved for another Spanish agent, Don Ignacio Fernandez de Castro, for Camino & Co., a Peruvian company with an office in Macao. This was known as the Spanish house, and a fourth house was granted to the French Maritime Agency.

The armies of the Allied Commissioners ended their occupation on 19 October 1861. With the termination of the Allied Commission in Canton, emigration became solely the responsibility of the Chinese government.[80]

Co-incident with this handover of responsibility, the emigration depots for Peru and Cuba closed their doors. However, British emigration efforts continued to be the responsibility of the Colonial Office, the Canton-based Consul, and the Emigration Agent based in Hong Kong. The depot was transferred from Hong Kong back to Canton in 1864. The French Maritime Agency also closed but reopened in 1865, a few doors down from the British Agency, in response to a record demand in Cuba, which saw ten shipments from Whampoa between 1865 and 1866.

**Whampoa from Dane's Island, 1843.
Departure port, 1852-1873.
Drawn by Thomas Allom.**

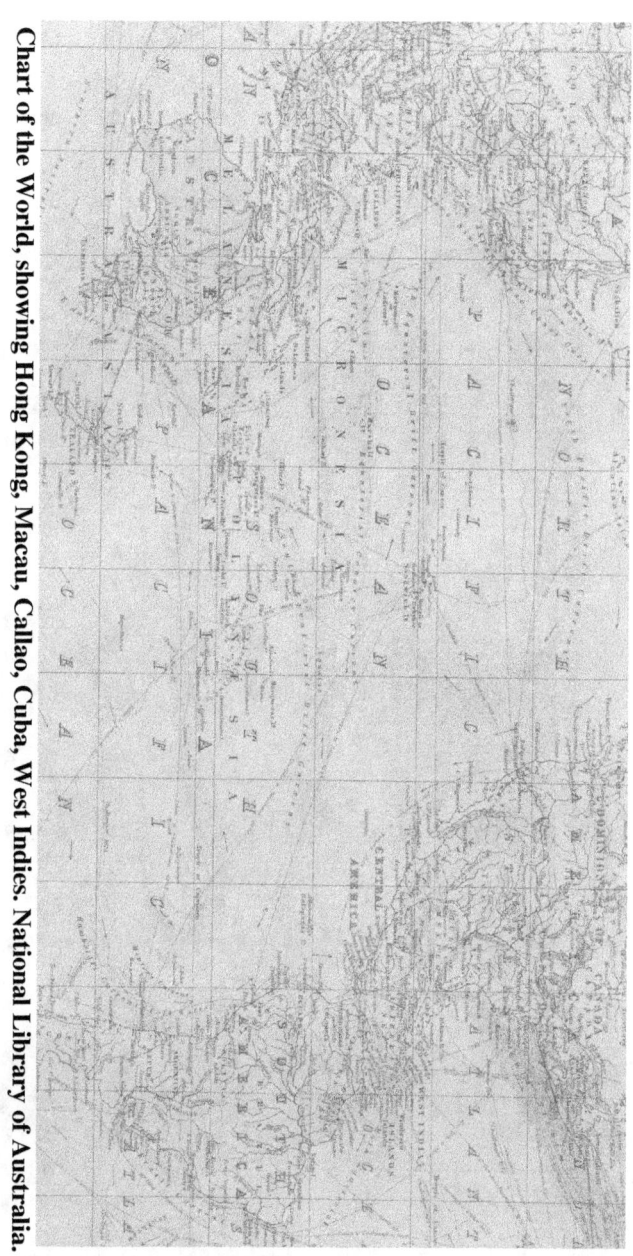

Chart of the World, showing Hong Kong, Macau, Callao, Cuba, West Indies. National Library of Australia.

Coolie Ships. Plate 1. Pp. 192a-192h

Hong Kong. Departure port, 1848-1870. Chinese artist. Photo: Martyn Gregory Gallery, London.

Macao. Departure port, 1851-1874. Chinese artist. Photo: Martyn Gregory Gallery, London.

Coolie Ships. Plate 3. Pp. 192a-192h

Whampoa. Departure port 1852-1873. Chinese artist. Photo: Martyn Gregory Gallery, London.

Amoy. Departure port, 1846-1869. Chinese artist. Photo: Martyn Gregory Gallery, London.

Coolie Ships. Plate 5. Pp. 192a-192h

Havana harbour, Cuba. Destination port, 1847-1873.

Kingston harbour, Jamaica, c. 1870. Destination port, 1852-54, 1858-1884.

Coolie Ships. Plate 7. Pp. 192a-192h

Port of Callao, Peru. From *Lima* by Manuel A. Fuentes, 1866. Destination port, 1852-1874.

7

Ships For The West Indies

The continual rise in the price of sugar sparked an interest among the planters in the Dutch, French and British West Indian colonies in recruiting Chinese labourers. The planters however needed to improve productivity to meet the strong competition from Cuba. The renewed interest for Chinese labourers began with two shipments for Surinam from Macao in 1858, one French shipment to Martinique from Shanghai and then another from Whampoa. British planters resumed recruiting Chinese labourers, first from Macao and then Whampoa in 1859.

This renewed interest began with two shipments from Macao to Surinam in 1858. However, after these, the Dutch suspended further shipments until 1865, when they resumed occasional shipments until 1869. The French had only two experimental shipments—in 1859 and 1860—and ceased further shipments, following strong resentment from the native population.

French West Indian shipments

With an official French presence in China, the Administration of Martinique entered into an agreement with the firm of Gastel, Malavois, & Assier on 25 November 1858 for the supply of up to 10,000 Chinese workers over a period of five years. The French Minister of Colonies however, would only allow an initial trial of two shipments. Accordingly, the Paris firm signed an agreement with Louis O'Lanyer of Bordeaux for the introduction of 600 Chinese agriculturists to the Colonies. The outcome is unclear.[81]

When the French 502-ton *Admiral Baudin* departed from Shanghai on 27 April 1859, she had 355 on board for Martinique. The British Consul reported two women were among the 331 who landed at St Pierre, on 29 September. Prior to that sailing, another French ship, the *Indien*, was reported by the *North China Herald* to have sailed on 6 April, in ballast for Guadaloupe. However, according to Jean-Luc Cardin,[82] the *Fulton* took 223 from the *Indien* to Martinique after the Guadalopeans refused 300 of the *Indien* contingent of 512 from Shanghai.

The 463-ton French ship *Gertrude*, under Captain LaBelle, had been lying in the Huangpo River near Woosung for some time, amid speculation that a good many people including children had disappeared.[83] One day a Chinese boy escaped from the ship just as the coolies on board began to mutiny. The coolies were fired upon by the crew and 60 or 70 of them jumped overboard, when the crew continued to shoot at them in the water. In explanation of the mutiny, it was said a French merchant had been contracted to furnish labourers for the French West Indies. His crimps had resorted to every sort of pretence to bring them in, brazenly taking people from the Bund, the hongs and sampans, and even the fields. The French Consul and Vice Consul were said to have agents among the Chinese, including policemen and even higher Chinese officials.

After waiting for more than three months, the *Galilee* eventually sailed from Whampoa for Martinique on 14 March 1860 with 426 Chinese. The shipment included seven families of from three to eight individuals, twelve married couples without infants, thirteen girls from three to seven years. There were 38 women on board including one aged 63 and an infant of tender age. There were 86 boys aged between 15 and 20, 226 men from 20 to 30 years old, 75 from 31 to 45 years old and one man aged over sixty.[84]

On 29 September 1859, the British Consul in Martinique reported the arrival of another vessel belonging to the same firm as having arrived at Guadalupe, but due to the reluctance of local planters to accept the Chinese, 225 of them were eventually transferred by Government steamer to Martinique, where they immediately found employment. Consul Lawless did not identify the ship that called at Guadaloupe, leaving it unclear as to which ship actually carried that shipment. The final three shipments to the French colonies were surprisingly undertaken by non-French vessels carrying 1,135 Chinese to Tahiti.

The French inducements were not enough, especially when compared with the contracts being offered by the Spanish for the same eight years servitude. The French contract was at the rate of four piastres a month, with 13 piastres advanced for clothing and other necessities to be repaid at one piaster a month. The Spanish contract of Don R. Bidau on behalf of Morales & Co. was for the same numerical number, but related to dollars rather than piastres. The piastre was introduced by the French in Annam. It was roughly equal in value to the dollar but was not well known in China. The big attraction of his contract however, was the payment of a $20 bounty, which was never to be recovered from wages.

British Emigration Agency in Hong Kong

With the British depot firmly established in Canton, Austin left Sampson in charge before returning to Hong Kong, where he met the Rev. William Lobscheid.[85]

Lobscheid had a deep understanding of the Chinese people, who trusted him, and he was able to promise to recruit 5,000 married families from the north and northeast of Hong Kong, areas where the women's feet were not bound. During December, Austin, with the able assistance of Lobschied's nominee, Wong Cheung Pak, was able to recruit 133 emigrants from the countryside who had been attracted by his notices, and another twenty, including seven women, in Hong Kong.

The first recruits in Hong Kong were held in temporary bamboo sheds, but Austin soon found it more economical to have a floating depot, with only an office and medical inspection room ashore. It also provided better supervision once advances had been paid.

The 977-ton *Whirlwind* was the first ship chartered by Austin. In Canton he placed 89 members of families, including 40 women and twelve children, on the ship taking them to Demerara. The first 127 single men from the Canton depot were taken to Hong Kong by steamer, joining 13 men and seven women already there. The final total of 372 persons included 47 women and eleven children and one infant sailing from Hong Kong on 23 December 1859. The *Whirlwind* was the first vessel to take Chinese women to the British West Indies. There was great scepticism as to the true relationship of these women, and that was soon borne out when so many of them were repudiated, even before the voyage commenced. In general, they were not of a strong nature, and most were not able, nor inclined, to perform any form of field work. The *Whirlwind* arrived at Demerara on 11 March 1860 after a speedy passage of 79 days, and without a single death. The British Guiana *Royal Gazette* of 23 March 1860 reported that the married folk lived in the after-part of the ship separated by a screen from the single men. Each couple had their own space, with the partitions dividing the berths only 5ft high to allow circulation of air. The men from Hong Kong were kept apart from those from Canton, while a few troublesome ones were housed in the longboat, away from all others.

Surgeon Superintendent J.A. Chaldecott was on the *Whirlwind* on her second voyage to Demerara. She was the last vessel of the season to sail from Hong Kong on 8 April 1861 with 365 men, women, and children on board. Nine men and four women died on the 114-day voyage which reached Demerara on 31 July 1861.

On 13 August, Dr Chaldecott wrote about the voyage, with remarks and suggestions under headings ranging from family emigration, opium smoking, the voyage itself, the lack of a receiving depot on arrival, the dearness of provisions, and the prospects for the Chinese in Demerara. He was sceptical of family migration, claiming that the women on board included two notorious prostitutes, four idiots, a helpless cripple, a hunchback, one deaf and dumb and several others disfigured by scars. He did not believe that opium addicts made good labourers, and decried the lack of medical comforts for the sick, even the very basic arrowroot and sago, which he claimed were very useful in sickness.

In 1866, in what may have been the same ship, but this time having a measurement of 868 tons, the *Whirlwind* left Hong Kong under Captain R. Hughes for Surinam with 409 Chinese. On this 76-day voyage, five deaths were recorded.

Given the success of the Canton emigration depot, Austin decided to try loading directly from that port. His next ship was the 720-ton *Red Riding Hood*. With little understanding of the operational constraints on ships, Austin had expected her to anchor very close to his depot on Shameen Island. But ocean-going ships could not go that far up the river, being able to progress only as far as Whampoa, some ten miles downstream. With 314 men, women and infants on board, the *Red Riding Hood* left for Demerara on 19 January 1860, having being cleared by Acting British Consul Winchester in his capacity as Emigration Officer. She left in a cacophony of 10,000 firecrackers. There was some excitement on that very fast 75-day voyage, when, on the twelfth day out, a disturbance erupted. The two ringleaders were seized and put in irons. With increased vigilance, no further disturbances occurred, and the men in irons were eventually released along with the rest of the passengers. She arrived at Demerara on 8 April 1860 having suffered only three losses.

The *Red Riding Hood* was built in 1857 with dimensions of 184ft in length, a beam of 29ft and a depth of 14ft. She is the only ship which can be regarded as engaging in the Chinese equivalent of the triangular trade. Her voyage pattern was to sail from England with a cargo of general merchandise for China. Then to replicate the Middle Passage with a cargo of Chinese indentured labour for Demerara. On completion of that leg, she then took on a cargo of sugar back to England.

She made three consecutive voyages from Whampoa to British Guiana between 1860 and 1862. Her second was in January 1861, also with 314 Chinese. She arrived at Demerara on 13 April 1861 with four deaths during another fast voyage of 84 days. On her third voyage, she departed from Whampoa on 19 January 1862 with 326 men women and children. With three deaths and the birth of a baby the arrival count was short by just two. The average mortality rate for the three voyages was 1.05%. On a subsequent fourth voyage to Trinidad in 1865, two deaths only were reported out of the 327 Chinese who embarked. On that 82-day voyage, just 0.61% did not survive.

At least two of the men who had escaped from the *Greyhound*, as described above, were subsequently found on the 908-ton ship *Sebastopol*, which was loading for British Guiana. About 5 December 1860, a group of coolies rushed the crew in broad daylight, severely wounding several of them. They failed in their attempt, which was speculated to be attempted robbery rather than mutiny, as the vessel was still in port. Captain Lowther sailed from Whampoa on 23 December 1860 with 333 Chinese.

British Branch Agencies
In his letter to the Emigration Commissioners on 15 March 1860, Austin said that, from the tenor of communications from the West Indies, he had not expected to have to set the emigration programmes in train, and the requirement for families was a complete surprise to him. Nevertheless, through his resourcefulness and attention to detail, Austin had succeeded in shipping 1,974 emigrants, including 299 women and 108 children, to British Guiana. As an added achievement, all this was accomplished within the budget allowed, recording a saving of nearly $50,000. He had fully complied with the wishes of the British Guiana planters.

Looking to the future, Austin was confident that, through the prudent counsel of the commissioners of Canton, and supported by the European consuls, the Governor-General of Kwangtung had driven the slave-ships from the Canton River. Also, with the surveillance of emigrant ships at Swatow by European customs officers, a healthy emigration system to relieve a superabundant population was now possible.

An increased quota was requested for the next season, and, in preparation for this, Austin appointed W. Maxwell to open a branch agency at Hang tai, about 50 miles from Hong Kong. It was a dangerous area. A price had been placed on every foreigner. And on one occasion, Maxwell was beaten and robbed. Austin never openly disclosed his movements, and always carried a revolver.

Rev. Lobschied had promised the Chinese parishioners whom he had sent to British Guiana, that, should he ever return to Europe, he would call on them on his way over. When he took ill, late in 1860, he sought to return to Europe to recuperate. When Austin learned of this, he offered him a free passage to Demerara on any ship he chose.

Lobschied chose the 1,074-ton *Mystery* which left Hong Kong on 1 March 1861 with 360 men women and children. Lobschied was effusive about the ship, claiming that the decks were so high and well-ventilated that he could sit among the emigrants without feeling claustrophobic among so many people.

On the other hand, he was highly critical of the recruiting methods he had experienced on a recent visit to Canton. The example he used was that of a Portuguese crimp who had gathered up a group of emaciated men. He coached them into declaring that they did not understand the local dialect, but were willing to emigrate as a group. The crimp then began offering them around the various brokers. Lobschied claimed that Austin yielded to this fraud, even when he saw that the advance he had given them was immediately passed on to the Portuguese man.

Lobschied claimed he was shocked at the sight of those men on board, where at least two-thirds were opium addicts. Teeming with vermin, full of sores, nothing but skin and bone, scaly and spotted all over from former diseases, they could hardly walk. At least ninety of the men were opium addicts, and even though Lobschied tried to nurse them, at least sixteen of them died, while two others attempted suicide on the first day out. Nevertheless, only five other men, and two women, died, leaving 337 Chinese emigrants to walk off the *Mystery* on 9 June after a 97-day voyage.

Austin was quick to respond, writing to Lobschied on 19 December 1861. Austin reminded Lobschied of the first voyage on the *Whirlwind* in 1859 saying that despite Lobschied's knowledge of the language and active interest in Chinese emigration, it did not free either of them from the deceits of native agents. Lobschied's agent, Wong Cheung Pak, had collected sixty women, whom he presented to Austin as having led a previously impure life. Lobschied would have known the Doctor's wife was the only *bona fide* wife of any standing. All the others became wives only on the day of embarkation.[86]

The 714-ton *Agra*, under Captain Philip de St Croix, left Canton on 26 November 1861 with 285 men and women, and two boys. After a very speedy voyage of just 81 days, she arrived at the Demerara on 15 February without loss. The *Agra* was the first to carry a Chinese medical practitioner only, Tsoi-a-fai. He and the interpreter Ko-wan-Ki were both praised for their part in the successful voyage and their intelligence.

The next ship to sail was the 738 ton *Earl of Windsor*. Captain Dick departed Hong Kong on 3 December 1861 with 325 Chinese, including six children. On the 104-day voyage six men and seventeen women died, and one man jumped overboard. There were two births during the voyage. Captain David Dick reported that he tried in vain to maintain separation between the sexes, but was not very successful.

British Recruiting problems

The 1,332-ton *Maggie Miller* arrived in Hong Kong, and was being offered for charter just as Austin was gathering recruits for the *Earl of Windsor*. Austin was in a dilemma. He had an annual quota to fill. As the CLEC could not source sufficient ships in England to meet the quota, Austin had to find ships out East at a price within his budget. He did not have barracoons to hold men waiting for a ship so he could only recruit small numbers until he had ships chartered. He was already having trouble recruiting for the *Earl of Windsor* for Britih Guiana, when the *Maggie Miller* be came available. He had to charter her to fill his Trinidad quota but did not have enough recruits waiting for this second ship so soon after the *Earl of Windsor*. He called on Captain Frederick Johns and explained his situation on 30 October. No contract was entered into at that time. Later, Austin maintained that the verbal agreement was that he (Austin) would sign the charter party when he knew when the *Earl of Windsor* could sail. He declared his ability to do so on 2 December with 40 lay-days. Like most captains, Johns was a cunning man, and when he knew about Austin's dilemna, saw his chance possibly to claim demurrage earlier than discussed. Johns on the other hand said the agreement was to commence on 1 November, the day after they first met, even though his ship was still discharging cargo on 10 November.[87]

On 12 November, Austin sent Johns the list of provisions required. Within two days, Johns notified Austin of his readiness to take on the emigrants and requested the Harbour Master to inspect the vessel. Johns also told Austin that all the stores had already been placed on board by the 10th, which was not true as the *Maggie Miller* was still discharging her cargo of rice.

When Austin learnt that the *Earl of Windsor* could sail on 2 December 1861, he immediately advised Jardine, Matheson & Co., agents for the *Maggie Miller*, that he was ready to sign the charter party to commence on 3 December 1861, with 40 days to complete, known as lay-days. This was communicated to Captain Johns, who immediately responded by saying that the ship was taken by Austin on 30 October, and to be despatched in all of November, meaning the *Maggie Miller* was to be available to Austin from 1 November. Johns told Jardine to claim demurrage from 1 December 1861. Austin rebutted that interpretation and refused to go on board until the charter party was signed.

Following very heated arguments between the two, Captain Johns finally agreed that continued delay only compounded the dilemma, and signed the charter party on 9 December 1861. In a spirit of compromise, Austin offered to provide twenty more emigrants, even though he was struggling to provide even the original number.

But things were about to get stressful for Austin. He speculated that the check at the branch agency at Hang tai was due to the meddling of the German missionaries, not aligned with Rev. Lobschied, who had begun circulating adverse reports from some of the Chinese who had earlier arrived in British Guiana. They were not happy with the arrangements under which they worked as cane workers. Recruitment from the original areas ceased almost immediately, and Austin found he needed to open another depot at O'tau near Swatow with James Jones in charge, and a sub-depot under M. Fitzgibbon at Tat hao pu near Changchow. Swatow by then had been opened to foreign trade and was now therefore a legitimate loading port. Austin personally went on to Swatow to oversee a contingent of emigrants.

In anticipation of 49 more men from Swatow arriving on 10 February, Austin had the Government Surveyor re-measure the *Maggie Miller*. The new measurement allowed for 541 adults. At the ratio of two children being counted as one adult, Austin's total of 364 men, 170 women, and fifteen children was acceptable.

Three days before the *Maggie Miller* was due to sail, the captain of the *Persia*, also loading at Hong Kong, confided to Austin and the Harbour Master that Captain Johns had spoken of a serious incident on his ship. Apparently, a petty officer had molested and treated with great harshness some of the females on board the *Maggie Miller*. When the chief mate learned of this, he sanctioned the action with no rebuke. The Harbour Master, in his capacity as Emigration Officer, immediately held an investigation after which he ordered the dismissal of the petty officer, reprimanded the chief mate, and warned Captain Johns.

When at last the *Maggie Miller* sailed on 12 February 1862, it was still not without controversy. In his haste to be rid of Austin, Johns left without his full complement of seamen. For a ship of *Maggie Miller*'s tonnage and rig, a normal crew complement would have been between thirty and thirty-five, but it was stated that he had fifteen men only. Some of the crew refused to sail short-handed, but without the prospect of replacements anytime soon, he slipped away during the night. He planned on recruiting additional hands from amongst the emigrants if necessary.

But fate was not kind to Captain Johns. He had enjoyed a swift passage down the China Sea, through the Gaspar Straits, and only glimpsed Anjer as he sailed through the

Sunda Straits. But then, on 28 February, the *Maggie Miller* encountered a severe hurricane in the Indian Ocean. The vicious storm battered the 1,332-ton ship, and with only fifteen experienced seamen, she was tossed about with bare masts. The depleted crew were not able to rig or handle sails, which would have been torn to shreds anyway. When the main mast came away, the falling timber stove in the deck, breaking beams and carlines. Three of her boats were carried away, and the seas breaking over her destroyed bulwarks and rails. Then the rudder sprung, and a quantity of copper sheathing was stripped off the bottom. Stores and the cargo became waterlogged, and one man was washed overboard, while another was severely injured.

When the storm passed, Captain Johns managed to rig a jury rudder, and with only the stump of the mizzen-mast left, limped towards Mauritius, arriving on 25 March. Fifteen men and two women had died by the time she got to Mauritius. There, the Chinese were placed in quarantine on Flat Island until 2 April, when 345 men, 165 women and 15 children were placed on the *Wanata* to continue their journey.

The *Wanata* was a slightly larger vessel at 1,442 tons, but her dimensions were much smaller, being 174 by 38ft compared with the 214 by 39ft of the *Maggie Miller* A previous conveyor of emigrants from England to Australia, she was on her way home when Captain Johns contracted with Captain John Henry to take the remaining passengers on to Trinidad for a lump sum of £5,000, irrespective of the number actually disembarking. *Wanata* sailed from Mauritius on 7 May 1862 with 345 men, 165 women, and 15 children, calling at St Helena on 6 June before arriving at Trinidad on 3 July 1862.

Governor Robert W. Keate wrote to the Duke of Newcastle on 7 July 1862 reporting the arrival of the *Wanata*, and again on 18 July. Keate confirmed that several of the immigrants had been employed by Captain Johns to assist in working the ship, and had been paid wages of $5 per month for doing so. Keate went on to detail the interim payments made, and the sum to be retained pending the settlement of claim against Johns for sailing short-handed. He raised questions about the Charter Party and queried the payment of gratuities only to "inferior" officers rather than follow the established practice of paying the captain and chief mate. He was also very critical of the quality of females, and the advances paid to the men as inducements for bringing a wife, and children.

In response, Austin explained that the chief mate had nothing to do with the emigrants. The second and third mates were the ones in hourly contact with them, distributing provisions etc. Austin considered it good policy to depart from the established system, especially as it was common for captains to appropriate the whole bounty, and not necessarily distribute a portion to the officers.[88] The *Wanata* was the first ship to deliver Chinese women to the island of Trinidad, as all previous shipments there had consisted only of men.

Persia, a ship of 1,683 tons, arrived as the *Maggie Miller* was preparing to sail from Hong Kong. Captain J.H. Smith promptly presented his Notice of Readiness. Austin was still stressed from not being able to revive his recruitment from Hang tai. With the spectre of having to pay demurrage, Austin called upon his depots at Canton, Swatow, and Amoy to provide the necessary numbers. Including the few men he had gathered in Hong Kong, he was able to send off 531 men, women, and children on 19 March 1862. After a voyage lasting 113 days during which one man and five women died, the *Persia* arrived at Demerara on 10 July.

On board the *Persia* was a cabin passenger bound for Cape Town, Lieutenant Shinkwin of His Majesty's 59th regiment. For some reason Shinkwin took a dislike to Clarence Chapman, the Surgeon Superintendent, accusing him of ill-treatment of the emigrants. He began to keep a diary of the injustices inflicted. But it was only after the *Persia* had left Cape Town that Shinkwin made a declaration before a Justice of the Peace in that town. He used extravagant language in his accusations of the doctor. The Governor of Cape Town forwarded the declaration to the Duke of Newcastle who then ordered an inquiry into the matter by the Emigration Commissioners. The Secretary of the Commission, Stephen Walcott, explained the situation by enclosing a letter from Chapman detailing the steps he took in maintaining discipline on board. A statement from the Interpreter on the *Persia* said that the doctor was not generally liked because of his free use of the cane, but the punishments on the *Persia* would not have been considered punishments at all in China.

Dr Chapman was well known to the Emigration Commission, having previously been in their service for eight years, and he had made nine voyages in their vessels; to Australia, to Madras with soldiers; with coolies from India, and from China. In his defence, Chapman admitted to using the several modes of punishment as alleged, but denied that they were used to excess. He also asked how he was to maintain discipline between men who came from four very different districts, and speaking two different dialects. They were fighting among themselves even as they boarded. This continued almost daily with the parties yelling and screaming at each other and throwing dangerous objects about in great abandon.

He first tried remonstrance and reasoning, then locking up the more boisterous ones in the hospital. He admitted to placing caustic marks on offenders in order to identify them. The marks disappeared after a few days. When placing them in irons did not deter them, he resorted to using the cane. He was adamant that they were not excessive, and never broke any skin. The only time when three dozen were inflicted was when a plot to kill the Chinese interpreter was discovered. He administered the punishments himself, as he did not wish revenge to be inflicted on any other person who might have been nominated to do so. Mr Chapman's statements were confirmed by the chief mate and the Interpreter who were then in London. The Emigration Commissioners considered that Chapman was exculpated, but disapproved of his liberal use of the cane, especially against women, however lightly used.

With difficulty in recruiting being experienced in Canton in 1862, Austin despatched the *Lady Elma Bruce* to Amoy to load her complement that April. Even then, the numbers were insufficient, and had to be supplemented by a contingent from

Swatow, risking the outbreak of disturbances between men from different regions.

While contingents from Swatow were also placed on each of the *Genghis Khan* and *Sir George Seymour*, which also had a third group from Canton placed on board, there is no record that those vessels actually made direct calls at Swatow to take the labourers on. It is more likely that the Chinese had been transhipped to Hong Kong. With all this stress, Austin's health necessitated his return to England on 15 April 1862, leaving Sampson to supervise the loading of both ships in Hong Kong without incident.

The cost of shipping in the first period under White was about $110. That for the two ships under Gerard reached nearly $144 a head, while in Austin's first season it was $125 a head. It fell to $120 in 1860-61 then up to $139 the following year. The Emigration Commissioners had allowed $145 a head during his first season.[89]

British Emigration Agency transferred to Canton

Sampson, now in sole charge of the British Emigration Agency in Hong Kong, supervised the only two sailings in the 1863 season. The 839-ton *Ganges*, owned by and sailing under Captain James Nourse, left Whampoa on 4 April 1863 with 413 Chinese, and the larger 1,323-ton *Zouave* under Captain J. Malcolm on 19 December 1863, with another 517. Both vessels had speedy voyages and sustained minimal losses.

In 1864, Sampson transferred the headquarters of the agency to Canton from Hong Kong. He cited among his reasons the extensive river system to the interior, its political importance, and his own personal influence and knowledge. Whatever the reason, only two shipments were required that year. Both the *Brechin Castle* for British Guiana and the *Montrose* for Trinidad had no difficulty in loading, or on the voyage.

But by 1865 Sampson was having difficulty in sourcing sufficient numbers from the Canton region. At Whampoa, he was only just able to load the *Queen of the East* with 490 labourers for British Guiana, among them 112 women and 16 children, and the *Paria* with 213 men and 76 women for Trinidad. In an attempt to meet the full requirements of the colonies, he then commissioned a mercantile firm in Amoy to procure sufficient numbers to fill two other ships. Unfamiliar with the requirements of the British colonies, the agents recruited emigrants of such a nature that it led to complaints that insufficient attention had been paid in their selection.

Meanwhile Sampson struggled to fill the *Sevilla* which had sailed from Whampoa on 7 March 1865, and the *Arima* which sailed on 30 March. He then had a month in which to find recruits for the last shipment of the season, the *Bucton Castle*, with 266 men, 74 women, 10 children, and 3 infants.

This led to the question being asked whether Canton could still be relied upon or whether the agency should be moved to Amoy. British Consul Morrison had drawn attention to the lack of suitable emigrants in 1858 and predicted it would need time for a proper system to be organised. But as Sampson was also not confident that sufficient females could be found in Amoy, the move to that port was no longer considered. Alternatively, Sampson considered providing overall supervision from Canton, with a sub-agency at Amoy. Even though Sampson had to have his finances approved in Hong Kong, he never contemplated returning the headquarters to Hong Kong, much to the chagrin of the Hong Kong Government.

On 27 April 1865 Sampson complained that competition from the French-Cuban emigration depot, situated just a few doors from the British Agency was causing him great difficulty in recruiting the 1,950 Chinese, requested by British Guiana and Trinidad. With a nearly identical prospectus, the French were unscrupulous in securing the most and the best emigrants. As a consequence Sampson was forced to raise the advance offered to $20.

It was not until 1865 that Amoy was resorted to again. This time Sampson placed the *Light of the Age* on the berth in March 1865 to load 480 Chinese—among them 16 women and three children—for a new destination, British Honduras. The request for Chinese labourers to that colony was made by J. Gardiner Austin, who was by then the Lieutenant-

Governor of the colony. This was the first and only shipment of Chinese to that Central American colony. Two shipments from Amoy to Trinidad followed later that year, both without incident. The *Dudbrook* left in October arriving in Trinidad on 12 February 1866 with 272 of 286 passengers put on board, among them a solitary female. The *Red Riding Hood* arrived two weeks later, with 325 out of 327 embarked, among them six females.

The 1,214-ton *Light Brigade*, previously the *Ocean Telegraph*, left Amoy on 18 January1866 with 493 emigrants including five women. Captain H. Evans landed 487 of them in British Guiana 86 days later equalling the low mortality rate of 1.22% achieved by the 977-ton—also British—ship *Whirlwind*, which had left Hong Kong three days earlier for Surinam. This was her third coolie voyage as she had made previous such voyages in 1859 and 1861.

British disasters

Britain prided itself on the manner in which its recruiting practices for the West Indies were being conducted. With strict rules and regulations, Britain was confident that the horrors of the African Middle Passage could not be associated with the West Indian programme. It was not anticipated that the problems of the main participants in the coolie trade would also flow on to the British. Even though mutinies had been reported onboard the *Samuel Boddington* in 1852, and the *Sebastopol* in 1861, both had been unsuccessful, and the ships had made their way safely to their destinations. It was therefore with great astonishment that they learned of two successful insurrections in 1866 on British ships bound for British Guiana.

The *Pride of the Ganges* loaded her emigrants bound for British Guiana and sailed from Whampoa early in 1866. Within a day of leaving, a mutiny broke out and the master was thrown overboard. The mutineers compelled the chief mate to proceed to Hainan, where all the emigrants abandoned the ship. The ship was afterwards taken to Hong Kong by the mate. The alleged cause of the mutiny was the indifferent quality of the rice on board, but as the rice was subsequently sold in open market at the highest price of the day, it seemed to disprove the truth of that allegation. The mutineers did no injury to the ship and took away from it nothing but provisions. Sampson then placed another group of 305 fresh emigrants on board and on 31 March 1866 the ship sailed again for Demerara. Nothing untoward occurred on this 122-day voyage, with just three deaths reported on arrival on 31 July.

Jeddo was to become the only total loss of a ship in the British recruitment programme. On 18 March 1866, the 1,059-ton British ship *Jeddo*, under Captain Joseph West, sailed from Amoy with 480 Chinese emigrants; and a little cargo, for Demerara. Typhus fever broke out soon after she sailed, and about 20 of the emigrants died. On the 27th, one of the interpreters informed the Master that there was a plot to kill all the Europeans and seize the ship. When the ringleaders were identified, he had them flogged, and kept in irons on the poop till the 15th April, when apparently they were allowed to return to the other emigrants.

About 8am the next day, while the *Jeddo* was standing through the Straits of Sunda, a fire broke out in the fore hold where all the fuel was stored. After a vain attempt to extinguish the fire, the Master determined to run the ship ashore to save life. As she was close to Anjer at about 9pm, Captain West managed to carry a line ashore, by which he, and Dr Lang the surgeon, succeeded in passing a large number of the emigrants through the surf to land. Eventually 319 were saved, but the number drowned was no less than 141. The chief mate, an apprentice, and two European seamen were also drowned.

All the Europeans and some of the Chinese were drowned in an attempt by the latter to seize a boat. The surgeon remained on the ship, assisting the emigrants as long as he could without endangering his own life, but when he finally left, 60 of the emigrants were still left on board.

The survivors entered the service of the Netherlands Inland Railway Company at Semarang, with the company reimbursing the expenses incurred in China. A court of enquiry on the loss of the ship was held at Singapore. The finding of the court was that, under the circumstances, the master acted judiciously in flogging the leaders of the conspiracy. Though there was no positive evidence as to the origin of the fire, there were strong grounds for suspecting that it was caused by the coolies themselves. The court recorded that the conduct of the master and surgeon in their efforts to save the coolies was in the highest degree praiseworthy, and the master was fully acquitted of all blame for the loss of his ship.

Kung Convention and the end of British migration

On March 1866, the English and French Ministers at Peking entered into a convention with the Chinese government. This convention, commonly known as the Kung Convention, contained 22 articles to regulate the engagement of Chinese emigrants by British and French subjects. British and French merchants had not been consulted, and protested vigorously at the great increase in the expense of emigration which would result. The main opposition centred around the article that entitled every Chinese emigrant to be conveyed back to China at public expense at the end of five years. If the emigrant wished to remain in the colony, the sum which would otherwise have been paid for his passage should be handed over to him. If he entered into a second five years he should receive a gratuity equal to half the cost of his return passage, his right to a return passage at the end of his engagement remaining as before. Invalids, or men incapable of work, should be entitled at any time to claim payment of the sum necessary to cover the expense of their return to China.[90]

Expense was not the only objection. There was great concern that the 12,000 Chinese in British Guiana and the 1,600 already in Trinidad, without any stipulation as to a return passage, would be greatly discontented and irritated. Under those circumstances, there was no alternative but to redirect the vessels, which had been taken up for Chinese emigrants, to India. Sampson was to suspend all operations, and the British Government eventually decided not to confirm the convention.

This was a subject of much regret, because, that October, there was a proposal from the local Chinese officials for Sampson to provide passages to the West Indies for a number of Hakka families, comprising in all several thousand persons. These people, all of the agricultural class, had been defeated, and reduced to destitution, in their clan-fights with the Puntis. The Chinese government was anxious to find the means of disposing of them in a humane and satisfactory manner. Theo Sampson offered to take them, provided the emigrants would consent to a monthly deduction from their wages to cover the expense of the return passage stipulated for by the convention. The Chinese Viceroy did not consider himself at liberty to agree, and the negotiation dropped. No further British shipments were made, but the Dutch, not being party to the convention, continued to recruit for Surinam.

Coolies for Surinam

Chinese emigration to the Dutch West Indies commenced from Macao in January 1858, when two Dutch vessels—the 777-ton *Minister Pahud*, and the 710-ton *Twee Guzusters*—took 500 coolies between them to Surinam. No further shipments were made until 1865, when the *de Surinaamsche Immigratie-Maatschappij* (Immigration Corporation) was founded in Amsterdam for Dutch recruitment in China. In his 1866 Annual Report, Hong Kong Harbour Master Thomsett (1825-1892),[91] gave details of the efforts to encourage Chinese emigration to Surinam. The liberal terms provided each emigrant with two suits of clothing in Hong Kong, together with bedding and other comforts for the voyage. In addition, each was given $11 to spend as they wished. Their contracts were for five years at $7 a month, and there was no work on Sundays or public holidays. At the end of their contract, they were to receive a bonus of $60 to pay for their return passage or to engage in shopkeeping. Alternatively, they could opt to cultivate their own plot of land which the Government gave to settlers.

The 1,497-ton British ship *Tricolor*, under Captain James G. Price, left Hong Kong on 2 May 1865, with 356 men, 120 women and 17 boys for Paramaribo. The large number of females and children were the direct result of the involvement of the Rev. Lobschied. Unfortunately, the *Tricolor* suffered from a high mortality rate, losing 190 on the voyage, and Lobscheid was held to account for the quality of the people embarked.[92] Successful shipments were then made in 1866 on the British vessels *Whirlwind* and *Golden Horn*.

Lobschied had also been careless in lending his name to recruiting leaflets utilised by Chinese crimps, known to be kidnappers. In 1867, he, together with Bourjan Hubener, was arrested for breaches of the Emigration Ordinances in Hong Kong. When key witnesses failed to appear, the matter was not pursued, but not before Governor MacDonnell put on record his lack of faith in the Rev. Lobschied. Harbour Master Thomsett had discovered that Chinese women had been kidnapped and transported to premises close to the Sailors' Home in Hong Kong, there to await transportation on the British ship *Portland* to Surinam. When Lobschied learned of this, he immediately visited the premises and freed the women, and at the same time threw up the charter for the ship. The Dutch Government, not aware of the full facts, protested to the Hong Kong Authorities.

In defence of his reputation, Lobschied wrote a letter to the Governor on 17 May 1867 referring to the Governor's remarks at the Legislative Council. He started by claiming that the mortality on the *Tricolor* did not stand alone in the annals of history. He cited the 8,000 pilgrims who had left British India in 1865, of whom only 2,000 returned. The *Tricolor* could carry 663, but he chose to send only 486—men women and children—in consideration of the advanced season. The Commission of Inquiry that sat in Surinam distinctly stated that there had been an abundance of excellent water and provisions on board but that the presence of beriberi must have prevailed. Lobschied wanted to know what means MacDonnell had to stop an epidemic.

Lobschied claimed he had frequently been on board the *Tricolor* and the emigrants were quiet and satisfied, and left with cheerfulness. He then went on to say that if the Governor continued making remarks upon his character, he demanded the right of reply to the letter he was sent when he had solicited MacDonnell's interference in the action commenced against him by Police Superintendent Deane and Registrar General Tonnochy. He was of the opinion that MacDonnell's declaration of incompetency to interfere was not convincing, as MacDonnell had sufficient discretional power to intercede on his behalf.

Lobschied continued in his bitter condemnation of the injustice done to him, claiming that, as the Government servant Ho Aloy, was aware of the house, he would have been aware of the illegality of the proceedings. Barricaded windows were a violation of the law. The notices explaining the conditions of the contract which Lobschied had placed there had been altered by Ho and the people had been prevented from seeking his (Lobschied's) advice.

Continuing Surinam shipments
With the Kung Convention coming into effect, no shipments were made to the British West Indies, leaving Hong Kong with just one departure for Surinam in each of 1867 and 1868. However there were two sailings in 1869.

The British ship *Veritas* left Hong Kong on 6 November 1867 with 291 Chinese emigrants including nine or ten females, wives of the emigrants bound for Surinam. The women had each received a bonus of $20. The men had signed agreements before the Harbour Master to serve for five years at $7 per month. The year was to consist of 300 working days, with Sundays and festivals observed as holidays. They had received advances of between $8 and $11 and two suits of clothes, the value to be deducted. They were to receive a bonus of $60 at the end of their contracts and the option of re-engaging or returning home.

The *Veritas* was described as a fine strong British-built ship with lofty 'tween decks with two tiers of bunks with a small portion partitioned off for the women. Ventilators were placed along the deck and there was a fire engine on standby.[93] Five headmen were chosen to look after the men together with twelve cooks who were all paid. The emigrants were allowed on deck during the day while one man continually patrolled the 'tween decks. The crew of twenty had a good supply of firearms in case of an untoward event, so it was a surprise to learn of an attempted mutiny on the voyage. No details were forthcoming.

In 1868, a certain Mr Baak approached Hong Kong Harbour Master Thomsett, saying he was acting for a company of Dutch planters in Dutch Guiana, and was authorised by his Government to enlist Chinese for services in that Colony. He was about to despatch coolies from Hong Kong on the *Marie Therese*, as he had done by other ships. Thomsett immediately had the ship properly surveyed and measured by a Government Surveyor, and examined her himself as to her capabilities for the voyage. A house had been hired near the Sailors' Home, in which the coolies were lodged until the ship was properly fitted and provisioned. He visited the house occasionally, and had printed copies of the contract they were about to sign posted. He was accompanied by an Interpreter who explained the nature of the contract.

When the vessel was ready, the first batch of 100 was placed on board. He then visited the vessel along with the Dutch Consul and Mr Baak, explaining the contracts to the men again as they were being signed by the consul and himself. As they accepted their contracts, they were handed their bonus and clothing, and individually asked if they were desirous of proceeding. The same procedure was followed as each batch of coolies was brought on board. Occasionally a coolie objected to proceeding and he was immediately landed, as were those whose relatives petitioned for their release. Thomsett wondered what would have happened if the Agent had objected, but this did not eventuate. On the day of departure, 1 May 1868, Thomsett made a final inspection of the ship, and remained on board until she weighed anchor, many of the coolies assisting with the sails.

But the coolies mutinied soon after leaving port. No details of the mutiny were published, as was the case with a previous attempted mutiny on the British-flagged *Veritas*, which had also sailed from Hong Kong for Surinam the previous November, as mentioned above.

On 30 November 1868, the British ships *Omba* and *Veritas* were reported to have shifted anchorage in Hong

Kong to load 395 and 301 Chinese emigrants respectively for Surinam.[94] Each was carrying a Chinese doctor and interpreter. Each had water for 144 days and the accommodation was described as very good. The provision and clothing however was proving a problem with a considerable quantity having to be sent ashore as rotten and worthless. The *Vertias* did eventually sail (her second voyage), carrying 202 labourers from Hong Kong on 6 February 1869. Captain Ingram disembarked 180 Chinese labourers 112 days later, the highest mortality rate to date.

Despite being extensively advertised as sailing for Surinam, the *Omba* eventually sailed for Whampoa in January 1869. Her charter for Surinam was taken over by the Russian *Ferdinand Brumm* making her second voyage carrying Chinese coolies. She departed from Hong Kong on 28 April 1869 with 298 of them. Captain A.F. Voss also took 112 days to Surinam, but there were only 225 left to land on arrival.

After this, the Amsterdam-founded *de Surinaamsche Immigratie-Maatschappij* was wound up, the Dutch Government assuming direct control. But with the cessation of indentured labour from Macao no further shipments were made directly from China.

Workers for Tahiti

In April 1862, the Rev. Lobschied had planned to return to China by way of Trinidad and British Guiana, where he hoped to collect any labourers who might wish to return home, in the expectation that they would there expound the virtues of their recent home. He volunteered to the West India Committee that he was prepared to undertake the task on a pro bono basis.[95] His offer was declined, but this did not deter him from continuing his involvement in Chinese emigration. No further British shipments were being made from Hong Kong, but, after an interview with Governor Hercules Robinson, Lobschied successfully started recruiting labourers for the new destinations of Surinam and Tahiti.

In 1864, Harbour Master Thomsett explained the system under which the Russian vessel *Ferdinand Brumm* was to load 337 males for Tahiti. They had been contracted by the Rev. Lobschied, with the assistance of a highly respectable Chinese merchant named Wohang who had been for many years engaged in forwarding emigrants to the goldfields of Australia and California. The arrangement was that, for a stated sum per head, he would procure the emigrants, and fit and victual the ship by which they were to be sent. Thomsett approved of this, as Wohang knew the stringency of the laws and rules respecting emigration, and would be sure to engage only such men as were willing to go.

As the intended emigrants arrived in Hong Kong, they were to be kept, either in the houses licensed for the purpose under Ordinance 8 of 1858, or placed at once on board the ship if ready, as was done with those whose destination was British Guiana. The contracts were then completed and their advance wages, or bonus, paid in his presence.

Two further shipments were made to Tahiti the following year. The 845-ton British ship *Spray of the Ocean* with 351 emigrants and the 1,209-ton German clipper ship *Albertine* with 347 Chinese.

Hawaiian resumption

In 1865, shipments to Hawaii were undertaken from Hong Kong. The 653-ton Chilean *Alberto* carried 250 Chinese, and the 508-ton British *Roscoe* carried 276. In 1866, the 769-ton British *Mary Frances* left with a part shipment of 62 for Honolulu on her way to San Francisco.

On 3 October 1866, the 642-ton Dutch ship *Antonia Petronella* left Hong Kong for Honolulu with 200 Chinese. She encountered bad weather soon after leaving, and was so badly damaged she had to call at Manila, where she was condemned. The British barque *Eastfield* under Captain Worth was despatched to Manila to collect her passengers and cargo. She arrived in Honolulu on 23 April 1867 after a passage of eighty days.

As with other destinations, the Chinese caused grave concern in some circles and shipments were stopped until 1870, when two Hawaiian vessels, the 377-ton *R W Wood* and the 1,021-ton *Solo* brought 249 Chinese to the islands in

June and the 381-ton British *Violette* brought another 112 in December.

Louisiana shipments

Following the American Civil War, Louisiana planters learnt of the productive Chinese workers in Cuba. They tried first to recruit some of them from the Hawaiian islands, and then from California, but with little success. They then turned directly to China, but this was met with serious opposition from the American government.

In his Annual Report for 1870, the Hong Kong harbour master noted that the opposition in the USA to Chinese emigration was having an effect. However, this did not prevent 8,879 Chinese embarking for San Francisco that year, along with 1,121 to Portland.

Another 195 were despatched to New Orleans on the 374-ton French barque *Ville de St Lo* on 9 February 1870 and another 213 on another French barque, the 740-ton *Charles Auguste*, on 2 April 1870.

Lingering British Interest

The West Indian colonies were still interested in Chinese labour, and in 1867 Governor Hamilton-Gordon of Trinidad instructed his Calcutta emigration agent to visit China to inquire and report on Chinese emigration. Thornton Warner arrived on 7 May 1868 and was received by Governor MacDonnell, who introduced him to the consuls at Canton, Swatow, Amoy and Foochow. He also met J. Gardiner Austin (who had returned to Hong Kong as Colonial Secretary), Harbour Master Thomsett, and Emigration Agent Sampson.

In his report[96] Warner was full of enthusiasm for the Chinese, praising Austin's plans but was less pleased with the way in which Sampson conducted business. He considered Swatow was a good place for a sub-depot, as was Amoy, but overall considered Hong Kong the best place to maintain the office.

He was informed that the cost of placing kidnapped and destitute paupers into the Macao barracoons ranged from $40 to $50. The Peruvian Consul at Macao was offering $100 a head. With the cost of the passage money, a coolie could be delivered for less than $200. At Callao, contracts were being sold for between $300 and $350, while in Cuba the price was between $400 and $500. He could not believe the costs, but they had been given to him on good authority.

As the demand for Chinese labour was still extant, the Governor of Hong Kong was asked if it was possible to continue recruitment from the colony. Sir Richard MacDonnell replied that it could be done only by employing native agents on the mainland, which would breach Chinese law. The Emigration Commissioners however found it difficult to understand how it was impossible to procure a small number for the British colonies without resorting to illegal practices to entice them from the mainland, yet possible for the Hong Kong Government to allow the establishment of depots for emigration.[97]

The planters of British Guiana were still optimistic of receiving Chinese immigrants. In view of their prolonged residence and assimilation in the colony, it was proposed that consideration be given to the provision of back passages as available to Indians after a period of ten years. The offer was for a period of ten years, the first five under indenture, and the remaining time at their own disposal. In anticipation of an agreement, British Guiana planters applied for 1,225 Chinese immigrants in 1871-72 and 3,000 for 1872-73. The planters in Trinidad too were convinced of the superiority of the Chinese and submitted an application for 400 of them for the same year (1872-73). The proposal had been sent to the British Minister in Peking but there was no agreement from the French Minister.

A compromise with the Governor General of Kwangtung was reached in 1873, and on 14 February 1874 Theo Sampson re-opened an emigration house in Canton. But very few prospective emigrants applied. The Taiping Rebellion was over, and the need to escape no longer existed. As the shipping season was about to end, the depot was closed until September when marginally sufficient numbers came forward to enable Sampson to charter the 1,199-ton *Corona*. After much difficulty combating crimps, who were luring away his recruits, Sampson managed to sail the *Corona* from Whampoa on 23 December 1874. Captain Bate conducted one of the fastest passages to Georgetown—62 days—in the large spacious vessel. The only death of a single man was offset with the birth of an infant, leaving the count of 388 souls embarked and 388 disembarking.

This contingent left after extensive consultations between the British and Chinese governments involving a modified form of indenture, now termed a contract, under which $50 would be paid towards a return passage if desired on the expiry of the contract.

Chinese non-contract shipments

Despite the demand, no more Chinese were shipped until 24 December 1878 when the 915-ton *Dartmouth* left Hong Kong with 516 emigrants. On the 81-day passage, only one man did not reach Demerara on 17 March 1879.

On 3 November 1881, the Emigration Officer in Hong Kong cleared the 939-ton *Clara*, Captain A.S. Cutler, with 308 men, 11 women and 3 boys bound for Antigua. Four of the men were identified as being shipped under a contract of service, the rest were emigrating on their own initiative.

The Hong Kong Harbour Master's Returns for 1884 showed the German steamer *Prinz Alexander* of 1,911 tons, as having left Hong Kong on 7 May 1884 under Captain R. Eckert, with 509 men, 109 women, 59 boys and 17 girls making a total of 694 passengers bound for Jamaica.[98] After calling at Gibraltar on 24 June 1884, the 501 men, 105 women, 54 boys, 17 girls, and 3 babies arrived in Jamaica on 12 July 1884. They were the last direct immigrants from China.

Light Brigade
**Left Amoy on 18 January 1866 with 493 emigrants
including five women.**

8

Peruvian Focus On Macao

The abrogation of the Peruvian "Chinese Law" in 1856 was never fully accepted by the Peruvian plantation owners, who continued to lobby the Government for its re-introduction. On the plea of absolute necessity, special licences were then granted for introducing fixed numbers of coolies under direct contract wth the recipients of the licences, most of them issued to planters.[99]

A.F. da Cunha, the Macao Port Captain, reported that the 750-ton Sardinian (Italian) barque *Guiseppe Rocca* had departed on 23 June 1858 with Captain Lavagna, taking 300 Chinese to Callao.[100] She had arrived only six days before. The Port Captain also recorded the 581-ton Peruvian ship *Maria Natividad* as having departed on 12 January 1859 with Captain Nissour Arue, carrying 321 on to Callao. There were at least two other sailings to Peru in 1859, both from Swatow. The 370-ton Colombian (New Granadian) brig *Napoleon* arrived at Honolulu from Swatow on 15 November 1859 with 200 Chinese, and departed on 19 November for Callao, but with only 160.[101] The other was the 420-ton Peruvian ship *Victoria* under Captain Henley, which sailed on 24 December 1859 with 426 Chinese. It turned out to be an extraordinarily long voyage of 190 days, with only 205 of the Chinese being able to disembark on 1 July 1860. The mortality rate was 51.88%.

With special licences being freely issued to farmers on a one-off basis, demand rose to eight shipments in 1860 and seven in 1861, before falling back to four in 1862. Mendoza lists five ships which arrived in Callao in 1860. The first was an unusual shipment. The 1,188-ton American clipper ship *Florence Nightingale* had a 'tween deck of 192ft by 34ft with a height of 8½ft to the beams and 9ft 4 inches to the ceiling.

The space was capable of accommodating 300 to 340 passengers. However, on this voyage departing from Macao on 20 January 1860, Captain E.W. Holmes only brought 20 Chinese, whom Mendoza classified as passengers.

The 1,633-ton Peruvian dedicated shuttle ship *Westward Ho* managed to perform two voyages in 1860. Captain A. de Araucoa conducted the first, in February, in 78 days with a loss of 4.98%. The second voyage, in November, took 110 days with only 12 deaths out of the 670 embarked.

The 281-ton Spanish brig *Neptuno* sailed on 1 June 1860 taking the north Pacific route past the Sandwich Islands. The *Daily Alta* reported her at San Francisco as the *Natoma*, arriving on 23 July. Captain Echevarria did not report his arrival, and when the US Marshall learned of her presence, he sent the revenue cutter *Wm L Marcy* to detain the vessel on the grounds of being a slaver and of not reporting her arrival within 48 hours. The *Neptuno* left before the cutter could reach her. She arrived at Callao on 31 October 1860 with the 130 Chinese she had taken onboard. This was the last sailing from Amoy to Peru.

In October 1860 Don F. Pineyro, the Consul for Peru in Canton, had placards advertising the sailing of the *Empresa* for Peru. The notice called for intending passengers to register their names, and declare their willingness to go to Peru of their own accord. They were invited to board the vessel from boats at four boarding points along the river. On declaring before the Allied Commissioners and Chinese Authorities their willingness to proceed, they would be free to leave at any time before the ship sailed. On signing an agreement after a second notice, they would be given a $12 advance, but would then not be free to leave the ship.

The Allied Commissioners had the placards torn down, because the Peruvian Consul did not have an establishment on shore, as required under the rules established by the Commissioners. The aggrieved Consul protested. But with no resolution in sight, the *Empresa* sailed for Siam. However, she later returned and eventually sailed for Callao on 27 June 1861 with 280 Chinese.

Macao attempts at regulation

With the establishment of the British, French, and then American emigration depots in Canton, under strict supervision, and the prohibition of receiving ships at Whampoa, brokers and crimps curtailed their activities in the immediate vicinity. With seemingly unlimited amounts of money to bribe their Chinese brokers and Portuguese officials, Spanish and Peruvian agents concentrated their recruiting efforts at Macao.

Events were to reveal that the existing Macao Regulations were not only unable to control the abuses connected with the recruitment process, but were also a cause of the numerous conflicts generated on the voyages themselves between men from different districts. Many of these conflicts derived from the faulty recruitment process itself, but many also resulted from circumstances arising on the vessels. Whether the events were disorder and rebellion among the coolie passengers, or high mortality and sickness debilitating passengers and often the crew, many voyages became a hellish experience which justified the term, "a new Middle Passage", which the china-coast newspapers and critics of the coolie trade began to apply indiscriminately to the voyages to Latin America.

In yet another attempt to stem abuses, another Regulation for the Shipment of Colonists, dated 30 April 1860, established an Office of Chinese Emigration in Macao.[102] The first Superintendent of Chinese Emigration was A. Marques Pereira. He was to receive a fixed fee not dependent on the number of emigrants passing through the port. He was to have an Interpreter also on a fixed salary. He would be required to be present at the presentation of every migrant prior to embarkation, to sign each contract in the same manner as the Procurador, and was to maintain a register of all applicants, listing name, age, and native place, along with employment and state of health. With existing regulations tightened, prospective emigrants, on first presentation, were to be given a copy of the contract, the terms of which were to be explained to them. They would not be permitted to sign such contracts until six days had elapsed and, if under the age of 25, without the agreement of a parent.

Like the House Rules which Austin had instituted at Canton, similar rules, agreed to by the Chinese Superintendent, were to be prominently displayed in every depot. While in the depots, Agents were to allow recruits free egress from the barracoons, and refunds were not to be extracted from the emigrants for the cost of food, accommodation, or expenses for the voyage. On confirmation that the emigrant was willing to go, he was to sign the contract and be given his advance payment while awaiting shipment. Should he change his mind before sailing, the emigrant was bound to refund all expenses incurred by the agent.

A Supplement to the Regulations[103] was published on 12 October 1860, strengthening its provisions, but most commentators were of the opinion that, while the Ordinance established an official superintendence over the engagement and embarkation of coolies, lack of supervision would impair the effectiveness of the strengthened regulations.

Watt Stewart credits the Macao authorities with definite regulations concerning the ship itself. The between decks had to be at least 6ft high and the space for each person to be at least 2.5 metres. Three suits of clothing, a small chest about the size of a tea chest, a blanket, and bamboo pillow were to be supplied for each man. They were also to be provided with eating utensils, and if the ship was to approach a cold climate, winter clothing was to be issued.

Before the ship could embark passengers, it was to be thoroughly disinfected with chloride of lime. The regulations extended to what was to be done at sea, but as they were impossible to supervise, it was up to the captain to see that the ship was disinfected regularly and that clothing was changed often and laundered once a week in boiling water and bleaching powder.

Following the Spanish Royal Decree of 1860, which restricted the number of passengers allowed on ships arriving in Cuba to one per two tons of the ship's register, a Portuguese Decree was issued on 5 September 1861, applying the rule to all ships sailing for Cuba.[104] However, the 1½ ton rule was still to apply to all other destinations. But then, on 13 August 1864, another Decree was issued by the new Governor Amaral.[105] He decreed that the tonnage rule was to be superseded by one based on the light available in the cabin and the ventilation of the ship. From 1 January 1865, for ships with side ports and air funnels, 2 cubic metres, approximately 55 cubic feet, would be required for each passenger. For ships with side ports but no air funnels, the space allowed was to be 2.5 cubic metres, and for a ship with neither, 3 cubic metres per passenger would be required.

But it was not until 1868 that Macao implemented regulations requiring shipmasters to apply for a certificate stating the number of passengers that could be carried for a particular voyage.[106]

Peru re-introduces Asiatic colonists

The onset of the American Civil War in 1861 provided Peru with the opportunity of great profits in the production of cotton. But this required labour, and the Government was forced to pass a new "Chinese Law" on 15 January 1861. This new law cancelled the 1856 legislation and allowed for the re-introduction of Asiatic colonists to cultivate rural lands and for domestic service. It specifically prohibited the transfer of contracts without the consent of the colonist, and significantly, incorporated the old British standard of only allowing one passenger for every two tons of the ship's registry on a potential penalty of 500 pesos for each person in excess of that number.

President Ramon Castilla was not in favour of the legislation and had initially vetoed it on the grounds, inter alia, that the Chinese were weak, sickly, degraded, and corrupted. Experience had shown that Chinese men had either died at their hard tasks with great frequency, or abandoned their obligations not to pillage or engage in other occupations. The Castilla objections were not accepted and the law was promulgated on 14 March 1861.

Pacific Islands recruitment

Just as the Peruvian Immigration Law of 1849 was intended to encourage European migrants, but was turned into the "Chinese law", so too, was the new "Chinese Law" of 15 January 1861 manipulated. The law was finally passed on 14 March, and by 1 April, permission was sought by, and granted to, D.J.L. Byrne to bring colonists from the islands of the South Western Pacific for a period of six years. The rules of the 15 January 1861 law were to be followed.

The expectation was that they would be better workers than the Chinese. The practice that followed, which was to become known as "blackbirding", became a scandal, with recruitment practices even more abhorrent than that practiced in China. Islanders would be entertained on board, and while there, were persuaded to go to Peru. In some instances, the ships simply sailed away with their bewildered visitors trapped on board.

No fewer than 32 vessels were employed in this dark period of Peruvian immigration from Polynesia. They were mostly small Peruvian brigs and schooners. The number of South Pacific islanders transported in the two years between 1862 and 1863 amounted to 3,483. This may explain the dip to 1,459 in 1862 in the exponential growth of Chinese immigrants which had steadily risen from 2,552 in 1860 to the first peak of 9,037 in 1865.

Persistent representations from foreign governments eventually forced the Peruvian Government, on 28 April 1863, to cancel the special licences, referred to above.

The 205-ton barque *General Prim*—previously Prussian, then British, and now Peruvian—arrived in Callao in 1852. On 26 November 1862, she joined the lengthening list of vessels engaged in roaming the South Pacific in search of labour. On the first of her two "blackbirding" expeditions, she succeeded in deceiving 115 Polynesians from Easter Island into emigrating; and after discharging them in Callao on 6 January 1863, turned around and set off again on 2 March 1863 on another expedition, but now as a Peruvian vessel. She returned on 19 July with 174 Polynesians.

234

Captain Aureliano Olano then headed for Macao, arriving on 12 December 1863. With his usual efficiency Emigration Agent Ignacio F. de Castro filled the vessel with 182 coolies after only 24 days. *General Prim* left on 6 January 1864 on a 101-day voyage back to Callao where he handed 163 of the coolies to Ugarte y Santiago.

The *Rosa y Carmen* was also a "blackbirder". She had the distinction of being the only Spanish ship to participate in that trade. On 11 July 1863 she discharged 128 disoriented South Sea islanders in Callao and headed for Macao. She too was handled by de Castro who placed 228 Chinese on her after only 21 days. Captain J. Maristoni took the 368-ton barque away on 31 January 1864 and after an even speedier passage of 96 days delivered 194 of them once more to Ugarte y Santiago.

High mortality

High mortality was a continuing concern in the coolie trades. There were seven sailings from Macao in 1860, three with high mortality rates. The 517-ton Spanish barque *Maria Clotilde* arrived on 17 October 1860 with 241 Chinese. When Captain J. Luis Basseterre left Macao on 5 June 1860, he had 319 on board, suffering a 24.45% loss on the 134-day voyage. Then the American 549-ton ship *Tarolinta* lost one third of her complement, landing only 221 of the original 330 whom Captain David Moreley had taken on board on 24 October 1860.

The third vessel, the 407-ton Peruvian ship *Loa*, suffered a 37.97% loss on a 89-day voyage, which commenced in Macao on 4 November 1860 with 237 coolies. It was reported that an outbreak of coolies occurred on the 20 November.[107] The cause was indeterminate. The crew fired on the many who jumped overboard, and only a few were re-captured. On arrival, Captain Aureliano Olano was able to deliver only 147 men. The mortality was 37.97%. One further shipment, with a mortality loss of 21.86%, was undertaken by the 495-ton Spanish barque *Agustina*, which left Macao on 14 January 1861. Captain Juan Echevarria took 247 *colonos* on board, but only 193 were able to walk off.

In 1863 the 219-ton Peruvian brig *Maria* called at Payta, prior to going on to Lima. She had lost 45 men or 34.09% of the 132 packed on board in Macao. The 550-ton ship *Perseverancia* lost even more, 129 of the 400 boarded not reaching their destination, a loss of 32.25%. She was the last of the American ships to be reflagged in Macao, this one to the flag of Peru.

On 23 March 1864, the 836-ton Dutch barque *Onrust* left on her first coolie voyage. Captain W.J. Jonquer took 89 days to deliver 390 of the 500 Chinese he had taken on in Macao. The mortality rate of 23.53% was exceeded by Captain Menard of the 536-ton French barque *Bacalan* which left Macao on 8 June 1864 with 308 coolies. With only 208 men walking ashore, the mortality rate was 32.47%.

The peak years of 1865 and 1866 were disastrous years in terms of high death rates The 834-ton Portuguese ship *Juliao* sailed on 22 February 1865 with 516 Chinese. With a passenger/ton ratio of 0.62, no less than 43.99% of her complement died on their way to Callao. The *Juliao* made another voyage the following year with a passenger ratio of 0.57 but still with a loss rate of 32.91%. The 796-ton Italian *Don Jose* had an even higher passenger/ton ratio of 0.63. She lost 44.36% of the 505 taken onboard on 14 May 1865. A third tragedy was on the 890-ton Italian ship *R Pratolongo*. Formerly the American *Starlight*, she took on 503 Chinese on 23 June 1865. With a passenger/ton ratio of 0.57% for that voyage, she lost 49.11% of her complement.

Three vessels had passenger/ton ratios in excess of 0.73 with one even reaching 0.90. The 389-ton French *Flore* registered this exceedingly high figure when she sailed on 8 July 1865 with 350 coolies. The mortality loss was 25.43%. Captain LaFontaine must have been a very callous man. On his second coolie voyage, to Cuba in 1866, he took on 310 men at a 0.80 ratio. However, the loss rate on that voyage amounted to only 0.32%

Two ships, each with a ratio of 0.73, had different experiences. The 550-ton Peruvian *Perseverancia*, previously mentioned, had a 32.25% loss, while the 393-ton French

Marie Laure lost 19.65%. The 487-ton Italian *Rosina*, with the slightly higher ratio of 0.76 had a 27.57% loss.

The 849-ton Italian ship *Liguria* sailed from Macao on 30 July 1865, with 513 coolies embarked for Callao. It would appear that she suffered a mutiny and had to call at Tahiti to land some of the men. However, when he eventually arrived at Callao on 3 February 1866, after an 188-day voyage, Captain A. Pezzolo did not explain what had happened. He was able to land only seventy-two of the original 513 embarked at Macao. This remarkable figure—a 85.96% loss—can be ameliorated to 75.44%, considering that, as recorded by Mendoza, fifty-four of the passengers were unexpectedly landed in Callao from the 213-ton French ship *Tampico*, on 11 June 1866. No explanation was given other than that the *Tampico* had taken 42 days to bring these men on from Tahiti.

The 894-ton Italian ship *Dea del Mare* arrived at Macao on 27 July 1865 to take coolies to Callao. In the evening of 31 August, while still in port, a fight broke out over gambling debts amongst the 379 coolies then on board. Captain Ansaido Giacomo testified that in the struggle which lasted twelve hours, some 47 of them tried to escape by seizing the long boats, while others simply jumped overboard. During the quelling of the riot, one man was shot and 23 drowned.

The *Dea del Mare* sailed on 8 September 1865 bound for Callao with 506 men on board. The unrest at Macao continued such that a mutiny occurred, details of which are not clear. It was severe enough to have the ship call at Tahiti before continuing on to Callao. On arrival on 21 January 1866 only 268 emigrants were landed. A mortality rate of 47% was incurred in quelling the mutiny.

The 344-ton Italian barque *Amalia* did not have a good voyage. Sailing with 241 Chinese on 10 April 1866, Captain Joao B. Bollo needed 138 days to reach Callao where he was able to produce only 149 men. The mortality rate was the highest for 1866 at 38.17%. Her passenger ton ratio was 0.70.

In 1851, the US built 1,334-ton *Challenge* was the fastest clipper built. The British, not to be outdone, built the *Challenger* in 1852 to challenge her in the competitive tea races from China to Britain. The Americans in turn then built their own *Challenger* in 1853, but she was to become employed in the San Francisco rather than the China tea trade. In the general exodus of American shipping in 1863, the *Challenger* was sold to Peruvian interests. She was renamed *Camillo Cavour*, and became the longest-serving vessel in the coolie trade.

Camillo Cavour arrived at Hong Kong on 21 October 1863, having carried 71 Chinese passengers back from San Francisco. After fitting out, she arrived at Macao to load her first cargo on 15 November. Her first captain was Stefano Caravagno, who left on 7 December 1863 with 700 coolies bound for Callao. The 118 men who lost their lives on this voyage represented a mortality rate of 16.86%. On her subsequent voyage on 11 August 1864 under Captain F. de Landabaso, the rate had improved to 10.95%. Captain de Landabaso completed four sailings averaging 630 Chinese on each voyage, with death rates in the twenties. Captain Antonio Astorquia took over command from 1868 to 1872, undertaking six voyages during that period.

The final two shipments for the 1865-66 season were on the 820-ton Italian ship *Asia*, on her first coolie voyage, recoding a rate of 20.60% and the 1,283-ton Portuguese ship *Dolores Ugarte* on her first voyage showing a rate of 25.37%.

In 1867 the 1,078-ton Italian ship *Galileo* sailed from Macao with 413 *colonos* for Callao. After a long passage of 143 days, Captain Stepheno Splivalo was able to deliver only 302 of them on 13 December 1867. The mortality rate was 26.88% compared with the 2.30% he had achieved on the *Compania Maritima del Peru 2*. Another Italian ship in 1867 was the *Luisa Canevaro*, which suffered a 30.92% loss on her second voyage. The 757-ton French *Henri IV* was also on her second voyage, having left Macao on 31 July 1868. Captain J. Monillot chose the northern route via Honolulu and in doing so lost 31% of the 458 Chinese he had taken on.

Mutinies

There were eight mutinies on ships to Peru between 1860 and 1869, three of which were successful, in that the ships did not reach their destination. Another three—the *Loa, Liguria* and *Dea del Mare*—all previously mentioned, also suffered high mortality rates.

The Spanish 567-ton barque *Encarnacion* commenced her employment in the coolie trade on 4 December 1853 when Captain Gandia took 400 Chinese from Macao to Havana, losing only eight on her 130-day voyage. After a long period of inactivity in Hong Kong, the 567-ton Spanish barque *Encarnacion* resumed carrying coolies, sailing from Macao on 2 August 1860 with 324 Chinese emigrants for Peru. The official *Boletim de Macao* reported on 11 August that she returned in the afternoon of the 8th, due to armed insurgency against the thirty crew members. The ship reported 72 dead and 20 seriously wounded. The Government inquiry revealed that, incited by two of the emigrants, more than 80 men had planned to take the ship and seize the large sum of money which they thought to be in the Captain's cabin. More than 200 had been on deck at the time of the uprising and in the consequent struggle, 20 had been injured, five of them seriously.

Captain Ambrogue was severely criticised for not taking sufficient precautions. He gave the false opinion that the reason for the revolt was the water rations. Others thought greed for money was the only cause of the disorder. Complete freedom to roam the ship, including the fact that the cabin area was open and accessible,[108] contributed to the mutiny. The uprising took place in the morning of the sixth day. After a bloody fight lasting more than an hour, the crew managed to confine the men in the hold. Of those interviewed, only one said he did not want to emigrate and was taken ashore.

The *Encarnacion* departed on her second attempt on 1 September 1860. The number of men embarked was not reported, nor were details of the reason for her return 25 days later. No reports of a mutiny were published, and with the long period since her departure, it is presumed that she encountered a storm, and was dismasted. Major repairs at Whampoa from 27 October 1860 kept her there until 14 December. *Encarnacion* eventually departed for a third time on 14 January 1861 with a new captain, J. Manio, and 308 labourers, this time for Havana. She arrived on 16 May 1861 with 290 landing, suffering a loss of eighteen on the voyage.

One of the famous American clipper ships, noted for their speed, was the *White Falcon*. Built in 1853 at Pittston, Massachusetts, she was sold in 1864 to Canevaro & Co. of Lima for $28,000. Renamed *Napoleon Canevaro,* Rafael de Moro was her first captain and she successfully completed two voyages to Callao without incident. On her third voyage, the *Napoleon Canevaro* sailed from Macao on 8 March 1866, with a crew of 40, and 662 coolie emigrants, again bound to Callao. Part of the cargo consisted of 8,000 boxes of Chinese fire crackers.

A few hours after leaving port, the officers discovered a plot among the coolies to poison them, and that 200 of them had agreed to revolt, and capture the ship. Some of the ringleaders were flogged, while others were placed in irons. At 4 o'clock the next day, the interpreter reported to Chief Mate Alexander Francis Faw, that the coolies intended to revolt at 5 o'clock. At 5.30pm the coolies revolted, and broke up the sleeping benches into which they had driven spikes for weapons. They also had several knives, spades, and two cutlasses, taken from the men on guard.[109]

The crew fired on them, and after about thirty had been shot, the captain called on them to surrender. They refused, and set fire to some straw in the hold of the vessel. The fire rapidly increased but the coolies again refused to surrender. Two boats were lowered and swamped, but a third was lowered in safety, and several of the crew got into it and put off from the ship's side. The captain, chief mate, and supercargo were saved by swimming to one of the swamped boats, from which they were taken by the crew in the third boat; but the doctor, store-keeper, interpreter, and some of the crew perished. At 10 o'clock on the 9th the vessel blew up, the fire having reached that part of the hold in which 8,000 boxes of Chinese fire crackers were stowed, and all those on board perished.

After they had been 48 hours in the lifeboats, they sighted the Hamburg barque *Madeira,* bound for Saigon from Hong Kong. Captain Pollock received the survivors on board and took them on to Saigon where, on 17 March, they were transferred to the French Admiral's frigate. They remained there until they were placed on the steamer *Far East* which sailed for Hong Kong on 27 March 1866.

On 23 April 1866 the 1,064-ton Italian ship *Theresa* dropped anchor in Macao. She had previously been the American *Saracen*. Captain Sebastian Bollo had arrived to collect 613 Chinese for Peru. It took him 40 days to assemble them and she sailed on 2 June 1866. Captain Sebastian was not as successful as his brother Joao, and after a 122-day voyage he was able to pass only 497 of them to the consignee, Molfino.

Nevertheless, *Theresa* returned to Macao on 14 October 1867. Sebastian Bollo could muster only 293 Chinese coolies after 141 days. They must have been the very dregs of society and a rebellious collection. On 3 March 1868, she departed on her second voyage for Callao with 293 coolies and a considerable amount of silk, tea, and Chinese goods for Callao. All went well for the first 62 days. On 5 April, off the coast of New Zealand, the coolies rose, while most of the 38-man crew were asleep. After wounding many of the crew and killing 12 of them, the coolies demanded to be taken back to China. The chief mate, the captain's brother, had seventeen wounds and was placed in irons by the mutineers. After eighty days of torture, including having nails driven into his head, he was killed on 6 July, two days before the ship arrived off Cha-fo on the south China coast.

They spared the life of Captain Sebastian Bollo and his wife, and directed the captain to steer for Tin pak some 120 miles to the southwest of Macao. Soon after the mutiny, the Puntis and Hakkas on board had a free fight, lasting over two to three hours, and which saw some fifty of them killed. The heads were removed and placed in boxes in the hold where, after sixty days, they emitted a dreadful stench. The remaining coolies then plundered the ship, taking away most of her precious cargo, before absconding. The ship's name was taken off all her boats.

The *Theresa* arrived back in Macao on 14 July 1868 with a crew of eight Europeans including the captain's wife.

Five coolies who refused to join the pirates returned with the ship. It was considered that the mutiny was in fact piracy as many of the men had an understanding of navigation. In the days following the arrival of the *Theresa*, seven men were caught and brought to trial as pirates in Macao. Three of them had boldly re-entered a barracoon seeking to emigrate. *Theresa* was eventually put up for auction in Macao on 22 May 1869.

The 660-ton Italian ship *Providenza* arrived in Callao on 23 December 1868 with 376 of the 382 that had embarked in Macao on 23 July 1868. This was Captain Alberto Nattini's fourth voyage in the coolie trades and no report was made of a mutiny on board. It is probable, however, that there was some unrest on that voyage, as the following account, which mentions the *Providenza*, suggests.

The 350-ton Peruvian barque *Cayalti*, owned by John C. Codina, sailed from Callao on 16 January 1869 bound for Pacasmayo, also known as San Pedro, some 315 miles north of Callao. Along with a mixed cargo, the *Cayalti* took on between 50 and 60 coolies in total from the Italian ships *Providenza* and *Camillo Cavour*, both of which had been lying at Callao for some time.

On the second morning, as the steward was preparing breakfast, the Chinese rose, seized him, and bound him to the foremast. They then killed the second mate and attacked the man at the wheel. On hearing the commotion, the captain and mate checked to see what was happening, then jumped overboard, hoping to reach the shore some eighteen miles distant. The enraged coolies lowered a boat and chased them then killed them mercilessly. On return to the ship, they tied the rest of the crew to an anchor and threw them overboard. The Chinese crewman was spared, as it was he who had told the coolies of the bounty on board. Codina was next, but was spared on the intercession of his steward.

They then demanded that Codina take them to China, but he pleaded that he was no navigator and didn't even know where China was. One of the ring-leaders then dismissed him saying he knew the way. Apparently, he had been a pirate on the China coast until the British Navy put a stop to that practice. There were three other ex-pirates in the group, together with two fishermen, and between them they took the ship in a north-westerly direction. Later, the steward told Codina that they had originally intended to take the *Providenza* on her outward passage to Callao. One of the ex-pirates still had scars from the flogging he received after an unsuccessful attack on that voyage.

Without a proper crew, she drifted when she encountered calm. Then she encountered storms so severe that most of her sails were in tatters. After about 77 days, they saw land, and after 118 days made their first landing and were given deer meat by the natives. Three days later, they landed on Crag Island, where Codina was allowed ashore, with his steward. When the boat was returning to the ship Codina refused to go, and was abandoned. His Chinese steward of four years faithfully remained with him. They were eventually picked up by Captain James A. Hamilton of the whaling barque *Sea Breeze*. Captain Hamilton calculated that their first sighting of land would have been the Kurile Islands at the entrance of the Okhotsk Sea.

Japanese newspapers[110] reported that, on 19 August, a foreign-built barque, with a full poop, and of 350 to 400 tons, entered Hakodate from Namba (Osaka). She was an old ship and in a very dilapidated condition, topgallant masts gone, and all rigging in disorder and disrepair. She displayed no name, and had no ship's papers, nor other means of identification. Her name had been torn off, and erased from the two boats remaining. On one of the bells was the name "Bertha 1836", which had possibly been her previous name.

On board were 42 Chinese, common coolies, not sailors. Through a Cantonese interpreter, the men pretended that the vessel was Chinese-owned, that she had left Macao about 70 days previously for Foochow, with a European captain, five officers, and 50 Chinese sailors. They claimed the Europeans had abandoned the ship during a gale, taking with them two boats, the davits for which stood empty. A thorough examination of ship and crew discovered that seventeen of the coolies had contracts written in Spanish, with dates ranging from May to July 1867 and made out for the Italian barque *Providenza*.

There was considerable speculation over the identity of the ship, with surveyors in London and Hakodate confirming that the ship was the *Providenza*. On 11 September 1868, Barao do Cercal, Italian Consul at Macao, wrote to the Editor of the *Overland China Mail* confirming the supposition that the ship was the *Providenza*. Cercal said that the *Providenza* under Captain Nattini cleared from Macao with twenty-eight European crew members and 382 Chinese coolies for Callao. Barao de Cercal ended by commenting on the practice "of allowing a coolie ship to lay in the roads for two or three months, with those wretches on board, in sight of land but still confined, allowed them doubtless much time to form plans to regain, on the high seas, their lost liberty".

Captain José Peres Saul of the *Dolores Ugarte* however was adamant that the ship was the *Cayalti*, citing several characteristics of the ship and providing the previous names of the vessel. He was not, however, able to confirm that, in 1836, she was the *Bertha*. Then in October, the Italian Consul in Yokohama advised that new information confirmed the ship was the *Cayalti* and not the *Providenza*.

After yet another name and flag change, the *Pedro 1* became the 1,552-ton San Salvadorian ship *Callao*. She arrived at Honolulu on 15 August 1869, with 650 Chinese, 55 days out from Macao. The 21 August 1869 issue of the *Pacific Commercial Advertiser* criticised the Government's *Hawaiian Gazette* for quoting Captain Luiz Lavarello as saying only that, "the health of the passengers has been good, with a few exceptions, four deaths having occurred on the voyage". The paper sarcastically wanted to know why the *Gazette* did not go on to say that, "the ship had been the scene of a slight misunderstanding, and in the endeavour to bring about a correct state of feeling it was necessary to kill one 'emigrant', wound several and place many more in irons, and to prevent the recurrence of any misunderstanding, the backs of several had been excoriated to such an extent as to sicken the beholder and render it disagreeable for the parties to wear clothing." The *Callao*, which had left Macao on 19 June 1869 with 653 labourers, then continued on to Peru where 628 were landed at Payta north of Callao.

Foreign correspondent Curtis J. Lyons said that he had visited the *Callao* two days after her arrival.[111] He did not meet the captain but wandered about on his own. He saw the heavy iron barricade with two gates manned by armed guards. He spoke to a guard who told him that soon after leaving Macao the coolies attempted to take the ship. The leader was killed and several wounded. There were at least 14 kept in irons. The men were served breakfast when he was there. It looked good, with 60 baskets of clean rice, each accompanied by a dish of meat and potatoes and also greens.

After breakfast, some of the men came on deck. About a dozen chained men were made to scrub the decks while others were set to scouring the metal sheathing on the railings. Several had ugly wounds, with patches of raw flesh showing on their hips. The carpenter explained that they had been flogged a hundred lashes or more. A number of them had been appointed overseers. They walked about with a short double knotted piece of rope. He also saw some of them physically assaulted.

He said the accommodation was apparently ample and neater than he had seen on other ships. Some of the coolies seemed emaciated, but most were in good condition, but with scanty clothing. Overall, he did not think the surroundings and circumstances suggested a voluntary and free emigration, but acknowledged that some people might think otherwise.

In the period between 1869 and 1873, the *Callao* completed three voyages as a Salvadorian ship under Captain Luiz Lavarello, then another three as a Peruvian national carrier under Captain Antonio de Araucoa. At least eleven children were among the 4,033 Chinese passengers she took on board in the four years, landing 3,901 of them, recording a mortality rate of 3.27%.

After a spell ashore, Antonio de Araucoa resumed his position in the coolie trade, commanding the *Callao* from 1872 to 1873. With three more voyages to his name, Captain Araucoa can be credited with having undertaken more coolie voyages than any other captain. The number was nine.

Following the proclamation of the new "Chinese Law" on 14 March 1861, shipments of Chinese labourers to Peru rose slowly from 947 in 1859 to 2,552 in 1860 and 2,240 in 1861.

Stress of weather and leaky vessels were common problems in wooden ships. On 17 July 1861, the 682-ton Peruvian ship *Petronila* under Captain Felipe Compodonico left Macao with 300 Chinese bound for Callao. Meeting heavy weather in the Bashi Channel north of Formosa (Taiwan), on 5 August she met up with a gale, during which she lost all her sails. She made Honolulu on 10 October where she had repairs done before continuing on her voyage on 29 October 1861. Tenders for cash were advertised in the *Polynesian* of 12 October in the name of the owner Thomas Conroy in Callao and the charterer Ugarte Santiago of Lima. It was a surprise when the *Petronila* returned to Honolulu 40 days later, on 8 December, in a leaky condition. She eventually departed once more on 23 January 1862 and arrived in Callao on 18 April 1862 still with 279 Chinese on board.

Chinese people are generally very superstitious, with many believing in ghosts. About midnight on 2 August, the crew of the *Petronila* were awakened by a fearful uproar and confusion from the coolies below deck. Fearing a mutiny, the crew fired down the hatchway but did not injure anyone. On enquiry, it was determined that the commotion was caused by the Chinese seeing a ghost. It took a long time to convince the Chinese that this was not so.[112]

The same thing happened for three nights in a row. The mate eventually asked them to show him where this devil was. They pointed out a position and the mate shot at it. He did this for several places, and then invited the Chinese to see for themselves the results. They found nothing, but one man who did not believe it jumped overboard rather than continue the journey.

On 16 March 1861, the *Friend of China* quoted the *Javasche Courant* as reporting the American ship *Marion* as having passed Anjer on 31 January, 23 days out from Kwangchowan, with 350 Chinese bound for Callao. As was the practice, Captain Fred. A. Goss reported to the Anjer signal station as she passed through the Sunda Straits. No mention of the ship had been made in the local papers of the time, and it was fortunate for Captain Goss not to have experienced the fortunes of the *Ville d'Agen*.

The 715-ton French vessel *Ville d'Agen* arrived in Hong Kong on 18 April 1861 and left on 26 June for East Coast ports. However, on departure with 120 coolies, Captain de Fourrau opened his sealed orders and headed west to Kwangchowan on the Liuchow Peninsula instead. There he was met by *Lorchas No 45* and *No 46*, one under a Portuguese named Manoel, and the other under a Peruvian named Juan Pastor, the latter claiming to be the Peruvian Vice Consul.[113] First, 120 coolies were transferred from the two lorchas to the *Ville d'Agen*. Then, between 1 July and 15 August, another 243 coolies were similarly transferred. Further attempts to bring more coolies were thwarted when some tried to escape and the lorchas were scuttled. The *Ville d'Agen* then set sail but struck a bar and was substantially damaged.

She arrived in Hong Kong on 30 August 1861, but it was not until the next day that French Vice Consul Vaucher and Mr Helguero of Camino & Co. (of Peru), called on the Harbour Master to report her arrival with coolies. When the Harbour Master boarded he found everything in order except for the stanchions to confine the passengers. He informed Helguero that the *Ville d'Agen* was now in British jurisdiction, and that the provisions of the Chinese Passengers' Act would apply. He would need to interview each passenger and fresh contracts would need to be signed. In interviewing the coolies, the Harbour Master was told of widespread kidnapping to fill the ship. Just prior to sailing, some tried to revolt but were not successful.

The captain, lorcha captains, and agent were detained. The French Consul demanded the captain's freedom as he had done nothing wrong, and the latter was about to walk free, when a French gunboat arrived. The gunboat commander did not agree and said he would take Captain de Fourrau prisoner and send him to France for trial. At the subsequent trial he was acquitted for lack of evidence, but was prohibited from being in command of a French vessel again.

There were only four shipments to Peru in 1862. The *Marion* made another voyage on 26 January 1862, but this time from Macao with 225 coolies. Her arrival in Callao on 14 May 1865 still with 224 of them was a proud moment for Captain Goss. That was the last voyage by an American-flagged ship in the coolie trades. The *Westward Ho* carried her sixth shipment and the *Empresa* her fifth. The 498-ton French barque *Claire* began her participation in the coolie trades carrying 312 Chinese to Callao on 2 October 1862.

The ten shipments for Peru in 1863 were for more diverse importers. Ugarte had two shipments on the *Westward Ho*—handled by Castro—and a third shipment on the *Eliza*, handled by Manuel Antonio de Ponte. Two shipments for Canevaro were recruited by Leathold. These ten sailings took on board 3,740 emigrants, with 3,394 able to walk ashore in Callao. This presented an average mortality rate of 10.45%, but this figure hides the large losses suffered by the two Peruvian vessels mentioned above, the *Maria* and *Perseverancia*.

Captain Joao Bollo had two shipments with undisclosed consignees. Garcia and Fernandez each had one consignment and there was one unknown consignee.

The 671-ton Portuguese ship *Donna Maria Pia* dropped anchor at Macao from Hong Kong on 15 October 1863. She had been the American *R B Forbes* and had just been bought by M.A. de Ponte of Macao. On her first voyage in the coolie trades, Captain E.A. Rodovalho took on board 424 Chinese, but lost forty-five on the 92-day voyage to Callao. She sailed on her second voyage on 4 August 1864, but a week out encountered a typhoon, during which she lost a mast and was unable to proceed. A steamer with no identifying marks approached and offered to tow her for $6,000 which Captain F. Botelho declined. She was managing to make her way slowly back to Macao when she was spotted by the steamer *Maggie Lauder* on her regular voyage from Hong Kong to Macao. A towing fee of $250 was negotiated and *Donna*

Maria Pia was brought back to Macao on 24 August. After repairs she sailed once again on 3 November 1864 with all her original 425 men. After a speedy 81-day voyage, under replacement Captain J.F. dos Santos, 400 of those men were landed in Callao.

Her next two voyages were extended ones to Havana. Captain E.A. da Souza had taken over, and on her fourth voyage in November 1867, she took twelve soldiers to Luanda, and another thirty to Lisbon, in addition to 248 Chinese to Havana. Her extended voyage took 140 days during which twenty-two men were lost. Da Souza remained with the *Donna Maria Pia* for the rest of her time as a coolie carrier, twice back to Callao, and then a final voyage to Havana on 9 November 1871. Over her seven voyages, she took on 2,518 men and landed 2,283 of them. The mortality rate averaged 9.33%.

The 240-ton Chilean brig *Theresa* arrived in Macao on 26 November 1862. Captain Joao B. Bollo did not have an agent in Macao and directly recruited 132 Chinese before sailing on 12 January 1863 for Callao. The brig took 131 days to get there, but was able to land 130 men. She then took on her true colours of Peru and returned to Macao. As before, Captain Joao Bollo recruited his own men and now took 140 of them to Callao on 21 December 1863. After a 130-day voyage he was able to land 128 of them in Callao. *Theresa* returned once again to Macao for a third voyage with Chinese coolies. This time Joao Bollo had Sebastian Bollo to help with the recruitment of 143 Chinese. Sailing on 24 December 1864 with his 16-man crew, Captain Joao Bollo landed 141 of the 143 men embarked, 108 days later.

There was another Peruvian vessel with the name of *Theresa*. This 796-ton ship left Callao for Macao, arriving on 6 December 1863. There Agent Aramburn was asked to find 500 Chinese coolies which took him all of 55 days. Captain Miguel Sicard sailed on 30 January 1864, and after a somewhat longer voyage of 104 days, 427 of them were able to walk ashore in Callao. These coolies were consigned to Pratolongo.

Two Peruvian vessels arrived at Macao from Callao on the same day, 12 November 1863. Captain Sebastian Bollo of the 357-ton Peruvian barque *Clothilde,* was to join his brother Joao who was still in command of the *Theresa.* The *Clothilde* was yet another American ship to be sold overseas. Elias had bought the *Our Union* and placed her under the Peruvian flag. It would appear that the Bollo brothers had established a connection with Bianchi y Profumo, importers of Chinese coolies.

O Boletim listed *Clothilde* as having sailed on 17 January 1864 with 220 men. This was repeated in the 1864 summary of coolie departures. However Mendoza was quite clear in showing her as arriving at Callao on 12 May 1864 after a 114-day voyage with 275 men on board. The Mendoza table shows 292 as having embarked and 27 not surviving the voyage. These are the figures used here.

The 258-ton Peruvian barque *Mandarina* under Captain Francisco Xavier Rossi departed from Macao on 14 May 1864 with 152 men bound for Callao. She encountered a heavy typhoon 28 days out and began taking in water at the rate of 8 inches per hour. She eventually arrived at Honolulu on 23 July with 150 coolies. Her condition was such that she could not continue on to Callao, and all her passengers were transferred to the 268-ton British brig *Argo.* Captain Hamen had arrived in Honolulu on 14 July after a 143-day voyage from Liverpool. *Argo* sailed on 18 August and arrived at Callao on 25 October 1864 with 146 men.

Peruvian Regulatory Decree

On 9 October 1864 the Peruvian Government issued a regulatory decree recognising the excessive number of colonists embarked in cramped and badly equipped boats, with bad and scanty food, suffering careless and even cruel treatment, as well as a general lack of hygiene. The regulations restricted the number of passengers embarked to one per registered ton, stated that the food was to be healthy and sufficient, that there should be appropriate clothing, and a spacious, clean, and sufficiently ventilated bedspace for each immigrant. Additionally, a doctor and sufficient medicines were to be carried. The Peruvian Consul in Macao was charged with ensuring the non-exacting directions were enforced. He was also to certify that the ship was compliant with the regulations.

Peruvian flag changes

The Chincha Islands War with Spain from 1864 to 1866 had a profound effect on the Peruvian fleet. This war was provoked by Spain which seized the Chincha Islands in an attempt to regain its former possessions of Peru and Chile. This failed.

Of the 21 sailings in 1864, 13 of them were by Peruvian ships. By 1865 only six of the twenty-two departures flew the Peruvian flag, while the number flying the Italian flag had risen from none to twelve. The total number of sailings in 1866 had fallen to nineteen, with only one Peruvian flag compared with thirteen Italian ones.

Aurora was another British ship which had been sold and reflagged. She had earlier been the American *Peerless*. Captain George Hill sailed her under the Peruvian flag for two voyages in 1864 and 1865. In 1866 another Briton, Captain W.C. Linscott, sailed the now Italian-flagged ship from Macao with 272 Chinese bound for Callao. Then, in a reversal of past practice, the *Aurora* changed her registration to San Salvador, but under a Peruvian Captain, Narciso Garcia y Garcia. On her five voyages between 1864 and 1868, including one to Havana, she took on 1867 passengers, and disembarked 1791 of them, achieving a low mortality rate of 4.07%.

Canevaro was not the only Peruvian entrepreneur investing in shipping. The Compania Maritima del Peru was formed with the express purpose of engaging in the coolie trade. Represented by N. Larco in San Francisco, two of the first ships purchased were the 1,482-ton *Twilight* bought at auction in San Francisco for $6,500 while the 1,068-ton *Telegraph,* originally the *Harry Brigham*, was similarly bought on 10 May 1865 for $10,000. They were unimaginatively named, respectively, *Compania Maritima del Peru 1*, and *Compania Maritima del Peru 2*.

The first sailed from Macao on 30 October 1865 with 659 Chinese for Callao. After a 96-day voyage, 604 of them were safely landed. With fear of being captured during the Peruvian war with Spain the *Compania Maritima del Peru 1* became the Portuguese-flagged *Pedro 1*, still under Captain Angelo Fulle. She subsequently became the *Callao* under Captain Luiz Lavarello for three voyages and then under Captain Antonio de Araucoa for a further three, until the end of trading.

The Log of the ship *Compania Maritima del Peru 2*, completed by Captain Stephenio Splivalo commenced on 26 September 1865 when she left San Francisco with 144 Chinese passengers bound for Hong Kong. She called at Honolulu on 18 October for water before proceeding on 21 October 1865. On arrival in Hong Kong she immediately discharged her passengers, but did not commence preparing for her coolie voyage until 5 December 1865 when a company of carpenters began fitting berths in the 'tween deck, and a house aft for the crew. From 15 December, a series of deadlights were cut in the hull for light and ventilation. No mention was made of other fittings such as for cooking or sanitation. Neither was there any reference to gratings or other fittings for the confinement of the passengers.

Compania Maritima del Peru 2 arrived in Macao on 28 December 1865, and accepted her first 52 Chinese coolies on 6 January 1866, along with an interpreter and three watchmen. On the seventh intake on 21 January, the 53 coolies brought the total to date to 304, but three had been returned ashore without explanation. A boatload of water and a lighter of firewood was sent to the ship along with 1,053 bags of rice on 22 January. Provisions, water casks and more water and firewood together with nine packages of clothing, were taken on board in the following days. The final batch of 90 coolies boarded on 2 February 1866 making a full cargo of 435.

The ship sailed early in the morning of 3 February 1866 in thick heavy rain, and made a good passage to Anjer where she arrived on 14 February. Buying all the fruit a boatman had brought, *Compania Maritima del Peru 2* then sailed south to round Australia. All went well until 16 March when coolie No 383 died soon after encountering the Roaring Forties. These strong westerly winds, found between the latitudes of 40 and 50 degrees south, were a major aid to sailing-ships making for Australia and South America. However they carried cold winds from Antarctica, and with little clothing provided, one coolie after another died, presumably from the cold.

Captain Splivalo may never have approached Callao from the south before, but in any case could not have been a very good navigator. He made landfall on 21 April 1866, but had no idea where he was. Unable to find the port, he sent a boat ashore on successive days, only to learn he was somewhere to the north of Callao.The ship eventually arrived at Callao on 28 April 1866 to learn that war had been declared between Peru and Spain. The coolies and their provisions were hurriedly discharged, as well as part of the crew, and *Compania Maritima del Peru 2* departed on 2 May 1866 before she could be blockaded by the Spanish fleet. She arrived in San Francisco on 11 June 1866 where she was renamed the *Galileo* and reflagged to Italy still under the command of Captain Splivalo. *Galileo* sailed from Macao on 23 July 1867 with 413 coolies, but only 302 were landed in Callao on 13 December 1867.

Eva was a 224-ton Peruvian barque first registered in Hong Kong in 1864 as the *Dom Pedro II*. She arrived in Macao on 31 August 1865, but it was not until 16 December that she was able to sail with 120 men for Callao. The 104-day voyage for Captain N. Christopher was a successful one with 119 of them landing safely. *Eva* reverted to being the Hong Kong barque *Dom Pedro II* in 1868.

The 1,206-ton Italian-flagged ship *Luisa Canevaro* was originally the American *North America* and bought by Canevaro & Co. of Lima in 1865. She arrived at Hong Kong on 8 November 1865, bringing with her 22 Chinese returning from Peru. Instead of loading for Peru, the *Luisa Canevaro* left for Havana under Captain D.A. Cavassa with 698

Chinese on 10 April 1866. The voyage took 129 days during which 78 coolies died.

After her maiden voyage to Havana, *Luisa Canevaro* became a dedicated carrier in the Peruvian trade. Captain Rafael de Moro awaited her return to Hong Kong on 23 July 1867, and took command of her for the next five years even when she changed her flag to that of San Salvador.

Her first voyage to Callao was not a good one. On 22 September 1867, she sailed from Macao for Callao with 663 labourers. Captain de Moro had an extremely long voyage of 163 days during which he lost 205 of his passengers. The mortality rate was 30.92%, the highest for 1867. However his next voyage was much better with only 27 deaths out of the 721 embarked on 3 October 1869.

Despite the mutiny on the *Napoleon Canevaro,* Rafael de Moro was a caring captain earning the praise of the Honolulu papers in 1870 when the *Luisa Canevaro* called there for provisions. The *New York Times* of 13 October 1870 quoted the *Advertiser*, saying that on 29 August she had arrived at Honolulu with 700 Chinese after a 56-day passage from Macao. It reported that the coolies had been allowed the full freedom of the ship, the 'tween deck was admirably ventilated, and there was no evidence of coercion in sight.

When Captain Francisco Venturini took over the *Luisa Canevaro* in 1872, her flag was changed to that of Peru. On his first voyage, leaving Macao for Callao on 18 February 1872, he lost 192 out of an original complement of 739 Chinese. His next voyage in July 1873 did not go well either, having to put back after only four days into the voyage. *Luisa Canevaro* returned to Hong Kong on 13 August 1873 before going on to Macao on 27 September. On 11 January 1874, with 759 passengers, she sailed on her last voyage. The mortality rate for the *Luisa Canevaro* over her seven voyages came to 6.29%, despite the good record of Captain de Moro.

Another vessel purchased by the Compania Maritima del Peru was the 1,454-ton British ship *Red Rose*, which arrived in Hong Kong on 20 August 1866. After a quick completion of the fitting-out for her new owners, she sailed for Macao on 1 September 1866 as the *America* under Italian colours, still with British Captain Evans, who was to take her to Callao before his return to England.

When the *America* arrived at Macao there were nine ships already there, awaiting their cargoes of coolies. By the time she left on 10 November, ten other ships had left, all but one for Havana. The *America* spent 69 days awaiting her 622 passengers, the largest contingent of the season.

For her next three voyages, the *America* flew the flag of San Salvador. Then, Captain Eduardo Perks sailed with her on her first voyage as a Peruvian ship, before going on leave in preparation for joining in 1874 what was to be the first Peruvian steamship specially built for the coolie trades, the *Florencia*. The *America* completed seven coolie voyages, one to Havana and a sixth to Callao on 19 November 1873. In all, the *America* embarked 4,703 Chinese passengers including six children and landed 4,451 of them. The death toll of 251 corresponds to a mortality rate of 5.34%.

The name of Captain Ramon Mota was synonymous with the 561-ton ship *Fray Bentos*, which first carried fare-paying Chinese passengers as a German vessel to Vancouver Island in 1865. She sailed from Macao under the Italian flag on 20 June 1866 under Captain J.B. Castaynhola and then Captain A. Bollo. In 1869, her flag was changed to that of San Salvador, when Captain Mota took command. He remained in command even when her flag was changed once again to that of Peru in 1871. In Captain Mota's five years of service, the *Fray Bentos* undertook six voyages and was awaiting a seventh, when emigration from Macao was stopped. Ramon Mota must have been a very caring captain. Under his command, the highest deaths recorded were 30 on one voyage and 21 on another. Just nine, two, six, and six deaths were recorded on the other four voyages, a mortality rate of 3%. Over 350 passengers were embarked on each of his six voyages.

A period of reassessment followed the peak of 1866. Due to the Civil War, Peruvian shipments in 1867 fell to twelve, carrying 5,848 Chinese. There was only one death, with the *Asia* having to put back in August 1867 after being dismasted in a typhoon on her second voyage to Peru. The

820-ton Salvadorian ship left Macao on 21 August 1867. Captain B. Calderon had taken 513 Chinese on board at that time. The *Asia* had had to be towed back to Hong Kong where she arrived on 9 October 1867. From her full complement, about 511 were transferred to the *Pedro 1*, which sailed on 17 November 1867 with a total of 680 Chinese.

The 1,326-ton Austrian ship *Johanna* sailed from Macao on 21 July 1867 with 619 coolies. By the time Captain Steggman called at the northern Peruvian port of Payta he had only 529 left on board. He had lost 90 on the voyage and had to send another 241 to hospital. He then went on to Callao, arriving on 2 December 1867 with 288 of his original complement. The 241 Chinese left in Payta were eventually brought to Callao. On the short coastal voyage twenty-three died, leaving 218 to join the remaining 288 off the *Johanna*.

Treatment of coolies in Peru

An incident in Peru in 1868 enraged international and Chinese public opinion. On 17 June 1868, Don Narciso Velarde, the Portuguese Consul-General in Lima, advised the Governor of Macao that he had protested to Peruvian Minister of Foreign Affairs Don M. Polar over an article in the local newspapers. It claimed that, "an agriculturalist from this coast took 48 contract Chinese men in Callao, and fearing probably that he might lose them, marked them with a hot iron as if they were slaves".

Her Majesty's Chargé d'Affaires in Lima, Wm. Stafford Jerningham, reported the branding incident to the Earl of Clarendon, adding that, "the coolie trade, under its best aspect, can hardly be looked upon as much other than a kind of white slave trade".[114] He described the difficulties the Chinese "colonists" faced, and some of the methods they used to overcome them, including suicide and rebelling against their employers. As very few of those who had served out their contracts were able to find their way home, most became vendors of the necessities of life. They were not harassed by the authorities as long as they did not break the law. Their assimilation into the community was looked upon with indifference by all concerned. He predicted that the children of those who actually obtained Peruvian wives did not have better prospects and would evince a greater aptitude for evil tendencies and immorality. In Jerningham's despatch, he also gave an example of Chinese who were not so enchanted with their position. He was referring to the events relating to the barque *Cayalti*.

When the Earl of Clarendon heard of the branding, he requested Sir Charles Murray, in Lisbon on 20 May 1869, to convey the substance of the communication, in guarded language, to the Portuguese Government. Senhor Mendes Leal, the Portuguese Foreign Minister, did not agree with his Consul General in Lima, curtly replying that the branding did not happen.[115] His response was dated 8 January 1870.

But Governor Antonio Sergio de Souza in Macao had already acted. In a decree on 18 November 1868, he declared that, until further notice, the permission by the Government to establishments of emigration for Callao was suspended. Asiatic emigrants or colonists would not be matriculated for that port, nor would there be contracts signed in the Procurator's office.

It is not known how many ships had been trapped by the sudden ban on shipping to Peru. The *Callao* had departed for Hong Kong the day before the Proclamation. The *Macao* arrived from Callao on 21 November 1868 and left for Hong Kong on the 28th. It was the normal practice for ships to proceed to Hong Kong for repairs and provisioning prior to their next voyage. After the ban was eventually lifted, the veteran *Camillo Cavour* was the first to leave on 17 June 1869 with 586 labourers. This was her seventh coolie voyage. During the seven-month ban, 16 ships sailed for Havana, including the Peruvian-owned, Salvadorian-flagged vessels, *Dolores Ugarte*, and *Aurora* which had found alternative charters to Havana.

The *New York Times* of 20 March 1869 carried an article from their Peruvian correspondent describing the horrors of the coolie trade. It commenced with the assertion that yellow fever was greatly on the increase in Lima. Doctors had begun protesting against the arrival of coolie ships loaded with

Chinese men destined for the plantations up and down the coast of Peru. The doctors maintained that the yellow fever had been brought by these coolies.

The correspondent said he knew of no sadder sight than to see the poor wretches huddled into such close and dirty quarters as to be incapable of lying down. They sat, half bent, half lying in the dark hold covered with sores and vermin, with the coolies around them indifferent to the fate of a dying comrade. So jealous were they of the extra space vacated, that he actually saw dying wretches being picked up and tossed overboard even before they had died. Twice a day they would be given a pint of rice, so mouldy and wormy that it was almost impossible to eat. So hungry were the men that the poor wretches would lick the outside, bottom, top, sides and handle of the tin, as a ravenous dog would gnaw at a bone.

The correspondent said the captain claimed that he was powerless to prevent this as the ship had its own Chinese physician. The Chinese themselves were so cruel and indifferent to the sufferings of others that, despite care and watchfulness, they would rid themselves of their fellow sufferers. He said that he himself had seen men playing dominoes beside a dying man, and as he fell one of the men pushed him to one side. When transferring between ships, those suffering from scurvy and disease were rolled in a blanket, their arms clasped to their knees. Sailors would then lift them by their clasped elbows and dump them into the hold, pulling them by the ears and making them sit up exactly as he had seen dead hogs being loaded into freight cars. When asked what happened to them, the reply was that they were thrown overboard into deep water as soon as they died. He remarked that under those circumstances it was no wonder that yellow fever could not be controlled.

There were 10 sailings to Peru in 1869 with one attempted mutiny. It was an exceptional year with no ship recording mortality rates higher than 3.83%. The average was just 2.11%. There were only two newcomers to the trade, both French. They had excellent records with the 440-ton *Jourdain* losing only four men and the 627-ton *Ango* just two. The veteran Portuguese *Donna Maria Pia* also had a good voyage with just three men lost. Another veteran, the *Uncowah*, also lost only three men on her voyage.

The other seven departures were all by Salvadorian flags all on at least their third voyage to Callao. As was becoming the practice, the off-season departures took the northern route via Honolulu while the seasonal ones took the shorter route via Anjer.

Dolores Ugarte
made four coolie voyages.

Top: Guano bed mining, Chincha Islands, 1875.
Bottom: Loading lighters with guano from chutes.
Both photographed by Gardner, Washington, D.C.

9

Cuba Overwhelms Macao

Cuban demand for Chinese labourers had doubled in 1865, but then more than doubled again in 1866 when there were 52 shipments for the year. In the peak year of 1866, a total of 18,437 Chinese labourers embarked on 44 ships from Macao, seven ships from Canton and one from Swatow. Of these, 16,624 landed alive in Cuba. There were 29 shipments to Cuba in 1867 on which 10,849 Chinese were taken on and 9,837 able to land.

Shipments to Cuba in 1868 declined to 23, with 8,835 Chinese coolies embarking and 8,084 able to walk off. The average mortality rate was 8.50% with only one over 40% and another over 25%. There were two mutinies only on Cuba-bound ships that year.

By 1869, shipments to Cuba were down to twelve, but it was not a good year. One mutiny involved a large loss of life. Three other shipments had a mortality rate in excess of 30%. In all, only 3,852 Chinese disembarked of the 5,027 who were taken on in Macao and Amoy. The mortality rate for the year was 23.37%.

Prospective Polynesian recruitment

The Spanish Royal Decree of 1860 (referred to above) was intended to encourage new entrants to the trade. But the decree seems also to have inspired merchants to seek labour from alternative sources.

The decree seems also to have inspired merchants to seek alternative sources of supply. On 6 September 1860, US Vice Consul General Thomas Savage advised US Secretary of State Lewis Cass that the Governor Captain-General of Cuba had, on 4 September, granted permission to José and Antonio Carbaga and Canet & Gavalena, merchants of

Havana in connection with Charles Burrill of Boston and James C. Jewett of New York, to import 5,000 colonists from the islands of Polynesia, by way of experiment. The regulations to be followed were those in existence for governing the importation of Chinese. While the permission was subject to approval from the supreme government in Madrid, Savage was confident that there would be no obstacle from Her Majesty's government.[116] However, it appears that the Spanish Government did not approve this permission as nothing further has come to light about this application.

Carbaga however did maintain their interest in coolies and in 1865 made just one shipment in conjunction with the Campbell brothers. This was on the 493-ton French barque *Amiral Trehouart*, which left Macao for Havana on 29 November 1865. Captain P. Cotte took 313 Chinese onboard and delivered 280 of them 106 days later.

However, the question of Polynesian immigration remained in the minds of the influential planters, Marcial Dupierris and Augustin,[117] as they made a presentation on 25 February 1863 to the Royal Economic Society of Friends of the Country of Havana, requesting a grant for five years. They praised the superiority of the race of inhabitants of the islands of Oceania, such as Penrhyn. Sugar *refaccionista* Ferran said that they were a race of men far superior to that of the "celestial empire". The request was dismissed by the Commission of Population of the Economic Society, which insisted that the elements of mortality and order were indispensable in all immigration and colonization.[118]

Merino Gilledo y Cia

Joining the trade in 1864, Merino Gilledo operated with the assistance of Castro in Cuba and his agent Virana Garcia in Macao. The three shipments in 1864 were by Spanish ships dedicated to the coolie trade—the *Emigrante* on her fifth voyage, the *Encarnacion* on her fourth and the *Guadaloupe* on her third. The only shipment in 1865 was by the 597-ton Spanish barque *Arizona*, on her second coolie voyage.

Merino Gilledo did not make any shipments in 1866 and their only shipment in 1867 was by the 399-ton French barque *Bangkok*, which sailed from Macao on 1 February 1867 with 233 coolies. Captain E. Chappot had to quell a mutiny, details of which were not released, before disembarking 218 of the coolies after a 113-day voyage. They had been recruited by a little-known agent, A.G. de Ville.

Mariano del Pielago worked for Merino Gilledo in the final two years of the company's participation. Del Pielago was not as well-known as the other emigration agents, making his first shipment on the 495-ton French *Mysore*, which departed from Macao on 20 February 1868 with 294 Chinese.

He was the emigration agent who made the last two coolie shipments from Amoy in 1869. The number of coolies on the 1,076-ton *Macao* was put at only 290, but the *Boletin de Colonizacion* listed 400 as having arrived. The number embarked is unclear but in her previous life as the *Compania Maritima del Peru 2,* and on each of her following three voyages to Callao, the *Macao* embarked 436 coolies. On this basis the number embarked would also have been about 436. With a reported mortality figure of 36, this was in line with those on other Merino Gilledo vessels.

The other voyage in 1869 was undertaken by the 542-ton Spanish barque *Villa de Comillas*. The Dutch barque *Padang Panjang* had been lying in Amoy for some time undergoing repairs, when she was sold by Tait & Co. to a Spanish subject, Don Mariano.[119] She received her papers to sail for Havana as the *Villa de Comillas*. Customs officials refused to grant clearance until a second payment of tonnage dues was paid. The passenger list shows that 290 Chinese were embarked in Amoy on 7 June 1869. This is the same number which Luzon mentions as being on the *Macao*.[120] The *Villa de Comillas* arrived in Havana on 17 November 1869 with 267 Chinese.

Even though foreign recruitment from Amoy had all but ceased, the merchants of Amoy were concerned enough to protest to the British Consul over the exportation of coolies in vessels belonging to non-treaty powers. They were concerned that, while abuses in recruitment was still being carried out, shipments on ships of Treaty nations could be prohibited, whereas those on non-treaty ships could not. In the event, no further coolie shipments were made from Amoy.

Merino Gilledo made only nine shipments, over a period of six years. Of the 2,632 Chinese taken on board, 2,429 were landed. The mortality rate was a creditable 7.71%.

Aldama

Domingo Aldama and his son Miguel Aldama were slave owners who owned sugar mills in Matanzas, east of Havana. In 1864 they decided to import directly for their own account. They employed their own emigration agent in Macao, a Colombian named G. Sagues.

The partnership was very successful. Among 4,176 Chinese embarked overall, the mortality rate was a low 6.87%. The highest mortality rate on the 13 shipments was 17.09%. This was on the 671-ton Portuguese ship, *Donna Maria Pia*, which, departing on 24 March 1866, made a cross-over trip, taking 351 Chinese to Cuba, instead of to Peru, as usual. Captain E.A. da Souza took 144 days on this unfamiliar voyage and as a consequence lost 60 before reaching Havana.

The ship *Bella Gallega* was on her third voyage to Havana with 373 Chinese when she encountered an off-season typhoon soon after leaving Macao on 5 April 1867. She lost her masts but all her passengers were taken safely to Saigon. The men were quickly placed on the French ship *Nouvelle Penelope*, which set sail from Saigon on 17 June 1867 with the 330 survivors from the *Bella Gallega*. She arrived at Havana on 6 October 1867 with 318 Chinese labourers. The *Bella Gallega* had previously been dismasted in 1853, on her first voyage as a coolie ship.

Empresa

This consortium, originally known as the Colonizadora, changed its name to Empresa in 1863.

There was a rather unusual result for the 242-ton French brig *Perseverant*, which left Macao for Cuba on 4 February 1863. Captain Ducit was taking 121 Chinese to Havana on consignment to the Empresa. There were no revolts or riots, but in May, just when she was about to enter the Caribbean, she was struck by an un-seasonal hurricane. Unable to hold her course, the *Perseverant* was wrecked off Barbuda in the Leeward Islands. Most of the coolies managed to struggle ashore. When the surviving 110 coolies were questioned at St John's, the capital of Antigua, they emphatically refused to carry on to Cuba. They were granted permission to stay, becoming the first Chinese labourers to land on that tiny island. They must have been very successful, as the Government of Antigua subsequently requested a shipment of Chinese workers.

There were 16 shipments made by Empresa between 1863 and 1865. Despite the very high losses on two of the Portuguese ships in 1863 (the *Donna Maria de Gloria* and *Vasco de Gama*), the mortality rate for the period averaged 15.20% of the 5,591 Chinese embarked. There were six sailings by French ships and eight by Portuguese ships (including the two previously mentioned). The latter all previously flew the American flag. The Chilean *Mercedes* in 1863 and the Italian *Avon* in 1865 carried the other two shipments.

Reflagged American ships

The US Congress passed "An Act to prohibit the 'Coolie Trade' by American Citizens in American Vessels" in 1862. With the possibility of forfeiture and fines, the last American-flagged ships used were the *Messenger* to Cuba in 1861 and the *Marion* to Peru in 1862.

The American Civil War started in April 1861 and lasted until May 1865. Faced with the possibility of being lost to Confederate forces, and strong competition from iron steamships, which were being built in great numbers, American wooden ships, including the fast clipper ships, were being sold off to foreign buyers as quickly as possible.

In 1863 eight American ships changed their flag in Macao. Five of the six that became Portuguese vessels then sailed for Cuba. The sixth sailed for Peru along with two which had been reflagged to Peru. Another five American ships arrived in Macao to be sold in 1864. One was reflagged to Portugal and sailed for Cuba while the other four took on Peruvian registry and were placed in the Peruvian trade.

On 16 August 1863, Captain Jordan of the American ship *Fanny Fern* dropped anchor in Macao.—The *Fanny Fern* was originally a 594-ton ship built at New Ireland, Maine in 1854.—In Macao she was bought by Filomena M. de Garcia and renamed the *Luisita*. She was remeasured at 685 tons, which allowed her to take on 343 coolies when she sailed on 30 October 1863. She had taken 75 days to load the men. Captain Jordan remained unofficially in command, but it was the Portuguese national Joao A. Nunez who signed the necessary documents. After the 114-day voyage, 283 disembarked at Havana, a mortality rate of 17.49%. Her eventual true owners are not clear, as she was still listed as *Luisita* in 1865, Liverpool then being given as her home port.

The American 848-ton *Julia G. Tyler* arrived at Macao from Hong Kong on 3 September 1863. She maintained her tonnage on remeasurement, and sailed as the *Camoes* with 418 Chinese on 2 November 1863. The men had been held in barracoons for up to 60 days.

On 7 January 1864, the Port Captain at Cape Town reported that the Portuguese ship *Camoes* had just arrived. The captain (Captain Cooper), the officers and crew were mostly the same as when she had been there before. As the ship had been placed under Portuguese colours, a nominal master (J.V. Marques) appeared before the Portuguese consul to sign papers, etc.

The American ships arrived in Macao just as cholera had taken hold in the Portuguese colony. In the 18 November 1863 issue of *The Times* of London, a quarantine notice in the Ship News section advised, from Lisbon, that on 6 November 1863 the Board of Health declared Macao free from cholera morbus, along with the ports of Hong Kong, Canton, Amoy, and Foochowfoo.

The epidemic was waning when the *Alfonso d'Albuquerque* (formerly the *Carrington*) departed on 11 December 1863. She still suffered a loss of 13.87%, but losses on the *Don Fernando* (formerly the *Independence*), which had left on 3 January 1864 had dropped to 3.46%. These two percentages may however have been an anomaly, as another ex-American ship, the *Versailles*, renamed *Perseverancia*, recorded a loss of 32.25% on her voyage to Callao. She had left three days earlier and took only two more days for the longer journey. This was despite having to divert to Mauritius, not normally a port of call.

Lombillo

Gabriel Lombillo was a founding partner of the Empresa, but by 1866 had begun importing Chinese labour on his own account in conjunction with Montalvo. The first five shipments by Lombillo in 1866 were by one Spanish and four Portuguese ships; all achieved with no disruptions and mortality rates below ten percent.

The shortage of properly-trained men to captain Portuguese vessels was again highlighted in 1868.[121] The *Nina* was once the American *Spirit of the Times*. She sailed from Macao on 2 November 1866 with a cargo of 549 Chinese bound for Havana. She arrived on 10 March 1867 and landed 510 men. C.J. Sequeira was the nominated captain who was to be relieved in Havana by Charles la Blanche, a British subject. He had been engaged to take the *Nina* from Havana to Glasgow and then on to Hong Kong, Macao and back to Havana. His reward was to be £18 per month and 10 shillings for every coolie landed in Havana. Under Portuguese law, he was not permitted to command the Portuguese-flagged ship, and so a nominal captain, F.D.P. Almeida, was engaged for that position. La Blanche was to sign on as piloto or mate, but was in reality expected to command the vessel with entire control. Shortly after leaving Havana, a dispute arose between the two men. Blanche left the ship in Glasgow, and lodged a claim for £324 for wages and £285 for bonus expected from the proposed 570 coolies to be taken on. The claim was disputed and the ship was arrested then released, with costs awarded against Blanche. It was re-arrested in Cardiff, and again Blanche lost. He was again ordered to pay costs. The *Nina* was the second ship chartered for Lombillo Montalvo and did not return to Macao.

Alianza

When the Empresa merged with La Compania de Seguros y Creditos to form La Alianza y Cia the business of importation of Chinese coolies changed from one financed by merchant creditors to one of plantation capitalists in their own right.[122] Alianza easily became the major importer of Chinese labour, but not all planters were in Alianza.

Alianza recruited the large number of 23,508 Chinese coolies and suffered an average loss of 10.40% over the 55 shipments they made between 1865 and 1873. Calderon was their agent until the end of the 1867-1868 season when Tuton took over the agency.

French ships conducted all five shipments for Alianza in 1865. Averaging 121 days for the voyage, 1,312 Chinese were landed from the 1,372 taken on board in Macao. The average mortality for the year was 4.37%.

With the high mortality rate on auxiliary steamships, it was not until 1866 that another attempt was made to utilise them. On 12 May 1866 the 1,300-ton steamer *Cataluna*, under Spanish colours and Captain M.L. Vaello, sailed from Macao with 473 Chinese for Alianza to begin the regular transportation of coolies by steamer for Havana. By then, technology had progressed such that steam engines were the prime form of propulsion; with sails used only when the engines failed, or to supplement the engines.

Captain V. Escajadillo took command of the *Cataluna* in June 1867. He had to abort the voyage and return to Hong Kong with a fouled hull. She sailed again on 5 July 1867 but not without controversy as it had been claimed that several Annamites had been kidnapped and placed on board without proper authorisation. On her five voyages to Havana between 1866 and 1871, the *Cataluna* embarked 2,532 Chinese passengers and landed 2,296 of them, suffering a mortality rate of 9.32%.

High mortality concerns

There were 14 shipments between 1863 and 1869, with mortality rates above 20%. The *Bilbaina* shipment for Troncoso and the three shipments on Caro vessels have previously been mentioned. High mortality losses were suffered on three Empresa and also on three Alianza voyages. Lombillo however suffered high losses on four of their voyages.

The 570-ton *Sarah Chase* dropped anchor in Macao from Hong Kong on 12 September 1863. Captain E. Evans was there to hand over command and see his ship being reflagged and remeasured. As the 592-ton *Donna Maria de Gloria*, she loaded 296 coolies after 48 days and set sail on 30 October along with the *Luisita*. However, she took 45 days longer to reach Havana, which would account for her horrific loss of 143 men. The mortality rate was 48.31%.

The fourth American ship to arrive from Hong Kong at Macao in 1863 was the 1,001-ton *Parliament*. After a 39-day wait for her coolies, she was renamed *Vasco de Gama*, remeasured at 1016 tons, and took on 508 on 15 November 1863. Captain A.A. McCaslin had officially handed over to José da Silva, but remained on board. Despite the shorter 109-day voyage, the death rate on arrival was 39.96%. Like the *Luisita*, the *Vasco de Gama* had her home port changed to Liverpool, and continued to trade elsewhere. She was still in the American Lloyds Register in 1871.

The third shipment, which departed on 23 February 1865 was on the *Camoes*, previously mentioned, with a loss of 26.08% on her second voyage.

For Alianza, the Spanish *JAU* had a mortality rate of 23.22% in 1866. The *Antares*, making her first voyage as a coolie ship, suffered a loss 25.86% in 1868. In 1869, the *Italia*, on her second voyage as a coolie ship, lost 30.77%. After a journey of 129 days, Captain Raymundo de Zulueta was able to see only 360 of the original 520 coolies walk off. The mortality rate amounted to 30.77%.

The 1,345-ton French ship *Carmeline* left Macao on her second voyage to Havana under Captain C. Gallet on 7 November 1867 with 653 Chinese. All was well until she met a storm in the Indian Ocean. In circumstances similar to those experienced by the *Maggie Miller* she became dismasted and eventually made it to Mauritius on 9 January 1868. Captain Gallet needed more than five months to have repairs effected and it was until 5 June 1868 that the *Carmeline* was able to proceed with a greatly depleted complement. When the *Carmeline* eventually reached Havana, only 344 Chinese were landed. Her mortality rate was 47.32%.

The average mortality rate for the twenty-three Lombillo shipments amounted to 12.97%. However, four of these shipments incurred mortality rates in excess of 25%. The lowest was a shipment on the 1868 voyage of the *Maria Morton* during which she lost 57 of the original 215 Chinese taken on board in Macao. This 26.51% mortality followed a 40.03% loss on the *Dolores Ugarte* departing Macao a month earlier. The 13 April 1869 departure from Macao by the *Nelly* resulted in a mortality rate of 61.49% with only 171 Chinese landed from an original complement of 444. The following sailing on 2 May however was a little better at 31.65%. Lombillo made no further shipments after that.

The 848-ton French *Nelly* commenced her second voyage on 13 April 1868 with 444 Chinese for Lombillo. Captain J. Poilbout was unable to keep the mortality rate below 61.49%, with 273 of the 444 men embarked dying on this extremely long 192-day voyage. Another French ship, the 1,006-ton *Mongol* left Macao on 2 May 1869 with 496 Chinese, also for Lombillo. This time the voyage was only a little shorter, taking 160 days, and Captain L. Courbe managed to produce only 339 men on arrival. The mortality rate was 31.65%.

The clipper ship *Dolores Ugarte* was on her first charter to Cuba for Lombillo having already undertaken two voyages to Peru. Captain José Peres Saul took the 1,283-ton now-Salvadorian ship from Macao on 28 October 1868 with 602 coolies on board. On arrival at Havana 116 days later, only 361 were disembarked. The mortality rate was 40.03%. On her return voyage to China, she was driven ashore on 19 May 1869, six miles SE of Riding Rocks, Bahamas. She was assisted off and Captain Saul continued on the voyage.

Macao barracoons

On 1 November 1866, British vice-consul William S. Frederick Mayers in Canton reported to Sir Rutherford Alcock (now the British Minister Plenipotentiary in China)[123] that the decline in the African Slave Trade had led to a greatly increased demand for Chinese coolies in Cuba, such that it had become known that no fewer than 80,000 Chinese coolies would be required in the 1866-67 shipping season. The immediate result had been a large influx to Macao of speculators of various nationalities. The number of barracoons had risen from six or eight the previous season to between thirty-five and forty in 1866.

Mayers told of the practice of shipping coolies on the daily river-steamers running from Canton to Macao and explained that coolies were collected in the barracoons by various speculators[124] until bids were made for them by the agents of companies despatching vessels to Havana. The price per head paid fluctuated with demand. Each barracoon keeper replenished his stock by means of brokers or crimps; but the latter were abusing their legalised status by practising abuses, such as kidnapping and fraud.[125]

A long article in the *Daily Press* of 29 October 1866 further explains the process. On the daily steamer from Canton to Macao, there were always groups of deluded men loosely huddled together under the watchful eye of a crimp. On the Purser going around to collect the fare, they would not be able to produce the 50 cash and so would be confined in the lower hold with the threat of being taken back to Canton. On arrival at Macao, there was always a cluster of boats to meet the steamer. Manned by Chinese and Portuguese brokers, they were prepared to pay the penalty fare of two dollars to secure the release of the men into their care.

In a memorandum, "System of Inspection of Coolies at Macao",[126] British West Indian Emigration Agent, Mr Sampson, told of his experiences on one of the ferries. On arrival, the 20 or 30 coolies on board were handled, just as sheep might be discharged from a vessel. They were grabbed by the shoulders and lowered down until taken by the men in the boats waiting to take them to the barracoons. All looked forlorn and dejected as if knowing that they were now the property of someone else; hopeless resignation and callous indifference seemed to have full possession of them.

Sampson went on to say that he had witnessed the first stage of official surveillance in Macao. From the barracoons, the coolies were taken before the Portuguese officials to have the contract explained to them. After some days they were again taken before the same officials in order to sign the contracts. They were securely escorted on both journeys. At the first appearance about 50 coolies in six or seven batches belonging to different owners, were placed two or three deep before a railing, each batch supervised by a barracoon employee and roughly handled into position. The Portuguese official who explained the contract appeared to speak different Chinese dialects "with facility" and certainly spoke Cantonese "admirably". He harangued the coolies at length, explicitly explaining that they were going away for eight years and would be paid $4 a month. The $8 advance they would receive would be deducted from their wages, and at the end of the contract, they would be free to remain or depart as they chose. He repeatedly invited them to say if any person had brought them there by force or fraud, then finally asked each coolie individually if he was willing to go or not.

The barracoons of Macao had only limited capacity to hold men awaiting the ships. It was therefore a common practice for the men there to be presented to the Portuguese officials and then taken on board in batches of about fifty. The *America* had accommodation for 700 men, and received her first fifty within a week of her arrival, but took 69 days to complete her complement. A pattern soon developed where consignments were normally made on Wednesdays and Saturdays, but always dependent on the number of recruits available.

After visiting a barracoon in Macao, which Aldus thought looked like a, "large, commodious, county-jail-looking structure",[127] he saw two companies of men preparing for embarkation under the watchful eye of Europeans. After marching down to the jetty, they were put on to junks for conveyance to the ship, some four miles distant. As soon as the junk was moored, they were unceremoniously walked, or dragged, on board, some resisting while others cried. Those who refused to move were simply hoisted on like common merchandise.

On deck, the men, each with a small piece of small bamboo bearing his bed space number hanging around his neck, were stripped and examined for physical defects, while their little boxes of personal goods were critically examined for opium and weapons. On completion of the examination, the interpreter and coolie master introduced them to their respective bed spaces.

In his report to Alcock, already mentioned, Mayers would merely have repeated the greatly exaggerated numbers required as reported in the local newspapers. The number of barracoons opening as a consequence, as stated in this study, are based on conjecture. A statistical report on the occupations of Chinese in Macao showed that, as at 14 June 1867, there were 163 employees working in 17 "estabelecimentos de emigracao chineza".[128] The number of broker licences issued in 1865 was thirty-two. In 1866 the number had jumped to 90, but then fell back to 41 in 1867 and just 17 in 1868.

Peak years

In the 1865-1866 season from September to June there were 55 sailings for Peru and Cuba. The numbers taken on board were 19,575. The peak month was March 1866 with eleven sailings taking a total of 3,606 emigrants. The average time taken by these vessels to gather their complements was now 62 days. The greatest delays occurred the following month, when the average time extended to 80 days.

In the 1866-1867 season up to June 1867, 47 vessels took 17,586 Chinese emigrants. There were eight sailings to Cuba in October 1866, with seven to Cuba and one to Peru in December 1866. The December ships took an average of 108 days to gather their complements. This was at the beginning of a lengthy period, during which ships had to wait an average of 119 days in March 1867.

The strong demand from Cuba importers would have resulted in premium prices being paid for their 41 shipments of Chinese coolies in the peak season. Three Peruvian shipments only were made in the peak months and another three in what would be considered the off-season of May and June. At least two of these shipments did not head south, but instead used the alternate route, passing the Sandwich Islands and down the California coast.

Mutinies

The 357-ton *Emmanuel*, departing from Macao on 4 March 1865, under Captain L. de Condray, suffered a mutiny on her 130-day voyage and recorded a loss of just on 10%. Details of the mutiny were not made available. The mutiny on the *Bangkok* has already been mentioned above. There was also another mutiny, reported on the first voyage of the *Nelly*, which sailed from Macao on 29 November 1867. Again, no details were published. After 109 days Captain Poilbout was still able to land all but fifteen of the 444 men he had taken on board for Lombillo.

An unusual sequel to a mutiny occurred on the only Portuguese ship used by the Alianza consortium, *Josefita y Almira*. She sailed from Macao on 24 January 1866 with 537 coolies bound for Havana. (Prior to her first voyage in 1864, she had been the British ship, *Abissinian*.) As was the practice with ships changing to the Portuguese flag, the British captain, Richard Lee, remained on board as supercargo and navigator, but the Portuguese national, Valerio A Remedios, was the official captain in charge.

On this, her second voyage, when off Java on 8 February 1866, the Chinese seized knives from the kitchen and advanced to the cabin to capture weapons. The mutiny was suppressed by the crew. Two Chinese jumped into the sea, and another died from injuries, and eleven ringleaders were shackled. On arrival at Batavia, the crew accused Captain Remedios of not fulfilling his obligations, and demanded that he be replaced, claiming that he did not attempt to subdue the revolt even though he was well conversant with the Chinese language. On enquiry and receiving written petitions from the crew, the Port Captain at Batavia agreed to the captain being relieved in favour of Chief Mate Antonio Ribeiro. The *Josefita y Almira* arrived at Havana on 20 May 1866. Only fourteen did not survive the voyage (including the three mentioned earlier), 523 landing safely.

On 7 October 1866, the French barque *Eugene et Adele* left Macao bound for Havana with 466 coolies consigned to Alianza. Two days out, the coolies mutinied. Captain J. Giraud was killed and the chief mate severely wounded, as were many of the 24-man crew. The great bravery of the crew led to thirteen of the coolies being killed and many others wounded. The ship put into Saigon on 15 October where the chief mate and wounded sailors were sent to hospital. One of the ringleaders was shot by the French authorities.[129] The French Consul arranged for a temporary captain, subject to an officer of the Imperial Navy, who also sailed on to Havana. *Eugene et Adele* arrived in Havana on 26 March 1867 with 376 able to walk ashore.

The 937-ton French ship *Orixa* faced a revolt on Sunday, 1 December 1867, when preparing to depart from Macao. That afternoon the rebels attacked the crew with knives and wooden sticks. In the ensuing repulsion, five of the Chinese were killed and several crew wounded. These attempted mutinies prompted suspicion of a plot to have bogus emigrants board the ships with the intention of forcing the abortion of the voyages. Mr Marques, the British Consular Agent, reported that the outbreak originated with some Chinese who had been induced to go on board the vessel to make up the numbers the broker was bound to furnish to a barracoon by a certain date, being told that they would be replaced by voluntary men after some days. When the ship sailed, the men grew desperate and revolted. The *Orixa* eventually sailed under Captain A. Guiraud on 17 December 1867 with 556 Chinese bound for Havana.

On 5 January 1868, the 397-ton French ship *Esperance* left Macao under the command of her owner Captain E. Boju with 300 Chinese bound for Havana, again for Alianza. Fifteen days out a sudden strengthening of the winds was so intense that the crew was not able to reduce sail quickly enough. The captain then called upon 50 of his passengers to assist in the shortening of sail. But instead of assisting, they rushed the cabin to capture arms while the crew was aloft. The captain who was at the wheel saw this and called his crew down as he rushed the mutineers with a cutlass. He was severely wounded but was saved by his men who after a long fight managed to subdue the mutineers. Their leader was killed and thrown overboard. Captain Boju was so wounded that he was left at Anjer and the *Esperance* continued on to Cape Town under acting captain Noel. She arrived there on 25 March, departing on the 28th after taking on provisions. *Esperance* arrived at Havana on 31 May 1868 with 279 survivors of the voyage.

Yet another mutiny was reported on the 615-ton French ship *Lucie*, which left Macao on 8 December 1868. Again, no details were provided. She arrived after 123 days with 327 of her original complement of 360 consigned to Alianza.

The 545-ton French barque *Tamaris* left Macao on 7 February 1869 under Captain Phillipe Raunie for Havana with 300 coolies. On 9 February, the captain was warned that something mutinous was going on among the Chinese coolies, and he maintained a watch throughout the night. Next morning 15 of them were brought on deck and the ringleader given 18 strokes and his assistants 12 each. On 20 February, the chief mate, Lecoeur, was caught gambling with the coolies, and soon after, the supercargo was found selling them necessaries, which they were entitled to receive freely. The chief mate was found sleeping on watch and was logged. Coolies were dying each day. The last entry in the log was on 8 March. What happened next is unknown, but it appears that, for whatever reason, the captain and crew decided to abandon the ship on that day, render the rudder unserviceable and leave the Chinese to their fate. When the captain had second thoughts, the crew simply rowed off and left him to jump overboard to reach the boats. He was thrown a piece of wood, but he did not make the boats. The crew reached Batavia on 22 March, and on hearing their story, the Director of the Marine Department despatched two ships to look for the *Tamaris*. The Dutch naval ship *Borneo* eventually found the ship at Padang on 8 April, when, on boarding, the captain found 269 Chinese still on board. On 24 April, two officers and sixteen of the original crew were taken to Padang to rejoin the *Tamaris*. She eventually arrived at Havana on 6 November 1869, but with only 68 survivors. In commenting on this figure, the *Chicago Tribune*, in its report of 21 November 1869, attributed the high loss of lives to the coolies committing suicide by cutting their throats or by jumping overboard. The consignees were not identified.

The 624-ton Austrian barque *Niemen* sailed for Havana on 8 February 1867 with 410 Chinese. Her recruits were provided by little-known agents, Bowen y Yngram, for a one-time importer, F.D. Drain. Built in Nantes in 1859, *Niemen* first appeared on the Hong Kong Register as a ship, but two years later had her registration amended as she had been re-rigged to that of a barque. Later that year her port of registration was recorded as Trieste, and flying the Austrian flag.

As the coolies were mutinous, Captain N.W. Beckwith armed his crew, killing three and severely wounding several more. On being driven below, they set fire to the ship. Captain Beckwith poured water down the ventilators, raising so much steam that the coolies themselves had to extinguish the flames.[130]

Russian-flagged ships

In 1865 a Russian national, William Rudolf Landstein (1840-81), was a partner in the firm of Landstein and Co. of Stanley Street in Hong Kong. Landstein had been born in Warsaw of Jewish parents. The Italian Consul in Macao identified him as being a first grade merchant resident who had been buying ships and obtaining temporary certificates from the Russian Consul before despatching them to Macao where they took on coolies for various ports in South America.[131]

The first was the Troncoso-chartered 571-ton barque *Sovinto* which left Macao for Havana with 317 Chinese on 4 January 1866. The next, in October, was the *Suomi*, a 942-ton ship built in Lovisa, Finland, in 1856. She made two voyages to Cuba for Alianza as a Russian ship under Captain C.V. Nordberg with no incidents.

Built in Glasgow, the 462-ton ship *Falcon* was registered in Hong Kong. In 1865 her flag was changed to that of Peru for one voyage to Callao. She reverted to the Hong Kong Register on her return to Hong Kong and in 1866 was once again re-flagged. This time regular British Captain Mortimer O. Sullivan had to raise the Russian flag for her voyage from Macao on 18 October 1866. With 259 coolies consigned to Empresa he took 115 days to deliver 250 in Havana.

The 1,086-ton ship *Avon* was the American built *Cyclone*, sold off as a consequence of the American Civil War. She became a Hong Kong-based British ship in 1864, but almost immediately became an Italian vessel, taking 543 men to Havana on 24 January 1865.

The *Avon* changed her flag to Russia before proceeding to Macao, when on 16 November 1866, British captain Warwick took on 551 Chinese bound for Havana. Two days later the British gunboat *Opossum* left harbour to render assistance to a coolie ship off Aberdeen on the south coast of Hong Kong. HMS *Salamis* also went to the rescue and found the *Avon* at anchor off Lamma Island. It was claimed that intelligence had been received that the coolies had risen against the crew, but that was disputed by the captain.

The *Avon* was taken in tow and taken to Green Island where she was boarded and asked for her papers. But they had been taken ashore by her owners who had boarded in the meantime. Unable to provide papers, the Russian flag was torn down driving the captain into a rage, and the ship was towed further into Hong Kong harbour. There it was alleged that kidnapped children had been placed on board and that they had not signed any contracts.

The *Avon* returned to Macao on 23 November 1866, but with only 537 on board. No explanation was given as to the fourteen missing persons. Representations from Hong Kong barristers to the Attorney General in Macao elicited a promise to look into the matter, but in the event, he was not permitted to do so by the Governor who caused a Notice to be printed in

O Boletim do Governo on 26 November, declaring that such an investigation was to be conducted by the relevant authorities. Governor Horta pointedly told the Hong Kong delegation that his officers were quite capable of conducting their own enquiries and there was no need for interference from people of high office in Hong Kong.

The investigation committee determined that proper procedures had been followed and that the nine children were of legal age and understood the contracts. Nevertheless, together with twenty-four others, they were taken off the ship before she sailed again for Havana on 5 December 1866. But this time she had only 502 Chinese on board. In Macao, Captain Warwick was replaced by E. de Vildosola. The sequel to this episode came a few days later when the Portuguese gunboat *Camoes* delivered twenty-four children off the *Avon* to the Chief Mandarin of Canton. The *Avon* went on to make another voyage in 1868 without incident.

In among this turmoil was the 635-ton *Glenlee*, another American-built ship sold off as a consequence of the American Civil War. She made one uneventful voyage for Caro on 4 December 1866, but subsequently changed her name to *Vistula* with a new measurement of 733 tons. She retained her Russian identity, however. *Vistula* made one voyage to Cuba in 1869 for Alianza and one to Peru in 1870.

The 1,142-ton *Neva* under Captain J.D. Onate was to undertake two voyages to Havana in 1869 and 1870 both without incident. But then confusion arose when a new 1,626-ton *Neva* made one voyage to Callao on 28 February 1871. This new *Neva* was originally the American *Francis A. Palmer*, built in Brooklyn in 1854 and registered in New York. From 1867 her new owner was James A. Duck of Liverpool. In 1869 she changed to the Salvador flag for two voyages, carrying fare paying passengers from Hong Kong to San Francisco in 1869 and 1870.

The last Russian ship used in the coolie trades was the *Naples* which made a single voyage to Havana on 11 October 1871. She was possibly the 926-ton American ship of the same name but there is no record of her changing her flag.

Challenge, New York Clipper Ship.
She made a journey from Swatow to Havana in 1857.
Library of Congress.

10

The Final Years

In the final five years of the Chinese coolie trade no fewer than 102 shipments, with 47,564 Chinese taken on board, were made to Peru, all but one from Macao. Thirty-eight shipments carried 19,740 Chinese to Cuba. There were six mutinies, four on ships bound for Peru and two for Cuba.

On 10 October 1868 what became known as the Ten Years' War began in Cuba. Many landowners and slave owners freed their slaves and fought along with Spanish troops. Freed slaves fought on both sides, and many disgruntled Chinese sided with the revolutionaries. With the prospect of prolonged uncertainty because of the struggle, the sugar estates began reducing their labour programmes.

Cuban Decree to suspend immigration

In 1870 imports of Chinese labourers fell to fewer than 2,000, but this reduction was not enough to appease the Governor of Cuba. On 27 April 1871, the Spanish Minister for the Colonies, Lopez de Ayala, wrote to the Superior Civil Governor of Cuba agreeing to his second request to prohibit the further importation of Chinese on the grounds that they did not fulfil their obligations, infringed the laws of hospitality, disturbed public order, resisted with the enemies of the nation and kept the interest and tranquillity of the island in constant alarm.

Taking all things into account, King Amadeo invoked Article 81 of the Royal Decree of 1860 and suspended the introduction of Chinese labourers eight months from the publication of the notice in the Havana Gazette. The trade was abolished in 1871, however imports were allowed until 1874.[132]

Last Cuban shipments

Alianza was the only importer in 1870 and had only two departures. The first was on the 1,142-ton Russian ship *Neva* which commenced her second voyage on 6 January with 537 Chinese on board. There were only three casualties on the 121-day voyage, with Captain J.D. Onate happily landing the remaining 534.

The 1,069-ton Italian-registered ship *Italia* under Captain A.V.Vidaurrazaga left Macao on 19 March 1870 with 527 Chinese emigrants bound for Havana. After a long passage down the South China Sea, she arrived at Anjer on 18 April to take on water and provisions. But she anchored too close to shore, where the bottom was chiefly of coral. She had intended sailing on the 20th, but strong currents and winds prevented her from doing so. The next day a gale parted her cable and she was driven on to rocks. Despite heroic efforts by the European and local populations, they were unable to save the ship. A line was taken to the *Italia* by which most of the passengers and all the crew were rescued.

Captain W.P. de Jong was the pilot at Anjer and was instrumental in the saving of so many lives. Not until the *New Batavia Handelsblad* published a letter of appreciation from Captain Vidaurrazaga of the *Italia* in 1872, did his heroic efforts become public.[133] In the letter, Captain Vidaurrazaga praised the 65 year-old pilot for his tireless efforts, which he continued until he was totally exhausted. When finally forced to leave the ship, he did so by way of the mizzen boom, together with his dog. Captain de Jong fell into the water and his faithful dog saved him. Vidaurrazaga called for full recognition of the old man.

In all, 474 Chinese were taken off, leaving 49 lost. The survivors were taken to Batavia. Alianza immediately looked for another ship to take the Cuban consignees on to Havana. On 9 November, the French ship *Esperance*, now with owner Captain Boju back in charge, embarked 248 of the rescued Chinese from Batavia on to Havana. She arrived at the Mariel quarantine station on 18 February 1871, only 162 surviving the voyage. Three more died at the quarantine station before the *Esperance* docked in Havana on 20 February 1871.

The Suez Canal was opened on 17 November 1869, one week after the *Cataluna* sailed from Macao on a fourth voyage which took 125 days. It was not until 1871 that the *Cataluna* sailed for Cuba by way of the Suez Canal. This fifth voyage took the auxiliary steamer 99 days. However it was not as fast as the second voyage in 1867 which took just 91 days via the Cape of Good Hope.

Alianza required eight ships to carry the 3,347 Chinese whom Tuton had recruited for them in 1871. A total of 142 died on these voyages. The 496-ton French barque *Papillon* was the only ship making her first voyage in the trade. The seven others had made previous voyages, six in their own names. The seventh was the Russian *Neva*, on her second voyage, but now reflagged as the 1,652-ton Spanish ship *China*.

Alianza was joined by two new entrants in 1871, following the announcement that Article 31 of the 1860 Decree invoking suspension of Chinese labourers would soon come into effect. Francisco Ibanez immediately commenced operation in conjunction with Emigration Agent Francisco Abella y Raldiris in Macao in 1871. That same year, La Compania de Hacendados was formed with the intention of providing an alternative to la Alianza. It seems strange that, though Emigration Agent Armero, who had recruited so many Chinese for Cuban patrons, was in Macao at the time, Hacendados chose to employ Emigration Agent Tuton, who already represented Alianza.

There were no incidents on the three Hacendados sailings in 1871, but the 926-ton Russian ship *Naples* did suffer a mortality loss of 16.44%. Among the ships which Tuton chartered, the *Concepcion* was under the command of a family member, Captain Modesto Tuton. Hacendados shipped 1,317 Chinese with 1,214 disembarking that year.

The four other sailings to Cuba in 1871 were for Ibanez. Abella was the recruiting agent for these departures, on which 1,042 men were shipped, 979 of them being able to walk off after voyages which averaged 128 days. The Ibanez barques averaged half the size of the Hacendados vessels.

During the final two years of Chinese indentured labour shipments to Cuba, 21 vessels took on 12,970 men, leaving 11,824 of them at Havana. There were reports of women being on those vessels, but exact numbers were not reported. Alianza ended their shipments with six departures. Two had high mortality rates. The *Altagracia* on her fifth voyage suffered a loss of 28.53%; the auxiliary steamer *Alexandre Lavalley* on her second had a loss of 24.76%. The 725-ton Spanish ship *Maria* on her only voyage with coolies lost 17.19%, and the *Anduizas* lost just 17 men of 367 taken on board.

Hacendados made the final shipment of 510 Chinese coolies from Whampoa on the 1,880-ton Spanish ship *Salvadora*, which sailed on 27 January 1872. It was a 107-day voyage for Captain D. de Homachea and 499 healthy persons were disembarked. Hacendados had seven other shipments making the final recruitment of 4,742 coolies. The number disembarked was 4,470 giving a mortality rate of 5.74%. This result is distorted by the 28.42% mortality suffered on the 654-ton Spanish *Rosa del Turia*. Captain D.F. Vines had taken 387 on board on 27 March 1872 and lost 110 on the 136-day voyage.

Alexandre Lavalley was a 1,517-ton auxiliary screw 500hp steamer, rigged as a barque, built in 1870 in Nantes. Her dimensions were 245ft in length, with a 33 foot beam and 19 foot depth. She sailed on January 1872 losing only 18 men on a 77-day voyage via the Suez Canal.

Alexandre Lavalley was born in 1821 of Russian parents. Educated in France he became a mechanical engineer working on the construction of railways and bridges. He was recruited by Fredinand de Lesseps to construct the Suez Canal. He is credited with having done this on time and under budget.

Yrurac Bat was a 1,494-ton steamer built in 1871 in Sunderland, England. She was 287ft long with a 35ft beam and 23ft depth. Captain M. Balligui lost 27 of the 906 men embarked, a mortality rate of 2.98%, on her 104-day voyage.

Amboto was also built in Sunderland, in 1872. She was 260ft long with a 33ft beam and 19ft depth. On this her second voyage Captain L. Ansuatique took on board 905 coolies losing 6.85% of them on a 92-day voyage.

Glensannox and her sister the *Glendarroch* were the first steamships to be built in 1870 by Alexander Stephen & Sons at a new facility at Linthouse, Scotland. They were iron screw steamers of the following dimensions: 265ft. length by 33ft. beam by 24ft. 6 ins. from spar deck to top of floors, with a gross tonnage of 1,509 for the *Glendarroch* and 1,500 for the *Glensannox*. They were flush-decked fore and aft with a clipper bow, fully rigged with two masts, yards and sails.

The accommodation was similar to that of the sailing-ships, with captain and passengers below the spar deck aft, and in cabins on each side of a central saloon. The engineers and officers were berthed amidships, and the crew in the forecastle below the spar deck forward.

They had three cargo holds served by steam winches working the wooden booms, and her machinery was amidships, with one compound engine and two double-ended cylindrical boilers, and a small donkey boiler.[134]

In a last desperate attempt to recruit as many as possible the consortium chartered the large 1,776-ton Belgian steamer *Nelusko* to take on 1,099 men on 21 October 1873.

Nelusko also was launched at the Alexander Stephen yard at Linthouse, Scotland, on 3 December 1872, and delivered on 1 January 1873. Her dimensions were 97.5m long, with a 11.0m beam and a depth of 8.23m. She was a one-cylinder 250/900hp iron screw steamer rigged as a barque. Despite her being a steamer, Captain F. van der Heyden took 88 days before discharging 1,055 of his complement.

This low mortality rate of 4.00% had been bettered the previous year by another steamer, the 1,479-ton Spanish *Buenaventura*. Veteran Captain Juan B. Echevarria took only 79 days to land 843 of the 864 he had taken on board on 30 October 1872. The mortality rate was 2.43%.

Importer Ibanez would have been relieved to see the end of Chinese emigration. Five of his last six sailings were marred by controversy, including the indignity of one of them being the last Chinese shipment to arrive, 320 days after being placed on board.

Spain had officially stopped the importation of Chinese labourers in 1871, but the last shipment did not actually arrive in Cuba until 4 March 1874 when the unreliable steamer *Rosita y Nene* finally arrived after a 320-day voyage. First registered as the British-flagged *John Bright,* this 1268-ton steamer was sold "foreign", but then brought back in May 1871 and renamed *Venus.*

In May 1872, she was sold again, with her new Spanish owners renaming her *Rosita y Nene.* She arrived at Macao on 14 July and sailed on 11 August 1872 with 725 Chinese and two children for Havana. She was not long on her voyage when Captain E. Alcantara had to put back to Macao with boiler failure. When these repairs were found to be extensive, Francisco Abella transferred her passengers to the other ship he was loading, the *Fatchoy,* while the *Rosita y Nene* headed to Hong Kong for repairs on 27 August.

The *Rosita y Nene* returned to Macao on 23 March 1873, but had to return to Hong Kong once again on 1 April. She arrived back in Macao on 12 April and finally sailed for Havana on 18 April 1873, with 850 men and one child. Still beset with problems, the *Rosita y Nene* called at each of Cape Town, Rio de Janerio, and Puerto Rico, before finally arriving at Havana on 4 March 1874. She had a loss of 126 men, mainly from smallpox. The voyage took 320 days. It was also the last vessel to arrive from China. In the three years during which Ibanez was in the trade, he shipped 4,873 Chinese and received 4,409 of them. His success rate was 90.48%.

In 1873, despite the strong competition from Alianza, Hacendados and Ibanez, a small company, J. Prats y Cia became the last small importer of coolies from China. With no established contacts in Macao, the company appointed ex-captain Aurelio Olano, at that time an emigration agent for Peru, to recruit Chinese labourers.

The ship used was the 1,743-ton British steamer *Cailes,* was had been built in Newcastle in 1864. She had been sold to Spanish interests in 1872, renamed *Juan* and remeasured at

1228 tons. She arrived at Macao from Hong Kong on 24 May 1873, then sailed on 22 June 1873 for Havana. But the *Juan* got only as far as 60 miles off the Ladrones when she had to return to Macao, arriving back on 25 June, with a fouled hull, still with the 867 labourers and six children she left with. Disembarking her human cargo, she then left for Hong Kong for cleaning, and returned toMacao on 14 July to reload her coolies.

She sailed from Macao again on 20 July 1873 with only 657 of the original complement but still with the six children, arriving in Havana on 18 November with 602 coolies.

It would appear that Olano had had great difficulty in fulfilling this shipment. For, in the 1873 Macao list of departures, the *Juan* is shown to have 657 who actually left, 383 who were repatriated before the ship left, 127 who were returned to their parents and 447 who either stayed on in Macao or returned their deposits.

Perils of the sea

In his Annual Review for 1871, Hong Kong Harbour Master Thomsett reported that emigration from Macao had attained such unenviable notoriety that the captain (and owner) of the Belgian ship *Frederic* thought to try the experiment of despatching from Hong Kong to see if a system could be organised free from censure. A draft contract was submitted, and after some alteration, was approved by the Hong Kong Government.—It prohibited the employment of the labourers in the working of guano.—Two depots were opened at West Point where 200 were quickly medically-examined and registered. However, this progress did not last long, as many, after feasting on good food and lodging, left to seek employment elsewhere, or were inveigled by small advances and promises of a better contract in Macao.

The *Frederic*, now of 812 tons, and her owner, Captain A. Nicaise, were on their third voyage carrying coolies. On her previous two voyages she was known as the *Leopold Cateaux*. The *Frederic* did not get her complement until the first week in January, finally sailing on 15 January 1870 with 382 men after having had 762 originally registered. It appears that it was expected that the contracts would be honoured in Peru as the Home Government and Chargé d'Affaires in Lima were given lists of persons embarked and copies of the contracts.

The *Frederic* did not arrive at Callao, having caught fire off Batavia. Captain Nicaise had called at Batavia for water and fresh provisions on 4 February. While ashore the next day, the captain was informed that his ship was on fire. It was so intense that he was unable to get back on board. Unable to run the ship aground, the Chinese were told to jump overboard to save themselves. The crew and 52 of the Chinese managed to get into the boats, and many more were taken on board the rescue boats which quickly arrived on the scene. Four Chinese died in the rescue and 16 were missing, having been seen to swim for the shore. According to the interpreter, the disputes over gambling debts, which began while still in Hong Kong, continued on the voyage. He also said that the men had been talking continually about setting fire to the ship before they actually did so.

A large number of the survivors were subsequently contracted by Mr Baud of the Netherlands Trading Co. However, disorders of a serious nature broke out such that the police had to be called. Mr Baud then wished to get rid of them and called on Captain Nicaise to enter into new contracts to convey them to Cuba, not Peru as originally contracted. However, the Chinese were so pleased with life in Java, that they refused to undertake another voyage.

The 393-ton French barque *l'Olivier* left Macao on 5 September 1870 with 233 coolies bound for Callao. She was reported to have run aground, on 29 October, on the coast of Sumatra close to the Two Brothers. Captain Alexandre Aucan tried to lighten ship by throwing provisions and water overboard, but to no avail, and the assistance of a steamboat was requested. She was pulled off on 2 November by the French man-of-war *d'Assas* and towed to Batavia. Captain Aucan could not raise sufficient money to pay for repairs and had to persuade the authorities in Batavia to look after the men, while he looked for another charter. They were placed on Horn islet for the duration. She was eventually sold for 6,530 francs.

The *Camillo Cavour* departed from Macao on 27 July 1871 on her tenth voyage, with 632 passengers bound for Callao. She was in position 23N 127E on 8 August when she encountered a typhoon and was dismasted. She managed to limp back into Macao on 4 September. Her passengers then had to wait until 8 October when the *Mille Tonnes* carried 432 of them on to Callao. The remaining 179 were placed on the *Hong Kong* which departed on 12 October 1871 on her fourth voyage.

Camillo Cavour was advertised for sale but then headed to Hong Kong for repairs, and subsequently re-entered service. She returned to Macao and had to wait for over 50 days before leaving on her next voyage on 15 May 1872. On 12 August, she arrived at the northern Peruvian port of Payta, where ships had been required to obtain clearance, before going on to Callao. She left there on 18 August, and arrived at Callao on 31 August with 593 labourers, the 57 mortalities representing 8.77% of her complement.

She left Callao on 22 September for what was to be her last voyage with coolies. She arrived back at Hong Kong on 25 November 1872 unsure of a cargo. Captain Astorquia relinquished command to Ignacio Fernando Yriberri and was appointed Macao agent for the vessel. After varying periods in Hong Kong and Whampoa awaiting a cargo, the ship arrived at the Macao anchorage on 29 July, and departed on 6 August 1873 with 683 coolies. After a speedy 93-day passage, *Camillo Cavour* arrived at Callao on 7 November with 669 passengers surviving.

The *Camillo Cavour* was by far the longest-serving vessel in the coolie trades. She made 12 voyages between 1863 and 1873, during which 7,596 Chinese were embarked and 6,464 disembarked. The mortality rate of 14.90% is slightly distorted as one voyage was abandoned. Over the period, time she had only four Masters; Captain Stephano Caravagno for one voyage, then Captain F. de Landabaso for four, Captain A. Astorquia for six and finally—after Captain

Astorquia went ashore to become an emigration agent—Captain Ignacio Yriberri.

That the Macao anchorage was not a safe one was demonstrated when the Russian ship *Vistula* was shipwrecked between Kao and Kakiao on the night of 2 September 1871. She had arrived from Hong Kong only the day before and was awaiting her third cargo of emigrants for Havana, when a typhoon caused her to be blown ashore. Another ship dismasted was the *Manila*. She was due to leave Macao on 8 March 1872 on her second voyage with her full complement of 460 coolies bound for Havana, when a typhoon struck. The surviving coolies were transferred to the *Bengali* which took her maximum complement of 287 men and the remainder were placed on the veteran *Altagracia*.

Cruel Captains and mutinies

In the new decade of the 1870s, several ships did more to place the focus on Macao than at any other time.

On 3 December 1870, the *Straits Times* quoted Javanese papers on the loss by fire of the ship *Uncowah*, under the colours of San Salvador. She was under the command of Captain José Rosciano, an Italian, who reported that, after having sailed for a couple at days, the coolies began to grumble. On the morning of the 21st of October, the coolies were allowed on deck, but when ordered to go below, refused to obey. The sailors were provided with weapons, but the Chinese armed themselves with pieces of iron and wood and flayed about so effectively with them that the steward and carpenter were killed and several sailors wounded. After a struggle lasting half an hour, the Chinese were driven back into the hold.

With little hope of obtaining command by force, they coolies broke everything below and set fire to the ship. The crew became panic-stricken, got out a boat, and made away from the ship so hastily that the captain was left behind. He was obliged to jump overboard and swim after the boat, which picked him up. They pulled steadily for five days, during which time they were without food, before they reached the Great Natunas Island. They remained four days on the island, after which they were taken off by the San Salvadorian ship *Fray Bentos*, Captain Mota, and taken to Anjer where they arrived on the 9th of November 1870.

On the day of the mutiny, the British vessel *Juanpore* was proceeding down the China Sea from Shanghai to London, when smoke was seen from a vessel to the SSE. At sundown, fire was distinctly visible. Captain Augustus M. Haldane dispatched Second Mate Stewart to pull away in the gig in the hope of picking up any survivors. After about an hour, he returned with one of the *Uncowah*'s boats, manned by twenty-five Chinese and one European.

Captain Haldane requested the European—a Greek—to come on board. From him, Captain Haldane learned that the burning ship was the *Uncowah*, sailing from Macao for Callao with 537 coolies on board, that they had mutinied and set fire to the ship that same day. A fierce conflict had taken place between the officers and crew and the Chinese. Some of the Chinese bore strong evidence of the scene of slaughter, cutlass and pistol wounds being on several of them. The captain was also informed that, five days after leaving Macao, the coolies attempted to capture the ship, but had not succeeded, whereupon about one hundred of them had been put in irons. When the ring-leader of the mutiny and the man who set fire to the ship were identified on board, they were placed in irons.

Captain Haldane despatched the gig and the pinnace to the scene in the morning. The Chinese, seeing deliverance approaching, became frantic, plunging into the water from all quarters, nearly sinking the gig. On finding that there were 112 men on board his ship, the captain decided that no more could be done. The *Juanpore* sailed for Anjer, passing dead bodies, fragments of wreck, and various articles of cabin furniture fully twenty miles from the wreck.

When Captain Haldane put into Anjer, he was obliged to keep the coolies on board until they were placed on the steamer *Minister Van Staat Rochussen* for Batavia.

The *Hong Kong Daily Press* of 12 December 1870 reported the mutiny as having occurred on the Italian ship *Hankow*, placing "*Uncowah*" in parenthesis. Five of the coolies were put in irons, charged with the murder of the carpenter. The Greek, it is said, was also charged with having combined with the coolies, but the captain of the *Uncowah* denied that this was true.

The *Uncowah* was formerly under the American flag with the same name. She had been engaged in the Callao trade since 1866 when she was an Italian ship under Captain Tomaz Ordano. Captain José Rosciano took command in 1867 just prior to her registration being changed to that of San Salvador. On her five voyages to Callao, she embarked 2,527 Chinese passengers. Disregarding the 537 who were on the burnt-out final voyage, the mortality rate averaged 2.41% over four voyages.

According to a report in the *Straits Times* of 28 January 1871, the 112 survivors of the *Uncowah* were transferred to Horn islet, joining those, already mentioned, from the *l'Olivier*. The conditions on the islet were so bad that the Chinese were constantly threatening to murder the cooks who prepared their food. With the addition of the men from the *Uncowah*, persistent fighting between the two groups resulted in seven of the ringleaders being arrested. Some of the whole number of coolies had been murdered and thrown into the sea, while forty-five were found to be missing.

Captain Nicaise of the *Frederic* was still in Java, and had been joined by the Macao agent, A. Espantoso, who represented the Lima firm of Candamo in seeking a suitable charter for the displaced Chinese. The French barque *Bernice* of 320 tons was eventually found, and after much difficulty, some 280 from the *l'Olivier* and *Uncowah* were eventually persuaded to board the vessel for Callao. The *Bernice* departed from Batavia on 9 February 1871 and arrived at Callao on 26 May losing fifty men in the extremely cramped vessel.

The French ship *Nouvelle Penelope*, under Captain Le Vigoureux, left Macao on 1 October 1870 bound for Callao with 310 coolies on board. All went well for a day or two when suddenly a rush on deck was made by a group of Chinese, armed with belaying pins, billets of wood, etc. The master was knocked down, and his throat cut. Seven of the crew were overpowered and killed.

The remaining eight Europeans, including the mate, took to the rigging. They were assured that they would not be hurt, but had to navigate the ship to the land. This they did, and made the Bay of Tien-pak, some 180 miles on the coast below Macao. Three of the seamen were sent ashore to procure boats to land the coolies, but escaped instead. With the assistance of locals, they reached Macao after a fourteen day overland trek. In the meantime, after waiting for a day or two, and being unable to land, the pirates took the vessel further along the coast, where it was beached, then pillaged and abandoned.

On hearing the news, M. Dabry, the French Consul at Canton, had immediately set off in one of the Viceroy's gunboats for Macao, where he found the interpreter of the *Nouvelle Penelope*. Dabry then called first on the Governor, and then the Procurador who informed him that ten men had been arrested on suspicion. Dabry accused the interpreter of being the leader, but offered that if he confessed and pointed out his companions, his life would be spared. This he did, and incriminated three of the ten then present. He added that there were still others then in Macao.

Dabry and the Procurador then proceeded to the coolie barracoons with the four men, who pointed out eighty-three more who were all arrested. Dabry demanded their rendition to him as having committed piracy and murder upon French territory. The Portuguese authorities at first demurred, but subsequently consented to having them put on to a French ship then in the harbour. The chief of the pirates confessed that this was the third time he had been engaged in signing on with the intention of capturing a ship, returning to Macao, and re-entering the barracoons to be reshipped to do the same again.

Kwok A Sing, one of the ringleaders, escaped to Hong Kong, where he was arrested in January 1871 on a charge of being a suspicious character, and a person dangerous to the peace and good order of the colony. He was held in jail pending orders from Lieutenant General Whitfield.[135] Kwok's lawyer immediately applied for a writ of habeas corpus. On learning of his arrest, the Chinese authorities in Canton sought his extradition, as did the French Government. On 29 March, Chief Justice Sir John Smale ordered his release on the grounds that "the prisoner was beyond question under unlawful coercion on the *Nouvelle Penelope*, and had a right to take life to free himself from such constraint on his personal liberty".

When the French Government failed to proceed with the request, Attorney-General Julian Pauncefote immediately ordered his re-arrest on the grounds of piracy. Smale issued another writ of habeas corpus on the grounds of double jeopardy, and Kwok was released. This controversial decision set in train months of legal argument in Hong Kong and London, with the British Government ruling for Smale in the first case, but not the second. Smale's persistence that the Macao coolie trade was in fact a slave trade had embarrassing repercussions for the Portuguese government in Macao.

On 10 April, the Portuguese Governor demanded answers. Emigration Superintendent Hermenegildo Augusto Pereira Rodrigues replied on the 13th. He reported that on 16 September 1870, Macao emigration agent, José Tuton, submitted to the Emigration Superintendent a list of emigrants intended for the French ship. Open hearings were held between the 20th and the 22nd. With the contract placed before them and three interpreters speaking Punti, Hakka, and Chiuchow, one by one, each was asked the following questions:
- did he know where he was emigrating to?
- did he know the conditions of the contract?
- had he been cheated or abused?

They were advised that if anyone declared that he had been mistreated, he would have the protection of the Government, and even their repatriation if they did not wish to emigrate. Of the 257 presented, 176 declared they were willing to emigrate and 81 declined. This included six who were returned to relatives, having been claimed by them. In a second session, held between 25 and 26 September, another

134 agreed to emigrate with the remaining 66 of 200 presented refusing to go. Six brokers were punished for alleged mistreatment of the coolies.

Rodrigues said that a certificate from the warden of the jail showed that 253 settlers had been received at the jail, of whom 165 settlers from the *Nouvelle Penelope* had been made available to him. On examination, only 63 indicated a willingness to emigrate, with 23 being placed on the *St Iver* on 5 December and another 27 on the *Vistula* the same day. On the 14th, five were placed on the *Hong Kong*, and another eight on the *Nelly* on 21 December. Another twenty-two had shown renewed interest in emigrating, but were rejected by the agents as the captains refused to accept them on board.

The 1,281-ton ship *Dolores Ugarte* (mentioned above) first entered Macao in 1866 under Portuguese colours. The following year she was registered in Peru, and subsequently operated under the Salvadorian flag under Captain José Peres Saul.

She was still under Captain Saul in 1870 when she left Macao on 13 June with 609 coolies for Callao. Even before the ship had left port, a threatened mutiny had been sensed among the coolies. For the first three weeks of the voyage, they were not allowed on deck, but kept below decks in four rows of bunks, a space of only 16 inches wide being allotted to each individual.

After this, the coolies were allowed to go on deck in gangs of 50 for an hour's exercise each day. Fully armed sentries kept continual watch and guard over the coolies. On one occasion a scuffle did take place between the crew and the exercising coolies, which resulted in eighteen of the latter jumping overboard.

To add to the coolies' miseries, the ship's stores fell short, and they were put on an allowance of one lb. of boiled rice and less than a pint of water a day. The crowded state of the hold, together with the lack of water, caused the desperate coolies to thrust their dollars through the gratings of the hatches in exchange for cups of water from the crew. It is not clear why this dedicated coolie carrier still had a water problem in 1870. Water distillers had been commonplace on ships since the 1860s.

Disease soon broke out, and twenty-five died before the vessel reached Honolulu. The condition of the ship on arriving at that port was indescribable. The mate himself confessed that the stench from the main hatch was so overpowering that it was impossible to hold one's head over it "one minute without vomiting". Forty-three of those too ill to proceed were landed at Honolulu. Their plight was most pitiable. Twelve were in the last stages of decay—some with fever, and others with diarrhoea. Two were rendered blind for life, from ulcers that had formed in the corners of their eyes, and all were in a dreadfully emaciated condition. By the time the *Dolores Ugarte* arrived at Callao, she had only 490 of her passengers left alive.

Under the Macao Regulations, Portuguese consuls at the ports of destination of the coolie ships were to report their arrival, and the number of coolies landed. Consul General Narciso Velarde in Lima reported on 15 December 1870, that the *Dolores Ugarte* had arrived at Callao that day with 486 Chinese out of 605 who departed from Macao. His certificate showed that 43 were landed sick at Honolulu, and there were 76 deaths on board from natural causes. The difference in numbers, in the case of both embarkation and arrival, likely refers to at least four children, for children were not always included in the number count. As with every other report, the certificate from the consul simply stated that the passengers were well treated on the voyage.

The *Dolores Ugarte* returned to Hong Kong on 18 February 1871 with 39 Chinese passengers from Callao. She arrived at Macao on 16 April 1871 to load more coolies for Callao. On 21 April, D.H. Bailey, the American Consul in Hong Kong, drew attention to the atrocities committed on the previous voyage.

On 25 April 1871 the Secretary General and Port Captain announced, following American Consul Bailey's allegations, that the man who had been captain of the *Dolores Ugarte* on her two previous voyages, Jose Peres Saul, had been replaced at Lima by Captain D. Cecilio Garay. There was now also a new pilot and crew on the ship. On 27 April, Secretary General Henrique de Castro advised that the Governor had determined not to grant a licence for the ship to transport Chinese emigrants. The denial was based on the failure of the Captain and pilot to justify the public accusations that were made relating to the previous voyage.

In the 1 May 1871 issue of *Boletim da Provincia de Macau e Timor*, a notice, dated 26 April, advertised that the Peruvian ship *Dolores Ugarte* was granted the name of *Don Juan*. The notice had been placed by former emigration superintendent, B.S. Fernandes, who was now chargé at the Peruvian consulate. With the stroke of a pen, the *Don Juan* had resumed her original name, and she was placed on the Peruvian registry, Peru being the home of her owners, Compania Maritima del Peru. The crew consisted of 47 Europeans and a Chinese doctor. There were additionally seven Chinese servants, taken on in Hong Kong, to tend to the officers.

The *Don Juan* had three hatches, the fore-and-aft ones of about 6ft square, and the centre hatch a little larger. These were all closed by iron gratings. The aft hatch was never opened and the main one was opened only to pass meals down, but the fore hatch was left open most of the time. The only water closets were on the upper deck, which was divided into two by a high iron-rail barrier. The crew slept aft of this barrier, which had two gates. Four crew members always guarded the Chinese, two on deck by the open fore hatch, one immediately below, by the ladder, while a fourth mingled with the Chinese in the 'tween deck. There were also two sentries guarding the barrier gates.

Even before the ship had sailed, three of the coolies had tried to escape by jumping overboard. They were picked up and placed in irons until the ship sailed. On 3 May, while the Harbour Master was on board, he was intercepted by four coolies, who begged to be taken off. Instead, he told the captain to put them in irons. A Portuguese, dressed in chinese clothes came on board with the Harbour Master, and stayed overnight, mingling with the coolies. As he left on 4 May, just before the *Don Juan* was being towed out by the steamer

White Cloud he warned the captain that the coolies were planning a mutiny two days out. The coolies had numbers painted on their jackets. He wrote down the numbers of the ringleaders.

On 4 May 1871, the captain of the port reported that the *Don Juan* had passed inspection, and was granted a certificate to carry 655 coolies. They all had their contracts, and all were going voluntarily. Significantly, unlike the usual statement in accordance with another regulation issued in 1871, there was no declaration from the captain that "the ship carried on board no decoyed coolies, nor such as were suspected of being pirates". It must have been a tremendous act of faith for captains to make such a declaration. On the morning of the 5th, the captain told the crew to arm themselves. He then called for the twenty Chinese whom the Portuguese broker had identified. He had them placed in chains, and exhibited them to about 100 of the others, as an example of what would happen to them too.

On the morning of the 6th, a coolie jumped overboard. He was picked up and placed in irons with the rest. Later that morning, a number of the men complained that there were three dishes short for breakfast. The interpreter came below and said he would fetch more. But some of the men accosted him as he was leaving. He used his cane to free himself, and drew his revolver as he escaped up the ladder. The two crewmen below immediately raced for the ladder, and the grating was slammed down on the heads of several Chinese trying to get on deck.

The hatch gratings were then padlocked, and the Captain ordered the crew to fire into the hold, but it was not known if anyone was killed. The Chinese responded by breaking up the furniture and breaking everything they could, initially in the fore part of the ship, but then continued towards the after part where there was a small paint room. As the Captain and some of his men watched through a grating in the cabin, they saw men breaking into the store, and soon after a fire broke out.

The crew quickly manned the pumps, and a hose was sent below, but was immediately pushed out. Again, it was pushed in, and again it was pushed out. At the third attempt, a

Chinese did take the hose, but before he could direct it at the flames, another coolie struck him on the head, killing him. The hose was pushed out again, this time through a port hole, which had its glass broken. When the masts fell over, the crew took to the boats, throwing spare masts and spars into the water. The hatches were not opened, and only a few Chinese managed to get out when a padlock was eventually broken.

All of the crew were saved, but only about 50 of the 650 Chinese emigrants managed to make land. Some of the survivors that managed to reach Hong Kong gave statements commencing with their recruitment, then life on board, and then their experiences on being picked up by the fishing junks in the vicinity. Leung Ashew was one of the lucky ones. He had money. Many of those who did not were simply left to drown. A 20-year-old native of Sunning, he had no parents and no employment.—The following account is based on his testimony.

Before the ship sailed, the coolies were allowed on deck, but after the ship sailed, they were not allowed on deck at any time, not even for necessary purposes. There were buckets in the hold for this purpose. Nobody was allowed to smoke. Twelve men were told off to act as cooks. They were allowed on deck. The hatch gratings were opened only to lower down the meals. There were about ten foreigners acting as sentries in the hold. They had swords and rattans, but Leung never saw them use the rattans. They were on duty night and day. The fare on board was inferior to what Leung was accustomed at Sunning. The treatment on board was very good. They could play dominoes or dice in the hold.

Shortly after breakfast on the third day, there was a fire. The fire occurred in the aft part, in a room adjoining the hold. The smoke entered the hold in a great volume, with a strong smell of gunpowder. The ship had a great quantity of ammunition on board—muskets and swords. No explosion was heard and there were no foreigners in the hold at the time. The hatch grating was not opened and, with the thick smoke, a great many were suffocated. After more than an hour, the grating was torn off. In the rush for the opening

Leung was partially suffocated and could not climb up. By the time he was pulled up, the fire had reached the hatchway, and his face was severely burnt.

When he eventually emerged, the ship, from the mainmast to the stern, was a mass of flames. The foremast however had not caught fire by then. About twenty men clung to the rigging, and there were more than ten others holding to the bowsprit. Leung held on to the anchor-chain, with the anchor dangling over the side. When the fire reached the woodwork that held the anchor-chain, Leung was tumbled into the sea with the anchor. Luckily, he could swim a little, and swam to a burnt spar floating nearby. It was a small one, and three or four others had got to it before him. There was a larger spar close by with more than ten men holding on it. Leung's smaller spar was carried away by the current, and he did not see what had become of the larger one and its men. He was carried so far away from the burning ship that he could hardly see her. As he left the burning wreck, Leung said he saw blood ooze out from the sides of the vessel; from the hold where the coolies were lodged.

That evening a fishing junk appeared. The junkmen wanted money before they would pick up the survivors. From his advance of $8, Leung still had $5, which he handed over to the junkmen. They refused to take his four companions who had no money. Those men wanted to get into the junk too but the junkmen pushed them back and they had to remain on the spar. After picking Leung up the junkmen went on, picking up any wrecked property they could find. The junk took in nine others on the way. The junk got money from all these men. There were many others in the water, but the junk would not receive them, as they had no money. The junk then took them to Hong Kong, and put them all ashore.

Leung could hardly walk, but struggled to a stone-cutter's shed, where he was refused shelter for the night. He walked on, and came to a bridge and stopped under the arch for the night. Next morning he went further up the hill and came to another stone-cutter's shed. This time the men received him, but they gave him nothing to eat or anything to lie down upon for the two days he stopped there. When he left the shed, he came to a shop and sheltered from the rain under the awning. The shopkeeper turned him away, but a seamstress took pity on him and asked an elderly man to take care of him. He took pity on him and conducted him to his house. The elderly man wanted to adopt him, but his own son prevented him from doing so.

The survivors were taken to Hong Kong where they were cared for at the Tung Wah Hospital. A subscription, organised by the hospital, was raised to return them tho their places of origin. The sum raised was sufficient to pay for their fares with the remainder then distributed amongst them.[136]

On 9 September 1872, the *Chicago Tribune* quoted a 6 September report from Havana, advising the arrival of the French ship, *Jacques Sevrin*, which had departed from Macao on 7 April 1872. The coolies had mutinied shortly after commencing on their journey, such that Captain Achilles Heu had to fire on them, killing several. Whipping was practiced throughout the voyage and the coolies arrived in a terrible condition. Of the 300 who had embarked, 65 died, and many of the remaining 235 were unable to walk ashore on 3 September.

Consul General Graham Dunlop in Havana was the first to alert Earl Granville of another case of mutiny on board a Havana-bound ship. The steamer *Fatchoy*, formerly the British *Vixen*, was sold at Hong Kong to Messrs. Paul Ehlers & Co. early in April 1872, and placed under the German flag. Then, on 30 July, Ehlers sold her to the Spanish Emigration Agent, Francisco Abella. She was then put under the Spanish flag, registered at Havana. She had been chartered to the Havana Coolie Importing Society for two trips, but on her first (and only) arrival at Havana, she was listed as having been consigned to Ibanez.

The master had applied to have her fitted out at Hong Kong for the conveyance of emigrants. The only fittings approved were sleeping berths, a hospital, ventilators, and cooking places. After this work had been done, she took in water and coal and proceeded to Macao on 1 August 1872. Earlier, a French ship, the *Charles Albert*, had iron gratings on the hatches, around the hatches, in the between decks, and at the side ports fitted out in Hong Kong. Iron barricades were also installed on deck. This was against the direction of the Harbour Master, and the captain was fined for disregarding the instruction. The *Fatchoy* wisely chose to have these fitted in Macao.

While *Fatchoy* was lying at Macao, the steamer *Rosita y Nene*, which had left some six weeks earlier, returned to Macao in distress. Her cargo of 700 coolies were in a sad state, many of them had been cruelly flogged and otherwise ill-used on board. These coolies were transferred to the *Fatchoy*.

Every one of these men gave indications that the vilest deception had been practiced upon them, and once having realized the utter hopelessness of their situation, they gave themselves up to frantic despair. Some threw themselves overboard whenever an opportunity offered, but two boats were constantly alongside to pick them up and return them on board.

The *Fatchoy* left Macao on the 26th August 1872, with 1,005 coolies. All went well until the fourth day out when a cry of "mutiny forward" was raised. The coolies had attacked the guards, throwing one overboard while the other took to the rigging. The coolies made a rush to the Chinese galley, expecting to find knives or other weapons. The mate and second mate shot into the crowd and wounded three of the coolies. The officers then rallied, and succeeded in catching a number of the coolies. They were tied by their long hair to the barricade of iron gratings, the rest driven below. About 150 were put in irons.

The next morning the Spanish captain had them brought up. Some bags of rice were placed on the deck and the prisoners were laid across them, then unmercifully flogged and beaten by two men keeping time with their whips or sticks. In a short time, the deck was covered with blood. As each coolie was flogged, he was washed with salt water and sent below.

The *Fatchoy* arrived at Anjer on the 9th September, and remained there two days before proceeding to Mauritius, where she took in water and coal, the ship remaining in quarantine. From Mauritius, the *Fatchoy* went to the Cape of Good Hope. At each of these ports, the coolies were kept below; and while coaling was going on, the hatches were put on, and the hospital bulkheads for the sick were closed. The heat was intolerable even in the open air.

For the coolies, the voyage was one of the most unimaginable sufferings. They were struck, kicked, flogged, and otherwise treated with the greatest brutality. The filth and stench was something horrible. The hospitals were not cleaned during the whole voyage.

There was on board a man styled, in sailor parlance, a "paper captain". He was the supercargo in charge of the coolies. He had full control of the coolies, superintending the beatings and other punishments inflicted on them throughout the voyage. A more merciless ruffian never lived. He was not named, but it was known that C.R. Menser, a partner in the firm of Paul Ehlers & Co., had been placed on board the *Fatchoy* as supercargo.

The other "captain" was a German. On the ship's papers, he was styled the "sailing-master". The chief, second, and third mates, and the carpenter, were all Germans. The chief engineer was an American. The other members of the crew were English, Scottish, and Irish. The crew came from several nations, but all of them understood English. There were two or three only on board who spoke Spanish. The officers always spoke English or German.

The statements relating to the *Fatchoy* were attributed to the American chief engineer, who had made them in conversation with the American Consul General in Havana. The statement from the American chief engineer continued, "I venture to say that in the annals of the African Slave Trade all the horrors of the 'middle passage' never surpassed those of this China slave-ship".

On learning of these revelations, Paul Ehlers & Co. wrote to the *China Mail* on 10 April 1873, refuting the exposure, and challenging the American and British governments to impound the ship, which was then in Liverpool.

The *Fatchoy* returned to Hong Kong on 1 May 1873 where she was boarded by Boarding Officer Sampson of the Harbour Master's Office, who saw iron barricades and gratings lying on the 'tween decks. Menser was on board as a passenger, and when Paul Ehlers went on board, he ordered Captain Paraja not to anchor but to proceed directly to Macao. The Harbour Master was unable to search the vessel before she left the port. After disposing of any incriminating evidence, she left Macao on 8 May, back to Hong Kong where she stayed until 14 June 1873 when she departed for Manila.

Macao Emigrant Committee

Following the tragedies of the *Nouvelle Penelope* and *Don Juan*, Governor Antonio Sergio de Souza appointed a committee charged with proposing measures, "to more effectually ensure the condition and freedom of the Chinese emigrants". Formed on 12 May 1871, the six-man committee reported on 23 May. It noted that under the present regulation, the men would have undergone the appropriate examinations and the men emigrating could not have been doing so under an illusion. Nevertheless, as a great number of them were indigent and desperate, they would have believed any promises made to them, in the expectation that their lot would improve.

The committee noted that the men found conditions in the barracoons so comfortable they were prepared to say anything to foreigners, as dictated by the brokers. However they would subsequently declare that they had been deceived and were therefore released prior to shipment. Men had been known to have passed through the superintendent's office more than once, with no intention of emigrating.

To defeat this practice, the Committee proposed 12 points, the first of which was to diminish the number of barracoons, with one or at most two for each agent. Only persons approved by the Procurator and Superintendent would be responsible to the Government. Another proposal was for a Committee of three independent individuals to assist in controlling emigration activities up until their presentation to the Superintendent. Finally, once in the "establishments" (i.e. the barracoons), no contact was to be allowed with the brokers.

The Maritime Police were to be notified of all colonists (that is, those going to emigrate) arriving in Macao. The police in turn were to provide a daily list of arrivals, which could be matched with one from the establishments specifying those arriving by steamer and by other means. The Fiscal Committee was to determine the space allocated to each man, and to ensure that those leaving did not exceed the numbers listed. Only colonists were allowed to reside in the establishments. Brokers were to live in registered houses, with the number of brokers in each to be reported.

The Committee then recommended that the $8 advance be discontinued but the agent would be free to furnish articles demanded and to provide advances to families. The Committee had reason to believe that immorality occurred on board and to prevent this money should not be allowed to be taken on board.

Each ship was to have two interpreters examined in different dialects by the procurator's office. Ports to which the emigrants were sent to should have consulates to protect them as though they were Portuguese subjects. The committee also considered that 3 cubic meters should be allocated to each person, and steamers should have distillers to provide fresh water, and be equipped with at least one lifeboat and a few safety buoys. Finally, in order that the committee's recommendations could be rendered useful, they reminded the Governor of the urgent necessity of embodying into one code of regulations all the various reforms at present in force.

Governor de Souza acted on these recommendations immediately, proclaiming an Ordinance, dated 27 May 1871, declaring improvements in the regulating of Chinese emigration to ensure that the colonists embarked of their own free will.

He ordained that individuals in charge of emigration establishments would be bound to exhibit a certificate extracted from the Criminal Register, and have a declaration from the Procurator for Chinese Affairs and Superintendent of Chinese Emigration to prove their fitness for the office in question.

Secondly, brokers were expressly forbidden to enter the "establishments", after delivering the colonists to the person in charge of those establishments. For a first infraction, the person in charge would incur a fine equal to half the surety bond ($500). Any further relapse would incur a similar fine, and he would also be rendered unfit to manage any affairs relative to emigration. One quarter of the fine would be given to the informer, with the remainder to the Public Treasury. All brokers, even those expressing a wish to emigrate themselves would not be admitted into the barracoon, but be kept away from the coolies and sent immediately to the Superintendent's office for questioning.

Increased Peruvian demand

There were 25 sailings for Peru in 1871. On them were 11,494 men, women and children, and 9,695 were able to go ashore after between 78 and 153 days. The longest journey was by the 271-ton French barque *Ville de Grenade* under Captain M. Chansel. The Port Captain in Macao allowed 198 Chinese to board the small vessel, but only 115 of them were able to walk ashore. The mortality rate was 41.92%, surpassed in recent years only by the *Uncowah* the year before.

The highest number of sailings for Peru was in 1872. On the 31 departures were 13,800 Chinese, placed aboard predominantly Peruvian-flagged vessels, making regular voyages back to Callao. There were 1,185 deaths that year, three vessels only having mortality rates above 20%. The highest was on the 401-ton French ship *Antares*, leaving from Macao for her second voyage on 21 March 1872. Of the 263 taken on by Captain G. Nolte, also making his second voyage, only 181 made it ashore. The mortality rate was 31.18%. The *Luisa Canevaro*, on her sixth voyage, had a 25.98% mortality rate. On 26 February 1872, a new entrant to the trade commenced her first of two voyages from Macao to Callao. This was the 962-ton Portuguese ship, *Emigrante*,[137] and she had a loss of 21.44% on this voyage. She did only slightly better on her next voyage in 1873, with a loss of 14.94%.

The drop to 13 sailings to Peru in 1873 may have been a precursor to a changing pattern in shipping. In 1872 the 13,800 Chinese taken on board the 31 ships averaged 445 per vessel. In 1873 the 7,170 who embarked averaged 552 on each of the 13 ships used. Shipments were abruptly cut short in 1874 but the average for the only four ships which carried the 2,371 Chinese who left that year was 593. The number carried would have been even higher had the large new steamers dedicated to the work (which had arrived only as the termination of shipping was announced) been utilised.

The *Maria Luz* affair

An event, which was eventually to lead to the end of indentured emigration from China, occurred when the Peruvian 408-ton *Maria Luz* left Macao on 28 May 1872, bound for Callao with 225 Chinese coolies on board. Captain R. Herrera chose to take the northern route before turning south to Peru. Buffeted by a typhoon, the *Maria Luz* was forced into Yokohama. On arrival, some Chinese jumped overboard and swam to a British warship, HMS *Iron Duke*, where they claimed they had been kidnapped.

With the publicity and great outcry generated, the Japanese government accepted their story and released the Chinese on board, sending them back to China. Peru, who had no treaty relations with Japan, threatened war unless Japan apologised, and indemnified the owners. The British government then intervened and warned Peru that any hostile act would result in retaliatory action by the Royal Navy. France was asked to arbitrate, and agreed with the Japanese action. The Peruvians were forced to back down. The trial was widely reported in the international press, and both Peru and Portugal were criticised for their participation in the disreputable coolie trade.

Costa Rican experiment

On 20 June 1871, the Government of Costa Rica signed a new £1,600,000 contract with the Meiggs family to build a railroad across the country within three years.[138] With a shortage of labour in the country, Keith Meiggs wrote to President Don Tomas Guardia pleading with him to allow 1,000 Chinese into the country under a government-appointed commission to assist in building the railroad. This was approved, and Otto Hubbe was appointed Costa Rican Government Agent for the Recruitment of Chinese workers. A native German, Hubbe had previous experience in Chinese recruiting in Hong Kong, and returned there in October 1872.

His arrival in Macao caused great consternation there. The local authorities were not at all sure how to handle his application. On 12 November, Governor Januario Correia de Almeida announced that Hubbe had been approved by the Colonies Minister as Commissioner of the Government of Costa Rica, to recruit settlers for that country. As Hubbe had shown willingness to meet the conditions set down in the regulations, he had been granted permission for one shipment to that country. The Governor emphasized it was Hubbe's duty to ensure that the settlers would be given protection on arrival similar to that in Cuba and Peru. As there was no consular representation in any Central American country, the plan was to have the settlers placed on an Italian steamer, and on arrival have the Italian Consul oversee disembarkation. Barao Cercal, the Italian Consul in Macao had agreed with the proposal.

With this authorisation, Hubbe appointed Nicholas Tanco Armero as the employment agent. Armero had originally chartered the *Glensannox* for a voyage to Callao. He had already received his certificate from Port Capitan J.E. Scarnichia as well as one from the Head of Public Health allowing 739 passengers to board. But with Hubbe's appointment, Armero changed the ship's destination to Punta Arenas in Costa Rica. This unique alteration from all previous departures caused considerable confusion among the Government officials. Secretary Henrique de Castro wanted to know if Punta Arenas was on the Pacific or Atlantic coast.

Following several exchanges, the confusion was cleared, and following the formal examination on 9 November, the *Glensannox* was cleared to sail. Captain Domenico Capello finally left on 17 November 1872 with 685 Chinese coolies. He had made the usual declaration that the settlers were happy and that there were no pirates on board. As required, a doctor and interpreter were also embarked, as part of the crew.

With all the bureaucracy exchanges publicly aired, the *New York Times* of 3 January 1873 quoted a San Francisco report of news from Hong Kong dated 27 November 1872. According to the article, it appeared that the Superintendent of Emigration in Macao had refused to sign the contracts of coolies bound for Costa Rica. The Governor threatened to dismiss him if he refused. In reply, the superintendent said he would report the incident direct to Lisbon. The impasse was broken when the superintendent took two weeks leave, during which time his Deputy signed the contracts.

En route to Costa Rica, the *Glensannox* called at Honolulu for provisions and bunkers. The Honolulu *Pacific Commercial Advertiser* reported her arrival on 20 December 1872, thirty-three days after she had sailed from Macao. In his manifest, Captain Capello neglected to add punctuation to his list, resulting in the 685 Chinese being listed as part of the captain's personal effects. Immediately prior to sailing, three Chinese refused to re-board claiming to have been illegally held by the captain. Presiding Judge Hartwell held that the contracts were not valid until the parties arrived at their port of destination. Two of the men returned to the ship, but one remained in Honolulu.

The *Glensannox* left Honolulu on 28 December with glowing reports from the *Pacific Commercial Advertiser*, declaring that on inspection of the ship, the covers were found to be clean and airy, and the occupants well-fed and healthy. Nevertheless, by the time she arrived at Punta Arenas, 31 had died, leaving 654 Chinese to learn about their new home. On 3 November 1872, Otto Hubbe was appointed Italian Consul in Punta Arenas. He met the ship on her arrival on 15 February 1873.

The *Glensannox* returned to Macao, from where Captain D. Capello undertook a second voyage, departing on 24 September 1873—this time to Cuba. This was the last shipment on behalf of La Compania de Hacendados, which made no further shipments after the termination of the coolie trade to Cuba.

Macao Regulations of 1872

On 28 May 1872, new Regulations for the Emigration of Chinese were published.[139] Ten Sections containing 83 Articles covered the agents and their employees, the contracts, and the ships employed.

Schedule A gave an example of what was to be placed on board. A blackboard would show that Havana and Peru were in America and that it would take about three months to reach them from China. As the coolies had already had an opportunity to declare their unwillingness to emigrate, had received their down payment, and signed a contract, they would not be able to return ashore. Schedule B contained instructions to be practiced on board and the scale of medicines to be carried. Schedule C referred to the form of certificate to be issued by the captain of the port (i.e. the Macao harbour-master), and Schedule D referred to the instructions to be followed on going to sea.

Table A provided a list of the daily rations to be issued, very similar to the Hong Kong provisions. Table B listed the duration of voyages for which the groceries for the Chinese colonists were to be provided. It followed the British example of having two columns corresponding to the seasons. As with the British declaration, the number of days to Callao was deemed to be 120 throughout the year, while to Cuba, 147 days was the requirement between October and March inclusive, and 168 in the off-season.

Once again the new regulations did not seem to have any great impact on recruitment. The treatment of coolies continued to be harsh.

Unrecognised record of achievement

Each week in the *Boletim*, a table was published listing the number of Chinese who had been repatriated to their homes. Formal exchanges with officials of the major surrounding districts were published for the men returning to the more than 100 villages from whence they came. In reality, as C.A. Montalto de Jesus maintains, "When found out in Macao, the victims were handed over by the authorities to the charge of the district mandarins; but instead of being sent home as requested, the men were detained, sold to the crimps, and again brought to Macao for shipment".[140]

In 1868, the Government of Macao began publishing statistics as to the number of Chinese accepting contracts to work in Peru or Cuba, and also the numbers who had been returned to their home villages, or otherwise not proceeding overseas.—Prior to this time, the number of arrests in relation to emigration infringements had been included in the weekly police reports. With the advent of this new statistical summary, such arrests were published annually.

Table 10. 1 Macao recruits (and brokers punished) October 1868-March 1874

	1868	1869	1870	1871	1872	1873	1874
Repatriated home	1,394	2,477	3,637	5,572	7,365	3,596	371
Returned to parents	17	72	82	304	1,329	1,312	127
Remained in Macao	69	17	40	1,391	928	1,092	432
Returned deposits		37	14	46	221	165	11
Changed mind		6	21	58	394	624	3
To different country					113	142	
Total not proceeding	1,480	2,609	3,794	7,371	10,350	6,931	944
Emigrants shipped	3,738	9,000	13,392	16,518	20,855	12,838	2,320
Percentage not shipped	60.4	71.0	71.7	55.4	50.4	46.0	59.3
Brokers punished	30	56	58	100	267	282	17

Source: Author's compilation

The table showing the number of emigrants shipped ("Macao recruits (and brokers punished) October 1868-March 1874") is compiled from one set of data only, published in *O Boletim*, and this data does not precisely match figures published in other lists which also appear in the official Government bulletin.The various figures are however relatively similar and it is reasonable to be confident that the data used provides a good understanding of the degree of success which the Portuguese authorities achieved in limiting the transport of Chinese coolies who did not wish to be taken away from home.

The table, "Macao recruits (and brokers punished) October 1868-March 1874", shows that, over the six and a half year period, October 1868 to March 1874, almost 30% of the recruits asked to be returned home. In the final three months of indentured labour (January to March 1874) alone, as many as 15.99% of the men, put forward, refused to go, while 18.62% elected to remain in Macao.

With the publication of these statistics, the number of children returned to their parents increased steadily each year as parents learned of their incarceration. The increasing number of brokers fined for infringements also illustrates the seeming effectiveness of the regulations.

Cuba Commission

Following years of reports, telling of the atrocious conditions—bordering on slavery—endured by the Chinese in Cuba, the Chinese government eventually made a formal complaint about the harsh treatment of their nationals. But the Spanish refuted the allegations. The exchanges became heated, and Samuel Wells Williams, the American Chargé d'Affaires in Peking, suggested a visit by the Chinese government to see for themselves. The Spanish reluctantly agreed.

Chen Lanpin, the Chinese Officer in Charge of the Educational Mission in the United States, together with Messrs. Macpherson and Huber, Commissioners of Customs at Hankow and Tientsin, respectively, formed the official delegation to inquire into the condition of the Chinese in Cuba.[141]

On 19 March 1873, they met with the Captain-General (who also had the title, Governor of Havana), and later the also with consular representatives of the major powers. The Commission of Inquiry lasted until 8 May, during which the commissioners interviewed more than 2,500 Chinese, took 1,176 depositions, and received 85 petitions, the latter supported by 1,665 signatures. The Commission Report summarised their findings in 1876.

The depositions showed that 80 percent of the Chinese labourers declared that they had been either kidnapped or decoyed into signing contracts. They confirmed the deceitful methods used by their countrymen from the earliest days of recruitment from Amoy in the 1850s. "I was decoyed here by wicked men." "We were conveyed on board by violence." "Portuguese and Spaniards, acting in concert, and aided by vicious Chinese, make a practice of decoying and selling men." And so it continued.

Among the 1,176 depositions, at least 65 claimed to have been kidnapped, 689 decoyed, and 50 others entrapped into signing contracts in the belief that they were merely doing so in the place of others temporarily absent. Ninety-three others were victims of traps set after they had gambled and lost, but at least 81 volunteered that they had embarked willingly. While most of the men came from Macao, Amoy, Swatow and Canton, at least five came from Manila, one from Shanghai, and at least ten from Wenchow in faraway Chekiang.

The questions raised by the Commissioners were various, including the following: "Did you sign an agreement, and did you understand it?" "What was your position on the plantation and were the agreement stipulations carried out?" And even, "Do you support the rebellion?"[142]

In answer to the question, "Were the laws adequate for the voyage?" one answered, "When we proceeded to sea, we were confined in the hold below; some were shut up in bamboo cages, or chained to iron posts, and a few were indiscriminately selected and flogged as a means of intimidating all others." Another stated, "Three months had passed but we had not arrived; no water was issued, and we had to pay a dollar for a single cup of water." In their thirst, some stole water, only to be flogged when caught; one even being struck dead by the Master. The hatchway was only wide enough to allow one man to go up or down at a time, and the stench from below was most offensive. The deaths were without number. They confirmed that mortality during the voyages exceeded ten percent, mainly from wounds caused by blows, from suicide, or sickness. But several said that they were well looked after, and that the Master was kind.

The commissioners formed the view that, on arrival, they were sold into slavery on the sugar plantations, with only a very small proportion being sold to families and shops. Cruelty was practiced by both classes of employers, more so on the plantations, where it often became unendurable. The work was excessively severe, and the food insufficient; the hours were long, and chastisement by rods, whips, chains, stocks, etc. produced great suffering and injury. Apart from those killed by blows and wounds, many hanged themselves, cut their throats, poisoned themselves with opium, or threw themselves into wells and the sugar cauldrons. Scars and mutilations were evident on many of the coolies.

On the termination of their contracts, the employers invariably withheld the certificates of completion, insisting on renewal of engagements; on the same terms, and with the same system of cruelty. If they failed to renew, the Chinese were placed on chain gangs, repairing roads, until such time as they agreed to sign the new contracts.

In the "men-market" in which they were placed on landing in Havana, "intending purchasers insisted on removing their clothes, and examining their persons in order to ascertain whether they possessed strength, just as if an ox or a horse was being bought." Those who objected to having their queues cut off were beaten almost to death. When asked if they were more comfortable in Cuba than at home, one replied "I hold a Letter of Domicile and Cedula, and work independently, yet I am subjected to outrage. Here we are regarded as appertaining to the same class as the Negro; indeed sometimes these latter are treated better than we are". Many said even beggars at home were better off than they were. Another stated that he had enough to pay for a passage home, yet he was seized, placed in prison, and forced to labour.

The Cuban Commission Report, like Yung Wing's Peru report (see the section, 'Peruvian Mission to China and Japan', below), dealt the final death blow to the system of coolie contract recruitment, determining, as it did without any shadow of doubt, the true situation of the Chinese labourer in Cuba. All emigration henceforth would have to be placed on a new footing.

Continued concern for coolies in Peru

The *New York Times* continued to lament the coolie trade in Peru. In its 19 July 1873 issue, it carried an article from "An Occasional Correspondent", which claimed that the coolie trade was nothing more than a slave trade. Citing supporting statements from others, "An Occasional Correspondent" described the Chinese character, and then the coolie depots in Macao. He acknowledged that there were ordinances regulating the clothing, amount of food and water allowed, as well as the requirement for a doctor and sufficient medicines to be carried on all ships. But as he pointed out, they were port regulations, and only lasted as long as land was in sight.

On the face of it, "An Occasional Correspondent" wrote, contracts appeared to be very reasonable. In practice, it could well be a completely different matter. With captains not deterred by the desire to present a fine article in the market, coolies were often driven to desperation by repeated acts of cruelty. The inevitable revolt led only to more cruelty, and when landed with scars and bruises, their pleas for help were often to deaf ears.

Once in Peru, "An Occasional Correspondent" continued, the coolies were not entitled to the benefits written into their contracts. Should a coolie become sick during the passage and unable to work, the contract was annulled and the coolie was abandoned, leaving him to the mercies of an uncaring community. Should he perchance recover, his master could immediately reclaim him and force the man to start his eight-year contract again.

Life on a plantation, as "An Occasional Correspondent" described it, commenced at 4.30 in the morning, when the coolies were hustled off to collect their daily provisions and cooking utensils, before being taken to the fields until at least 6pm. They were constantly watched, and if found slacking, immediately subjected to beatings from negro ex-slaves, who themselves had been treated in the same manner.

Should a coolie survive his eight-year servitude, "An Occasional Correspondent" testified, he would be so crippled and weakened by diseases that he would be fit only to beg. And to a Chinese man in Peru, that meant death by starvation.

Governor Jui-lin acts against the coolie trade

In 1872, Jui-lin, Governor-General of Kwangtung and Kwangsi, on instructions from Peking, began a concerted effort at disrupting and ending the trafficking between Canton and Macao. (This was after the Tsungli Yamen—the Chinese Foreign Office—had received a report from the American Minister to China, accusing local officials in Kwangtung of complicity in the coolie emigration traffic at Macao.) Kidnapping and forcible or deceptive recruiting became crimes punishable by death, and gunboats were despatched to the Pearl River Estuary to police all sea traffic between Canton and Macao. The recruiters attempted to evade the authorities by shifting to a region west of Macao in southwest Kwangtung, but the campaign shifted its efforts to this area as well.

In April, when about 20 vessels sailed into the region in an attempt to recruit coolies, Governor Jui-lin ordered gunboats into the area. They intercepted three vessels under the command of Portuguese, and found 60 kidnapped Chinese. The American Chargé d'Affaires in Peking reported to the US State Department in November 1873 as follows. "The severe measures adopted by the authorities at Canton to prevent coolies of all kinds going to Macao, in order to stop as much as possible the delivery of those who may have been engaged by contract to go abroad, and the summary execution of all crimps and kidnappers who have been caught, have, I hear, made the business so dangerous and losing that most of the barracoons are empty."[143]

Hong Kong prohibits fitting out of ships

Sir Arthur Kennedy arrived in Hong Kong to take up the role of Governor on 16 April 1872. In his despatch of 7 June 1872 to the Earl of Kimberley, Governor Kennedy reported that he had been credibly informed that there were no fewer than 300 barracoons and more than 800 coolie brokers in Macao engaged in the trade "so vividly described" in the translation he attached of a document handed to him by a deputation of "very influential" Chinese inhabitants of Hong Kong. After several interviews with the delegation, Kennedy, as he wrote, "was impressed with the sincerity and earnestness of their desire to put an end to the cruel and disgraceful traffic at Macao".[144]

The Earl of Kimberley enquired whether there was any truth that persons in Hong Kong derived great profits from supplying the coolie ships. Kennedy's despatch in reply, dated 19 October 1872, stated that, "the Macao coolie ships are mostly invariably fitted in the port of Hong Kong". He also said, "that these fittings are made here I have no doubt, but they are carried to sea, and put up elsewhere." Responding in a despatch in reply, dated 17 December, Kimberley wrote that the state of things described in Kennedy's 19 October despatch, "is most unstisfactory" and confirmed the opinion that fresh legislation was required.

Kennedy then hurriedly amended "The Hong Kong Emigration Ordinance 1870", to take Kimberley's instructions into account. The new Ordinance would have the same title, replacing the date 1870 with the new date of 1873, and he forwarded it to London on 22 January.

In a further despatch, Kennedy said that he had personally inspected two of the coolie vessels. He also reported that the Macao Governor had proclaimed that emigrants to Peru were to receive gratuitous return passages, or a sum of money in lieu.[145] He was at a loss to conceive how the Government was going to insure that the promise would be faithfully discharged.

Following amendments, as required by the Foreign Office, Ordinance No. 3 of 1873, entitled, "Chinese Emigrant Ship Fittings Ordinance, 1873", was passed by the Legislative Council of Hong Kong on 24 April 1873. Ordinance No. 5 entitled, "The Hong Kong Emigration Ordinance 1873", was passed on 6 May 1873, and Ordinance No. 6, "For the Better Protection of Chinese Women and Female Children", was passed on 8 May1873.

In the *Hong Kong Gazette* of 2 August, Kennedy Proclaimed Ordinance No. 3, in which notice was given to owners or agents and masters of vessels engaged in the Macao coolie trade lying in Hong Kong waters. Five of the seven ships in port cleared at once, the *Glensannox* cleared soon after, and the *Columbia* was given seven days to complete repairs. These ships took refuge at Whampoa. The Canton consul, now Sir Brooke Robertson, reported that, following long consultations, the viceroy of Kwantung had instructed the Imperial Maritime Customs Acting Commissioner, H.O. Brown, to issue notices to masters, requiring them to leave Whampoa and adjacent waters at once. No vessel destined for the carriage of Chinese coolies and belonging to non-treaty powers would in future be allowed to enter the port. The provincial judge and the provincial chancellor issued the formal proclamation on 17 October 1873.[146]

Macao Capitulation

On 27 December 1873, the Governor of Macao proclaimed that in obedience to the orders of His Majesty, King Amadeo's Government, the Chinese emigration carried on in the port of Macao was henceforth prohibited. The determination was to be complied with within three months of the date of the proclamation.

However, in a somewhat surprising footnote to this affair, on 31 January 1874, Governor Januairo de Almeida tried to publish new Regulations for Asiatic Passengers and their transport from Macao. The response of Governor Jui-lin was immediate. He informed Governor Almeida that, if emigration resumed in any form, he would despatch gunboats and troops to Macao to arrest and punish those involved. Governor Almeida rescinded his decree, promising that no further emigration would take place. Upon further consultation with Governor Jui-lin in Canton, he was able to ensure that the more than 20,000 Chinese in Macao connected with the emigration traffic, now unemployed, would be allowed to return to the mainland without fear of punishment, provided they renounced all further participation in coolie recruitment in Macao. In August 1874, this agreement was formalised between the two parties in an official ceremony in Macao.

The Portuguese proclamation did not have any effect on Cuba. The last vessel to load at Macao for Havana was the 1,776-ton Belgian steamer, *Nelusko* on 21 October 1873, carrying the largest contingent of Chinese on a single ship. Of the 1,099 who were embarked, 1,055 were able to disembark on 17 January 1874, the 44 deaths amounting to a mortality rate of 4%.

Peruvian shipments had peaked in 1872 with 31 shipments that year. The Portuguese proclamation had a devastating effect in Peru. Shipments in 1873 had dropped to 15 but plans had been underway to introduce steamships to the trade which had been dominated by dedicated shuttle ships capable of only one voyage a year.

On the date of the Proclamation (27 December 1873), fourteen ships—all Peruvian—were at Macao awaiting their coolies. The *Oracle, Macao, San Juan, Providencia, Colombia, Agustina,* and *Fray Bentos*, all stayed on in Macao in the hope of a reversal of the decision to halt Chinese emigration. The *Emigrante* arrived on 23 January 1874, and, on 26 February 1874, the *Camillo Cavour* became the last ship to arrive direct from Callao with the expectation of obtaining a return cargo.

The *Peru*, which had been lying in Macao since 19 August 1873, left in ballast on 17 February, together with the 818-ton steamer *Francisco Calderon*, which had arrived in Macao from Cape Town on 1 February in need of urgent repairs. On 3 February, the *Francisco Calderon* continued on to Hong Kong, where Captain Eduardo Perks had to call for tenders for major repairs.

One of the more conspicuous coolie ships made redundant was the Peruvian steamer *Florencia* which arrived in Macao on 24 January. With no prospect of a cargo, Captain Guillermo Garcia y Garcia took the 855-ton steamer to Hong Kong on 20 March. Her agents, Pustau & Co., then applied to the Hong Kong Government for permission to take Chinese from Hong Kong to California. This was refused, as all traffic between the two places was reserved for British and American ships.

In his *Chinese Bondage in Peru*, Watt Stewart quotes unnamed sources as saying that the 1873-built 883-ton ship was fitted up in a costly manner, having between-decks ventilation, separate quarters for the sick, an admirable means of cooking, a distilling apparatus for use should the 50,000 gallon water tanks be exhausted, and iron decks covered with cement to prevent fire. On her maiden voyage from Cardiff, she arrived in Macao on 24 January 1874 only to find that there would be no coolies to take to Peru. Ironically, the *Francisco Calderon* and *Florencia* were to be the first steamships employed in the Callao trade. Up until then, steamships had been utilised only to Havana.

With only three months notice, only four vessels were able to load before the deadline. The *Luisa Canevaro*, with 759 coolies, and the *Nuevo Providencia* with 524 coolies, departed in January 1874; while the *Isabel*, with 713 emigrants, left in March.

The 890-ton *Lola* had the distinction of being the last coolie ship to load at Macao. A speedy vessel, she made two voyages in her debut year, 1871. She took only 95 days to transport 479 Chinese on her first voyage to Callao. Four deaths only were recorded on those two 1871 voyages under Captain Pio de Elorrieta. Originally registered in San Salvador, she changed her flag to Peruvian for her second voyage. She carried over 2,000 passengers, including 21 children, on her four voyages, sustaining a low mortality rate of 2.08%.

On her last voyage, she departed Macao on 27 March 1874, and arrived at Callao on 2 July after a 97-day passage. The 375 Chinese on board, consigned to Juan de Ugarte, did not fill the ship to its capacity. With that last departure, there were still nine Peruvian vessels left in Macao. The *Callao* eventually departed on 27 October 1874.

Peruvian Mission to Japan and China

Up until the time of the *Maria Luz*, Chinese migration to Peru was conducted under an 1853 Consular Convention between Peru and Portugal (which Peru recognised as the sovereign power in Macao). The Convention had been replaced by one signed between the two countries in February 1872. Having no diplomatic representation in either Japan or China, the Peruvian Government decided to improve relations with those countries. Captain Manuel Aurelio Garcia y Garcia was appointed Special Envoy to the two countries with power to sign treaties and to appoint consuls if he considered a permanent mission was required.

Garcia was to proceed in his flagship, the *Independencia*, together with the screw steamer *Union*, which was then being repaired in Britain. On realisation that a naval expedition was too expensive and probably not appropriate, the delegation eventually set off by commercial steamer for Japan on 22 December 1872. There Garcia was received with full honours and grandly hosted. He even had an audience with the Emperor. Reparations for the *Maria Luz* were settled and a Treaty of Peace, Friendship, Trade, and Navigation was signed on 21 August 1873.

Flushed with the success of the Japanese mission, Garcia headed for China, where he was received by Viceroy Li Huang-chang. The hostile reception he met with was a complete contrast with his experience in Japan. The Chinese were deeply resentful of the treatment of their nationals in Peru.

In his *My Life in China and America*, Yung Wing, a Commissioner of the Chinese Educational Commission in Hartford, Connecticut, wrote that he happened to be back in China, on a mission to sell the Gatling machine gun, for which he had the sole agency in China, at the same time as the Peruvian envoy Garcia.

Yung was in Tientsin when the Viceroy requested him to call on Garcia. Yung wasted no time in telling Garcia that he had seen for himself in Macao in 1855 a string of poor Chinese coolies tied to each other by their queues, and led into the barracoons like abject slaves. He vividly described the horrors of the middle passage and how whole cargoes revolted or jumped overboard rather than endure the sufferings those Chinese had experienced on their voyages to Peru. He pointedly told Garcia that he would dissuade the Viceroy from entering into any treaty with Peru.

Yung was then recalled to Harvard to prepare for a mission to Peru to learn at first hand the condition of the Chinese coolies in Peru. He was to be accompanied by two Americans, the Rev. J.H. Twichell, and Dr E.W. Kellogg. A fellow Commissioner, Chen Lanpin, would be conducting a similar but separate study in Cuba.

After a short but intense investigation in Peru in September 1874, Yung's study was completed within three months, and sent to Viceroy Li Huang-chang in December 1874.

It contained:
- Field reports on Chinese labourers in the agricultural and construction sectors in Peru;
- testimonies of witnesses;
- a petition from Chinese residents in Lima;
- interviews with 14 Chinese in Lima, and
- 24 photos of lacerated and torn backs of some of the coolies, perpetuated by some owners of the haciendas.

There were three separate rounds of negotiations between the Peruvian envoy and Viceroy Li between October 1873 and May-June 1874. Garcia was still in China when the reports from Yung and Chin were received. Garcia denied all the allegations and continued to expound on how well the Chinese were prospering in Peru. The incriminating photographs were withheld until Garcia had exhausted himself, and when eventually shown to him, he was taken by surprise, dumbfounded, and he retired completely crestfallen.

Yung Wing's Peru mission did not take place until September 1874, when the treaty with Peru was already signed (26 June 1874). His report did in fact cause a delay in the formal ratification of the treaty by China, but this was eventually done by February 1876.[147]

Treaties with Peru and Spain

With encouragement from Britain and the United States, on 26 June 1874, China and Peru eventually signed a Treaty of Friendship. By now, the emigration of Chinese from Macao had already ceased. Nevertheless, a supplementary treaty to protect the rights of Chinese was agreed. Hereinafter Chinese migration to Peru was to be on a free and voluntary basis.

To encourage this free migration, the Peruvian Congress in 1875 granted an annual subsidy of 160,000 Peruvian *soles* to any steamship company bringing coolies from China. The American steamship company Olyphant and Co. was granted a contract in April 1877, but this was rescinded the following year for failing to comply with the contract terms. With the failure of a direct service to China, the Peruvian Government then granted a licence to Grace Brothers and Company, another company based in San Francisco, but with strong ties to Peru, to bring Chinese from California. The first shipment was with 23 Chinese, with the expectation that one or two thousand could be enticed to work in Peru.[148] But the War of the Pacific (1879-84) between Peru and Chile prevented any further importation of Chinese.

With the Report of the Cuba Commission, the Chinese government finally took steps to formalise the emigration of their nationals. As with the treaty signed with Peru in 1874, the Treaty of Peking of 17 November 1877 between China and Spain prohibited the transportation of Chinese labourers under contract to Cuba. But free emigration was permitted. Under the treaty, Cuba granted most favoured nation status to Chinese subjects, and they were free to leave as they pleased. Spain also volunteered to return certain classes of Chinese workers. The era of the pseudo-slavery of Chinese people had ended. Nevertheless, slavery was not officially abolished in Cuba until 1886.

After Macao introduced a regulation for Chinese Emigration in 1856, on 21 October 1857, the Legislative Council of Hong Kong enacted, "An Ordinance for Licensing and Regulating Emigration Brokers",[149] to prevent abuses of the emigrants who were increasingly passing through Hong Kong on their way to other lands.

With strict laws governing against any abuse in the recruitment of Chinese passengers, Hong Kong was not an attractive port for those engaged in the indentured labour trade. However, it very quickly became the predominant port of departure for credit-ticket emigrants leaving for San Francisco, Sydney, Melbourne, and Victoria (Vancouver Island).

A Portuguese Retrospective

On 24 March 1874, four days before the last coolie ship departed from Macao, , the Portuguese Minister for Foreign Affairs, Joao de Andrade Corvo, presented a report to the Cortes, the Legislative Council in Lisbon.[150] Corvo opened his address by saying that the Government, while recognising the importance of this lucrative commerce, had constantly endeavoured, through active vigilance and the severest measures, to restrict the abuses inseparably connected with the system. These abuses had been known to the Portuguese authorities, but had been, "more than once unjustly treated by artificially excited opinions, not always animated by sincerity and disinterestedness".

Señor Corvo then sketched the origin of Chinese emigration from 1845 up to the time of the British Government's questions to its Consuls in 1852, when Britain was looking to import labour for its sugar-producing colonies, following the loss of slave labour. He claimed that the British Government, in pursuing this emigration, was well aware of the danger to emigrants. While English agents tried to promote the system and improve conditions, they had, in contrast, markedly hostile dispositions to any emigration which might seek shores other than those of the British colonies. He thought that Britain could have given the Portuguese more credit in their attempts to diminish the abuses and crimes of the coolie trade. Hong Kong's efforts at superintendence over the coolie trade through the institution of licensed agents and the establishment of warehouses and depots, as well as the measures regulating voyages, were all followed by the Macao authorities. By 1856-57, the essential abuses connected with the system were well recognised; yet emigration was still encouraged by England. Portugal had hoped that England, knowing these abuses, would stop emigration from Hong Kong. As this did not happen, Portugal followed suit by allowing emigration from Macao.

Various repressive measures had been implemented, beginning from 1853, but had been ineffectual. This was chiefly because both the origin of the emigration, and its ultimate destination, were out of the control of the authorities.

In another interpretation of the Kung Convention, Corvo claimed that it was aimed at restricting emigration to the powers who had signed the 1866 Treaty of Peking, namely France and England. He added, "As may be gleaned from the instructions given to Lord Elgin, the idea of supplying their Colonies in the tropics with labourers pre-occupied the agents of the European Powers in China more than any other object".

Despite all the efforts of Portugal to come to an agreement with China, Señor Corvo was particularly disappointed by a letter from the Viceroy of Canton to the Governor of Macao, full of hostility to Macao emigration. Corvo was of the opinion that China's refusal, backed by European diplomacy in Peking, to enter into an agreement on emigration through the port of Macao, was one of the principal causes for the perpetuation of abuses in emigration from Macao. The presence of a mandarin at Macao raised great objections, but if the mandarin's powers had been limited by Treaty, those objections might have ceased to exist.[151]

Señor Corvo did not approve of the 1872 Regulations, which he said were framed to favour emigration agents rather than the coolies. In April 1873, the Governor admitted that the

Portuguese Government was totally powerless to prevent the abuses and horrors of the system, maintaining that these were entirely perpetuated before the emigrants came under the influence of Portuguese rule.

The Christian population of Macao had increased marginally since 1822, reaching 5,375 in 1871, while, during the same period, the number of Chinese had risen greatly, from 8,000 to 64,029. In contrast, the number of Portuguese residents in Hong Kong had outnumbered the British by one third, and as the coolie traffic developed, so did the Portuguese population in Hong Kong increase.

Emigration from Macao increased after emigration from Hong Kong ceased, but the real interests of the Portuguese colony had been sacrificed by an illusory prosperity which not only destroyed the energy of the population but also discredited the Portuguese name. Increasing hostility with China did not help. From 1868 to 1872, 57,883 coolies had emigrated, and, during the same period, 15,138 had been repatriated on the grounds of having been deceived.

Señor Corvo considered that the coolie traffic had undoubtedly corrupted the morals of the colony. This was particularly shameful because it did not promote legitimate prosperity and because the emigration business was concentrated in a few hands, almost all foreigners. He concluded that the abolition of the trade was necessary for the honour of the Portuguese name.

Peru
Returned 140 Chinese in 1890.

11
Coolie Shipping In Review

The Chinese indentured labour trade lasted for 29 years between 1846 and 1874. The 732 ships involved took on board 291,484 Chinese emigrants. These were mainly men with a few children and even fewer women. They embarked from six main ports and landed mainly in Cuba, Peru and the West Indies.

The Departure Ports

Table 11.1 Shipments from Various Departure Ports

From / To	Amoy	Cum sing moon	Hong Kong	Macao	Swatow	Whampoa	Other	Total
Number of ship departures								
Cuba	23	0	4	266	45	18	2	358
Peru	4	16	2	224	15	11	2	274
West Indies	9	0	23	4	2	22	3	63
Other	18	0	13	1	4	1	0	37
Total	54	16	42	495	66	52	7	732
Numbers Embarked								
Cuba	8,653	0	1,237	111,720	18,581	6,452	0	146,643
Peru	1,291	4,945	790	95,447	6,402	4,443	593	113,911
West Indies	3,262	0	8,549	1,261	759	7,452	562	21,845
Other	3,802	0	2,741	685	1,489	368	0	9,085
Total	17,008	4,945	13,317	209,113	27,231	18,715	1,155	291,484
Numbers Landed								
Cuba	6,659	0	920	97,450	15,114	5,820	304	126,267
Peru	772	3,110	0	82,131	4,149	4,029	0	94,191
West Indies	2,589	0	7,903	1,201	737	6,721	536	19,687
Other	3,215	0	1,577	654	1,448	368	0	7,262
Total	13,235	3,110	10,400	181,436	21,448	16,938	840	247,407

Source: Author's compilation

Amoy

Amoy was the first focus of foreigners looking for cheap Chinese labour and the main port for traditional departures for the Nanyang. From the time when two French ships took 290 Chinese to Bourbon in 1846, up to 1869 when the last two ships to sail from Amoy took 726 more to Cuba, Amoy saw the departure of 54 ships sailing for foreign lands.

The Spanish were the biggest users of the port with 23 of the 54 departures. They took 8,653 of the 17,008 indentured Chinese who left from Amoy, representing 51% of the total.

Table 11.2 Shipments from Amoy, 1846-1869

	No. of Shipments	No. Embarked	No. Landed	% Died	Notes
1846	2	290			
1847	2	642	594	7.48	
1848	1	120	120	0.00	
1849	1	150	138	8.00	
1850	2	392	373	4.85	
1851	7	1,678	1,551	7.57	
1852	14	4,258	2,989	29.80	5 mutinies
1853	4	1,209	1,026	15.14	1 mutiny
1855	3	1,505	1,266	15.88	
1856	2	1,100	634	42.36	
1857	2	710	454	36.06	
1858	3	1,097	869	20.78	
1859	1	120	82	31.67	
1860	2	560	530	5.36	
1862	1	385	384	0.26	
1865	3	1,093	1,071	2.01	
1866	2	973	487	1.22	1 mutiny
1869	2	726	667	8.13	
Total	54	17,008	13,235	22.18	

Source: Author's compilation

The first opposition to indentured Chinese emigration occurred in 1852 when the recruitment of large numbers of men created a strong reaction from the locals. This resulted in five mutinies and a riot, with ships having to divert to Namoa (Swatow).

Amoy continued to be a loading port, primarily for Cuba, until 1860, and again in 1869, but, although there were six shipments to the British West Indies in the 1860s, the port was no longer considered a major source for indentured Chinese labourers. However, it remained the main port for emigration to the Nanyang.

Swatow (Namoa)

Following the Amoy riots in 1852, recruiting agents unable to fulfil their contracts diverted their ships to Namoa, just 100 miles to the south.

The Namoa anchorage was first used by the opium ships which sheltered in the bay on the north coast of Namoa Island, just to the east of the main town of Swatow. The seven ships which were diverted to Namoa in 1852 included four destined for Cuba, two for the West Indies and one for Australia. As Swatow did not become a Treaty Port until 1858, the 23 British ships loading at that port were technically breaking the terms of the 1842 Treaty of Nanking between Britain and China.

Table 11.3 Shipments from Swatow, 1852-1866

	No. of Shipments	No. Embarked	No. Landed	% Died	Notes
1852	4	1,402	1,342	4.28	
1853	3	1,074	984	8.38	
1854	8	3,585	2,857	20.31	1 shipwreck
1855	12	6,304	5,110	18.94	2 mutinies
1856	11	4,598	4,017	12.64	
1857	17	6,135	4,366	28.83	4 mutinies
1858	7	2,451	1,632	33.41	
1859	2	626	365	41.69	
1860	1	612	343	43.95	1 mutiny
1866	1	444	432	22.82	
Total	66	27,231	21,448	21.24	

Source: Author's compilation

Comfortable with the arrangement, the Cubans then continued to use Swatow until 1860 with one break only, in 1859. In all, 45 shipments were made to Cuba, carrying a total of 18,581 Chinese, which was 67% of the total number of coolies shipped from there.

Peru began using Swatow in 1854, and shipped 24% of the total of 27,231 men in the 15 ships which departed for Callao. Even though Swatow became a Treaty Port in 1858, Britain did not directly use that port again after the transgressions in 1853 (i.e. British ships using Swatow when it was not a Treaty port).

Cumsingmoon

Like Namoa, Cumsingmoon, 20 miles to the north of Macao, was not a port but an opium anchorage. Remote from official surveillance, it was a convenient place to load desperate paupers from the area. Between 1849 and 1854, 16 ships loaded 4,945 destitute men, all for Peru.

Table 11.4 Shipments from Cumsingmoon, 1849-1854

	No. of Shipments	No. Embarked	No. Landed	% Died	Notes
1849	1	75	75	0.00	
1850	5	1,400	669	52.21	2 dismasted
1851	1	350			1 mutiny
1852	3	925	547	40.86	1 abandoned
1853	5	1,870	1,541	17.59	1 mutiny
1854	1	325	278	14.46	1 mutiny
Total	16	4,945	3,110	37.11	

Source: Author's compilation

Two of the five ships which departed Cumsingmoon in 1850 failed to reach their destination, one (the *Albert*) suffering a mutiny and the other (*Manuelita*) having to abandon her voyage after being dismasted. Another ship was also dismasted but managed to make Manila, where her passengers were transferred to another vessel (*Orixa*) for the rest of the voyage. Only four died in the process with 176 men eventually sent to Chincha. The mortality rate for the voyage was 48.89%. The first vessel bound for Chincha (*Lady Montague*) suffered 45.23% mortality after a 129-day voyage. In 1851, the *Victory* was unable to complete the voyage because of a mutiny.

The plight of the men on the five horror ships made an everlasting impression on the world. Coolie shipping to Peru became synonymous with the killing fields of the Chincha guano islands.

Canton (Whampoa)

Canton was the prize Treaty Port. But the shallow river waters of Canton did not allow ships of any significant draft to reach it. Whampoa, some six miles from Canton, was the anchorage which serviced the Provincial capital.

Table 11.5 Shipments from Whampoa, 1852-1873

	No. of Shipments	No. Embarked	No. Landed	% Died	Notes
1852	2	259	256	1.16	
1853	1	350			voyage aborted
1855	3	1,540	1,436	6.75	
1856	3	1,084	961	11.35	1 dismasted
1857	1	770	723	6.10	
1859	2	1,180	1,073	9.07	
1860	6	2,112	1,869	11.51	3 mutinies
1861	9	2,981	2,875	3.56	1 mutiny
1862	1	326	324	0.61	
1863	2	930	905	2.69	
1864	2	590	582	1.36	
1865	10	3,279	3,000	8.51	2 mutinies
1866	8	2,416	2,047	15.27	3 mutinies
1872	1	510	499	2.16	
1873	1	388	388	0.00	
Total	52	18,715	16,938	9.50	

Source: Author's compilation

Only two ships, carrying 259 Chinese, used the port in 1852. The sole departure in 1853 was aborted and there were no departures in 1854. It was not until 1859 that recruiters began to look to Whampoa seriously as a possible place to load coolies. Strict supervision by the local officials, however, banned holding facilities which had not been approved as depots. This effectively favoured the British Emigration Agency which became the major user of the port until 1866, when the French Maritime Agency re-established a depot there to service Cuban requirements. There were 11 shipments to Peru carrying 4,443 men, and 18 shipments to

Cuba with 6,452 Chinese. The British West Indies took the most shipments with 7,452 labourers in 22 shipments.

Hong Kong

Hong Kong was the only port which shipped both indentured and free labour. The first ship leaving Hong Kong for Australia with Chinese on board was recorded in 1847. There were only seven of them however, and it is doubtful whether they went as indentured labourers. Single shipments of two and six men were recorded in the next two years. However, in 1848, the *London*, making her second trip in two years, carried 149 indentured servants, thus marking Hong Kong's entrance into the role of a "coolie port".

Table 11.6 Indentured Coolie Labour Shipments from Hong Kong, 1848-1870[152]

	No. of Shipments	No. Embarked	No. Landed	% Died	Notes
1848	1	149	149	0.00	
1854	2	718	267	3.87	1 aborted
1855	1	375	375	0.00	
1856	2	635	373	41.26	1 mutiny
1857	1	227	172	24.23	
1859	1	372	372	0.00	
1860	4	1,308	1,289	1.45	
1861	6	2,301	2,200	4.39	
1862	4	1,914	1,761	7.99	1 dismasted
1864	1	337	0	-	numbers landed
1865	5	1,700	755	-	not all known
1866	4	1,087	1,049	3.50	
1867	1	291	270	7.22	1 mutiny
1868	1	252	246	2.38	1 mutiny
1869	2	500	405	19.00	
1870	6	1,151	717	37.71	1 mutiny
Total	42	13,317	10,400	21.90	

Source: Author's compilation

Strict British supervision, however, ensured that Hong Kong was never to become a major port for indentured coolie labour. The only two ships that loaded there for Peru did not reach their destinations. The *Topaz* was shipwrecked and the

Frederic suffered a mutiny. Cuban planters were prepared to use Hong Kong as an emigration port with four shipments but after the Chinese Passengers' Act of 1855 came into force, they turned to other load ports. British West Indian planters however had a preference for Hong Kong and over 14 shipments between 1854 and 1862 took 5,369 men women and children. Between 1865 and 1869 Surinam was the destination for 2,344 coolies in seven shipments.

Macao

Table 11.7 Shipments from Macao, 1851-1874

	No. of Shipments	No. of Agents	No. Embarked	No. Landed	% Died	Notes
1851	2	1	813	800	1.60	
1852	1	1	250	233	6.80	
1853	7	3	2,327	1,885	18.99	1 mutiny
1854	1	1	60	60	0.00	
1855	5	4	1,955	1,586	18.87	1 mutiny
1856	7	3	2,608	1,566	39.95	2 mutinies
1857	16	4	7,855	6,166	21.50	4 mutinies
1858	19	9	10,000	8,676	13.24	
1859	15	7	8,477	6,291	25.79	2 mutinies
1860	22	6	8,931	8,030	10.09	4 mutinies
1861	10	7	3,953	3,686	6.75	
1862	6	4	2,111	2,007	4.93	
1863	19	9	6,663	5,563	16.51	1 shipwreck
1864	33	16	10,784	9,915	8.06	
1865	38	13	13,624	11,387	7.37	3 mutinies
1866	63	18	23,563	20,585	12.64	3 mutinies
1867	41	13	16,697	14,422	13.63	4 mutinies
1868	31	10	12,208	10,959	10.23	4 mutinies
1869	20	5	9,136	7,918	13.33	2 mutinies
1870	30	7	13,412	11,548	13.90	2 mutinies
1871	40	8	17,200	15,093	12.25	1 mutiny
1872	44	6	21,098	19,063	9.65	2 mutinies
1873	21	8	13,017	11,658	0.57	
1874	4	4	2,371	2,339	1.35	
Total	495	-	209,113	181,436	13.23	

Source: Author's compilation

Macao became a coolie port in 1851 when a second Peruvian entrepreneur was granted permission to import Chinese labour. Unhappy with the sorry outcomes of the Cumsingmoon shipments, José Sevilla preferred to utilise the nearby port of Macao rather than the troubled port of Amoy.

The grand total of 495 ships which left Macao between 1851 and 1874, inclusive, took 209,113 Chinese coolies away. By 1858, the number of sailings from Macao regularly exceeded the sailings from all of the other ports. In the ten years between 1860 and 1869, 283 ships left Macao for Latin America, compared with 73 between 1851 and 1859, a fourfold increase in the traffic. A further 139 sailed between 1870 and 1874, the last year of the trade. With the exception of four ships to the West Indies in 1858-59 and one ship to Costa Rica in 1872, all were destined for Cuba or Peru.

The peak year was 1866. In that year, eighteen emigration agents recruited 23,563 coolies to leave on 63 ships. There were three mutinies in that frantic year—one ship did not reach its destination because it was burned by the mutineers. The mortality rate for the year (12.64%) is also worth noting, being below the overall average.

In 1871, Cuba indicated that its migration programme would terminate in 1873; and on 27 December 1873, Macao proclaimed an end to emigration from that port. In the last full year of the programme (1873), eight ships took 5,847 labourers to Havana while thirteen ships took another 7,170 to Callao. Only four ships were able to load 2,371 Chinese for Callao in 1874, leaving twelve ships stranded in Macao with no cargoes.

In the 447 departures where lay days can be calculated, the average time was 47 days ranging from 4 to 225 days. The median was 36 days.

Destinations from all ports

Chinese coolies were sought after from a diverse number of places. The main destinations, as already said, were Cuba, Peru and the West Indies. This latter grouping included the French West Indies—to which two sailings were made—and

Dutch Guiana (better known as Surinam), to which nine departures were made.

Table 11.8 Ship arrivals from various ports w. no. embarked, no. of agents used, no. and % successfully landed

Sending ports \ Arrival ports	Cuba	Peru	West Indies	Other	Total
Departures and Arrivals from Various Ports with Number of Agents Used					
Amoy	23	4	9	18	54
Cumsingmoon		16			16
Hong Kong	4	2	23	13	42
Macao	266	224	4	1	495
Swatow	45	15	2	4	66
Whampoa	18	11	22	1	52
Other	2	2	3		7
TOTAL departures	358	274	63	37	732
TOTAL Arrivals	348	255	61	37	701
Agents used	44	34	7	-	-
Numbers Embarked at Various Ports					
Amoy	8,653	1,291	3,262	3,802	17,008
Cumsingmoon		4,945			4,945
Hong Kong	1,237	790	8,549	2,741	13,317
Macao	111,720	95,447	1,261	685	209,113
Swatow	18,581	6,402	759	1,489	27,231
Whampoa	6,452	4,443	7,452	368	18,715
Other		593	562		1,155
TOTAL	146,643	113,911	21,845	9,085	291,484
Numbers Landed from Various Ports					
Amoy	6,659	772	2,589	3,215	13,235
Cumsingmoon		3,110			3,110
Hong Kong	920		7,903	1,577	10,400
Macao	97,450	82,131	1,201	654	181,436
Swatow	15,114	4,149	737	1,448	21,448
Whampoa	5,820	4,029	6,721	368	16,938
Other		304	536		840
TOTAL	126,267	94,191	19,687	7,262	247,407
% Landed	86.11	82.69	90.12	79.93	84.88

Source: Author's compilation
Note: "Other" refers to Kwangchow, Manila, Panama and Shanghai.

Cuban importers undertook 358 shipments of which 348 were completed. (Table 11.8) They utilised 44 identified and three unidentified emigration agents to recruit 146,643 Chinese coolies, of whom 126,627 were landed. This represents 86.11% of the number engaged.

Peru was less successful. (Table 11.8) From the 274 shipments undertaken, only 255 reached their destination. Peruvian importers employed 34 identified emigration agents (68 shipments did not show the agent employed). They engaged 113,911 Chinese labourers, with 94,191 of them able to walk ashore. The success rate was 82.69%.

West Indian plantation owners differed from their Cuban and Peruvian counterparts in that they had access to Indian labour. Some 144,257 Indians were taken to the British West Indies, 9,783 men women and children to Guadaloupe and 5,553 to Martinique, with a further 2,175 Indians from Pondicherry in 1872. The Dutch Government entered into an agreement with the British Government in 1870 to bring Indians to Surinam. Actual numbers are not known.

West Indian importers differed from the Cubans and Peruvians in another way also, they were state-sponsored. The British government employed five agents to recruit their 18,013 emigrants while France used one company. The Netherlands had one agency in Hong Kong with an unidentified agent for their two shipments from Macao. Two of the 63 shipments carrying 21,845 Chinese to the West Indies did not arrive, leaving 19,687 to disembark. That represented 90.12% of the total recruited from China. (Table 11.8)

Data on the 37 shipments to other destinations is insufficient to draw meaningful comment.

Cuba

Cuba first used Chinese labour in 1847, but it was not until 1852 that allocations were made for controlled importation of Chinese coolies. The demand was cyclical. There were only three shipments in 1854, but this rose sharply to 34 in 1857. After falling to just two shipments in 1862, demand slowly rose before reaching the all-time record of 52 in 1866. Shipments again began to fall after that, reaching a nadir of only two shipments in 1870 with the advent of the Ten Years'

War. Shipments resumed in 1871 and 1872 before falling to eight in 1873, the final year of importations. (Table 11.9)

In the 26 years between 1847 and 1873, 146,643 Chinese were embarked on 358 ships for Havana. The number who landed amounted to 126,267, giving an average mortality rate over the entire period of 13.89%. However 10 ships did not reach their destination, seven because of mutinies and three from shipwreck. If we discount the number of men on those ships, the mortality on ships arriving at Havana was 11.56% of those embarked.

Table 11.9 Shipments to Cuba, 1847-1873

	Shipments	Embarked	Passengers Per Ton ratio	Average Voyage Days	Landed	% Died
1847	2	642	0.66	130	594	7.48
1852	8	2,651	0.63	128	1,984	25.16
1853	11	3,842	0.64	142	3,212	16.40
1854	3	1,453	0.73	117	1,416	2.55
1855	10	4,617	0.45	108	4,278	7.34
1856	20	8,239	0.55	142	5,948	27.81
1857	34	14,217	0.52	134	10,880	23.47
1858	25	12,448	0.49	119	10,166	18.33
1859	16	8,995	0.52	123	6,681	25.73
1860	21	8,338	0.44	118	8,046	3.50
1861	10	4,090	0.45	108	3,876	5.23
1862	2	752	0.43	127	730	2.93
1863	9	2,923	0.47	122	2,214	24.26
1864	12	4,469	0.52	112	4,328	3.16
1865	21	6,079	0.55	123	5,655	6.97
1866	52	18,437	0.55	133	16,624	9.83
1867	29	10,849	0.55	126	9,784	9.82
1868	23	8,835	0.55	126	8,084	8.50
1869	12	5,027	0.50	149	3,852	23.37
1870	2	1,064	0.48	121	693	34.87
1871	15	5,706	0.53	122	5,398	5.40
1872	13	7,123	0.56	102	6,518	8.49
1873	8	5,847	0.58	137	5,306	9.25
Total	358	146,643	0.53	122	126,267	13.89

Source: Author's compilation

The number of men embarked on each ship averaged 412, ranging from a low of 113 in 1858 to 1099 in 1873, the final year of importations. The number of passengers permitted to be loaded was generally taken as being one passenger per two tons of the vessel. Any factor above 0.5 would have been a breach of the regulations. The load factor on Cuban-bound ships ranged from 0.21 to 1.04. The average was 0.53.

There was only one sailing route to Cuba and the West Indies.—First, down the South China Sea to Anjer, into the Indian Ocean. Ships then crossed either north or south of Mauritius to Cape Town, where supplies could be replenished if required, or directly for St Helena in the South Atlantic. The island of St Helena was an important resupply port for ships heading for the West Indies as well as to North America and all of Europe. The distance to Cuba was about 10,830 miles.

Under the Chinese Passengers' Act ships sailing for the Caribbean were to carry provisions for a voyage of at least 147 days during the season from October to March and for at least 168 days in the off-season between April and September. The average time taken for the 358 voyages was 128 days.

The *Carpentaria* has been credited with the fastest voyage time of 64 days from Macao to Havana in 1855. The mortality rate on that voyage was 4.61%. The longest voyage was also the last shipment, and did not arrive until 4 March 1874 when the unreliable steamer *Rosita y Nene* finally arrived after a 320-day voyage. The mortality rate was 14.81% of the 851 who embarked.

Although Spain officially gave eight months notice in 1871, stopping the importation of Chinese labourers as from that same year, shipments continued until October 1873. The last vessel to load at Macao for Havana was the 1,776-ton Belgian 300hp steamer, *Nelusko*, bringing the largest ever contingent of Chinese on a single ship.[153] Of the 1,099 who were embarked, 1,055 were able to disembark, the 44 deaths amounting to 4% of the whole.

Cuban Consignees and their Agents (Table 11.10)
The first merchants to bring in Chinese labourers were Villoldo Wardrop. They recruited 3,153 men on only nine

ships, but problems on the ships resulted in 2,397 only being able to land in Cuba. Pereda was given a similar allocation to Villoldo, and also suffered initial losses. But he persisted, eventually utilising 33 vessels to bring 13,324 men to Cuba. The overall result was that he was able to on-sell the contracts of more than 90% of those men.

Table 11.10 Cuban Consignees and their Principal Agents, 1852-1873

Consignee	Agents	Active Years	Shipments	Embarked	Landed	% Died
Villoldo	Tait	1852 - 53	9	3,153	2,397	23.98
Pereda	de Castro	1852 - 60	33	13,146	11,834	9.98
Drake	Armero	1855 - 57	19	7,838	5,606	28.48
Morales	Armero	1858 - 60	10	4,490	3,648	18.75
Torices	Ferran	1855 - 60	55	25,497	20,149	20.98
Colonizadora	de Hoyas	1858 - 58	3	1,596	1,305	18.23
Schimper	Laget	1859 - 60	3	1,566	1,262	19.41
Campbell	Flotard	1856 - 60	9	5,961	4,902	17.77
Caro	Caro	1859 - 67	16	5,774	5,150	10.81
Zangronis	Solares	1859 - 66	26	8,348	7,573	9.28
Troncoso	de Castro	1860 - 68	22	7,519	7,044	6.32
Bustmente	Garcia	1863 - 66	3	1,111	1,037	6.66
Empresa	Noronha	1863 - 67	21	7,219	6,342	12.15
Alianza	Calderon Tuton	1865 - 73	55	23,508	21,064	10.40
Aldama	Sagues	1864 - 68	13	4,176	3,889	6.87
Merino Gilledo	Garcia	1864 - 69	8	2,632	2,429	7.71
Lombillo	Armero	1866 -69	23	9,049	7,875	12.97
Hacendados	Tuton	1871 - 73	11	6,059	5,684	6.19
Ibanez	Abella	1871 - 73	10	4,873	4,409	9.52
Others	Various	1847 - 73	9	3,128	2,668	14.71
Total			358	146,643	126,267	13.89

Source: Author's compilation

The next two merchants to be granted allocations also had varying experiences. From 1855 to 1860, Drake—and then his partner, Morales—recruited 12,222 labourers between them, using 29 ships. The mortality rate was a depressing 21.58%. During the same period, Torices was the more aggressive importer. He needed 55 ships to take on 25,495 Chinese coolies, but lost 2,822 of them en route.

With import licences then no longer required, various partnerships—not necessarily formalised—emerged. Caro Campbell had a loose arrangement with Schimper, while Troncoso began in 1860 through a partnership with Bustamente. Individuals, such as Aldama, Zangronis and Lombillo had links with planters, and imported in their own right. Each undertook more than 20 sailings carrying in excess of 8,000 Chinese coolies.

Empresa was a consortium established by a group of planters. It later merged with banking interests to become Alianza, the biggest importer of Chinese labour. Between 1863 and 1873, they employed 76 ships to carry 30,727 coolies to Havana. Just over 10% of those died before reaching Cuba.

A new grouping, known as the Hacendados and, separately, a prominent planter, Ibanez, hastily entered the trade to recruit the last of the Chinese labour to be brought to the island.

Coolies returning from Cuba

Return passages were not offered to immigrants to Cuba. However, in the case of some of the ships dedicated to the Chinese coolie trade, those immigrants who had been able to accumulate their passage money were able to secure return passages at the end of their contracts.

The first ship to bring coolies back directly from Havana arrived in 1865. There were 16 Chinese on the *Lombard*, which arrived in Macao on 7 October 1865. The next year, 1866, the *JAU* arrived with 22, and in the same year, 15 came back on the shuttle auxiliary steamer *Cataluna*. Four ships brought 113 Chinese back from Cuba in 1867. In 1868, two ships brought back 65, and three ships brought 180 men in 1869. Another three ships brought 202 men back in 1870. There were none in 1871. Two final shipments brought just 58 men in 1872.

These were direct shipments. There would have been some who returned by way of the United States. The number of Chinese returning from Cuba has not been fully documented. In a Table dated 3 October 1873 the Comision

Central de Colonizacion[154] showed that 130 Chinese had obtained passports to return to China between July and December 1872, and another 135 between January and October 1873. One Chinese had gone to Spain, another to France and one to Mexico, and ten had left for the United States.

Another source[155] identified 14 ships which left Cuba in 1871 for Philadelphia, New York, New Orleans, and Tampico with a total on board of 111 Chinese.

Peru

Shipping to Peru commenced in 1849 and continued until 1874. As with Cuba, the demand was cyclical. It had three distinct peaks. The first was in 1855 when 13 shipments were made before the revocation of the "Chinese Law". Twelve shipments only were made between 1856 and 1859, inclusive, a period during which immigration was officially banned.

In anticipation of Chinese again being permitted to be brought to Peru, eight shipments were made in 1860 and seven more in 1861 when it became official again. Only four shipments were made in 1862 but, the next year, the number rose to ten. Following a slump from 1867 to 1869, shipments rose sharply to 29 in 1870 and 31 in 1872. Following the *Maria Luz* affair (described above), shipments fell back to 13 in 1873, but were expected to rise again when emigration from Macao was stopped.

Between 1849 and 1874, 113,911 Chinese were embarked on 274 ships for Callao. The number known to have landed amounted to 94,191, giving an average mortality rate of 17.31% over the entire period. However, 19 ships did not reach their destination. When the number of men on those ships is discounted, the mortality on ships arriving at Callao was 11.86%. Six other ships did not reach their destination either but were able to transfer some of their passengers to other ships for oncarriage to Callao. Of these 25 voyages, 12 were the result of successful mutinies, two from unsuccessful insurrections, four ships were dismasted and three shipwrecked. Four others, including the *Maria Luz*, were abandoned.

Table 11.11 Shipments to Peru, 1849-1874

	Ship-ments	Embarked	Passengers Per Ton Ratio	Average Voyage Days	Landed	% Died
1849	1	75	0.17	139	75	0
1850	5	1,400	0.67	140	669	52.21
1851	3	1,163	0.6	124	800	31.21
1852	6	1,760	0.7	134	945	46.31
1853	6	2,070	0.64	125	1,739	15.99
1854	5	1,691	0.73	130	586	65.35
1855	13	6,694	0.52	107	5,127	23.41
1856	5	1,786	0.59	132	1,603	10.25
1857	3	1480	0.55	100	1001	32.36
1858	1	300	0.4	180	260	13.33
1859	3	947	0.69	141	680	28.19
1860	8	2,552	0.38	108	1,913	25.04
1861	7	2,240	0.52	156	1,535	31.47
1862	4	1,359	0.46	104	1,277	12.47
1863	10	3,740	0.51	106	3,349	10.45
1864	21	6,315	0.54	107	5,587	11.53
1865	22	9,037	0.56	107	7,030	22.21
1866	19	7,681	0.5	124	6,138	20.09
1867	12	5,848	0.48	120	4,638	20.69
1868	8	3,373	0.51	121	2,875	14.76
1869	10	4,835	0.51	106	4,733	2.11
1870	29	12,730	0.54	107	10,855	14.73
1871	25	11,494	0.53	107	9,695	15.65
1872	31	13,800	0.56	114	12,390	10.22
1873	13	7,170	0.56	110	6,352	11.41
1874	4	2,371	0.54	97	2,339	1.35
Total	274	113,911	0.53	110	94,191	17.31

Source: Author's compilation

Under the Chinese Passengers' Act, ships bound for the West Coast of America south of the Equator were required to carry sufficient provisions for a voyage of up to 120 days throughout the year. In the "off" season, vessels making for Callao could use the southwest monsoonal winds to carry them northwards towards Hawaii or Japan before taking advantage of the Kuro Siwo current to North America and then the California current southward.

During the northeast monsoon, captains could choose the southern route to Anjer in the Sunda Straits before continuing south to Australia, and then use the Antarctic Circumpolar Current and the strong westerlies that blow in the roaring forties to speed them to Callao. Alternatively, the captain could choose to sail across the Timor Sea, down the east coast of Australia and New Zealand, before joining the South Pacific Current. This route of approximately 11,000 miles would have been more than 1,000 miles longer than the northern alternative.

The fastest passage was 61 days, made by the Peruvian ship *Rosalia* under Mexican Captain E. Dias, which left Macao on 2 July 1873. The American clipper ship, *Winged Racer*, under Captain Gorman, had previously held the record of 68 days since 1855. The longest time taken was by the *Petronila*. Stress of weather caused her to seek repairs in Honolulu twice before eventually arriving in Callao 217 days after leaving Macao. The average voyage time over all three routes was 114 days.

Peruvian Consignees and their Agents (Table 11.12)

The Peruvian entrepreneur Don Elias made an experimental voyage in 1849 and five shipments in 1850. Nearly all the ships suffered casualties and there was a mortality rate of 18%. There were several mutinies, associated with the terrible conditions on board. Once this was known, the resulting outcry caused the world permanently to associate Chinese coolies with the horrors of the guano trade and to give Elias a lasting terrible reputation. He re-entered the trade in 1870 with two more shipments, but not for the Chinchas. His friend José Sevilla began shipping Chinese men to mainland Peru in 1851 (no more Chinese men were shipped to the Chinchas after Elias) and continued for three years during which he undertook 13 voyages taking on 4,766 in all.

Canevaro in conjunction with Emilio Althaus was the biggest importer of Chinese labour. They employed 50 vessels between 1857 and 1864. Most of the vessels were owned outright and dedicated to the trade. Of the 22,920 Chinese embarked, nearly 90% of them were able to land in Callao.

Table 11.12 Peruvian Consignees and their Agents (1849-1874)

Consignee	Agent	Active Years	Shipments	Embarked	Landed	% Died
Elias	Jorge	1849 - 70	8	2,127	1,353	36.39
Sevilla	Unknown	1851 - 53	13	4,756	3,336	29.86
Alson	Robinet	1852 - 53	2	500	426	14.80
Robinet	Robinet	1854 - 55	6	2,185	1,183	45.86
Ugarte	Olano Armero	1857 - 74	25	11,790	10,104	14.30
Canevaro	Landabaso	1863 - 74	40	19,395	16,308	15.92
Garcia	del Rio	1863 - 70	7	3,046	2,770	9.06
Althaus	Armero Leathold	1864 - 73	14	5,102	3,922	23.13
Figari	Tuton	1864 -74	25	9,173	8,662	5.57
Pardo	Pastor	1864 - 68	4	2,422	2,166	10.57
Maritima	Pearce	1865 - 73	29	15,702	14,716	6.28
Various	Various	1865 - 74	51	19,102	15,774	17.42
Unknown	Unknown	1852 - 74	50	18,611	13,471	27.62
TOTAL			274	113,911	94,191	17.31

Source: Author's compilation

The number of men embarked on each ship to Peru averaged 414, ranging from a low of 75 on the first ship to 593 in the final year of importations. The load factor on ships bound for Peru ranged from 0.02 to 1.20. Mortality rates ranged from 0.00% to 75.56% in 1852 when the load factor was 0.64. Mortality rates however, cannot be attributed solely to overcrowding. In 1850 the average load factor was 0.77, with the mortality rate showing 58.21%, whereas in 1853 the load factor was 0.73, but the mortality rate was 16.54%.

The other long-term participant in the trade was Ugarte who commenced operations in 1861 and based himself in Macao for a few years. Sometimes in conjunction with Santiago, he undertook 21 voyages, on which 9,558 Chinese labourers and servants were embarked. The success rate was similar to Canavaro's: nearly 90% landed safely in Callao. Ugarte was still active when the coolie trade was banned in 1874.

A company formed for the specific purpose of conveying Chinese colonists to Peru was the Compania Maritima del Peru. It bought its first three ships in 1865 and was active until the traffic was banned. On the 28 shipments the company made, 15,022 men, women and children were conveyed to Callao. There were only 959 deaths on the way giving the company a mortality record of 6.38%.

The figure was only bettered by another long-term participant in the trade. Figari and sons (there was at least two sons, Antonio and Juan), engaged 24 ships to take on 8,757 Chinese for Peru, of whom 501 did not complete the journey. The overall loss rate was 5.72%, the best in either the Cuban or Peruvian trades.

Smaller shippers included the Garcia family, Pardo and Cadamo. On the four Zaracondegui ships the loss rate was 24.65%, while Pratolongo, who had a ship named after him, suffered a loss of 29.90%.

On the 102 shipments between 1852 and 1874 where the consignee was not identified, 39,085 Chinese were placed on board but only 29,525 were able to walk ashore. The average loss rate on those ships amounted to 24.46%.

Coolies returning from Peru

Return passages from Peru were at the expense of the *"colonos"*.[156] Chinese returnees from Peru were first recorded when on 8 November 1865 the *Luisa Canevaro* brought 22 men back to Hong Kong. There was only one arrival with 20 on the *Camillo Cavour* in 1869 and two in 1870 with 43 men. In 1871 there were three ships bringing 131 Chinese back. In 1872, four ships disembarked their 68 passengers in Hong Kong while the *San Juan* went directly to Macao with an unknown number of Chinese returnees.

In his Annual Report for 1872, Hong Kong Harbour-Master Thomsett highlighted the contrast between Cuban and Peruvian returnees, mentioning two vessels bringing 58 Chinese back from Havana and 26 vessels arriving from Callao but only bringing 68 back. In 1873 however, the situation had somewhat improved with five vessels bringing 92 Chinese indentured labourers back from Peru.

No further returnees were recorded again until 1877, when the 173-ton Nicaraguan brig, *A. P. Christina*, brought 40 Chinese back from Peru on 31 July 1877 and another 29 on 3 December 1878. This was followed with another 141 males and the first two female returnees on the Belgian *Perusia*. The *Elvina Dovale* brought back 151 in 1881, including one female and 17 children, while the *Peru* returned another 140 Chinese in 1890. Between 1891 and 1894, the 480-ton British *Omega* brought back 116 men, women and children, while the Italian 794-ton clipper, *Lothair*, carried another 839 men, women and children. On the *Lothair*'s last voyage, 264 rushed to board her in an effort to get home before the Chinese New Year. Unfortunately, 55 of them died on the passage. When asked to comment on the large number of deaths, Captain Schiaffino simply replied "of old age".[157]

The West Indies (Table 11.13)

Shipping to the West Indies was characterised by the diversity of destinations, variously under British, French and Dutch rule.

Between 1852 and 1854, eight British ships were despatched to British Guiana, Trinidad and Jamaica. There were also two sailings from Panama taking stranded Chinese to Jamaica. Shipments ceased in 1854, on the grounds that the cost of shipping was too high.

Then, between 1858 and 1866, there were 48 sailings to the West Indies, carrying 17,726 Chinese. These totals include three sailings to Surinam and two shipments for the French West Indies from Whampoa.

The resumption of British shipping in 1858 was initially from Macao where Dutch Surinam had undertaken two shipments earlier that year. One shipment was undertaken in late 1858 followed by a second in early 1859. When the Chinese then condoned emigration from Kwangtung, British officials opened a recruitment depot in Canton with ships taking on migrants from both Hong Kong and Whampoa.

When the Kung Convention imposed unacceptable conditions for emigration, British shipments ceased in 1866. However shipments to Surinam were resumed in 1867 with four sailings, this time from Hong Kong.

A trial shipment of mainly non-contracted emigrants to British Guiana was conducted from Hong Kong in 1878, another to Antigua in 1881 and a further one to Jamaica in 1884. Those shipments have not been included in this study. In all 21,845 Chinese were taken to the West Indies. The 63 ships involved were able to land 19,687, with an average mortality rate of 9.88%. The high rate of 24.11% in 1866 was distorted by the only successful mutiny on a British West Indies-bound ship.

If we discount the 480 men who were on that ship, the mortality rate for 1866 would be 1.66%. Two other factors would have contributed to the lower mortality rates to the West Indies. The generally larger ships and resulting lower passenger tonnage ratios would have helped, as would the rather shorter times needed to reach their destinations.

Table 11.13 Shipments to the West Indies, 1852-1873

	No. of Shipments	No. Embarked	No. of Passengers Per ton	Average Voyage Days	No. Landed	% Died
1852	5	1,510	0.45	121	1,330	11.92
1853	2	664	0.47	109	305	54.07
1854	3	517	0.62	120	472	8.70
1855-1857	0					
1858	3	800	0.39	108	800	6.13
1859	3	1,188	0.51	108	1,153	2.95
1860	8	2,633	0.44	103	2,406	8.62
1861	10	3,498	0.37	103	3,350	4.23
1862	6	2,625	0.39	93	2,469	5.94
1863	2	930	0.43	79	905	2.69
1864	2	590	0.45	97	582	1.36
1865	9	3,356	0.41	102	3,059	8.85
1866	5	2,103	0.41	77	1,596	24.11
1867	1	291	0.46	83	270	7.22
1869	3	752	0.38	112	651	13.43
1873	1	388	0.32	62	388	0
TOTAL	63	21,845	0.41	97	19,687	9.88

Source: Author's compilation

The fastest voyage to the West Indies was undertaken by the *Corona* in 1873. Captain Bate took 62 days only on the 12,669 mile voyage to British Guiana. The 351-ton *Lord*

Elgin, under the unfortunate Captain M'Clelland, took 178 days —the longest time of any—and the voyage also took 168 lives. The average voyage time was 97 days.

In their haste to recruit Chinese labourers, the British Guiana plantation owners sent the *Lord Elgin* to China without adequate representation. It was left to Captain McClelland to decide who would be his agent. He chose James Tait. James White arrived in China on 10 October 1852, but had no authority to override the Tait appointment which White thought presented Tait with a conflict of interest as Tait was also representing Cuban importers. James White assumed responsibility after the first four shipments and arranged for another four, including the aborted voyage of the *Emigrant* in 1853.

Thomas Gerard was a West India Committee appointment who conducted two shipments before being superseded by J. Gardiner Austin in 1859. With failing health, Austin handed responsibility to Sampson who moved the Agency from Hong Kong to Canton.

The French and Dutch Governments chose to appoint third parties to arrange their Chinese requirements.

Table 11.14 Emigration Agents for the West Indies, 1852-1869

Agent	Principal	Active Year(s)	Number Recruited
James Tait	C LEC	1852	1,256
James White	C LEC	1852 - 1854	1,228
Thomas Gerard	West India Committee	1858 - 1859	761
J. Gardiner Austin	Colonial Governors	1859 - 1862	7,805
Theophilus Sampson	Colonial Governors	1862 - 1873	6,963
Gastel, Malavois & Assier	French Government	1859 - 1860	781
Immigratie Maatschappij	Dutch Government	1865 - 1869	2,344
Unknown	Others	1854 - 1858	707

Source: Author's compilation

Coolies returning from the West Indies

As in the case of Cuba and Peru, return passages were not offered to Chinese coolies. With no ships having returned directly to China, little is known of how many, and when any migrants returned from the West Indies. However, two Chinese paid for their own passage from Trinidad to Calcutta on the *Scindian* which left on 1 June 1855. On 10 December 1858, another three Chinese left on the *Morayshire* for Calcutta.[158]

The *Clarence* took just one fare paying Chinese passenger from British Guiana to Calcutta on 3 September 1865. Then in September 1869 the *Ganges* sailed from British Guiana for Calcutta with three Chinese men, four Chinese women and one child.[159] They travelled as cabin passengers who had paid their own fares to Calcutta. The head of the household was said to have deposited £333 6s 8d for transmission to India and had £833 in cash on him. He also held a letter of credit to the value of £33 to defray his expenses from Calcutta to Canton.[160] Also in 1869, five Chinese left Trinidad as cabin passengers on an unnamed ship. They were returning to China with a sum of $7,500 or £1,562 10s, equal to £312 10s each. They had expressed an intention of returning to Trinidad.[161]

In September 1870 the *Ganges* sailed once more from British Guiana, this time with 421 returning emigrants including ten Chinese.[162] However, a later report says the number was 407 exclusive of 14 Chinese who were embarked on the vessel.[163] On 22 September 1870, the *Wellesley* also sailed for Calcutta with one Chinese family of 15 persons who paid their own passage. They had £666 13s 4d between them.[164]

Then on 19 October 1872 the *Rohilla* departed British Guiana with 58 Chinese who had £1,416 13s 4d in cash, and on 19 October 1872 the *Enmore* left 80 Chinese who took away £6,312 10s.[165] The Chinese paid their own passages on both vessels. There were no Chinese from Trinidad that year.

The Annual Immigration Reports of British Guiana tabulate a total of 152 Chinese legally leaving the Colony for China between 1880 and 1905.[166] They would have done so by way of New York and San Francisco or via Montreal and Vancouver. The Annual Immigration Reports of British

Guiana tabulate a total of 152 Chinese legally leaving the Colony for China between 1880 and 1905.[167]

The Ships

Of the 732 voyages undertaken in the Chinese coolie trades 19 were by brigs, and 240 by barques. Voyages were undertaken by 391 ships with another 54 by what were known, sometimes loosely, as clipper ships. (Table 11.15) Steamers of the time were usually ships with small steam engines to provide propulsion when adverse wind conditions prevailed. Twenty-six auxiliary steamers were used in the trade to Cuba. There were also two small schooners which transported distressed Chinese coolies from Panama to Jamaica.

Of the 732 sailings identified in the various trades, 396 were undertaken by ships on a one-off opportunist basis. Sixty-five ships made two voyages, and 17 made three voyages each. With voyages to Peru and Cuba taking in excess of three months in each direction, it was unusual for any ship to undertake more than one voyage a year.

Twenty-seven ships can be considered dedicated coolie ships, having made at least four coolie voyages. (Table 11.16) Of these, ten made their first voyages in the boom year of 1866. Between them they made 151 voyages to Cuba and Peru. Only one British ship, the *Red Riding Hood,* made four voyages to the West Indies (between 1860 and 1865). Ten other ships made four voyages each. They were the Spanish ships, *Alavesa* and *Guadalupe*, travelling exclusively to Havana; the Portuguese *Cecilia*, and Italian *R Pratolongo* each travelling to Callao only, while the French *Claire* and Dutch *Onrust* called at both Havana and Callao. The four other ships were Peruvian controlled but sailed under various flags. They included the *Lola*, *Peru*, *Dolores Ugarte* and *Macao*.

Table 11.15 National flags used by ship type with tonnages

	Brigs	Barques	Schooners	Ships	Clippers	Steamers	Total
Minimun tons	168	191	73	342	520	1081	-
Maximum tons	391	1278	147	2078	2006	2134	-
Average tons	270	489	110	859	1314	1394	-
American	0	2	0	27	22	0	51
British	1	31	2	87	1	3	125
French	1	93	0	47	0	8	149
Spanish	3	33	0	41	0	12	89
Portuguese	1	8	0	27	2	0	38
Peruvian	4	30	0	65	11	0	110
Italian	0	6	0	28	8	2	44
Salvadorian	0	2	0	26	8	0	36
Dutch	0	13	0	16	0	0	29
Russian	0	2	0	14	0	0	16
Austrian	0	3	0	3	0	0	6
Belgian	0	1	0	3	0	1	5
Chilean	6	2	0	3	0	0	11
Colombian	1	0	0	1	0	0	2
Danish	0	1	0	1	0	0	2
Mexican	1	0	0	0	0	0	1
German	0	9	0	0	2	0	11
Noregian	0	4	0	0	0	0	4
Hawaiian	0	0	0	2	0	0	2
Swedish	0	1	0	0	0	0	1
Total	18	241	2	391	54	26	732

Source: Author's compilation

Five ships made five voyages each. The two ships sailing exclusively to Havana were the Spanish barque *Altagracia* and the steamer *Cataluna*—the only steamer to run continuously from 1866 to 1871. The Peruvian *Empresa* traded exclusively to Callao, as did the *Uncowah* sailing under the Italian and then Salvadorian flag. The *Aurora* sailed primarily to Callao, but made one voyage to Havana.

The *Emigrante* sailed under the Portuguese flag for one voyage before completing another five under Spanish colours to Havana. The Salvadorian *Callao* made six voyages between Macao and Callao between 1869 and 1873.

The *Westward Ho* made one voyage to Callao as an American clipper, before she was bought by the Peruvian entrepreneur Juan Ugarte in 1858 and placed under the Peruvian flag. Her one voyage to Havana was followed by another six to Callao before she was wrecked after discharging her passengers there.

Table 11.16 Dedicated Coolie Ships

Ship	Tons	Voyages	Embarked	Passengers per ton	Landed	% Died
Red Riding Hood	709	4	1,281	0.45	1,270	0.86
Lola	890	4	2,041	0.57	1,007	1.67
Cecilia	533	4	1,498	0.70	1,434	4.27
Claire	498	4	1,151	0.58	1,096	4.78
Macao	1076	4	1,744	0.41	1,647	5.56
Guadalupe	913	4	1,646	0.45	1,543	6.26
Alavesa	689	4	1,614	0.59	1,453	9.98
Peru	594	4	1,597	0.67	1,425	10.77
Onrust	836	4	1,865	0.56	1,621	13.03
R Pratolongo	890	4	1,825	0.51	1,508	17.37
Dolores Ugarte	1283	4	2,380	0.46	1,821	23.49
Aurora	668	5	1,867	0.56	1,752	6.16
Cataluna	1300	5	2,532	0.39	2,296	9.32
Empresa	446	5	1,724	0.77	1,546	10.32
Altagracia	618	5	1,804	0.58	1,580	12.42
Uncowah	988	5	2,526	0.51	2,188	13.38
Callao	1552	6	4,037	0.43	3,816	5.47
Emigrante	753	6	2,173	0.48	2,047	5.80
Hong Kong	470	7	2,147	0.67	1,806	15.88
America	1454	7	4,702	0.46	4,448	5.40
Westward Ho	1633	7	5,380	0.41	5,008	6.91
Donna Maria Pia	671	7	2,518	0.54	2,283	9.33
Luisa Canevaro	1206	7	5,018	0.59	4,483	10.66
Fray Bentos	561	8	2,866	0.64	2,780	3.00
Encarnacion	567	8	2,547	0.56	2,098	17.63
Providencia	660	10	4032	0.61	3,888	3.57
Camillo Cavour	1334	12	7,596	0.47	6,464	14.90
Average of all other ships	738	577	382	0.55	337	11.28

Source: Author's compilation

The Portuguese *Donna Maria Pia* was another American ship, bought in the general exodus of American ships from the United States. As a dedicated coolie ship, she made seven voyages to Callao and Havana. The *Luisa Canevaro* was yet another American ship. Bought by the Peruvian Canevaro family, she flew various flags in her nine-year history, undertaking seven voyages to Callao and Havana. The *America* was originally the British ship, *Red Rose*. She was bought by the Peruvian Maritime Company especially for the coolie trade. She also carried various flags in the course of her seven voyages to Callao and Havana. The *Hong Kong* started her career as a dedicated coolie carrier on a sad note, having succumbed to a mutiny on her first voyage in 1866 as a French carrier. She then changed her flag to that of Spain, when trading to Havana. When she switched to servicing Callao, she changed again to the flag of Peru.

The *Encarnacion* was a Spanish barque which entered the coolie trade first in 1853. After just one voyage to Callao in 1860, she returned intermittently to the Cuban trade during the period from 1861 to 1871. Over her eight voyages she carried 2,547 Chinese with an average loss of 4.91%. The *Fray Bentos* was a much smaller vessel. She made eight voyages between 1866 and 1872 over which she carried 2,866 Chinese coolies. With a loss of 86 passengers her mortality rate was 3.00%.

The *Providenza* was a stalwart of the Peruvian coolie trade. After she changed her registry in 1869 to that of Italy the spelling of her name also was changed, to *"Providencia"*. Beginning in 1865 and concluding in 1873, her ten voyages embarked 4,032 coolies in all, her average mortality rate being an impressive 3.57%.

The *Camillo Cavour* was the longest-serving ship in the coolie trades. Captain Caravagno, having served on the *Empresa* and *Westward Ho*, took command of the American-flagged *Challenger* when her name was changed and placed under the Peruvian flag in 1863. Between 1864 and 1867. Captain de Landabaso was in command for four voyages, first as a Peruvian ship and then, for the next three years, as an Italian one. In 1868, another change of flag took place, this time to that of Salvador. At this point, Captain Astorquia took command and remained there for the next four years and six voyages, seeing the ship revert to the Peruvian flag in 1870, when fears of a war with Spain were finally allayed. *Camillo*

Cavour's twelfth and last voyage was under Captain Ignacio Yriberri in 1873. Over her long career she took on 7,596 Chinese and carried 6,464 of them on to Peru. The mortality rate was 6.58%.

Mutinies

Throughout the 29 years when the coolie trades were in prosecution, mutinies were regularly reported in the newspapers of the world. (Tables 11.17 and 11.18) Mutiny is a strong word and not always an accurate description of what happened on board ship. In this study, out of the 732 sailings from all ports and to all destinations, 68 what we may call "insurrections" of varying degrees of severity have been identified. In other words, about one in ten sailings resulted in this type of disruption of the normal voyage. Of these "insurrections", 21 (30%) resulted in the ship not making its final destination.

The first successful mutiny in the coolie trades, which took place on the French *Albert* in 1850, was said to be in reaction to a cruel captain. The last mutiny, on the *Fatchoy* in 1872, was also a result of cruelty to the Chinese coolies. Cruelty by the captain was also the significant driver in the mutiny on the American *Robert Bowne* when, as in the case of the *Albert*, they began cutting the pigtails of the men on the grounds of cleanliness. In retaliation, the captains of the *Albert* and the *Robert Browne* were attacked, killed, and thrown overboard. In the case of the last two unsuccessful "insurrections" on the *Jacques Sevrin* and *Fatchoy*, both in 1872, cruelty was once again identified as the motivating factor.

An early factor in insurrections was also the quality and quantity of food and water granted to desperate men, almost all of whom were opium addicts, who had simply been picked up off the streets. This was rectified when captains realised that skimping on cheap food was not worth the risk of mutiny, but bad water in wooden casks was a problem until water distillers became commonplace. Another significant factor in early insurrections was the supposed deception of illiterate men as to their true destinations.

In 1859, Macao authorities began to suspect that mutinies were being conducted as part of a plan to exploit the weaknesses in the recruitment chain. Unscrupulous men willingly volunteered to emigrate in order to be well fed and kept comfortably, while waiting for a ship. Once on board plans would be made to capture the ship and plunder its cargo.

Of the 68 mutinies identified, there were seven from each of Amoy and Swatow, and four each from Cumsingmoon and Hong Kong. Two voyages from Amoy were aborted following mutinies. The ships in question were the American *Robert Bowne* in 1852 and the British *Jeddo* in 1866. The five other voyages from Amoy, undertaken by British vessels in the 1852-53 season, all suffered mutinies, with high mortality rates. From Swatow, one French and one Peruvian ship were unable to complete their voyages. The single British and four American ships also endured mutinies with extremely high mortality rates.

Table 11.17 Successful Mutinies

Departed	Ship	Flag	From	To	Notes
24/09/50	Albert	Fren	Cumsingmoon	Callao	Capt killed
5/12/51	Victory	Brit	Cumsingmoon	Callao	Capt killed
21/03/52	Robert Bowne	Amer	Amoy	Callao	Capt killed
8/03/53	Rosa Elias	Peru	Cumsingmoon	Callao	Capt killed
24/10/53	Adamastor	Port	Macao	Havana	abandoned
12/7/56	Resolucao	Port	Macao	Havana	Abandoned
12/07/56	Banca	Dutch	Macao	Havana	burnt
11/01/57	Port de Bordeaux	Fren	Macao	Havana	abandoned
29/01/57	Anais	Fren	Swatow	Havana	Capt killed
9/02/57	Henrietta Maria	Dutch	Macao	Havana	abandoned
1/03/57	Carmen	Peru	Swatow	Callao	burnt
8/10/59	Flora Temple	Amer	Macao	Havana	wrecked
2/08/60	Encarnacion	Span	Macao	Callao	Put back
23/01/66	Hong Kong	Fren	Whampoa	Havana	put back
8/03/66	Napoleon Canevaro	Ital	Macao	Callao	burnt
18/03/66	Jeddo	Brit	Amoy	B Guiana	burnt
3/03/68	Theresa	Ital	Macao	Callao	put back
15/01/70	Frederic	Belg	HK	Callao	burnt
1/10/70	Nouvelle Penelope	Fren	Macao	Callao	Capt killed
14/10/70	Uncowah	Sal	Macao	Callao	burnt
4/05/71	Don Juan	Peru	Macao	Callao	burnt

Source: Author's compilation

With no official supervision, three of the Cumsingmoon departures did not reach Callao with the fourth needing 190 days to complete her voyage suffering a loss of 14.46% of her coolies. Hong Kong, with strict supervision was not trouble free. The Belgian *Frederic* caught fire on her way to Callao. Details were not available for the two ships carrying Chinese to Surinam, whereas *Duke of Portland* which lost 40.72% of her passengers en route to Havana was the subject of a prolonged investigation by British authorities.

Table 18 lists the 47 departures that were reported as having had mutinies that failed. While undoubtedly some were genuine attempts at insubordination, the scant information provided in most cases makes it difficult to determine the extent to which they can be classified as mutinies. In each case the vessel continued on its voyage and can thus be classed as unsuccessful.

Table 11.18 Unsuccessful Insurrections

Departed	Ship	Flag	From	To	Notes
26/09/52	Panama	British	Amoy	Havana	crew left ship
12/10/52	Gertrude	British	Amoy	Havana	poor food
25/11/52	Samuel Boddington	British	Amoy	B Guiana	Forestalled
29/11/52	Lady Amherst	British	Amoy	Havana	crew left ship
8/01/53	Spartan	British	Amoy	Melbourne	2nd mate killed
20/02/54	Isabel Quintana	Peruvian	Cumsingmoon	Callao	Many killed
12/10/55	Waverly	American	Amoy	Callao	Opium
24/11/55	Samuel Enderby	British	Macao	Havana	
24/12/55	Winged Racer	American	Swatow	Callao	prior departure
2/04/56	Duke of Portland	British	Hong Kong	Havana	High mortality
11/03/57	Gulnare	British	Swatow	Havana	3rd mate hurt
4/04/57	Fernandez	French	Macao	Havana	set on fire
4/04/57	Francois 1	French	Macao	Havana	No details
15/10/57	Kate Hooper	American	Macao	Havana	set on fire
18/10/57	Challenge	American	Swatow	Havana	Over water
26/11/59	Norway	American	Macao	Havana	set on fire
22/01/60	Red Riding Hood	British	Whampoa	B Guiana	Minor attempt
20/02/60	Kitty Simpson	American	Macao	Havana	
22/02/60	Messenger	American	Macao	Havana	Piracy

Departed	Ship	Flag	From	To	Notes
22/02/60	Messenger	American	Macao	Havana	Piracy
10/03/60	Staghound	American	Swatow	Havana	High mortality
4/11/60	Loa	Peruvian	Macao	Callao	prior departure
20/11/60	Greyhound	Chilian	Whampoa	Havana	on departure
23/12/60	Sebastopol	British	Whampoa	B Guiana	on departure
18/03/61	Leonidas	American	Whampoa	Havana	3rd mate hurt
4/03/65	Emmanuel	French	Macao	Havana	No details
6/06/65	Louis	French	Whampoa	Havana	High mortality
30/07/65	Liguria	Italian	Macao	Callao	High mortality
8/09/65	Dea del Mare	Italian	Macao	Callao	High mortality
12/10/65	Caroline	French	Whampoa	Havana	12 shot
22/01/66	Ville de St Lo	French	Whampoa	Havana	12 killed
24/01/66	Josefita y Almira	Portuvian	Macao	Havana	Several hurt
10/02/66	Flore	French	Whampoa	Havana	on departure
31/03/66	Pride of the Ganges	British	Whampoa	B Guiana	Capt hurt
7/10/66	Eugene et Adele	French	Macao	Havana	Capt killed
1/02/67	Bangkok	French	Macao	Havana	No details
8/02/67	Niemen	Austrian	Macao	Havana	3 killed
29/11/67	Nelly	French	Macao	Havana	No details
17/12/67	Orixa	French	Macao	Havana	on departure
5/01/68	Esperance Marie	French	Macao	Havana	Capt hurt
1/05/68	Therese	French	Hong Kong	Surinam	No details
23/07/68	Providenza	Italian	Macao	Callao	No details
8/12/68	Lucie	French	Macao	Havana	No details
7/02/69	T amaris	French	Macao	Havana	Many suicides
19/06/69	Callao Jacques	Salvadorian	Macao	Callao	Ringleaders flogged
7/04/72	Sevrin	French	Macao	Havana	cruelty
26/08/72	Fatchoy	Spanish	Macao	Havana	cruelty

Source: Author's compilation

Of the ten departures from Whampoa, the three which took place towards the end of the Allied Commissioners occupation of Canton (this ceased on 10 October 1861) were suspected of being abetted by the Chinese authorities, while the five on French vessels in the 1865-66 season may have been the reaction to aggressive recruitment by the French Maritime Agency.

French ships accounted for five of the 21 successful mutinies and 16 of 47 unsuccessful insurrections reported. However very few details were ever published and the circumstances surrounding these presumed mutinies remain unknown.

In 1857 there were four mutinies and five insurrections. There was only one mutiny and one insurrection in 1859, but by 1860, unsuccessful insurrections had risen to seven with one successful mutiny. Of the 78 departures in 1866, three suffered mutinies which resulted in the ships not reaching their destination and five endured insurrections but were able to land their passengers.

The captains (Table 11.19)

The longest-serving captain in the coolie trades was Captain Antonio de Araucoa. He completed six voyages on the *Westward Ho* between 1858 and 1863, before she caught fire in Callao after discharging her passengers. After a period in other trades he returned to command the *Callao* for three voyages between 1871 and 1873 and was in Macao awaiting a further voyage when the trade was closed. Captain de Araucoa was responsible for 6,572 Chinese on his ships and was able to deliver 6,157 of them safely. The mortality rate varied from 1.44% to 26.65% at an average of 6.37%.

Rafael de Moro was the favourite captain of the Canevaro family, serving for eight years between 1864 and 1871. Over seven voyages between Macao and Callao he suffered the loss of the *Napoleon Canevaro* from a mutiny, and experienced a heavy loss of 30.92% on his voyage on the *Luisa Canevaro*. Overall, however his mortality rate was 8.07%.

Another long-time Peruvian captain was A.V. Vidaurrazaga. Six of his seven voyages were to Peru on the Figari-controlled *Providencia*. On his only voyage to Havana, Vidaurrazaga joined the *Italia*. In Anjer, while taking on provisions, the ship was blown aground while he was ashore and became a total wreck. Captain Viaaurrazago returned to Macao and was immediately returned to his command of the *Providencia*.

Two other Peruvian captains made six voyages each. Antonio Astorquia was in command of the *Camillo Cavour* between 1868 and 1872, and Ramon Mota commanded the

Fray Bentos between 1869 and 1872. The prominent Garcia family included two well known seafarers. Their first involvement in the coolie trade was on the *Amalia* in 1855. Narciso Garcia made five voyages between 1868 and 1872 while brother Guillermo made three.

One of the Spanish captains was Ignacio Fernando Yriberri. He was in command of the *Hong Kong* from 1867 to 1872, and transferred to the *Camillo Cavour* in 1873. As for the Portuguese captains, the most prominent was E.A. da Souza. He commanded the *Donna Maria Pia* for five voyages between 1866 and 1871, serving both Cuba and Peru.

Of the French captains, Captain L. Robert would have been the longest serving, commanding five voyages on three different vessels to Havana and Callao. The other known Frenchman was Captain F. Dubois. He was first on the *Port Durand* in 1865 and then made two voyages to Havana before taking the first contingent of Chinese to New Orleans.

Table 11.19 Longest Serving Captains

Captain	Voyages	Primary ship	Nos Embarked	Nos Landed	Average mortality
Joao B Bollo	5	Theresa	876	766	10.11
E A da Souza	5	Donna Maria Pia	1,669	1504	9.84
Narcisso Garcia	5	Clothilde	3,113	2937	5.53
L. Robert	5	Claire	1,729	1628	5.62
Antonio Astorquia	6	Camillo Cavour	3,746	3004	3.50
Ramon Mota	6	Fray Bentos	2,184	2110	3.43
Ignacio F. Yriberri	6	Hong Kong	2,254	2,180	3.53
Rafael de Moro	7	Luisa Canevaro	4,426	3452	8.07
A.V. Vidaurrazaga	7	Providencia Westward	3,107	2688	11.66
Antonio de Araucoa	10	Ho	6,572	6157	6.37

Source: Author's compilation

The Bollo brothers made eight voyages between them in the 1860s. Joao captained the 240-ton brig *Theresa* while Sebastian was captain of the 1,094-ton ship *Theresa*. They continued to confuse those in the trade by each commanding the 357-ton bark *Clothilde* for one voyage. Joao Bollo had the indignity of having the highest mortality rate of the dedicated captains at 38.17% on the 344-ton barque *Amalia* before experiencing a loss of just 0.91% on his following voyage on the *Clothilde*.

Flags utilised (Table 11.20)

Ships from 20 nations had engaged in the Chinese coolie trades.[168] They ranged from the one-off voyages of ships registered in Colombia, Mexico, or Sweden to those travelling under the national flags of Britain, Peru and Spain.

The American flag flew on 42 ships, making 51 voyages among them. When the United States banned American ships from participating in the coolie trades, at least 29 ships originally registered in American ports were subsequently employed under various flags, seven of them initially as Peruvian vessels and another nine flying Portuguese colours. Of these nine, six had been transferred to the Portuguese registry in Macao over a two-month period in 1863.

Reflecting the close ties between Peruvians and Italian nationals living in Peru, the Italian flag was prominent in the boom years of 1865 to 1867, mainly for voyages to Callao.— Thirteen of those 44 ships had been reflagged from other nations.—Seeking a flag of shelter during their war with Spain, Peruvian entrepreneurs turned to San Salvador. At least 35 voyages were made on Salvadorian vessels between 1867 and 1871.

Many of the vessels engaged in the Peruvian trade were employed as shuttle ships, plying between Macao and Callao. The 110 voyages to Callao were undertaken by 85 Peruvian-flagged ships. The number was arguably significantly greater as most of the Italian and Salvadorian—and many of the Portuguese—ships were Peruvian-owned. They were flagged in and out to avoid capture, or for financial reasons.

While nationalism was also prominent in Cuba, the strong financial position of the planters was reflected in their ability to secure British and American shipping. When these nations ceased participating in the coolie trade, French interests became the predominant suppliers of shipping to Cuba.

Table 11.20 National flags of vessels for voyages to various destinations

Flag	To Cuba	To Peru	To the West Indies	To ports elsewhere	Total
American	36	12		3	51
Austrian	3	3			6
Belgian	4	1			5
British	36	10	57	22	125
Chilean	4	6		1	11
Colombian		2			2
Danish	1	1			2
Dutch	21	5	2	1	29
French	106	36	3	4	149
German	8	2		1	11
Hawaiian				2	2
Italian	7	36		1	44
Mexican		1			1
Norwegian	4				4
Peruvian	6	104			110
Portuguese	23	15			38
Russian	12	2	1	1	16
Salvadorian	4	32			36
Spanish	82	6		1	89
ALL SHIPS	**358**	**274**	**63**	**37**	**732**

Source: Author's compilation

Mortality concerns

Not only mutinies, but the high mortality rates suffered on Chinese coolie voyages were also a cause for ongoing concern. As a port of departure, Amoy accounted for most of the voyages experiencing high mortality rates. From 1855 onwards, Swatow also gained a reputation as a port with high mortality rates. Even so, Cuban planters continued to use Swatow, despite the fact that six shipments, in each of 1857 and 1858, had losses in excess of 20%.

Two hypotheses have been put forward as to the causes for the high number of deaths on board—the first relates to the passengers' state of health at the time of embarkation; and the second suggests that the crowded and insanitary living conditions on board ship were to blame.[169]

The first hypothesis is supported by the following example. Dr Ely of the *Samuel Boddington* was very critical of the quality of the coolies being presented to him. He rejected many of them only to be told the ship would be sent away without a full complement if he continued to reject them. Following this, he allowed them to pass. The second hypothesis is supported by the fact that the high mortality rate (45.23%) on one of the first coolie ships, the *Lady Montague*, was attributed to the withdrawal of opium and to dysentery (the latter also claimed some of the crew). Opium deprivation—along with dysentery and scurvy—continued to be the main causes of death for many years.

The competence of the doctors on board would also have had a great effect on the number of deaths. Western doctors would be familiar with the mandatory list of medicines to be carried but the medicines would have been less than useful when native Chinese doctors were allowed to replace Europeans. In either case, many of the doctors seemed to be under a state of intoxication for most of the time.

The coolie master's log of the *Forest Eagle*'s voyage in 1861 does not refer to the doctor's nationality, but shows the complete inability of the man to arrest the outbreak of worms and dropsy that broke out. The captain had to administer medicines himself. Cholera was also a problem, but the high losses on ships out of Macao in 1863 was due to an outbreak of the disease on shore at that time.

The second hypothesis—relating to overcrowding—can be explored by analysis based on the passenger-per-ton ratio. (It would be more difficult to evaluate whether the use of this ratio had better results than the space allocation later adopted by the Portuguese in Macao.)

The difficulty in linking mortality to overcrowding is shown by reference to the 1,650-ton American clipper ship *Wandering Jew* which left Swatow on 5 February 1858 with 350 passengers. The passenger-to-ton ratio was 0.21, yet only 259 lived to disembark at journey's end. The mortality rate was 26.00%. At the other extreme, the 416-ton Spanish ship

Serafina left Amoy on 31 January 1860 with 430 passengers, which was more than the tonnage of the vessel. The passenger-to-ton ratio was 1.03, yet 400 were able to walk off after 117 days, a much lower mortality rate of 6.98%.

Space measurements could be interpreted very differently, as shown above, in the case of the *John Calvin*.

Other factors, such as the duration of voyages and the aftermath of mutinies, would also need to be considered.

There appears to be no study of the comparative mortality resulting when coolies slept in bunks rather than on cold decks. (The latter, it has been speculated, was a cause of death, especially in colder climes.)—The Chinese Passengers' Act and the various decrees by Spain, Peru and Macao make no mention of the provision of bunks.

The Colonial Land and Emigration Commission examined the statistics of Chinese emigration to British Guiana in the 1859-60 season. It found that, in the twelve ships of 900 tons and above, the death-rate among 5,312 emigrants averaged 2.4%. In the eight ships of under 700 tons, the death-rate averaged 2.5% on 2,373 emigrants. However in ships between 700 and 900 tons the death-rate was 4.4% on 3,987 emigrants. It concluded that the differences did not warrant them laying down strict rules on vessel sizes.[170]

From a quick look at the table, 'Dedicated Coolie Ships' it would seem that the second hypothesis may not hold. The table lists the 27 ships that could be considered as being dedicated to the coolie trades. As dedicated carriers it could have been expected that facilities on board would have been conducive to healthier conditions and thus lower mortality rates. The table shows that eight vessels averaged mortality rates in excess of the average for all other ships engaged in the coolie trades.

The second hypothesis would link ship masters to their ships. Ships undertaking one or two coolie voyages may not have installed all the fittings required for carrying passengers. Ships dedicated to the trade however, would have such fittings on board and their captains should be fully responsible for any unusually high mortality rates. The tables

'Longest serving captains' and 'Dedicated coolie ships' do show the value of having ships dedicated to the trade.

Table 11.21 Mortality by national vessel flag

Flag	Number	Total Embarked	Average tons	Average Passengers per ton	Average voyage days	Average mortality
American	51	26221	1134	0.48	112	12.34
Austrian	6	2,400	705	0.62	147	12.49
Belgian	5	2,680	1004	0.51	109	1.71
British	125	42,908	766	0.48	108	9.09
Chilean	11	2,416	415	0.56	120	16.47
Columbian	2	954	841	0.57	111	8.81
Danish	2	545	719	0.38	127	30.83
Dutch	29	11,459	741	0.53	130	9.89
French	149	51,605	612	0.59	130	10.37
German	11	3,000	539	0.54	121	8.67
Hawaiian	2	249	699	0.18	51	8.43
Italian	44	20,357	900	0.53	131	15.85
Mexican	1	200	237	0.48	144	1.00
Norwegian	4	1,025	456	0.57	134	20.74
Peruvian	110	47,420	801	0.57	114	10.00
Portuguese	38	15,299	718	0.59	115	12.26
Russian	16	7,308	886	0.53	112	8.18
Salvadorian	36	19,340	1063	0.53	117	7.45
Spanish	89	35,757	734	0.57	127	10.03
Swedish	1	341	507	0.67	127	12.90
ALL SHIPS	732	291,484	773	0.52	120	15.12

Source: Author's compilation

McDonald and Shlomowitz found that, "In the earlier period 1847-65 there was higher mortality on ships departing in summer, and the flag of the vessel, departure port, and length of voyage were important factors. Mortality was lower on British, French, and Dutch ships and higher on Portuguese and Italian ships. They used, as an example, transportation on an Italian rather than a French ship, assuming average voyage characteristics, resulted in approximately 71 extra deaths when 400 passengers embarked .... For the latter period 1866-74, mortality was lower. There was no significant seasonal effect, but the flag of the ship effect was highly significant. Mortality was lowest on Spanish, Italian, and possibly British ships".[171]

Table 11.21 attempts to relate the average mortality rates on ships of the various nations using average vessel sizes, average voyage days and the average passenger per ton ratio. It must be emphasized this is not a statistical analysis, and should not be used other than for superficial observation.

* * *

"Coolies Embarking"[172]

ENVOI

From conducting this study I have come to a better understanding of why I came across so many Chinese people in the different parts of the world that I visited in the course of my seafaring career. While many of the people I have described here were taken away by force or deception, it seems that most eventually settled in their new country even when there was an opportunity to return home.

Like humanity everywhere, some simply withered away and died, but there were many who, through hard work and frugality, managed to prosper. Some of those who did eventually make their way back home came to realise that they were better off in the new homeland and returned there of their own free will, sometimes with a newly-acquired wife and even home-born children.

The desire of people in poorer countries to improve themselves and the search for labour which complements this will undoubtedly continue through the ages. But this potentially mutually beneficial symbiosis should never cause suffering for any individual in this world.

I trust you have found this book informative and that neither you nor I will ever have to read stories such as those I retell here, about "horror ships".

Appendix I

The coolie master's Log on the *Forest Eagle*[173]

February 9 1861 Ship left Macao with 500 coolies. Mr Boye paid the head coolies, barbers and cooks their money. Some of the cooks were not qualified, and changed them for others. Coolie No. 67 wanted to go ashore after ship left, but he had not the money, and all the sampans had left the ship. Some little disturbance about the rice not being cooked properly, it being the first trial. The coolies were reconciled by being told that it would be better in future.

February 10 Strong breeze – rough sea. Coolies most more or less sea sick. Made them congee and gave them salt fish pickled lemons etc., but would not eat rice and vegetables. Coolie No. 67 is contented today and is about the liveliest of the lot – gave them victuals as usual. Doctor visited the coolies a number of times today. Three men in the hospital – one slight fever occasioned by constipation of long standing and gorged liver, one liver complaint, one had sore on the leg.

February 11 Pleasant weather. Coolies most all recovered or are recovering from sea sickness. Gave them food as per memorandum. 150 to 200 coolies on deck most all day. Cooks improving. Rice cooked very well today. Cleaned deck and sprinkled chloride lime between decks. Distributed dominoes cards instruments etc.

February 12 Pleasant weather. Coolies very well and contented. Put three coolies in irons for fighting last night – till breakfast time this morning. Gave three others a slight punishment for gambling for dollars and quarrelling. Gave the food as per memorandum. Eight coolies in hospital. None dangerously sick.

February 13 Coolies in hospital about the same. Cleaned deck and aired the coolies well. Coolies not requiring their full allowance of rice. Gave them 600 lbs rice today. No trouble at all with them.

February 14 Heavy sea. Coolies on deck about all day. Gave No. 405 one dozen on the hand for whipping a small boy for no provocation. Put No. 403 in irons at noon having heard something suspicious about him. At night learned that there was a scheme among some of the coolies to poison the Europeans aboard and then take the ship when she makes the land. Also put three others in irons; having been pointed out as the ringleaders. Some more are supposed to be implicated in the plot but have not found them yet. Searched for the poison and found two small bottles of white powder. Do not know what it was. Some of the coolies seasick again today. No. 413 is implicated in the same plot as the others. Coolies that are seasick are getting congee and other light food.

February 15 Rain and light drizzle. Put three others also being connected with those who were put in irons yesterday. At two am. after having asked them to tell where they put the poison, and to confess the plot, which they refused to do, gave them 3 dozen lashes on the back and kept them confined – keeping them on rice and water. They still refusing to tell anything concerning the affairs. At 6 am. one of the coolies informed against No. 67 as being also concerned. Brought him on deck and put him also in irons. On opening the baskets of pumpkins, find them decaying fast. Find it advisable to use them as soon as possible. A few of the men still seasick. Men in the hospital about the same. Cleaned the tween deck thoroughly today – a good proportion of the coolies on deck. All the coolies that are in irons were chosen in Macao for head and cooks.

February 16 Put No. 81 in irons. He also belonging to the same lot that was confined yesterday. No signs of repentance on the part of the prisoners. Gave No. 403 3 dozen for threatening to kill one of the coolies when he got clear of irons – supposed by his threat that he suspected him of informing on them. Cleaned deck thoroughly today, and had a number of the coolies bathing on deck. Coolies in general very quiet. Weather very hot. Seasick coolies recovering. Searched the boxes today for poison and knives – found one knife. Four coolies are informed of as having also a plot to heave gunpowder abaft the barricade and thus take the ship. These four are also implicated with the poison plot. They are very suspicious characters.

February 17 Two coolie prisoners owned up to the gunpowder plot. No. 403 (who seems to be the head) was very much agitated and was almost frantic with rage on hearing the confession. Cleaned between decks and had coolies bathing in salt water on deck. One coolie pretty sick in the hospital. Gave a coolie a punishment for gambling for dollars and fighting. The onions put on board in Macao are found to be perishing fast.

February 18 Land in sight. Anamba Is. Aired the coolies about 75 on deck at one hour spells. Gave two coolies a punishment for fighting. Just one in irons for fighting the same man again on going below after his punishment. Pumpkins very rotten, about three baskets of good out of five. Two baskets onions totally good for nothing. More overboard. Coolies very quiet. Allow the two coolies who confessed the plot full allowance of food, but kept them still confined. Cleaned decks and coolies bathing on deck etc. Sick some are recovering fast, others about the same.

February 19 Coolies quiet. Two or three coolies very sick – gave them light food. Deck cleaned thoroughly – coolies confined still obstinate as regards confessing the plot. Land in sight. Camels? ...... and other islands. About 75 coolies on deck at one time.

February 20 Cleaned deck and sprinkled chloride of lime below. Rice cooked very well. Got on deck all the sweet potatoes, as it was rather hot for them below. Sick coolies about the same. Coolies yet in confinement. Those that were put in irons for raising conspiracy. One sail in sight. One of the barrels of vinegar was found to have about 3 or 4 gallons in it.

February 21 Hot. Land in sight all day. Cleared the deck, gave the coolies bread today instead of vegetables. Very warm below, about 40 or 50 on deck at one time.

February 22 About 20 on the sick list. None very dangerous. Cleaned deck and sprinkled chloride of lime below. Number of coolies washing themselves in tubs on deck.

February 23 *Kate Hooper* passed us bound from Macao to Havana. Prisoners yet confined. One man very sick – rest not dangerous. Some seasick.
February 24 Land in sight. Coolies on deck. Sick coolies recovering fast with exception of No. 8 who is very sick – not expected to live. Coolie No. 2 offered $10 as a bribe to liberate one of the instigators of the plot, No. 125, and permit him to go below. Says that there were five kegs full of powder brought aboard in the food at Macao. Put him in irons with the rest. The leader of the conspirators was very agitated when he confessed it. Gave four coolies a light punishment for gambling and fighting for dollars.
February 25 Anchored at 11 am. No. 8 died of yellow jaundice and general derangement of the system produced by the use of opium. Buried him. Only four coolies very sick.
February 26 Ship off Anjer at 4 pm. Good breeze and cool below. Four coolies a light punishment for fighting below.
February 27 Opium seems to be almost exhausted among the coolies. Gave them bean soup with a little rice instead of tea at dinner.
February 28 No fighting, cleaned decks and fumigated hospital with tar.
March 3 Coolies consume 600 lbs rice.
March 4 Distributed tobacco package to each mess today. Coolie No. 2 liberated.
March 5 Report of spies say some talk of liberating the prisoners. Coolie 156 pretty sick. All opium gone.
March 6 No. 156 very sick – threw up a number of worms. Some with mumps.
March 7 No. 156 threw up more worms. Cannot get him to talk. One sick from effects of opium. Doctor sick from the effects of drinking too much rum put on board and meant for coolie use. Cannot attend to his business. Captain took liquor away from him.
March 8 No. 156 improving, doctor sick, prisoners still in irons. Some seasick, all sick sent forward.
March 9 No. 156 same, No. 150 very sick with yellow jaundice. Fresh vegetables below decaying. Advisable to use them as soon as possible, and hold on to the salt and bread.
March 10 No. 156 appeared little better but No. 150 died at sundown from opium withdrawal. Others now appearing sick from same cause as opium all gone.
March 11 No. 261 died from no opium. Doctor improving.
March 12 55 coolies on sick list. One discharged 10 worms. Doctor better. No. 73 covered with venereal sores.
March 13 Gave coolies 705 lbs rice today – largest amount used yet all consumed.
March 14 No. 156 died tonight after dead worms came from his nose. Other opium coolies very bad, others recovering. Overhauled water casks and found some leaking badly. Captain restricts water to 300 gallons and 700 lbs rice and 200 lbs vegetables per day.
March 15 No. 155 jumped overboard, couldn't save him, was a sick opium coolie. Supposed he was crazy.

March 16 Coolies stripped and examined and found on the whole pretty clean and not many cases of itch among them. Found 300 gallons water answered very well for all purposes.

March 17 Yams rotting fast. Sick coolies given sago, sweet potatoes etc.

March 18 Two released from irons after promising better behaviour. One very bad sick man with dropsy, some with fever. Fish getting bad.

March 19 Very cool below. Gave rum in tea with some complaining of belly aches.

March 20 No. 77 whipped and put in irons for stealing $30 from No. 75. He was among the plotters. Refused to say where the money was.

March 21 No. 20 died. Coolies rearranged in bunks below. No. 77 still refuses to say where money is.

March 22 Eggs in barrel broken and rotten. Sick opium coolies given vomitire. [*sic*]

March 23 No. 114 died. Some with mumps. Fresh pork getting rancid and fish decaying.

March 24 Head coolie 286 broken and punished for letting a boy steal opium and then taking it for himself. Made him pay for the opium. No. 64 died from opium withdrawal. A skeleton and sick for some time. Coolies given China cigars, a bundle to each.

March 25 No. 164 died of diarrhoea. Coolies cleaning themselves and shaving. Doctor visited patients. Bean soup instead of tea.

March 28 White-washed below. Boxes searched for opium and pipes and lamps, which were confiscated.

March 29 Below sprinkled with vinegar instead of lime. Coolies fed eggs, and bean broth instead of tea.

March 31 Counted coolies – 487 on board. One short, No. 326 who had not been seen for several days. Presumed fallen or jumped overboard. Can't find his contract. Some coolies probably sick from eating too much. Given exercise such as pulling ropes and cleaning decks etc. Cigars distributed. No. 77 released without confessing.

April 1 Passed Cape of Good Hope. Washed coolies mouths with vinegar today.

April 2 Doctor among the sick more often now. Several cases of venereal.

April 3 No. 451 jumped overboard and would not take the rope thrown to him. Was in hospital and out of his mind. Told the interpreter that he had died the previous night. No. 6 prepared to drown himself as he had stolen a pipe and when found out could not pay for it. Shackled to a ring bolt. No. 2 accused of sodomy. No. 6 claims he performed the man's part. Both whipped. No. 2 friend of the prisoners and always in trouble. He is only a boy but he is a devil.

April 4 No. 6 given 3 dozen for attempting to drown himself and No. 162 also for threatening to kill No. 6 on shore if he did not pay the $20 for the stolen pipe.

April 5 Coolies counted at 486.

April 6 Ship rolling badly. 2 died today and several pretty sick. All berths thoroughly cleaned.

April 7 Think Doctor could do more for the sick than he does. Capt visited sick twice today, and administered medicine himself. Coolies prefer bean soup to the tea.

April 8 Getting warmer. Doctor gives vomitire to 15, and Capt visits sick two or three times.

April 9 2 more died today, and several very sick. Can't understand why. Hopes Doctor will pay more attention to his business and not try to be the professional gentleman on board a coolie ship.

April 11 Arrived St Helena.

April 12 Water and fresh vegetables purchased. Departed 7 am.

April 13 5 or 6 steady sick cases. Heard some opium purchased at St Helena. Bought from the water tank men. Found and took it away. Fresh cabbage given out and rum put in the water supplied.

April 14 Doctor pays good attention to the men now.

April 18 No. 314 missing. Head coolie 117 found him lurking about at 10 am. night before, took his number and sent him to bed with warning that he would be reported for not obeying instructions. Not seen since. Coolie count 477. Found more opium on No. 400. Doctor administered vomitire to 42 coolies.

April 21 No. 276 bad with worms. Getting warm. Stopped putting rum in the water as it made it sour.

April 22 No. 322 with piles and worms. Doctor amongst coolies all the time now. Think excessive eating is cause of sickness. All except sick look fat.

April 23 Saw several ships off Ferdinando Noronha.

April 24 No. 383 died suddenly. Not on Doctor's book for a week.

April 30 No. 288 died. Was known as No. 300. Found he had swapped cards with a friend. Last of the St Helena vegetables.

May 2 Cooler. Will start giving pork again. Think pork was too heating in the hot weather.

May 4 Killed pig today. Coolies will get fresh pork for breakfast tomorrow.

May 6 35 coolies rather too fleshy! No. 147 threw up 18 very large worms. Three with swelled testicles and dropsy of the bag. Coolies not allowed to eat below as they eat to excess and get sick.

May 10 Big stout coolies placed on diet and exercise. Lazy devils, look like NY aldermen than coolies.

May 13 Lower tier of bunks removed and cleaned the deck under. Stout men not allowed to eat too much and no pork or fish. Bean soup recommended by Mr Souza.

May 14 Fresh pig for dinner today. No. 32 died of dropsy and swelled penis. Land in sight.

May 15 Finished white-washing below. Anchored off Great Isaacs (Bimini Bahamas) at 8 am. Coolies enlivened on seeing land.

May 17 Underway for Havana. Several coolies with swelled penis etc.

May 19 Coast of Cuba in sight. Coolies excited. Washing and cleaning themselves. Salt fish and prunes thrown overboard. Opened side ports. Got clothes ready for distribution. No. 367 hove up a very large worm and No. 207 all skin and bone with some kind of consumption. Off Moro at 7 am.

May 20 Took steamboat tow into Havana at 8 am. New clothes for the coolies. No. 250 died. Captain of Port counted coolies and examined sick. Into quarantine.

May 21 6 died by 4 pm. Awnings spread for the hot weather. Congee for dinner.

May 22 6 more died. Doctors can't determine why.

May 24 2 more died. Ship sent to Mariel in quarantine. Doctors say there is no contagious disease on board. Coolies frightened. Pumpkins sent on board.

May 25 Only 1 died. Coolies not eating much. Fresh vegetables and bean broth.

May 27 4 died of dropsy of the penis and bag. Looks like scurvy. Coolie count 433. Coolies restless. Talk of building barracoon ashore and sick put on a small boat coming from Havana. Hope it would be done soon. Large number on sick list.

May 29 3 died. Doctor neglecting to dress sores. Mr Souza the interpreter does it instead. The doctor is lazy and dilatory.

May 30 Fresh provisions came on board. Potatoes, onions and vinegar for the coolies. Soup of rice and meat for dinner. One died.

May 31 3 died. Raw potatoes onions vinegar given to coolies. All down hearted and need a change.

June 3 No. 408 tried to hang himself – twice. Second time No. 284 made the rope fast for him. Got a licking for that and shackled to a ring bolt.

June 4 3 died. Altercation with crewman who struck 2 coolies.

June 5 One died. Permission to build barracoon ashore. Consignee will build it.

June 8 Fresh provisions. No deaths. Coolie count 418. Barracoon being built.

June 9 No deaths. Shore doctors examined coolies. Counted 418.

June 19 No deaths, fresh provisions. Spanish doctors say fresh and good food will bring the coolies back to health.

June 20 Ship to return Havana at expiration of 40 days quarantine.

July 1 Two doctors examined coolies and found no contagion on board, also examined crew. Coolies washing and shaving.

July 4 Man overboard found ashore and brought back. One died. Steamer alongside and took 387 coolies off. Coolies lively and glad to go. Interpreter and Doctor went with them.

Appendix II
Summary of Macao Regulations

No. 39   5 June 1856
Regulations for Chinese Emigration at Macao[174]

The Governor of the Province of Macao, Timor and Solor determines as follows:

Whereas it is necessary that all practicable measures be taken to the end that, without interfering with the right of Chinese to depart from Macao, those abuses be prevented which might occur in the transportation of such as may embark for foreign countries as Colonists or emigrants, and to unite in one single regulation all the enactments heretofore prevailing in this respect, in order that they may the better come to the knowledge of all, - and the Council of Government having been heard, I deem it right to determine as follows:-

Section 1 Concerning Brokers
1. Brokers will require a license from the Procurador.
2. Brokers to deposit a one year $200 security bond
3. Any Chinese engaged by a Broker shall produce him at the Procurador's office where he will be informed of the country he is emigrating to, the service entered into, and the conditions thereof; the regulations of the depot and all other circumstances which the Procurador deems necessary, such that the Colonist is thoroughly informed of the obligations he is about to contract.
4. The Procurador shall visit the Brokers' houses from time to time, should he find any who have been kept against his will, is to free him and fine the Broker $100. Any repetition of the offence will result in the withdrawal of his license.
5. Every Broker who does not produce any Colonist he has engaged within 24 hours in Macao or after arrival shall incur a similar penalty.
6. Brokers are to repatriate all Colonists who have been rejected by the Emigration Agents, and to pay their passage home. Failure to comply will incur a $30 penalty.
7. Any Broker resorting to violence or coercion to compel a Colonist to enter his house or depot shall be prosecuted and fined as per Article 4.

Section 2 Concerning Emigration Agents and their Depots.
8. Emigration Agents are to advise the embarkation location, the number of persons for each vessel and their destination.
9. Each depot is to have a place for sick persons.
10. The Surgeon Major shall from time to time inspect the locations occupied, ensure precautions required for public health are observed; give appropriate instructions as required, and propose measures to ensure public health as well as the good treatment and comfort of the Colonists are met.

11. Medical practitioners appointed in the depots are to report the method is which they discharge their duties.
12. Emigration Agents are to send a copy of the regulations in their depots.
13. Contracts shall be registered in the same manner as contracts between Chinese and Christians. Registration is to be before two witnesses.
    1. Contracts are to be in Chinese and the language of the destination country.
    2. The Contract must specify the name, sex, age, and native place of the Colonist.
    3. A Colonist must be at least 18 years old or accompanied by his father or mother.
    4. The Contract is to specify the period of engagement, the amount of wages, food and clothing the Colonist is to receive.
14. The Procurador on his visits to the depots is to ascertain whether anyone is being held against his will or being deceived as to the destination of the vessel. Should anyone have been subjected to violence or fraud, he is to be freed at once and the Broker fined.
15. Timely notice by Agents of such compulsory visits are to be conducted on the evening prior to embarkation.
16. Chinese who have been fully informed prior to contracting before the Procurador are obliged to fulfil the contract, or repay the Agents for expenses if they not wish to proceed to their destination. The daily maintenance cost to be 100 cash.
17. Emigration Agents cannot keep the Colonists imprisoned in the depots; but may take measures to secure expenses incurred.
18. Emigration Agents are liable to fines of from $50 to $300 for infringement of any of the rules.

Section 3 Concerning the Vessels on which Colonists are shipped
19. No vessel shall leave without being inspected by the Captain of the Port.
20. The Port Captain shall ensure the sea-worthiness of the vessel, carries the requisite crew and equipment, and sufficiently ventilated for passengers.
21. Every vessel leaving with more than 20 Chinese passengers are subject to these regulations.
22. No Chinese can board without a passport or a Contract signed by the Procurador.
23. No vessel is to carry more than one passenger for every one ton and a half, Portuguese measurement, including crew.
24. The Port Captain is the ensure before embarkation of passengers, that the vessel has water and provisions as defined in Schedule A sufficient for the voyage length as computed in Schedule B.
25. A vessel with more than 20 passengers shall carry a doctor and medicine chest properly supplied.

26. The Captain is to disembark his passengers at the port for which the Colonists are engaged, except in cases specified in the Commercial Code.
27. The Port Captain will ascertain if any Chinese is on board against his will or subject to deception, or without a valid contract. Any such person is to be disembarked and reported.
28. No vessel shall leave without a certificate as per Schedule C signed by the Port Captain.
29. Any vessel infringing this Act will be subjected to a fine from $200 to $1000.
30. Consignees of vessels transporting Chinese shall give bonds of $1000 to be annulled on presentation of s legal certificate of arrival and of her having complied with the provisions of this Decree. This Certificate is to be presented within 18 months of sailing under penalty of forfeiture of the bond.
31. All Regulations contrary to this Decree are revoked.

Isidoro Fransicso Guimares
Macao   5 June 1856

Schedule A

Schedule of Provisions to be carried by vessels sailing with Chinese Colonists from the Port of Macao.

For each person per diem

Rice	1 ½ lbs
Salt pork, or 2/3 pork and 1/3 fish, or 1/3 pork, 1/3 beef and 1/3 fish	0 ½ lbs
Salted vegetables	0 ½ lbs
Tea	0 1/3 oz
Firewood	20 oz

Water at the rate of 13 canadas per week for each person.

1 canada equates to 1.4 litres.

Schedule B

Length of voyage for which provisions are to be calculated for sailing vessels:

As per the British Chinese Passengers' Act of 1855

Schedule C

Captaincy of the Port of Macao

I .... Captain of the Port of Macao hereby certify that the vessel (description, nationality, and name), Captain .... , ... tons burden, clears from the Port of Macao for .... carrying .... Chinese passengers, viz: .... males, ... females and .... children, engaged to serve as Colonists, and that all are aware of the place of their destination, and go of their own free will, which I have ascertained by personal inspection, as also that the contracts they carry have been duly registered in the proper department.

I further certify that the vessel is in a sea-worthy condition for the voyage on which she is bound, that she carries a sufficient number of crew, and that she is supplied with provisions and water in conformity with Regulation of the 5th of June 1856, as also that she has on board a physician, with Medicine Chest, and Chinese interpreter, and that the vessel has accommodation for the passengers she carries, and requisite means of ventilation.

Macao, ... 18 ...
(Signature of the Captain of the Port)
Macao, Government Secretariat
5th June 1856 José Carlos Barros
Acting Secretary of Government

No. 10   31 March 1857[175]

Resolved by the Governor of Macao:

It being necessary to take all practicable measures to the end that in the Depots for Chinese Colonists the provisions of Article 17 of the Regulation of 5 June 1856 be rigorously complied with:

I deem it right to determine that the Procurador of the Loyal Senate shall watch over the fulfilment of all that is enacted in that Article, and that he shall proceed against persons guilty of infringement thereof as culpable of an offence punishable under Article 330 of the Criminal Code.

Isadore Francisco Guimares
Macao 31 March 1857

No. 25   4 August 1857[176]

Resolved by the Governor of Macao:

Considering that all persons, both Chinese and Portuguese embarking as passengers from the Port of Macao, should be subject to the same rule with respect to the holding of passports, and considering moreover that many of the losses and accidents that have occurred to vessels laden with Chinese passengers have been the result of prolonged voyages to which those sailing with the contrary monsoon are exposed, after hearing the Council of Government whose opinion I adopt; I deem it right to determine the following regulations:

Section 1.

Chinese Colonists or emigrants embarking at the Port of Macao after the 31st October shall be required to take out their passports in conformity with the law.

1. Captains of vessels carrying Chinese emigrants shall present the emigrants with their passports before the Portuguese Consul at the port of disembarkation.

Section 2.

Emigration Agents shall be responsible for infringement of this Article, under the terms of Article 30 of the Regulations.

2. No. vessel shall be permitted to sail in the contrary monsoon when carrying more than 30 Chinese passengers. Schedule B annexed to the Regulations shall be taken as the rule whereby to determine at what time the monsoon is to be deemed contrary for voyages

Section 3.   to the various ports to which Chinese are in the habit of emigrating.

The provisions of this article shall not apply to vessels propelled by steam.

Isadore Francisco Guimares
Macao, 4 August 1857

No. 57   Regulation for the shipment of Colonists 30 April 1860[177]

Resolved by the Governor of Macao:

Whereas it is necessary to adopt in the regulations with respect to Chinese emigration from the Port of Macao some of the provisions that have been enacted by the authorities at Canton, to the end that in this Colony there be followed a system as nearly as possible similar to that which the aid authorities have deemed proper for the purpose of securing the liberty and good treatment of the emigrants. Having heard the Council of Government, I have seen fit to determine as follows:

1. The office is created of Superintendent of Chinese emigration, who shall be nominated by the Governor, and who shall be responsible to him for the execution of the regulations and other matters concerning the exportation of Chinese labourers engaged to emigrate to foreign countries.
2. The Superintendent of Chinese emigration shall draw a fixed salary from the Government and shall not receive any emolument depending upon the greater or less number of Chinese colonists embarking at Macao.
3. The Superintendent shall have under his orders an interpreter of Chinese, paid like himself by the Government, and who also shall receive no other fees.
4. The Superintendent shall be present at the examinations held at the Procurador's office in conformity with the Regulations of 5 June 1856, and shall sign the contracts in the same manner as is done by the Procurador.
5. Both the Superintendent and the Procurador shall keep a register, in which they shall enter the names of all Chinese coming before them to emigrate.
6. In this Register in addition to the name shall be entered the age, native place, employment and condition of the Chinese proposing to emigrate.
7. On Chinese presenting themselves when about to emigrate, there shall be given to them a copy of the contract and they shall be registered in the form laid down in the preceding article; and all explanations shall be made to them with reference to the contract offered to them, but they shall not be allowed to sign until the expiry of at least six days after registration.

8. During the time between the registration and the signing of the contract the Chinese registered shall be allowed to return to their homes or villages, or to reside in the depots, which they shall be allowed to enter and leave whenever they please (during the day) without any right on the part of the Emigration Agent to detain them or to require them to pay for their maintenance, clothing, travelling, expenses, or any other outlay prior to their signing their contract.
9. If the colonist presents himself on the expiry of the six days specified in Article 7, and states that he decidedly wishes to engage himself, the contract shall again be read and explained to him, and he shall then sign it, as well as the Superintendent and the Procurador, with two witnesses.
10. On the contract being signed, there shall be paid to the colonists the gratuity or advance made to them by the Agent, and they shall be sent on board the vessel that is to carry them to their destination.
11. The amount of the gratuity or advance received by the colonist must be noted in the contract, and delivered to him in the presence of the Superintendent.
12. No Chinese below the age of 25 shall be allowed to sign the contract unless he has obtained the consent of his parents if they are still living.
13. After having signed the contract, the colonist is bound to fulfil same, or, in case of change of mind, to repay the expenses lawfully incurred by the Agent, in conformity with Article 16 of the Regulations of 5 June 1856.
14. The advance paid to the Colonist and clothing given to him shall be considered part of the lawful expenses he shall be called upon to pay if he refuses to sail after signing the contract.
15. The contracts which Emigration Agents propose to enter into with Colonists must be previously laid before the Superintendent of Emigration, who will examine them and approve them if they are just and equitable, admitting no conditions that may be injurious to the Colonists.

Section 1
The Contracts shall not be for a longer period than eight years.
Section 2
Colonists shall not be allowed to renounce the benefit of the legislation in the countries for which they are engaged.
Section 3
On the expiry of the period of eight years, Colonists shall be free to dispose of their own services, no debt they may have contracted being allowed to serve as a pretext for prolonging the time of their engagement. Such debts must be recovered by process of law.
Section 4

Contracts shall be written in Chinese and in the language of the country to which the colonist is emigrating.

Section 5

Foreigners engaging colonists shall bind themselves to afford them every means for communicating with their families in China, and for remitting to them such monies as they may wish and be able to send.

16. Certain days shall be appointed by the Superintendent, in concert with the Procurador, for the appearance of intending emigrants at the latter's office, as also for the signature of the contracts.
17. Chinese wishing to emigrate shall present themselves at the Procurador's office to be registered, both by the Procurador and the Superintendent of Emigration, who will note in their respective books the depot to which the colonist is going until he signs the contract, and, in case he returns to his own home, the name of the Agent with whom he proposes engaging himself. In thus appearing, the colonists must go unaccompanied by the employees of the depots and by the Brokers.
18. There shall be fixed in the depots, both on the outside of the doors, and in different parts of the interior, the contracts and regulations of the Establishment, both in Chinese and Portuguese.
19. The internal regulations of the depots shall be submitted to the approval of the Superintendent of Emigration.
20. The depots shall be open from 8am until 4pm in order that all the relatives and friends of the colonists who choose to visit them may enter.
21. The Superintendent of Emigration shall visit the depots and vessels of the colonists from time to time, and shall muster the colonists in order to prevent any from embarking unless they have signed the contract, as provided in Article 9.
22. It shall be the duty of the Superintendent to watch over the execution of the regulations and to obviate any abuses that might occur, and in any case of infringement he shall proceed against the guilty party, accusing him before the Procurador if the delinquent is a Chinese, and notifying the Deputy Procurador of the Crown and Revenue whenever the individual should be dealt with by judicial power, and to the end that the functionary in question may take proceedings in conformity with the law.
23. All provisions of the Regulations of 5 June 1856, which are not affected by the present Order shall remain in force.

Section 1

The prohibition against the sailing of vessels with colonists in the contrary monsoon remains also in force, as well as the other provisions of the Orders of 31 March and 4 August 1857.

Section 2

It remains prohibited for Portuguese to go to any part of the Chinese territory in order to engage emigrants, as well as for

Portuguese vessels to transport them to Macao, or from one part of China to another.

24. Persons contravening the provisions of this Order shall be liable to the penalties of Articles 328 et seq. Of the Portuguese Penal Code. The authorities to whom appertains the cognizance and execution thereof shall attend to the fulfilment of the same.

Isidoro FranciscoGuimares
Macao, 30 April 1860

Supplement to the Regulations of 30 April 1860[178]

Resolved by the Governor of Macao:

1. Every vessel embarking Chinese emigrants at Macao under the Regulation of 30 April shall be anchored in the Taipa Roads, when her draft of water does not forbid, until she has completed the number of passengers she is to take on board.
2. No vessel shall carry a greater number of Chinese emigrants than one for every two tons burden.
3. On board all vessels receiving colonists internal regulations approved in the first place by the Superintendent of Emigration shall be observed.

Section 1

The Superintendent of emigration shall watch over observance of such regulations, on the occasion of the visits he is bound to make on board such vessels.

4. Without prejudice to the entire responsibility devolving on the Emigration Agent, the Captains of vessels intended to carry emigrants shall be responsible for the treatment of the latter on board.

Section 1

In the case of any offence on the part of an emigrant urgently necessitating confinement, the Captain shall be authorised to inflict the same, the fact being immediately communicated to the Superintendent of Chinese Emigration.

Section 2

No other punishment may be inflicted without previous report and authorisation.

Section 3

The superintendent of Chinese Emigration shall inquire whether any of the emigrants have just ground for complaint concerning the treatment they receive on board.

It shall be incumbent on the Emigration Agents to prevent the Colonists being injured in the purchases they may make at any of the shops established on board; rendering themselves liable to fine if they neglect to do so.

In the emigration establishment there shall not be allowed a greater number of employees than shall be considered strictly indispensable for the service and maintenance or order in the establishment.

Section 1

The persons in charge of each establishment shall deliver a statement of their employees to the Superintendent of Chinese Emigration, who shall point out the number allowed them, and exclude any person who owing to lack of security or for any antecedent reason may not be acceptable.

Section 2

In the statement above referred to must be entered the names of any employees who may be on board the vessel without belonging to the crew.

No Chinese who shall have twice declared himself unwilling to emigrate shall be allowed to sign the contract, although he may state that he has resolved to do so.

It shall not be lawful to engage colonists for a voyage when the northeast monsoon is unfavourable during the period extending between 31 March and 1 September.

The Government retains the right of closing all the establishments, or any of them, whenever it shall see fit, without being bound to give reasons for so doing.

The Government has the right to putting an end to the despatch of Chinese colonists from the Port of Macao six months after publishing a prohibition to that effect. The authorities to whom appertains etc. etc

Isidoro Francisco Guimares
Macao 12 October 1860

No. 35   5 September 1861[179]

Resolved by the Governor of Macao:

Whereas it is enacted by Order of this Government that in the despatch of Chinese colonists from Macao vessels be required to be of the capacity of two tons for every passenger, which measure has been adopted in order to assimilate the legislation on this subject to that instituted by the Spanish Government relatively to emigration into the island of Cuba, after hearing the Council of Government I have seen fit to declare that this provision shall henceforward be understood solely with reference to vessels carrying colonists to the island of Cuba, the Regulation of 5 June 1856 which prescribes the capacity of one ton and a half for each passenger remaining in force with respect to all other ports. The authorities to whom appertains etc. etc

Isidoro Francisco Guimares
Macao, 5 September 1861

No. 38   25 November 1863[180]

Resolved by the Governor of Macao:
Macao having been regulated by the Decrees of this Government of 5 June 1856, 31 March and 4 August 1857, and 30 April and 12 October 1860:
No clause being found in these Decrees which restricts the application of its provisions to emigration to certain specified countries; whence it should be understood that they are all applicable to emigration in general:
And whereas it is certain, nevertheless, that emigration to Havana and Peru alone has been subjected to the regulations adopted, and that all other has been carried on without any control (*fiscalisacao*) on the part of the Government.
And whereas it has become indispensable to obviate the abuses which may result herefrom: I see fit to determine as follows:
Art. 1   The observance of the Decrees above recapitulated is enjoined with respect to Chinese emigration from Macao for all countries without distinction.
Art. 2   The Superintendent of Emigration, the Procurador of the Loyal Senate, and the Captain of the Port, will take especial care, each in their own department, for the exact fulfilment of this Resolution. Other authorities and persons to whom appertains etc.

José Rodrigues C do Amaral
Governor. Macao, 25 November 1863

No. 19   13 August 1864[181]

Resolved by the Governor of Macao:
Whereas it is determined by Decree of this Government, No. 100 of 15 October 1860 that no vessel shall be allowed to carry a greater number of Chinese emigrants in proportion to her tonnage than at the rate of two tons for each person:
And whereas it has subsequently declared by Decree No. 35 of 5 September 1861 that this provision shall be understood solely with reference to vessels carrying emigrants to the Island of Cuba, the rule laid down in Decree No 39 of 5 June 1856 fixing the number of passengers, inclusive of the crew, at one for every one and a half tons, remaining in force with respect to vessels sailing for other ports:
And this distinction, based on the difference in voyages to countries where Chinese emigration usually proceeds are in all cases of long duration:
And inasmuch as the less reason exists for fixing the number of passengers that a vessel can carry in accordance with her tonnage or total capacity, since it is upon the amount of accommodation she possesses and her condition in respect to health that the number must essentially depend.

And whereas it is expedient to require implicit observance of Article 25 of said Decree of 5 June 1856, in which it is prescribed that there shall be a doctor and a medicine chest on board every vessel carrying more than 20 passengers; thus putting a stop to the abuse of substitution Chinese empirics for duly qualified practitioners.

For all these reasons, I have seen fit to determine as follows:

Art. 1 The greatest number of emigrants that a vessel may carry shall be regulated by the capacity of the accommodation destined for their use, and by the provision existing for the admission of light and of ventilation. In the most favourable case, that is, if the part of the vessel occupied by the emigrants receives air and light through sufficient apertures in the ship's side, and if, in addition thereto, air-funnels are used, the number shall be fixed by the condition that there be a space of two cubic metres (about 55 cubic feet) for each individual. If no side apertures exist, but air-funnels are used, two and a half cubic metres shall be allowed. In the absence of air-funnels the vessel shall not be allowed to carry a greater number of emigrants in proportion to her accommodation than at the rate of three cubic metres for each person.

Art. 2 Rigorous observance is enjoined of the provision contained in Article 25 of the Decree of 5 June 1856, to the effect that no vessel shall carry more than 20 emigrants unless she has on board a medical practioner and a medicine chest.

The provisions of this Decree shall take effect from 1 January 1865.

The authorities to whom etc. etc

José Rodrigues C. do Amaral
Governor, Macao 13 August 1864

Ordinance No. 25   24 August 1868[182]

The Governor of the Province of Macao and Timor determines as follows:-

In view of the necessity of obviating by means of due regulations the abuses that make themselves felt successively in the emigration of Chinese – abuses the origin of which resides for the most part without the limits of the jurisdiction of this Portuguese Colony, and to which, at the same time, it is only possible to apply a remedy whom their influence detracts from the beneficial intervention exercised by this Government in the act of engagement.

In view of the fact that some of the provisions of the last regulations for Chinese Emigration, although dictated by the necessity of repressing the abuses then prevailing, are at present practically superfluous, and even in some respects inconvenient, as for instance in the case of delay, not infrequently excessive, of vessels ay anchor in port with emigrants on board.

In view moreover of the advisability for judicial purposes of expressly defining the penalties applicable to each instance of infringement and offence, inasmuch as by this means a warning in afforded to persons of guilty intention and assistance is rendered to those invested with judicial power. And having given evidence to the Council of Government, to the Commission nominated by Decree of the 2nd April of the current year, and to the reports of the Procurador of Chinese Affairs for the Colony and the Superintendent of Chinese Emigration, I see fit to ordain as follows:-

Art I – Emigration Agents may obtain permission to open more than one establishment, on proof that they have an increased number of emigrants about to enter into contract with them.

1. It shall be lawful for the Government to fix the number of establishments allowed to each agent, in proportion to the number of emigrants he intends contracting with.
2. The establishments must fulfil the conditions as to space and ventilation that may be fixed upon, and in addition, must provide separate lodgings for the women and families who also intend to emigrate.
3. The establishments shall pay such a sum by way of police-rate, as may be determined.

Art II – It shall not be permitted to collect emigrants in 'cun-taus' (barracoons) or in any non-licensed building by way of establishment.

1. On detection of any case of infraction of this article, all persons interested in or responsible for the same shall be punished with a fine from $100 to $500, according to the circumstances, and in case of repetition of the offence, from three to six months imprisonment, with corresponding fine.

Art III – Emigration Agents shall accompany their applications for a license to open establishments with a list of the names of the persons in charge of the said establishments and with a copy of the agreements they have made with the said persons in charge.

Art IV – The persons in charge of the establishments shall deposit at the Superintendency caution money to the amount of $1000, and they shall be responsible for all offences or abuses practised in the said establishments.

1. For a breach of the regulations the person in charge shall be liable to a fine graduated according to the circumstances of the case from $50 up to the total amount of the caution money.

Art V – Every manager of an establishment, or contractor, or any broker, who being bound by any contract shall execute another contract with another Agent shall be liable to a fine of from $100 to $500.

Art VI – Every manager or contractor or any broker, who shall wilfully entice or receive emigrants who have been arranged for by the other brokers, employees or contractors of other agents, shall be liable to a fine of $50 to $200.

Art VII – Every broker who, having entered into an engagement with an Agent, an employee, or contractor from whom he has received money, shall offer to another person the emigrant or emigrants he may have obtained, shall be liable to a fine of from $50 to $200.

Art VIII – Any Emigration Agent proved guilty of connivance in a violation of Art VI and VII, shall be liable to the penalty of closing the Establishments for which he holds a license.

Art IX – Without prejudice to the responsibility of the Agents and managers or contractors, the persons employed in the Establishments shall be individually responsible for infringements of the internal regulations of the said Establishment.
1. The managers of Establishments shall be answerable, whenever necessary, for the fines imposed upon any of the employees.

Art X – It shall be the duty of the Police and the Superintendent of Chinese Emigration to see that the doors of the Establishments of the Establishments or licensed emigration houses remain open and that the emigrants enjoy free egress between the hours of 8 am and 4 pm.
1. Any police constable reporting any infringement of the emigration regulations on the same being proved, shall receive as reward the fourth part of the fine incurred by the offender.
2. A like reward shall be paid to any citizen who shall give information of any infringement of the rules, immediately on the same being proved.

Art XI – No corporal punishment of any description shall be inflicted upon the emigrants within the Establishments and any emigrant guilty of an offence shall be forthwith handed over to the Procurator of Chinese Affairs, and punished by that tribunal in conformity with the existing laws.

Persons infringing the above prohibition shall be liable to a fine of from $50 to $200, and the penalties provided in the Penal Code.

Art XII – Licensed brokers for Chinese emigration shall continue to receive their permits from the Procurator of Chinese Affairs, the process of security established by previous decrees being completed before issue of the license. The caution money for brokers is raised to the amount of $500.

Art XIII – The Emigration Agents shall keep suspended at the doors, and in all the rooms within, copies in perfectly legible characters of the contracts offered by the Agents respectively to the emigrants.

Art XIV – Notice shall be given to the Superintendent as soon as the Emigration Agent has collected emigrants having made up their minds to sign the contracts, in numbers sufficient to complete the despatch of the vessel in which it is intended to send them on.

Art XV – The Emigration Superintendency shall be established in a building of sufficient capacity to contain, during the period of four days, the entire number of emigrants to be despatched in each vessel.

Art XVI – Emigrants who are ready to embark, according to the notice given by the Agent shall be taken to the Superintendency where in open court they shall be examined by the Superintendent, and the contract shall be read and explained to them, a printed copy of the contract being delivered to each individual.

At this transaction, in addition to the persons employed in the Superintendency there shall be present the Procurador of Chinese Affairs, or his deputy, the interpreters of Chinese appointed for this service, the Commandant of Police, and two Chinese residents of the most acknowledged probity, during such time there shall be no Consular authority of that nation at Macao.

Art XVII – Such Chinese as on being examined, declare their readiness to emigrate and their acceptance of the terms of the contract, shall be collected in the lodgings provided for the purpose in the Superintendency, and during the period of four days, until the signing of the contracts, they shall not be allowed to communicate with the agents, managers or contractors or with the brokers.

Art XVIII – On the following day the emigrants shall publicly and at the hour appointed for the purpose, be summoned to the office of the Superintendency. And there, in the presence of the persons mentioned in the paragraph annexed to Art XVI, the contract shall again be read over to them, and the same questions shall be put to them, all who reply in the affirmative being thereupon sent back to their lodging place.

Art XIX – The same proceeding shall be repeated on the third day.

Art XX – On the fourth day in a similarly public manner after a fresh reading and examination, the contract shall be signed by each emigrant in turn. The contracts shall be in duplicate in accordance to the established rule, one being delivered to the Agent and the other to the emigrant.

Art XXI – All Chinese who have signed the contract shall proceed forthwith to the place where they are to be at the Agent's disposal and here they shall receive the advance and clothing and shall thereupon be at once taken on board the ship that is to convey them on their voyage.

Art XXII – Any Chinese who at the time of signing the contracts or in the preceding examination in the Superintendency shall declare themselves unwilling to emigrate shall be given a separate place, in order that they may be sent back to their homes, at the expense of the Agent to whom they shall be bound to reimburse the expense of their maintenance received and held the cost of their passage money, in conformity with Article XXVII.

Art XXIII – So long as the Superintendency shall not be established in a building capable of accommodating the total number of emigrants to be shipped bu any vessel, it shall be lawful to send them on board in two batches, no longer interval than ten days being allowed to elapse between the first embarkation, conducted according to the method laid down in this Decree and the last.

In view of the near approach of the ensuing North East monsoon the above period is extended to 20 days and the number of successive shipments to three, in the case of vessels having a larger amount of emigrants to take on board.

Art XXIV – Vessels about to carry emigrants must be in readiness to sail at the latest within 48 hours after the embarkation has taken place.

Art XXV – The medical men of the establishments must inspect the emigrants at the Superintendency, on the days during which the said emigrants are lodged there.

Art XXVI – To meet the expenses of the Superintendency and the maintenance of the emigrants while lodged there, each Agent respectively shall pay the sum of one dollar and a half for each emigrant so lodged.

Art XXVII – Any emigrant who shall have been for ten days in an Emigration establishment in the enjoyment of full liberty there allowed him, and who only withdraws after the lapse of the above interval, shall constitute himself debtor to the agent concerned in the amount of half the cost of his passage, and of his maintenance at the rate of 100 cash per diem.

Art XXVIII – Every breach of the Emigration regulations shall be reported by the Superintendent to the Government with minute particulars and evidence as to the fact. It shall be the duty of the Government to transmit the offenders when Chinese, to the Procurator of Chinese Affairs, and in other cases to the Judicial Tribunal, in conformity with the laws.

Art XXIX – All fines arising from the Emigration Regulations whether imposed by the Judicial Tribunal of by the Procurador of Chinese Affairs shall be forwarded to the Treasury in the shape or a warrant in order to their recovery.

Art XXX – All provisions of previous Regulations contrary to the present Decree are revoked, and this Decree shall be considered as annexed to the existing Regulations,

The authorities to whom appertain the cognizance and execution hereof, shall accordingly take note of the same and carry it into effect.

Macao August 24th 1868
Antonio Sergio de Souza
Governor

Decree No. 34 28 May 1872[183]

The governor of the province of Macao and Timor and their dependencies, in council, orders the following:

In response to the need to collect and codify various provisions scattered in different decrees and regulations on emigration:

Paying more attention to the convenience of increasing existing provisions other than giving emigrants full freedom to give new guarantees to their spontaneity, establishing the necessary precautions and restrictions to avoid and inhibit all kinds of violence or influence that they intend to exercise; thus ensuring the authority in its humanitarian principle, all the efficiency in the prosecution of the acts concerning the emigration made through this port:

I consider it convenient, with the affirmative vote of the government, to approve and order the execution of the regulation that is an integral part of this decree and signed by the secretary general of government. The authorities to whom you compose your knowledge and execution so understand and comply.

Government Palace in Macao, May 28, 1872.

The Governor of the province,
Viscount of Sam Januário.

CHINESE EMIGRATION REGULATION

Section I - EMPOWERED TO EMIGRATE.
Article 1
Any Chinese who has the health and age conditions specified in this regulation is allowed to emigrate from the port of Macao.
Article 2
Any individual who, having been brought to Macao as a settler, declares that he does not want to emigrate, will be repatriated immediately.
Section II - THE AGENTS AND THEIR DEPENDENTS.
Article 3
Any person who wishes to hire emigrants for the allowed ports, needs to be licensed by the Government of this colony, without which he will not be able to hire any settler; must declare which are the clauses of the contract proposed to the emigrant.
Article 4
The agent, or the person authorized by the license referred to in the foregoing article, before the entry of the settlers into the government Superintendência, will nominate the number of depots they wish to open by declaring their location, the number of emigrants they intend to gather, the name of the attendant in charge and the Chinese managers.
§ To grant the license, the Health Board on hygienic conditions will be inspect each house, and the Superintendent and Solicitor of Chinese Business on the competence and capacity of the attendants.
Article 5
Each depot will have two Chinese managers who must be authorized through a examination of their good conduct,
Article 6
The licenses granted to the Chinese managers will be annual, and these managers will have to place an acceptable bond of 1,000 (one thousand pesos) or deposit with the Procurador property titles worth 1,500 (one thousand five hundred pesos.)
Article 7
Chinese managers will always be responsible for the contraventions of this regulation by their subordinates and by the presentation of the transgressors to the authorities
Article 8
The assistant managers will deposit in the superintendência a bond of $1,000 (one thousand pesos) or a deposit of property titles worth $1,500 (one thousand five hundred pesos.)
Article 9
The attendants in charge are responsible for the contraventions of the present regulation
Article 10
Without prejudice to the responsibility of the managers, the other employees of the depots, they will be personally responsible for the

contraventions they practice; therefore, whenever necessary, those responsible will be liable for fines imposed on them.

Article 11
The Governor of the Colony may demand from the agents the resignation of any employee who commits abuses.

Article 12
The attendants will send to the Superintendência a list of the employees in their depots, and whenever there is modification in its staff.

Article 13
The Superintendent may refuse any of the junior employees of the depots and limit the number.

Section III - MARITIME POLICE
Article 14
The settlers who arrive in Macau must, before disembarking, be examined at the maritime police post, where a detailed list of the Colonists who disembark will be sent daily to the superintendência.

Article 15
The colonists who declared in the examination of the police that they do not want to emigrate will be sent to the office of Chinese Business as well as the people who would have presented themselves as voluntary migrants.

Article 16
Each depot will have one or two Chiptús, that is, employees to receive the settlers and conduct them to the depots, as well as to recognize the people who accompanied them to Macao.

Article 17
The Chiptús will have a Superintendência license.

Article 18
The Chiptús will sign a declaration of the number of settlers they take to the depots at the maritime police post.

Article 19
It is forbidden to bring migrants under 18 years of age or invalids to Macao.

Section IV – DEPOTS
Article 20
It is not allowed to have settlers, in depots that are not provided with the corresponding license.

Article 21
The depots will be open from 10 am to 2 pm so that the settlers can leave freely.

Article 22
The Superintendent, the Police Commander and the Attorney for Chinese Business will visit the depots after adequate examination of the colonists, and immediately repatriate those who declare that they do not wish to emigrate.

§ The Superintendent may, when deemed appropriate, send his assistant to supervise any depot.

Article 23
Those bringing settlers to Macao are forbidden to enter the depots.
Article 24
Only settlers and employees can stay in depots.
Article 25
It is prohibited to impose any kind of punishment on the settlers within the depot.
Article 26
Any individual, settler or employee who commits any crime or violation within the depot, will be immediately sent by the assistant manager to the Superintendência with written note of what happened.
§ If the criminals do not show up, the attendant will have to prove that there was an impossibility to do so, giving clarity to the clarifications that are necessary for the capture of the guilty.
Article 27
In the depots there will be placed in the most visible places of the interior and exterior, the deals that agents offer emigrants and clarifications in Chinese language according to Model A.
Article 28
In the depots there will be special accommodations for women and families wishing to emigrate.
Article 29
Each depot will have one or more doctors chosen by their respective agents, who will be responsible for the inspection of the settlers, their treatment when they feel sick and everything related to the hygiene of the rooms and the settlers.
§ Only minor diseases will be treated in the depots, the serious ones being cured in the hospitals.
Article 30
The Health Board or one of its members is responsible for inspecting the depots frequently, in order to ascertain whether the precautions required by hygiene are observed and to give to both those in charge and the doctors the instructions they deem appropriate.
§ There will be in the depots a special book signed by the Health Chief who will write down the observations of the visit.
Article 31
There will be in the depots a book signed by the Superintendent in which the authorities will write their observations.
Article 32
Depot managers will enforce the instructions given to them by the Health Board, who will inform them not only of how to execute them, but of any observations they may have made.
Article 33
The same doctors will visit their respective depots daily, and will be presented there or in the Superintendência for treatment of any sick colonist.
Article 34

The assistant and Chinese managers will examine the settlers one by one as they enter the depot, asking them if they came to Macau voluntarily and free of any coercion, and if they are willing to emigrate, telling them where they are going and the clauses of the contract they have to sign.

§ In case of recognizing that any settler was deceived or violated they will immediately advise the Solicitor of Chinese Business in writing, giving the name of the settler and that of the person who brought him to the depot.

Article 35
Chinese officials are responsible for presenting to the authorities, the deceived settlers or violated people who entered the depots.

Article 36
Settlers who do not have the precise age to emigrate, and those rejected in the Superintendência as unsuitable, may not remain more than 24 hours in their respective depots.

Article 37
The assistant managers will report daily to the superintendência the movement of settlers of their depots and the events of the day.

Article 38
When the number of settlers has gathered in a sufficient deposit to make a shipment, the respective agent will report in writing to the Superintendent who will determine the day on which the said settlers must enter the Superintendência to be examined.

Section V – SUPERINTENDENCE

Article 39
In addition to the Superintendent there will be an assistant who will be responsible for the internal service of the office.

§ The number of other employees in this office will depend on what the service requires.

Article 40
A doctor of the Health Board will decide on the age of the settler upon their entry into the superintendency, or in his absence the Superintendência Physician will decide.

Article 41
Gathered the settlers in an appropriate room will be read and explained clearly and in several dialects, the contract to which they are going to commit.

Article 42.
They will then be examined one by one by the Superintendent, and the clauses of the contract will be explained again.

§ The examinations will be public.

Article 43
The colonists who, after being examined, declared that they want to emigrate, and that they accept the contract terms will be collected in the Superintendência accommodation; and for as long as they are there until the time of signing the contract, they will not be able to contact the agents, managers or any depot clerk.

Article 44

On the second day after their entry into Superintendencia, the contract will be explained to them individually, then signed, by those who are willing to emigrate.

§ They will be present at this act, together with the Superintendent, the Solicitor of the Chinese Business and the Police Commander or his delegates, who will watch over the faithful observation validity of the present and the Port Captain will also attend so that he can recognize the identity of the settlers who embark.

Article 45

In the Superintendência there will be a record book where the name, age, native village will be recorded and the quality and profession of the settlers who come to emigrate.

Article 46

It is forbidden to introduce in the Superintendência together with the settlers and the people who bring them to Macao.

§ These people can be allowed to emigrate, if the assistant manager who presents them in the Superintendência declares them as such, so that they are in separate accommodation from others.

Article 47

After signing the contract, the settlers will receive advances, costumes and other stipulated objects.

Article 48

The settlers who sign their contract and receive the advances and costumes will be shipped immediately.

Article 49

Settlers who in the act of signing the contract clearly do not want to emigrate will be taken to a separate place and then sent to their country accompanied by a note from the Superintendência addressed to the Chinese authorities so that they may take them to their place of origin.

§ Any settler who is claimed by his relatives will be delivered immediately.

Article 50

Settlers are required to obtain a passport in accordance with the law.

Section VI – CONTRACTS

Article 51

The contracts that the emigration agents offer to the settlers will be presented. to the Governor of the colony to be approved, these contracts must have the following requirements.

1st - The duration of the contract may not exceed 8 years counted from the date of arrival at his destination.

2nd - At the end of 8 years the settler is free to dispose of his work and cannot serve of pre-order for continuation of the commitment any debt that the settler has contracted with his employer, which can only be made, according to the laws of the country where it is found;

3rd - Once the 8 years have elapsed, the settler may not be obliged to provide his services under the pretext that during his Contract he stopped working at any time for any reason whatsoever;

4th - The settler has the right to be cured and treated in any illness he suffers without any of his salary being deducted for this reason;

5th - The colonist cannot be forced to work more than 12 hours a day when the work is in the field or in the factories, and when employed for domestic service, will work the same hours as the natives of the country;

6th - The colonists who occupy the workings of the field or in the factories, will have 3 meals per day. They will have the same number of meals as the natives of the country, when they were occupied in domestic service. The groceries will be abundant and of good quality according to the custom of the country.

7th - On Sundays they will be resting for the settler, and when his employer needs his services these days, he will have to pay him as extraordinary.

8 - The settler who, upon arrival, went to the domestic or other similar service, may not be employed at the farm and factory sites;

9th - The settler is subjected to the legislation of the country where he will be;

10. - The contract will be written in Chinese and in the language of the country for which it is intended, well contain the name, sex, age, naturalness and profession of the emigrant;

11th - The contract will have to mention the salary, clothing and other guarantees that the agent offers a settler.

Article 52

No migrants may be forced to work that is recognized as being badly healthy.

Article 53

The contracts will be in duplicate delivering a copy to the settler and another to the agent.

Article 54

The contracts will be signed by the Superintendent, Solicitor or his delegate, Agent and Consul of the country for which they are destined; In addition, they shall bear the seal of the Procurature and reviewed by a clerk of this court in a book intended for this purpose.

Article 55

The settler, in the country where it is destined, is under the protection of the Portuguese government and its Consuls complies with the faithful compliance with the clauses of the contract protecting and collecting the interests of the Chinese who had gone as settlers of Macao to remit them to their families.

Article 56

There will be a Chinese interpreter in these consulates

Section VII – SHIPS

Article 57

Vessels that are intended to transport settlers from the port of Macao, must have at least two meters of headroom in the accommodation intended for settlers.

§ Any excess of 2 meters 30 is not counted, this being the maximum height that the housings should have.

Article 58
Any ship that is destined for the transport of settlers of the port of Macao, after arriving at this port will be carefully inspected by the Port Captain in order to make sure if it has the necessary capacity, armament and crew. The Captain of the Port will find out how many Portuguese tons are registered, and the number of settlers that the ship can transport will be given to the Government Secretary.
Article 59
A doctor of the Health Board will inspect the vessel to see if it has the hygienic conditions necessary.
Article 60
The Captain of the Port, upon entering the ship in the port, shall deliver to the Captain a copy of the model B instructions that are for the purpose of this regulation, and the Captain of the ship will sign a document for which he is responsible for the exact compliance with the instructions received.
Article 61
Any ship that embarks more than 20 Chinese passengers in the port of Macao, is subject to the provisions of the 7th and 8th section of the emigration regulation.
Article 62
All ships will have to carry interpreters of the different dialects of the Chinese they embark.
§ These interpreters must be examined and approved at the attorney's office.
Article 63
No settler can be received on board without presenting a pass from the Superintendência.
Article 64
No ship with more than twenty Chinese passengers can leave Macau, without carrying a doctor, a nurse and the corresponding kit.
Article 65
No ship may leave Macau with settlers without obtaining a certificate from the Port Captain according to Model C.
Article 66
No ship is allowed to leave carrying more than 20 Chinese passengers in the monsoon season.
Article 67
The maximum number of settlers that a ship can receive on board will be calculated according to the capacity of the accommodation allocated to them and by the conditions set. That is, for the entry of light and ventilation.
§ 1. With the vessel having good ventilation and light given by spacious openings, in addition to the hatches and ventilation pumps, the number of passengers will be calculated at the rate of two cubic meters for the accommodation of each passenger.
§ 2. For a vessel having only a ventilation pump, the number shall be calculated at 2.5 cubic meters for each passenger.
Article 68

394

Any ship that embarks 300 settlers must make their total shipment within 12 business days, and the one that ships 500, in 20 days, and so on.

Article 69

The ship that embarks settlers must sail twelve hours after dispatch, except in the circumstances of force majeure.

Article 70.

The consignee of a ship that transports colonists is obliged to place a bond of $1,000 guaranteed by a deposit in money at the Board of Finance or at any bank accredited, at the order of the Government, or in duly registered properties, and registered in the Conservatory as a guarantee of his bond. This bond will only be lifted if filed within 18 months, together with any legal document certifying that the ship has arrived at its destination, and having complied with the provisions of this regulation.

§ By not presenting this document within the specified period, the right to retrieve the bond is lost except in case of force majeure duly proven.

Article 71

The Captain of the ship upon arrival at the port of destination, must present the settlers with their proper passports to the Portuguese consul in the locality.

Article 72

The Captain of the ship may only disembark the settlers in the port for which he declared to be destined, except in the cases provided in the Portuguese commercial code.

Article 73

Any crime committed by the settlers on board, during their time in the port of Macao, will be reported by the Captain of the ship to the Captain of the Port, who will advise the Superintendent of what happened, but the Captain of the ship cannot punish, only detain the offender until he is sent ashore.

§ The captain of the vessel and the agent are both responsible for compliance with this order.

Article 74

The Superintendent will visit the settlers on board, when he sees fit.

Article 75

It is incumbent on the Port Captain to check, before the departure of the ship, if any settler has a complaint about the treatment received on board or if a settler has not gone through the Superintendência, and that it is not provided with its duly authenticated contract; and if there were any in these circumstances landed and sent to the Superintendência with a written report of what happened.

Article 76

From the first day of embarkation of settlers until the departure of the ship, there will be a police soldier from the port who will monitor the order, according to the model C instructions; give a written report of the daily events to the Captain of the Port for this to be recorded by the Superintendência.

Section VIII - STORES ON BOARD

Article 77

The person who wants to establish a store or sell anything on board a ship destined for the transport of settlers, will have to qualify for a Superintendência permit.

Article 78

The price list of the objects that are desired to be sold to the emigrants will have to be approved by the Superintendent.

Article 79

The store owner will have to give a deposit of $500 (five hundred pesos).

Article 80

The price rates for objects sold to emigrants must be placed in the most visible places on the ship, written in clear and well-legible Chinese characters.

Section IX – PENALTIES

Article 81

Those who secretly introduce settlers into Macau without giving the authority notification in the manner set out in this regulation, will be punished with a $50 to $200 fine.

Article 82

Any person who seduces the settlers or exerts any influence over them will incur the penalties that mark the laws and regulations in force.

Article 83

The contraventions to the prescriptions of the present regulation, mentioned below, will be punished with the corresponding fines.

	Contravention		Fines		
Section 3. -	Art.	14	$50	to	$100
	Fine or prison corresponding to the vessel's pattern.				
Section 4. -	Art.	20	$30	to	$800
		21	$50	to	$100
		23	$300	to	$800
		24.	$100	to	$200
		27	$50	to	$100
		34	$50	to	$100
		36	$50	to	$100
		37	$50	to	$100
Section 5		46	$100	to	$500
Section 8.		*	$100	to	$200

Section X - GENERAL DISPOSITION

Article 84

When the Portuguese government considers it appropriate to alter some fundamental provision of thisregulation, agents will be notified with; three months in advance.

Secretary of the Government of Macao
May 28, 1872
Enrique de Castro
General secretary

MODEL A
　　The settler who embarks cannot return to land. Havana and Peru are in America and to go from China to any of these two points it takes 3 months of travel a little more or less.
　　The Chinese who are in this Superintendência must know that it is in order to emigrate. Those who do not want to do so, can declare it on any of the two days of examination, without any fear, in the certainty that they can freely return to their homes.
　　The settler after receiving the advances and signing the contract is obliged to emigrate; It is previously notified. Those who do not want to emigrate do not sign without reflecting their contract, nor receive advances.

MODEL B
　　　Instructions to be carried out aboard ships carrying Chinese emigrants from Macau.
1. - The captains of ships destined to transport Chinese settlers from the port of Macao must adopt and follow the exact observance of the established hygienic precepts in these instructions.
2. - The settlers are not to be received on board without the accommodation being perfectly washed, dried and that the walls, ceilings and flooring are whitewashed with two or three hands of common water, united with a tail and a small amount of lime chloride. These operations will be repeated every time a trip is over, the ship is ready to transport new settlers.
3 - A room with the best ventilation and light conditions will be assigned to serve as a hospital, which will be completely separated from the accommodation and will receive the same preparations indicated. This location will vary according to the size and other conditions of each vessel.
4 – On receipt of the settlers on board, it will be treated as regularly as possible both in travel and in the ports, to clean, disinfect, wash and fix its effects, to demand the most scrupulous personal hygiene and finally to avoid all the causes of unhealthy even the ones that seem most insignificant.
5 - The accommodations will be swept twice a day or more if necessary. The fencing must be prohibited in this part of the vessel due to inconvenience to the settlers. The general or partial cleaning of the floor will be done when necessary, with sponges or moistened lampazos, having to rinse it immediately carefully.
6 - The floor and other wooden objects stained with vomiting materials, diarrhea, etc., They will dry thoroughly after washing with the following preparation:
　　　Dry Lime Chloride　　one part
　　　Common water　　　thirty-two parts
7 - The most rigorous vigilance will be observed to clean from the lodgings everything that can produce humidities and other exactions harmful to health, such as wet and dirty clothes, food

remains, fish and salted meat etc., these objects, which the settlers are observed to keep together.

8 - The custom of the colonists of smoking in the lodgings for which they constantly have a large number of lights there, is very harmful to the health, because the combustion products of the oil, the tobacco and the opium alter and vitiate the atmosphere, and therefore will be strictly prohibited. Smoking will be allowed only on the deck. The use of the opium that will only be smoked in an appropriate place must be stipulated poço a poço. Soon and little!

9 - The accommodation will be fumigated daily by first removing all of the colonists. All openings will be closed immediately where air enters, or most of they, mainly to windward. It will then be placed in the middle of the accommodation on hot sand or ashes, an ordinary clay casserole at two different points according to the size of the site, containing the following mixture;

Soda Chloride (common salt) powder	3	parts
Manganese dioxide	1	parts.
Common water	2	parts.
Sulfuric acid of 66 degrees	2	parts.

Sulfuric acid, which develops the disinfectant vapors of chloride, must be mixed last. One to two hours later, all the windows, doors, fans and hatches of the housings will be opened and kept open and all the media will be used to restore ventilation, without which it cannot be occupied by the settlers. This procedure, which is the most convenient, will be used not only on the occasions when the accommodation can be evacuated, but also on ships that have all the conditions for easy and prompt ventilation.

10. - If the circumstances do not allow all settlers to be at the same time in the rain, they will raise two thirds or half of the number, and the fumigation will be done as follows. The housings will be crossed with a casserole containing the indicated mixture, in which the sulfuric acid is made from time to time to avoid that there are vapors in so much quantity, that they cause the cough or other discomforts in the circumstances. Also avoid this inconvenience by spraying by means of nitric acid, for which the following substances are used:

Sulfuric acid 66.	2	parts
Common water	1	part
Nitro purified powder	2	parts.

The capacity that these substances must contain must be on hot ashes.

The nitro is mixed at the end and poço á poço.

11 - In the infirmary, and in the lodgings, when time precludes the leaving of the colonists, disinfection will be done by placing in the distance and for a few hours bowls containing the subsequent dissolution.

Dry lime chloride 1 part
Common water 3 parts.

12 - Fumigation of odoriferous substances, such as incense, essences, powder, etc., are inconvenient because instead of destroying miasmas, airborne products that are unfit for breathing are added to the air. When for in circumstances the disinfectants indicated in these instructions cannot be used, vinegar can be burnt with hot iron.

13. - The medicine cabinets of the ships in addition to the medicines for the sick, must be provided with the following substances, necessary for the fumigations indicated.

Dry lime chloride
Manganese dioxide
66 degree sulfuric acid
Nitro purified powder.

The quantities of these substances will be arranged according to the trip, by the Health Doctor who visits on board.

14. - Every day, the settlers will be screened in order to get some sick people out of the lodgings if there is one to transfer them to the infirmary. In no case of illness, even for those who seem milder, this move will be stopped.

15. - Dirty threads and scrub materials will be taken out of the infirmary and they will be thrown into the sea. The same will be done with clothing and bed objects that have been served in serious and suspicious diseases that cannot be used by means of disinfection and washing indicated in No. 21.

16 - The greatest care will be taken to throw the bodies into the sea with precipitation or not with too much delay, avoiding the colonists witness these painful spectacles.

17. - When there is no sick person, the infirmary will be washed and bleached, so atmosphere per fumigation medium as indicated in numbers 2 and 9.

18. - The settlers must remain for most of the day under cover, avoiding the perspiration and the colds that are caused by atmospheric variations.

19. - Blankets, and other bedding will be shaken, will be exposed to air and collected before the night, at least once a week. At the same time, the chests of the settlers will open on the deck in order to fix their effects.

20. - Personal cleanliness, which is an absolute necessity for the conservation of the health, not only from the individual himself but from those around him, must be demanded from the settlers. The mouth, face, hands, arms and feet will be washed every day in the morning before the first meal. The mouth will be washed with water and vinegar for what will be available to the settlers vessels containing this preparation. The rest of the body that is covered with clothing should be washed twice a week. The

bathrooms will be inspected on occasions that are convenient and possible.

For all these cleanings, individual circumstances and the state of time will be taken into account.

21.- Every week they will change their clothes, which will be appropriate to the variations of the weather. The laundry, mainly that of the sick, will be immediately put in boiling water containing a part of lime chloride, and then washed with soap and well dried.

22. - All these hygienic practices will be demanded more rigorously, on the occasions when an epidemic is declared on board, or serious and contagious diseases.

MODEL C
Captaincy of the port of Macao.

I X ... captain of the port of Macao certify: that the vessel (ship class, nationality and (name) captain ...... of ..... tons leaves the Macau port for that of .... taking on board ..... Chinese passengers, hired to serve as settlers, who all know the place of their destiny, and go on their own accord of what I duly inform myself, as well as the contracts that they carry were approved in the competent office.

I certify in addition, that in the visit I made to the ship I found that it is in a state of sailing, that it has enough crew to maneuver, and that it has the provisions and watering determined on the boards l. a and 2. to which they are part of the Chinese emigration regulations of May 28, 1872, as well as that there is a surgeon, apothecary and ..... Chinese interpreters and that the ship takes place for the passengers who are departing.

Macao ...... of ..... of 187--
(Signature of the port captain.)

MODEL D
Instructions for the guards that goes on board the vessels of settlers.

1st. - After receiving these instructions, the Superintendent will be presented, under whose orders remains for the duration of your service.

2nd - He will be on board during the day completely uniformed.

3rd - He will not consent to any colonist being on board without presenting a pass from the Superintendendência.

§ The fact of having already been on board and having disembarked due to illness does not dispense the presentation of the pass of the Superintendent.

4th - There will be no objection to the landing of any claimed settler, when presented he gives an order signed by the Superintendent.

§ The settler may keep this order in case the settler leaves; but of otherwise, he will have to return it.

5th - When any colonist leaves the ship for any reason whatsoever, the guard shall immediately inform the Port Police Commander so that he may notify the competent authority.

6th - Having addressed any disorder or serious conflict between the settlers, or between the crew, he will without loss of time communicate to the Commander of the Port Police.

7th - If a settler does not want to embark, he will be report to the Port Police Commander, and he will not be mistreated or forced to remain on board.

8th - No punishment may be inflicted on the settlers during the time of the ship in Macau, enforcing what is determined in article 73 of the rules of emigration of May 28, 1872.

§ In case the Captain or ship officers insisted on applying any corporal punishment he will make them observe that they cannot proceed like this and will report to the Port Police what happened.

9th - He will not allow the store to be on board without the person in charge of presenting him with the Superintendent's permission.

10. - He will not consent to the sale of any item that is not on the pre-order list approved by the superintendent.

11. - He will watch that the leaders do not mistreat the colonists.

12. - Of any extraordinary event that exists, he will send a report to the Port Police.

13. - When the Superintendent, Captain of Port, or Port Police Officers go aboard, he will tell them if there is anything new or not.

14. - Without ceasing to comply rigorously with his duties, he will act without compromise with the greatest prudence, avoiding conflicts and problems with the officers and crew.

TABLE 1

List of provisions to be carried by ships carrying Chinese settlers from the port of Macao.

DAILY RATION FOR EVERY CHINESE.

Rice	1 1/2 lb
Salted pork meat,	
or 2/3 of pork and 1/3 of fish,	
or 1/3 of pork 1/3 of cow & 1/3 of fish	0 1/2id.
Salted vegetables	0 1/2id.
Tea	0 1/3 of an ounce
Lena	20 ounces

Water at rate of 12 liters per week for each Chinese.

TABLE ll.
Duration of the trip for which the provisions for sailing ships that transport Chinese settlers must be calculated.

	October to March	April to September
California or West Coast of America, North of Ecuador	100 days	75
West Coast of America, South of Ecuador	120	120
Sandwich Islands	75	56
New Caledónia, New Hebrides, Fiji, Tahiti and Society	100	100
Sydney, Melbourne or Southern Australia	60	80
Western Austriala	45	60
Tasmania	65	80
New Zealand	75	90
Manila	20	20
Singapore	20	45
Batavia	30	60
Ceylon	45	70
Madras or Calcutá	50	75
Bombay	60	80
Mauritius, Bourbon	60	80
Cape of Good Hope	65	85
West Indies and East Coast of America	147	168

Secretary of the Macau government,
May 28, 1872.
Enrique de Castro, General secretary

Decree No. 11 January 28, 1874.[184]

Regulations for Future Emigration from Macao, as published in the "Government Gazette" styled "Boletim da Provincia, de Macau e Timor" 31st January, 1874.

(Translation)
Regulations for Asiatic Passengers and their Transport at the Port of Macao.

SECTION 1-Passengers.
Article 1. Embarkation at the Port of Macao is permitted to every Asiatic passenger who is in the enjoyment of his liberty and who is not in any way subject to the conditions of bondage.
Art. 2. The Portuguese Authorities in Macao shall not sanction nor recognize any transaction entered into under the pretext of inducing persons to emigrate.
Art. 3. Asiatic passengers shall be considered in all respects as any other passengers.

Art. 4. Passengers must provide themselves with individual passports obtained from the Government Offices by means of a proper security.

§ 1. If any passenger goes on board without a passport, or if the passport be not in order, he shall be disembarked.

§ 2. No passport shall be given to any individual whose arrest has been applied for, in conformity with the Treaties existing with the nation to which the said individual belongs.

§ 3. No passport shall be given to minors without the consent of their fathers or guardians.

Art. 5. No lodgings shall be permitted in Macao for Asiatics who intend or not to travel to foreign countries, except it be proved that such Asiatics are in a condition of perfect freedom.

Art. 6. It is not permitted that those vessels which are intended for the conveyance of Asiatic passengers shall be provided with gratings, chains, or other fittings which are intended for the purpose of confining or interfering with the perfect liberty of the passengers.

SECTION II-Emigrant Vessels.

Art. 7. The vessel which carries more than thirty Asiatic passengers for a voyage of more than seven days shall be considered an emigrant vessel, within the scope of these Regulations.

§ 1. The vessel which voyages for more than seven days, but which carries less than thirty passengers, shall only be subject to each of these Regulations as are framed to secure the freedom of the passengers.

§ 2. In both cases all the passengers must provide themselves with a proper passport.

Art. 8. Every individual who designs his vessel to be an emigrant ship for Asiatic passengers must obtain, through the Captain of the Port, a special licence from the Colonial Secretariat.

Art. 9. Every vessel intended as an emigrant vessel for Asiatic passengers shall be minutely examined by the Captain of the port, in order that it may be ascertained that said vessel has the necessary capacity, armament, and fittings.

§ 1. The vessel must have a space of at least 2 metres between decks for the accommodation of passengers.

§ 2. The number of passengers shall be regulated at the rate of 3 cubic metres for each adult passenger, or for two children under 12.

§ 3. A separate compartment shall be assigned to the women.

§ 4. The Captain of the port shall report to the Government Secretariat the result of the said inspection, and shall declare what is the number of passengers that can be carried in the said vessel.

Art. 10. A medical man, as health officer, shall see that the vessel is in a healthy condition; that the quarters assigned to the passengers are sufficiently roomy and ventilated ; that the various provisions, water and medicines, are of good quality and sufficient in quantity for the number of passengers the vessel is about to carry.

Art. 11. The captain of the vessel shall state a date by which he shall he bound to hand over to the Portuguese Consul of the port of destination, if there is any Consul, the passengers whom he has carried in his vessel. The captain is responsible for the fulfilment of this part of the Regulations, as well as for the carrying out the orders he has received from the Captain of the port and from the medical officer relative to the treatment of the passengers carried.

Art. 12. All the vessels destined to carry Asiatic passengers shall carry interpreters for the different dialects of the passengers on board.

SECTION Special. The said interpreters must be approved of by the Procurador of Chinese Affairs.

Art.13. No vessel shall leave Macao with more than fifty passengers without a doctor, a sick attendant, and the proper medicines.

SECTION Special. Carrying more than 200 passengers the vessel must have on board two doctors if they are Chinese.

Art. 14. No sailing-vessel will be allowed to start from Macao with passengers during the season that the monsoon is adverse to the voyage which it is proposed to make.

Art. 15. The consignee or captain of the vessel, in accordance with Article 5 for the regulation of emigrant vessels, shall lodge as security a sum of 4,000 dollars in such manner as the Government Secretariat may lay down.

Special. The said security can be withdrawn after the presentation within fifteen months of legal documents showing that the vessel had arrived at her destination, and had complied with these Regulations. Provision to be made for exceptional cases.

Art. 16. Any offence committed by any passenger on board during the stay of the vessel at the port of Macao shall be reported by the master of the vessel to the Captain of the port.

In no case shall the master inflict any other punishment than detention until the offender can be sent on shore.

Art. 17. It is not permitted that any vessel should keep passengers on board for more than three days before the time fixed for sailing.

Art. 18. Every vessel intended to convey Asiatic passengers in accordance with these Regulations, shall, three days before clearing, have on board a guard of police, whose duty it shall be to maintain order in conformity with the instructions received from a competent authority.

SECTION Special. This guard shall be relieved daily.

Art. 19. On the day proposed for sailing, the vessel carrying Asiatic passengers, before weighing, shall be visited by the Captain of the port and by an officer specially appointed by the Governor, accompanied by one or more interpreters.

§ 1. The passengers shall be counted and gone over with the list furnished by the masters, be tallied with their passports, and shall at the same time be asked individually whether they wish to proceed on the voyage or not.

§ 2. In case any passenger refuses to proceed on the voyage he shall be immediately put on shore, and shall have no claim for the return of his passage money.

§ 3. The number of passengers that the vessel carries shall be recorded in the ship's log.

§ 4. An examination of the ship's articles shall be held to ascertain that the number and proficiency of the crew is correct.

§ 5. A search shall be made on board the vessel to certify that she is not clandestinely carrying other passengers.

Art. 20. If after the examination it is considered that all or part of the conditions of these regulations are not satisfied, the vessel shall be detained until the Captain has satisfied them, and such penalty shall be imposed as the infractions committed shall require.

Art. 21. After the examination of the vessel and the questioning the passengers is completed, a document shall be drawn up by the officials present allowing the vessel to proceed on her voyage. This document shall be given to the Captain, and a copy thereof shall be sent to the Secretary of the Government, and the vessel shall immediately proceed on her voyage. Exceptional circumstances excepted.

Art. 22. After the visit of these officers, no passenger will be allowed to go on board. The Captain will be held responsible for the breach of this rule.

Art. 23. A duplicate list of the passengers shall be sent to the Portuguese Consul, if any, at the port of destination, for the purpose of comparing it with the list presented by the Captain.

SECTION III-General Rules.

Art. 24. The sanitary conditions, provisions, water, medicines, number of crew fittings, probable length and end of the voyages, shall be regulated by special tables and instructions.

Art. 25. Any infraction of the terms of these regulations shall be punished by the fines and penalties in accordance with laws and regulations now in force.

Art. 26. The terms of these regulations do not prevent the Government from contracting or authorizing contracts of emigrants, provided they are employed by our agricultural and industrial works in Portuguese possessions.

Colonial Secretariat, Macao, January 28, 1874.
(Signed) HENRIQUE DE CASTRO,
Secretary-General

Instructions which should be put in practice on board vessels carrying Asiatic Passengers from the Port of Macao

1. The Captains of vessels intended to convey Asiatic passengers shall adopt and promote the exact observance of the sanitary rules prescribed by these instructions.

2. No Passenger shall be received on board until his quarters have been perfectly washed and are dry, and the interior sides, roof, and cabin of

the ship have been washed two or three times with lime and water, to which is to be added a portion, of glue and a small quantity of chloride of lime. The same operation shall be repeated at the end of each voyage in case the vessel intends to carry new passengers.

3. A place with the best condition of light and ventilation shall be portioned off as a hospital; this shall be completely separate from the quarters of the passengers, and is to have the same advantages stated above. The place for the hospital will vary according to the tonnage or other circumstances of the said vessel.

4. Passengers must be treated with great regularity, both during the voyage and in port, with respect to cleansing, disinfecting, and ventilation of their quarters, likewise with respect to the disinfecting, cleansing, and airing their clothes; each individual is to be carefully advised to scrupulously attend to cleanliness, and to remove all causes of sickliness, even the most insignificant.

5. The quarters shall be swept twice a-day, or oftener if necessary. The daily washing by pouring water shall be prohibited in this part of the vessel on account of the inconvenience such would cause. A general or partial washing of the floor by sponge or swab shall be made when thought necessary, after which the quarters shall be carefully dried.

6. The floor and other wooden portions of the quarters soiled with vomitings or diarrhoeic matter, shall be dried after having been well washed with the following preparation

Chloride of lime	1 part
Common water	32 parts

7. Strict vigilance shall be used to remove from the, passengers' quarters everything which might cause dampness or other exhalations noxious to health, such as wet and foul clothing, the remains of meals, pieces of salt fish, meat, &c.

8. The custom of the passengers smoking in their quarters, by which constantly' number of lights are kept up, is prejudicial to health, as the fumes caused by the burning oil, tobacco, and opium vitiates the atmosphere, and should consequently be prohibited. Smoking tobacco is allowed under the awning. For the smoking of opium, a special place should be appropriated until gradually the practice can be forbidden.

9. The passengers' quarters are to be daily disinfected as follows:- In the first place, passengers are to be ordered to leave their quarters, then all or nearly all the openings by which the air enters are to be closed, specially those to windward. An ordinary earthen vessel is to be placed in the centre of the quarters, or two earthen vessels at fix distances, according to the size of the place. These earthen vessels are to be placed on hot sand or ashes and are to contain the following mixture:-

Chloride of sodium (common salt) in powder.	3 parts
Broxide of manganese	1 part
Common water	2 parts
Sulphuric acid, at 66 deg	2 parts

As sulphuric acid volatilizes the disinfecting vapours of the chloro it shall be mixed afterwards. After one or two hours open and keep open all the hatchways, portholes, and hatches of the passengers' quarters, and use all means to re-establish there a complete ventilation, without which the place is not to be reoccupied by the passengers. As this is a most convenient process, it should be done not only whenever the passengers' quarters can be emptied, but also in ships where there are the facilities of quick ventilation.

10. If circumstances do not allow of all the passengers being under the awning at once, then two-thirds or half of them should go up, and the disinfecting process should be conducted as follows:

Let a person walking through the quarters with a vessel containing the mixture above stated pour in the sulphuric acid from time to time so that the acid vapours will not rise in sufficient quantity to cause coughing or other inconveniences to the passengers. The inconvenience may also be avoided by the use of vapours of nitric acid, in which there are the following substances:-

Sulphuric acid, at 66 deg	2 parts
Common water	1 part
Pure nitre, in powder	2 parts

The vessel containing the above should be placed on hot ashes and the nitre poured in little by little.

11. In case bad weather prevents the passengers quitting the hospital or their quarters, the disinfection is to be caused by placing dishes at fixed distances for a few hours containing the following mixture.

Chloride of lime	1 part
Common water	3 parts

12. The fumes of odoriferous substances, such as incense, essences, gunpowder, &c., are inconvenient as they do not destroy the miasma, but have a contrary effect, and add to the air exhalations that cause a difficulty in breathing. When, by any accident, the disinfectants above indicated are not to be found on board, vinegar poured over hot iron way be substituted.

13. The medicine chests of the vessels, besides the medicines prescribed for the use of the sick, shall be provided with the following articles required for the fumigations above mentioned, namely:-

Chloride of lime, dry.	Broxide of manganese.
Sulphuric acid, 66 deg	Powdered purified nitre.

The quantity of these substances shall be regulated according to the length of the voyage by the medical man who has to visit the vessel.

14. A daily examination shall be made of the passengers for the purpose of moving the sick into the hospital, and this removal shall take place however slight the illness may be.

15. All the refuse and excremental matters shall be at once removed from the hospital and thrown into the sea. The same is to be done with the clothing and bedding of those suffering from graver or infectious complaints, and which cannot be made useful by means of disinfectants and washings.

16. Great care shall be taken that the corpses of the dead be not thrown into the sea in a too hasty manner; at the same time, it should not be

done too slowly, so as not to prolong the painful sight to the other passengers.

17. The hospital shall be washed, dried and whitewashed whenever there is no patient in it, and the atmosphere is to be disinfected by the means laid down in paragraphs 2 and 9.

18. Passengers should pass the greater part of the day under the awning, avoiding as much as possible the checking of perspiration and the chills that atmospheric changes might give rise to.

19. Bed clothes and other bedding shall be shaken, beaten, and exposed to the air and brought back before night at least once a week; at the same time the boxes of the passengers shall be brought on deck in order that their contents may be aired.

20. Personal cleanliness is absolutely necessary, not only for the preservation of the health of the individual, but of that of all who surround him. This should he strictly recommended to the passengers, they should be advised to wash their face, hands, and feet daily, to change their clothing, and wash such as is dirty.

21. All these sanitary arrangements should be the more punctually carded out whenever an epidemic should appear, or any serious or contagious disease manifest itself on board.

TABLE 1-Daily Ration for each Asiatic Passenger.

Rice	1½ lb.
Salt pork meat, or two-thirds pork, one-third fish or one-third pork, one-third beef, one-third fish	½ lb.
Preserved vegetables	½ lb.
Tea	1/3 oz.
Firewood	20 oz.

Water at the rate of 12 gallons a week for each Asiatic passenger.

Appendix III
Departures for Peru

Key: Departure Ports
A: Amoy   HK: Hong Kong   S: Swatow
C: Cumsingmoon   M: Macao   W: Whampoa

	Ship	Tons	Flag	From	Arr	On	Off
1849							
7-Jun	Fredrick Wilhelm	430	Dan	C	49/10/24	75	75
1850							
17-Feb	Lady Montague	763	Brit	C	50/06/26	440	241
13-Jun	Empresa	446	Per	C	50/11/12	300	252
24-Sep	Albert	292	Fren	C		180	
7-Oct	Chile	376	Fren	C		300	
14-Oct	Manuelita / Orixa	150	Fren	C	51/06/17	180	92
1851							
31-Jan	Mariner	685	Brit	M	51/06/01	409	400
21-Feb	Coromandel	663	Brit	M	51/06/28	404	400
5-Dec	Victory	579	Brit	C		350	
1852							
2-Feb	Beatrice	376	Per	C		300	
2-Feb	Susannah	514	Brit	C	52/06/15	325	319
21 Mar	Robert Bowne	504	Amer	A		410	
10-Apr	Miceno	290	Per	W	52/07/29	5	5
7-Jul	Empresa	446	Per	A	52/10/30	420	393
2-Dec	Ohio	373	Amer	C	53/05/25	300	228
1853							
2-Jan	Eliza Morrison	797	Brit	C	53/05/14	420	404
27-Jan	Isabel Quintana	514	Per	C	53/06/05	325	316
11-Feb	Nepaul	1006	Brit	C	53/06/01	500	492
11-Feb	Yaque	237	Mex	M	53/07/05	200	198
8-Mar	Rosa Elias	233	Per	C		200	
19-Mar	Empresa	446	Per	C	53/07/07	425	329
1854							
20-Feb	Amazon	370	Brit	S	54/05/22	250	248
20-Feb	Isabel Quintana	514	Per	C	54/08/29	325	278
25-Apr	Grimaneza	650	Per	S		648	
1-Jun	Topaz	482	Brit	HK		378	
14-Jun	Santiago	300	Per	M	54/09/28	60	60
1855							
6-Apr	Catalina	866	Per	S	55/07/25	500	492
28-Apr	Zetland	1283	Brit	S	55/10/01	400	336
1-May	Francisco	489	Chil	S	55/09/01	350	201
22-May	Delfshaven	643	Dut	W	55/09/01	342	340

	Ship	Tons	Flag	From	Arr	On	Off
14-Jun	Indiaman	1110	Amer	S	55/09/24	565	436
1-Aug	Amalia	415	Per	S	56/01/01	415	285
31-Aug	Dalmatia	560	Amer	A	56/02/01	331	249
6-Sep	Bald Eagle	1704	Amer	S	55/11/28	650	550
28-Sep	Buenaventura	359	Span	S	56/02/01	251	190
12-Oct	Waverly / Louise	749	Amer	A + S	56/04/15	450	110
14-Oct	Cora	1297	Per	M	56/01/31	710	480
27-Oct	Westward Ho	1633	Amer	W	56/02/04	830	728
24-Dec	Winged Racer	1767	Amer	S	56/03/01	900	730
1856							
28-Jan	Maria Natividad	581	Per	W	56/05/27	350	330
1-Feb	Ernani	292	Chil	S	56/05/21	202	155
1-Mar	Catalina	866	Per	S	56/07/01	500	487
29-May	Antonia Terry	690	Per	W	56/11/15	550	486
29-May	Theresa Terry	198	Per	W	56/10/15	184	145
1857							
1-Mar	Carmen	350	Per	S		260	
21-Mar	JCU	730	Per	M	57/07/17	450	278
1858							
23-Jun	Guiseppe Rocca	750	Ital	M	58/12/20	300	260
1859							
12-Jan	Maria Natividad	581	Per	M	59/05/03	321	315
10-Sep	Napoleon	370	Col	S	60/01/10	200	160
24-Dec	Victoria	420	Per	S	60/07/01	426	205
1860							
20-Jan	Florence Nightingale	1188	Amer	M	60/04/14	20	20
13-Feb	Westward Ho	1633	Per	M	60/05/01	522	496
1-Jun	Neptuno	281	Span	A	60/10/31	130	130
5-Jun	Maria Clotilde	517	Span	M	60/10/17	319	241
2-Aug	Encarnacion	567	Span	M		324	
24-Oct	Tarolinta	549	Amer	M	61/02/07	330	221
8-Nov	Westward Ho	1633	Per	M	61/02/26	670	658
1861							
8-Jan	Marion	564	Amer	Kwa	61/04/18	350	
22-Jan	Giovanna	568	Aust	M	61/06/01	308	308
1-Apr	Pamone	830	Fren	W	61/08/01	512	482
14-Apr	Agustina	495	Span	M	61/10/14	247	193
27-Jun	Empresa	446	Per	W	61/11/01	280	273
21-Jul	Petronila	682	Per	M	62/04/18	300	279
22-Sep	Ville d'Agen	715	Fren	Kwa		243	
1862							
26-Jan	Marion	564	Amer	M	62/05/14	225	224
19-Mar	Westward Ho	1633	Per	M	62/06/17	623	457
29-May	Empresa	446	Per	M	62/09/01	299	299
2-Oct	Claire	498	Fren	M	63/02/03	312	297

	Ship	Tons	Flag	From	Arr	On	Off
1863							
2-Jan	Westward Ho	1633	Per	M	63/03/15	665	652
12-Jan	Theresa	240	Chil	M	63/05/23	132	130
23-Jan	Eliza	249	Port	M	63/05/05	130	120
5-Apr	Maria	219	Per	M	63/09/05	132	87
1-Aug	Cesar	499	Per	M	63/11/20	317	317
18-Oct	Westward Ho	1633	Per	M	64/01/17	700	683
30-Nov	Donna Maria Pia	671	Port	M	64/03/01	424	379
7-Dec	Camillo Cavour	1334	Per	M	64/02/25	700	582
21-Dec	Theresa	240	Per	M	64/04/29	140	128
31-Dec	Perseverancia	550	Per	M	64/04/06	400	271
1864							
6-Jan	General Prim	205	Per	M	64/04/16	182	163
17-Jan	Clotilde	357	Per	M	64/05/12	292	275
18-Jan	Sol de Lima	222	Per	M	64/05/30	100	96
30-Jan	Theresa	796	Per	M	64/05/13	500	427
31-Jan	Sao Vicente de Paulo	423	Port	M	64/05/21	262	247
31-Jan	Rosa y Carmen	368	Span	M	64/05/06	228	194
14-Feb	Emma	391	Chil	M	64/06/03	160	160
6-Mar	Gaston	317	Fren	M	64/06/11	200	165
20-Mar	Cesar	499	Per	M	64/06/19	317	268
23-Mar	Onrust	836	Dut	M	64/06/20	510	390
24-Mar	Juliao	834	Per	M	64/07/09	500	448
7-Apr	Lima	328	Per	M	64/09/22	184	152
22-Apr	Vitalia	504	Per	M	64/10/16	260	214
14-May	Mandarina / Argo	258	Per	M	64/10/25	152	146
8-Jun	Bacalan	536	Fren	M	64/10/13	308	208
8-Jun	Napoleon Canevaro	1372	Per	M	64/09/17	300	290
11-Aug	Camillo Cavour	1334	Per	M	64/12/14	603	537
21-Aug	Claire	498	Fren	M	64/11/23	312	299
3-Nov	Donna Maria Pia	671	Port	M	65/01/25	425	400
12-Nov	Aurora	668	Per	M	65/02/24	377	367
24-Dec	Theresa	240	Per	M	65/04/11	143	141
1865							
2-Jan	Providenza	660	Ital	M	65/04/10	395	392
8-Jan	Clothilde	357	Ital	M	65/04/23	220	218
22-Jan	Johanna Roza Alcaras	360	Chil	M	65/05/12	225	205
22-Feb	Juliao	834	Port	M	65/06/27	516	289
4-Mar	Colombo	775	Ital	M	65/06/22	459	391
10-Mar	Napoleon Canevaro	1372	Ital	M	65/06/23	642	602
19-Mar	Lima	328	Ital	M	65/07/22	200	135
14-May	Don José	796	Ital	M	65/10/18	505	281
31-May	Camillo Cavour	1334	Ital	M	65/09/22	630	583

	Ship	Tons	Flag	From	Arr	On	Off
8-Jun	Christina	1206	Per	M	65/09/19	603	555
23-Jun	R Pratolongo	890	Ital	M	65/10/14	503	256
8-Jul	Flore	389	Fren	W	65/10/30	350	261
15-Jul	Cesar	499	Per	M	65/10/13	290	248
20-Jul	Falcon	462	Per	M	65/10/30	249	218
30-Jul	Liguria / Tampico	849	Ital	M	66/02/03	513	126
6-Aug	Aurora	668	Per	M	65/11/29	399	350
16-Aug	Claire	498	Fren	W	65/11/25	270	256
8-Sep	Dea del Mare	894	Ital	M	66/01/21	506	268
30-Oct	Co Maritima 1	1482	Per	M	66/02/03	659	604
14-Dec	Rosina	487	Ital	M	66/04/14	370	268
16-Dec	Eva	224	Per	M	66/03/30	120	119
17-Dec	Providenza	660	Ital	M	66/04/03	413	405
1-Feb	Carl	388	Ger	M	66/04/27	199	197
3-Feb	Co Maritima 2	1078	Per	M	66/04/28	435	425
17-Feb	Catalina	309	Ital	M	66/05/29	193	189
8-Mar	Napoleon Canevaro	1372	Ital	M		662	
22-Mar	Emma	391	Chil	M	66/06/28	125	124
10-Apr	Amalia	449	Ital	M	66/08/26	241	149
10-Apr	Uncowah	988	Ital	M	66/07/29	456	456
20-Apr	Colombo	775	Ital	M	66/09/11	370	364
21-Apr	Juliao	834	Port	M	66/09/20	474	318
6-May	Dolores Ugarte	1283	Port	M	66/09/05	670	500
10-May	Camillo Cavour	1334	Ital	M	66/08/17	634	503
31-May	Lima	328	Ital	M	66/10/22	148	141
2-Jun	Theresa	1094	Ital	M	66/10/02	613	497
9-Jun	Asia	820	Ital	M	66/11/01	500	397
20-Jun	Fray Bentos	561	Ital	M	66/11/09	360	352
21-Jun	R Pratolongo	890	Ital	M	66/10/20	455	448
23-Sep	Amalia	449	Ger	M	67/04/09	252	235
10-Nov	America	1454	Ital	M	67/03/08	622	584
14-Dec	Aurora	668	Ital	M	67/04/08	272	259
1867							
5-May	Marie Laure	393	Fren	M	67/08/28	285	229
23-May	Camillo Cavour	1334	Ital	M	67/09/20	600	586
9-Jun	R Pratolongo	890	Ital	M	67/10/07	403	352
5-Jul	Providenza	660	Ital	M	67/11/06	364	307
21-Jul	Johanna	1326	Aust	M	67/12/02	619	506
23-Jul	Galileo	1076	Ital	M	67/12/13	413	302
25-Jul	Dolores Ugarte	1283	Per	M	67/11/12	499	470
21-Aug	Asia	820	Salv	M		513	
22-Sep	Luisa Canevaro	1206	Ital	M	68/03/03	663	458
22-Oct	Uncowah	988	Ital	M	68/01/29	498	491
16-Nov	Blanche	533	Fren	M	68/03/08	311	284
17-Nov	Pedro 1	1552	Port	M	68/02/02	680	653

	Ship	Tons	Flag	From	Arr	On	Off
1868							
11-Jan	Aurora	668	Salv	M	68/04/14	400	392
3-Mar	Theresa	1094	Ital	M		293	
13-Mar	Fray Bentos	561	Ital	M	68/07/03	322	318
27-May	R Pratolongo	890	Ital	M	68/09/29	464	452
1-Jul	Camillo Cavour	1334	Salv	M	68/10/11	555	543
23-Jul	Providenza	660	Ital	M	68/12/23	382	376
31-Jul	Henri IV	757	Fren	M	68/12/08	458	316
31-Aug	Uncowah	988	Salv	M	69/01/07	499	478
1869							
17-Jun	Camillo Cavour	1334	Salv	M	69/09/19	586	567
19-Jun	Callao	1552	Salv	M	69/11/01	653	628
7-Jul	Fray Bentos	561	Salv	M	69/10/23	352	343
29-Jul	America	1454	Salv	M	69/11/12	669	667
2-Aug	Providencia	660	Salv	M	69/11/25	386	378
2-Oct	Jourdain	440	Fren	M	70/01/15	242	238
3-Oct	Luisa Canevaro	1206	Salv	M	70/01/14	721	694
24-Oct	Ango	627	Fren	M	70/02/18	320	318
6-Dec	Uncowah	988	Salv	M	70/03/01	536	533
23-Dec	Donna Maria Pia	671	Port	M	70/03/27	370	367
1870							
14-Jan	Mahela	444	Fren	M	70/04/23	247	243
15-Jan	Frederic	812	Belg	HK		381	
10-Feb	Camillo Cavour	1334	Salv	M	70/04/25	662	650
28-Feb	Fray Bentos	561	Salv	M	70/06/04	353	323
23-Apr	America	1454	Salv	M	70/08/23	694	630
1-May	Cecilia	533	Port	M	70/08/17	370	320
7-May	Providencia	660	Salv	M	70/08/29	416	410
27-May	Callao	1552	Salv	M	70/09/06	671	649
13-Jun	Dolores Ugarte	1283	Salv	M	70/11/29	609	490
4-Jul	Luisa Canevaro	1206	Salv	M	70/12/10	705	683
10-Jul	Maria Gavina	328	Salv	M	70/11/18	208	199
29-Jul	Clothilde	1311	Col	M	70/11/06	754	710
11-Aug	Macao	1076	Salv	M	71/01/22	436	427
20-Aug	Ephrem	389	Fren	M	70/12/08	285	280
1-Sep	Ferdinand Meric	459	Fren	M	71/01/11	310	296
5-Sep	L Olivier / Bernice	393	Fren	M		233	
16-Sep	Tanjore	479	Fren	M	71/01/16	327	290
24-Sep	Donna Maria Pia	671	Port	M	71/01/22	371	316
1-Oct	Nouvelle Penelope	490	Fren	M		310	
14-Oct	Uncowah / Bernice	988	Salv	M	71/05/28	537	230
20-Oct	Fray Bentos	561	Salv	M	71/01/21	366	364
7-Nov	Camillo Cavour	1334	Per	M	71/01/24	661	651
20-Nov	Couronnement	1284	Fren	M	71/03/08	557	515
28-Nov	Cosmopolite	450	Fren	M	71/03/10	300	297

	Ship	Tons	Flag	From	Arr	On	Off
9-Dec	Vistula	733	Rus	M	71/03/12	430	413
16-Dec	St Iver	640	Fren	M	71/03/14	363	354
20-Dec	Hong Kong	470	Per	M	71/04/10	313	299
26-Dec	Providencia	660	Salv	M	71/04/11	416	406
30-Dec	Nelly	848	Fren	M	71/04/02	444	410
14-Jan	Callao	1552	Salv	M	71/04/07	691	662
20-Jan	Peru	594	Salv	M	71/04/29	380	351
31-Jan	Cecilia	533	Port	M	71/05/30	370	369
14-Feb	Lola	890	Salv	M	71/05/20	479	475
15-Feb	Ville de Grenade	271	Fren	M	71/07/31	198	115
18-Feb	Casti	456	Fren	M	71/06/06	233	231
28-Feb	Neva	1142	Rus	M	71/06/02	762	717
19-Mar	Clothilde	1311	Salv	M	71/06/28	780	700
22-Mar	Joaquin Rigau	364	Salv	M	71/07/13	245	195
25-Mar	Pactole	448	Fren	M	71/07/01	278	233
28-Apr	Fray Bentos	561	Per	M	71/08/16	372	366
4-May	Don Juan	1283	Per	M		655	
19-Jun	Luisa Canevaro	1206	Salv	M	71/11/02	733	725
6-Jul	Rosalia	816	Per	M	71/10/15	461	440
6-Jul	Sara	708	Per	M	71/10/29	344	336
8-Jul	Constancia	191	Per	M	71/11/25	18	18
13-Jul	America	1454	Per	M	71/10/19	641	638
27-Jul	Camillo Cavour	1334	Per	M		632	
7-Aug	Macao	1076	Per	M	71/11/27	436	423
8-Oct	Mille Tonnes	755	Fren	M	72/01/20	432	393
12-Oct	Hong Kong	470	Per	M	72/01/21	314	306
15-Oct	Providencia	660	Per	M	72/01/24	416	411
5-Nov	Peru	594	Per	M	72/02/12	403	393
28-Nov	Callao	1552	Salv	M	72/02/12	629	610
22-Dec	Lola	890	Per	M	72/03/24	592	588
1872							
6-Jan	Fray Bentos	561	Per	M	72/04/12	375	369
16-Jan	Cecilia	533	Port	M	72/04/24	380	372
31-Jan	Clothilde	1311	Per	M	72/04/25	760	751
1-Feb	Johanna en Willem	494	Dut	M	72/05/16	260	247
18-Feb	Luisa Canevaro	1206	Per	M	72/05/17	739	547
26-Feb	Emigrante	962	Port	M	72/06/11	499	392
11-Mar	Rosalia	816	Per	M	72/06/12	457	393
17-Mar	America	1454	Per	M	72/06/13	690	585
21-Mar	Antares	401	Fren	M	72/06/30	263	181
5-May	Sara	708	Per	M	72/09/10	346	323
8-May	Onrust	836	Dut	M	72/09/28	455	410
15-May	Camillo Cavour	1334	Per	M	72/08/31	650	593
15-May	Macao	1076	Per	M	72/10/01	436	397
17-May	Peru	594	Per	M	72/09/27	408	374
20-May	Joaquin Rigau	364	Per	M	72/09/19	193	186

	Ship	Tons	Flag	From	Arr	On	Off
22-May	Hong Kong	470	Per	M	72/09/12	314	277
26-May	Canadienne	853	Fren	M	72/09/16	507	488
28-May	Maria Luz	408	Per	M		225	
12-Jun	Providencia	660	Per	M	72/09/22	422	412
19-Jun	Callao	1552	Salv	M	72/09/22	695	685
20-Jun	Emile	455	Fren	M	72/10/18	250	232
21-Jun	Radama	550	Fren	M	72/09/29	305	301
29-Jun	Nederland en Oranje	755	Dut	M	72/10/27	396	352
5-Jul	Manco Capac	1018	Per	M	72/11/01	577	560
15-Jul	Lola	890	Per	M	72/11/04	595	575
22-Jul	Bengale	677	Fren	M	72/12/17	375	333
7-Aug	Fray Bentos	561	Per	M	72/12/16	366	345
11-Sep	Colombia	979	Aust	M	73/03/26	500	439
19-Oct	Oracle	1231	Per	M	73/01/01	669	623
25-Nov	Blanche Marie	462	Fren	M	73/04/01	315	275
14-Dec	Cecilia	533	Port	M	73/03/26	378	373
1873							
9-Jan	Isabel	1311	Per	M	73/04/13	785	758
26-Jan	Agustina	947	Per	M	73/04/15	511	459
28-Feb	Peru	594	Per	M	73/06/01	406	307
20-Mar	Hong Kong	470	Per	M	73/08/01	316	295
26-Mar	Callao	1552	Salv	M	73/08/01	698	582
5-May	Providencia	660	Per	M	73/09/04	422	391
16-May	San Juan	1450	Per	M	73/09/10	816	607
28-May	Emigrante	962	Per	M	73/10/26	502	427
2-Jul	Rosalia	816	Per	M	73/09/01	463	371
28-Jul	Guillermo	328	Per	M	74/01/10	207	175
6-Aug	Camillo Cavour	1334	Per	M	73/11/07	683	669
19-Nov	America	1454	Per	M	74/03/02	776	737
13-Dec	Manco Capac	1018	Per	M	74/03/10	585	574
1874							
11-Jan	Luisa Canevaro	1206	Per	M	74/04/05	759	756
31-Jan	Nueva Providencia	947	Per	M	74/05/01	524	512
8-Mar	Isabel	1311	Per	M	74/07/01	713	702
27-Mar	Lola	890	Per	M	74/07/02	375	369

Appendix IV
Departures for Cuba

Key: Departure Ports

A: Amoy   M: Macao   W: Whampoa

HK: Hong Kong   S: Swatow

	Ship	Tons	Flag	From	Arr	On	Off
1847							
23-Jan	Oquendo	350	Span	A	47/06/03	212	206
6-Mar	Duke of Argyll	629	Brit	A	47/07/12	430	388
1852							
18-Aug	British Sovereign	450	Brit	A		321	
26-Sep	Panama	522	Brit	A	53/02/07	351	261
12-Oct	Gertrude	605	Brit	A	53/03/14	299	198
23-Oct	Blenheim	808	Brit	A	53/02/08	453	412
29-Nov	Lady Amherst	440	Brit	A	53/04/18	275	225
30-Nov	Inchinnan	565	Brit	S	53/03/24	355	335
23-Dec	Sir Thomas Gresham	594	Brit	S	53/05/11	347	320
31-Dec	Sophia	240	Port	M	53/04/17	250	233
1853							
3-Jan	Columbus	468	Brit	A	53/05/22	302	266
3-Jan	Julian de Unzueta	544	Span	M	53/05/15	351	348
14-Jan	Viajante	376	Port	M	53/05/02	300	249
20-Jan	Bella Gallega	499	Span	A	53/06/27	403	386
4-Feb	San Andres	573	Span	M	53/06/30	383	358
1-Mar	Medina	829	Brit	S	53/09/01	450	380
8-Mar	Victoria	894	Span	M	53/07/12	393	340
31-Mar	Sappho	446	Brit	A	53/08/30	250	194
24-Oct	Adamastor	400	Port	M		300	
4-Dec	Encarnacion	567	Span	M	54/04/13	400	392
26-Dec	Menzies	448	Brit	S	54/05/17	310	299
1854							
26-Jan	Emigrante	753	Port	S	54/05/23	550	539
1-Mar	Commercie Co	737	Dut	S	54/07/04	500	481
19-Dec	Bella Gallega	499	Span	S	55/04/08	403	396
1855							
15-Jan	Roxburgh Castle	1121	Brit	S	55/04/23	600	573
7-Mar	Sky Lark	1210	Amer	A	55/07/24	593	532
10-Mar	Martin Luther	1241	Brit	S	55/06/30	600	575
27-Mar	Carpentaria	1460	Brit	S	55/05/30	738	704
4-Apr	Hound	713	Amer	M	55/07/22	230	228

Ship		Tons	Flag	From	Arr	On	Off
30-Oct	Australia	1170	Brit	S	56/02/23	450	364
24-Nov	Samuel Enderby	395	Brit	M	56/03/04	200	196
10-Dec	Paquita	348	Span	M	56/03/02	250	246
24-Dec	Sea Witch	1600	Amer	A	56/06/09	581	485
27-Dec	Swordfish	1036	Amer	HK	56/03/22	375	375
1856							
22-Jan	Golden Eagle	1121	Amer	S	56/05/06	550	484
6-Feb	Teresita	459	Span	S	56/06/05	390	327
19-Feb	Resolucao	492	Port	M		450	
8-Mar	John Calvin	510	Brit	HK	56/09/02	301	175
14-Mar	Hope	819	Brit	S	56/06/14	504	452
28-Mar	War Hawk	1067	Amer	S	56/07/13	564	534
2-Apr	Duke of Portland	523	Brit	HK	56/08/30	334	198
15-Apr	Emigrante	753	Span	M	56/12/02	504	316
10-May	Bellona	885	Dut	A	56/12/22	500	319
11-May	Ellen Oliver	683	Brit	S	56/11/25	336	261
12-Jul	Banca	680	Dut	M		350	
19-Jul	Henry Miller	433	Brit	S	56/11/28	191	185
13-Sep	Dina	683	Dut	M	57/02/26	319	309
20-Oct	Cora	1297	Per	A	57/02/14	600	315
1-Nov	Johanna Maria	481	Dut	M	57/02/26	300	288
19-Nov	Vriendschap	707	Dut	S	57/04/07	399	352
28-Nov	Doggersbank	687	Dut	M	57/03/31	380	373
3-Dec	Vrouw Johanna	583	Dut	M	57/03/30	305	280
5-Dec	Catherine Glen	1327	Brit	S	57/04/08	597	437
10-Dec	Florida	688	Amer	S	57/04/03	365	343
1857							
9-Jan	Joseph Shepherd	630	Brit	S	57/04/29	300	299
11-Jan	Port de Bordeaux	675	Fren	M		450	
21-Jan	Succes	590	Fren	M	57/05/29	370	345
29-Jan	Anais	632	Fren	S		420	
2-Feb	Waverly	749	Amer	S	57/05/18	372	364
9-Feb	Henrietta Maria	636	Dut	M		350	
9-Feb	Maria Nativida	581	Per	M	57/06/14	350	342
2-Mar	Felix	560	Ger	S	57/06/14	260	236
9-Mar	Architect	520	Per	S	57/06/01	258	245
11-Mar	Gulnare	1002	Brit	S	57/08/19	432	268
12-Mar	Christina	342	Dut	M	57/06/20	200	192
14-Mar	Coldstream	756	Brit	S	57/07/17	220	202
19-Mar	Ville de Dieppe	1016	Fren	M	57/07/15	630	549
24-Mar	Tuskina	342	Amer	HK	57/10/04	227	172
1-Apr	Alianza	279	Chil	S	57/10/26	256	155
1-Apr	Robert Small	655	Brit	S	57/08/12	240	226
4-Apr	Fernandez	600	Fren	M	57/09/13	350	330
12-Apr	Admiraal Zoutman	669	Dut	S	57/09/19	402	349
16-Apr	Africaine	405	Fren	M	57/09/15	250	238
20-Apr	Maria	476	Nor	S	57/10/11	222	179

	Ship	Tons	Flag	From	Arr	On	Off
6-May	Tinita Torices	657	Per	M	57/11/07	370	167
8-May	Giscours	538	Fren	A	57/10/16	334	171
4-Aug	Francois 1	1583	Fren	M	57/11/25	900	842
15-Oct	Kate Hooper	1489	Amer	M	58/02/12	652	612
17-Oct	Charles Martell	1584	Fren	M	58/03/09	830	676
18-Oct	Challenge	2006	Amer	S	58/02/10	915	620
27-Oct	Admiral	783	Brit	A	58/03/20	376	283
9-Nov	Edwin Fox	892	Brit	S	58/03/19	310	269
14-Nov	Dream	1106	Brit	M	58/02/24	503	438
28-Nov	Kitty Simpson	698	Amer	S	58/03/19	430	337
3-Dec	Ticonderoga	1679	Amer	M	58/03/18	850	818
4-Dec	Earl of Eglinton	1278	Brit	S	58/04/03	488	357
23-Dec	Julian de Unzueta	554	Span	S	58/04/22	350	260
30-Dec	St Jean	576	Fren	M	58/05/06	350	339
1858							
20-Jan	Tasmania	1190	Brit	A	58/04/22	367	260
22-Jan	Don Julian	533	Per	M	58/05/12	326	326
22-Jan	Soolo	633	Dut	M	58/05/12	400	398
1-Feb	Flora Temple	1915	Amer	M	58/05/12	900	852
2-Feb	Mary Whitridge	978	Amer	S	58/05/15	500	415
5-Feb	Wandering Jew	1650	Amer	S	58/05/15	350	259
19-Feb	Kepler	567	Ger	M	58/07/15	364	292
20-Feb	Freya	1007	Dan	S	58/06/14	470	302
28-Feb	Travancore	584	Brit	A	58/06/26	266	235
28-Feb	Diana	168	Chil	S	58/07/12	113	74
15-Mar	Swallow	1432	Amer	M	58/07/01	650	644
17-Mar	Westward Ho	1633	Per	M	58/07/10	700	611
17-Mar	Eva Johanna	1015	Dut	M	58/07/26	604	495
19-Mar	Bella Vascondaga	575	Span	M	58/06/30	385	349
29-Mar	Competitor	871	Amer	S	58/07/05	382	225
30-Mar	Norma	440	Nor	S	58/08/23	276	139
31-Mar	Pieter Corneli zn Hooft	997	Dut	M	58/08/31	570	368
31-Mar	Admiraal Van Heemskerk	1145	Dut	M	58/08/29	610	482
1-Apr	Alavesa	502	Span	S	58/07/21	360	218
18-May	Mauritius	2134	Brit	M	58/09/15	741	659
31-May	Cleopatra	1089	Brit	A	58/10/22	464	374
24-Jun	Scotia	1195	Brit	M	58/10/24	570	431
20-Oct	Maria Elizabeth	825	Dut	M	59/02/08	510	483
6-Nov	Francois 1	1583	Fren	M	59/02/01	1000	835
15-Dec	Malabar	815	Fren	M	59/04/14	570	440
1859							
7-Jan	Succes	590	Fren	M	59/05/11	373	284
16-Jan	Alexandre Ralli	678	Fren	M	59/05/27	424	398
22-Feb	Emigrante	753	Span	M	59/06/20	400	378
4-Mar	Live Yankee	1637	Amer	M	59/06/02	800	778

Ship		Tons	Flag	From	Arr	On	Off
5-Mar	Ville de Dieppe	1016	Fren	W	59/06/26	530	521
15-Mar	Ceder	599	Ger	M	59/07/03	360	326
18-Mar	Bellona	885	Dut	M	59/06/27	500	427
2-Apr	Daguerre	566	Fren	M	59/08/08	356	325
2-Apr	Formose	780	Fren	M	59/08/18	465	400
13-Apr	Primera de Espana	1319	Span	M	59/09/16	749	543
17-Apr	Concepcion	1228	Span	M	59/08/10	480	423
3-Jul	Swallow	1432	Amer	W	59/11/09	650	552
26-Jul	Gravina	246	Span	A	59/12/18	120	82
11-Sep	Charles Martell	1584	Fren	M	60/02/06	900	340
8-Oct	Flora Temple	1915	Amer	M		850	
26-Nov	Norway	2078	Amer	M	60/03/10	1038	904
1860							
14-Jan	Ville de Lima	935	Fren	M	60/05/03	500	476
23-Jan	Emile Pereire	849	Fren	M	60/05/10	460	457
31-Jan	Serafina	491	Span	A	60/05/27	430	400
16-Feb	Solide	299	Fren	M	60/06/26	184	184
20-Feb	Kitty Simpson	698	Amer	M	60/06/13	350	313
22-Feb	Messenger	1350	Amer	M	60/06/08	380	359
10-Mar	Staghound	1534	Amer	S	60/08/10	612	343
19-Mar	Carmencita	236	Span	Manila	60/07/29		126
1-Apr	Guadalupe	913	Span	M	60/08/12	400	360
3-Apr	Maria Elizabeth	825	Dut	M	60/08/04	329	306
4-Apr	Brave Lourmel	534	Fren	M	60/08/02	302	300
4-Apr	Sigisbert Cezard	1015	Fren	M	60/08/12	410	399
4-Apr	Alexandre Delphine	456	Fren	M	60/09/03	201	196
5-May	Governor Morton	1429	Amer	W	60/09/14	557	552
20-May	Emigrante	753	Span	Manila	60/09/26		178
19-Oct	J Wakefield	1225	Amer	M	61/02/09	612	593
3-Nov	Live Yankee	1637	Amer	M	61/01/31	752	728
20-Nov	Greyhound	560	Chil	W	61/03/13	230	200
26-Dec	Francois 1	1583	Fren	M	61/03/31	790	773
26-Dec	May Queen	619	Amer	M	61/04/14	310	306
31-Dec	Reina del Oceano	1011	Span	M	61/04/01	529	497
1861							
14-Jan	Encarnacion	567	Span	M	61/05/16	308	290
15-Jan	Alice Thorndike	847	Amer	W	61/05/05	360	358
17-Jan	*Francis* P Sage	1146	Amer	W	61/04/30	550	520
7-Feb	Maria Clotilde	517	Span	M	61/05/24	258	256
9-Feb	Forest Eagle	1151	Amer	M	61/05/20	500	458
12-Feb	Kate Hooper	1489	Amer	M	61/05/13	589	556
7-Mar	Independence	733	Amer	W	61/06/20	342	337
12-Mar	Fides	685	Ger	M	61/07/20	338	282
18-Mar	Leonidas	690	Amer	W	61/07/09	290	275
20-Mar	Messenger	1350	Amer	M	61/07/02	555	544
1862							
3-Mar	Guadalupe	913	Span	M	62/07/16	336	314

Date	Ship	Tons	Flag	From	Arr	On	Off
5-Nov	Leopold Cateaux	832	Belg	M	63/03/03	416	416
1863							
24-Jan	Malabar	815	Fren	M	63/05/25	256	221
4-Feb	Perseverant	242	Fren	M		121	
17-Mar	Mercedes	746	Chil	M	63/07/12	373	315
30-Oct	Luisita	685	Port	M	64/02/21	343	283
30-Oct	Donna Maria de Gloria	592	Port	M	64/04/06	296	153
2-Nov	Camoes	848	Port	M	64/03/06	418	390
15-Nov	Vasco de Gama	1016	Port	M	64/03/03	508	305
11-Dec	Alfonso d'Albuquerque	621	Port	M	64/03/22	310	267
20-Dec	Arizona	597	Span	M	64/04/24	298	280
1864							
3-Jan	Don Fernando	827	Port	M	64/04/10	492	475
1-Oct	Medoc	697	Fren	M	65/02/04	324	315
29-Oct	Leopold Cateaux	832	Belg	M	65/02/24	416	411
31-Oct	Emigrante	753	Span	M	65/03/04	360	317
2-Nov	St Joseph	647	Fren	M	65/02/22	366	363
23-Nov	Encarnacion	567	Span	M	65/03/16	283	274
29-Nov	Josefita y Almira	1142	Port	M	65/03/09	571	566
8-Dec	Charlotte	485	Fren	M	65/03/28	270	264
8-Dec	Isabel	445	Fren	M	65/03/12	271	268
19-Dec	Guadalupe	913	Span	M	65/04/05	456	431
19-Dec	David	842	Fren	M	65/04/05	421	413
20-Dec	Emma	483	Port	M	65/05/05	239	231
1865							
3-Jan	Port Durand	357	Fren	M	65/05/18	178	177
14-Jan	Auguste et Gustave	477	Fren	M	65/04/23	238	234
17-Jan	Lombard	453	Fren	M	65/05/06	243	240
24-Jan	Avon	1086	Ital	M	65/06/20	543	539
12-Feb	Queen of England	1169	Ital	M	65/06/23	584	546
16-Feb	Nouvelle Pallas	385	Fren	M	65/06/17	192	192
4-Mar	Emmanuel	357	Fren	M	65/07/12	160	144
23-Mar	Camoes	848	Port	M	65/07/18	418	309
6-Jun	Louis	535	Fren	W	65/11/10	267	186
2-Oct	Tamatave	509	Fren	M	66/02/03	298	289
12-Oct	Caroline	666	Fren	W	66/04/16	360	352
14-Oct	Alphonse N Cezard	459	Fren	M	66/02/25	315	303
28-Oct	Mayotte & Nosse Be	291	Fren	M	66/02/26	210	193
5-Nov	Arizona	597	Span	M	66/02/23	280	243
10-Nov	Cote d'Or	416	Fren	W	66/03/03	245	243
25-Nov	Ange Gardien	486	Fren	M	66/03/20	290	277
29-Nov	Amiral Trehouart	493	Fren	M	66/03/15	313	280
1-Dec	Otilia	390	Nor	M	66/03/22	236	216
3-Dec	Verena Callet	336	Fren	M	66/03/11	231	225
17-Dec	St Julien	346	Fren	M	66/04/07	259	250

420

	Ship	Tons	Flag	From	Arr	On	Off
24-Dec	Emma und Mathilde	385	Ger	M	66/04/07	219	217
1866							
4-Jan	Mina	507	Swed	M	66/05/11	341	297
4-Jan	Sovinto	571	Rus	M	66/05/24	317	300
5-Jan	Ammerland	360	Ger	M	66/05/17	225	201
8-Jan	Italia	1086	Ital	M	66/04/23	486	479
12-Jan	Lombard	453	Fren	M	66/04/30	266	251
17-Jan	Emigrante	753	Span	M	66/05/21	359	319
22-Jan	Carmeline	1345	Fren	W	66/08/17	601	539
22-Jan	Ville de St Lo	374	Fren	W	66/05/23	260	233
22-Jan	Lieut Bellot	235	Fren	W	66/06/08	150	149
23-Jan	Hong Kong	470	Fren	W		260	
24-Jan	Josefita y Almira	1142	Port	M	66/05/20	537	523
1-Feb	Baron Kellner	381	Aust	M	66/05/28	268	177
7-Feb	Antoinette	378	Fren	M	66/06/11	240	208
7-Feb	Mousse de Nantes	365	Fren	M	66/05/29	210	206
10-Feb	Flore	389	Fren	W	66/08/11	310	309
11-Feb	Constantine	517	Nor	M	66/05/28	291	275
14-Feb	Guadalupe	913	Span	M	66/06/09	454	438
2-Mar	Bengali	432	Fren	M	66/07/01	290	283
2-Mar	Independant	569	Fren	M	66/07/06	331	313
9-Mar	Encarnacion	567	Span	M	66/07/07	263	248
15-Mar	Burdeos y Habana 1	446	Span	M	66/07/20	231	204
15-Mar	Altagracia	618	Span	M	66/07/08	361	350
24-Mar	Donna Maria Pia	671	Port	M	66/08/15	351	291
24-Mar	JAU	525	Span	M	66/08/09	323	248
24-Mar	Burdeos y Habana 2	440	Span	M	66/08/27	242	224
31-Mar	David	842	Fren	M	66/08/02	427	407
3-Apr	Gaulois	479	Fren	W	66/09/21	300	290
3-Apr	Granville	406	Fren	W	66/09/05	230	225
8-Apr	Denis	589	Fren	M	66/08/18	333	287
10-Apr	Luisa Canevaro	1206	Ital	M	66/08/17	698	620
12-May	Cataluna	1300	Span	M	66/09/07	473	409
18-Jun	Ste Croix	754	Fren	S	66/10/26	444	432
4-Oct	Suomi	942	Rus	M	67/02/14	526	508
4-Oct	Medoc	697	Fren	M	67/02/02	357	323
4-Oct	Loyola	567	Span	M	67/03/10	372	311
7-Oct	Eugene et Adele	858	Fren	M	67/03/26	466	374
15-Oct	Joven Tomaz	700	Port	M	67/03/13	400	356
18-Oct	Falcon	462	Rus	M	67/02/10	259	250
18-Oct	Bilbaina	673	Span	M	67/04/19	492	367
25-Oct	Luisita	1049	Span	M	67/04/14	558	516
2-Nov	Nina	1099	Port	M	67/03/10	549	510
11-Nov	Aureliana	483	Span	M	67/03/14	313	296
15-Nov	Sagittaire	329	Fren	M	67/04/19	165	123
15-Nov	Gica	499	Port	M	67/03/08	290	281
22-Nov	Dos Hermanos	305	Span	M	67/04/19	251	223

	Ship	Tons	Flag	From	Arr	On	Off
1-Dec	Manila y Bilboa	485	Span	M	67/04/14	251	236
4-Dec	Glenlee	635	Rus	M	67/03/20	433	393
5-Dec	Avon	1086	Rus	M	67/04/14	502	473
11-Dec	Nizam	460	Fren	M	67/04/21	262	254
20-Dec	Sao Vicente de Paulo	423	Port	M	67/04/21	296	287
22-Dec	Henri IV	757	Fren	M	67/04/21	456	447
30-Dec	Egmont et Hoorn	768	Belg	M	67/04/19	367	361
1867							
4-Jan	Delangle	411	Fren	M	67/05/03	275	270
4-Jan	Hong Kong	470	Span	M	67/04/21	314	313
8-Jan	Confucius	362	Ger	M	67/05/12	218	213
30-Jan	Mina	506	Span	M	67/06/12	284	282
30-Jan	Reina des los Angelos	504	Span	M	67/06/03	384	343
1-Feb	Esperanza	1067	Span	M	67/06/03	518	474
1-Feb	Bangkok	399	Fren	M	67/05/25	233	218
8-Feb	Niemen	624	Aust	M	67/08/11	410	396
10-Feb	Victoria	352	Aust	M	67/06/13	295	274
17-Feb	Josefita y Almira	1142	Port	M	67/06/08	535	511
4-Mar	Krimpen aan de Lek	703	Dut	M	67/06/27	368	363
10-Mar	Ephrem	389	Fren	M	67/08/02	285	278
15-Mar	Onrust	836	Dut	M	67/08/27	447	436
16-Mar	Altagracia	618	Span	M	67/07/13	360	303
20-Mar	Justa	429	Span	M	67/07/18	290	273
21-Mar	Alavesa	689	Span	M	67/07/22	418	415
3-Apr	JAU	525	Span	M	67/07/19	319	312
5-Apr	Bella Gallega / Nouvelle Penelope	499	Span	M	67/10/06	373	318
5-Apr	Encarnacion	467	Span	M	67/07/19	340	298
6-Apr	Ariosto	837	Fren	M	67/08/19	409	409
7-Apr	Cervantes	1025	Span	M	67/08/27	541	372
5-Jul	Cataluna	1300	Span	M	67/10/04	487	430
3-Oct	Tamatave	509	Fren	M	68/02/10	317	255
3-Oct	Claire	498	Fren	M	68/01/26	257	244
23-Oct	Antifer	549	Fren	M	68/02/20	271	245
6-Nov	Donna Maria Pia	671	Port	M	68/03/25	248	226
7-Nov	Carmeline	1345	Fren	M	68/09/16	653	344
29-Nov	Nelly	848	Fren	M	68/03/17	444	429
17-Dec	Orixa	937	Fren	M	68/04/03	556	540
1868							
2-Jan	Malabar	815	Fren	M	68/04/25	500	493
5-Jan	Esperance	397	Fren	M	68/05/31	300	279
9-Jan	Hong Kong	470	Span	M	68/04/25	316	316
25-Jan	America	1454	Salv	M	68/05/20	610	607
14-Feb	Avon	1086	Rus	M	68/06/09	551	536
20-Feb	Ville de St Lo	374	Fren	M	68/06/26	281	274

Ship		Tons	Flag	From	Arr	On	Off
20-Feb	Mysore	495	Fren	M	68/07/02	294	279
23-Feb	Altagracia	618	Span	M	68/06/23	361	326
8-Mar	Guantanamo	348	Fren	M	68/08/03	213	205
18-Mar	Eugene et Adele	858	Fren	M	68/07/11	466	455
25-Mar	Encarnacion	567	Span	M	68/07/05	302	286
31-Mar	Alavesa	689	Span	M	68/08/01	418	406
8-Apr	Suomi	942	Rus	M	68/08/03	525	508
23-May	Cataluna	1300	Span	M	68/09/19	517	503
3-Oct	Niagara	726	Fren	M	69/02/15	406	385
18-Oct	Confucius	362	Ger	M	69/03/03	218	196
28-Oct	Dolores Ugarte	1283	Salv	M	69/02/21	602	361
3-Nov	Antares	401	Fren	M	69/03/17	263	195
8-Nov	Pactole	448	Fren	M	69/04/10	245	220
17-Nov	Maria Morton	401	Fren	M	69/04/28	215	158
24-Nov	Aurora	668	Salv	M	69/03/26	419	384
8-Dec	Lucie	615	Fren	M	69/04/10	360	327
25-Dec	Onrust	836	Dut	M	69/04/21	453	385
1869							
5-Jan	Vistula	733	Rus	M	69/04/17	430	364
15-Jan	Nadesda	487	Rus	M	69/05/20	353	307
27-Jan	Neva	1142	Rus	M	69/04/30	537	485
7-Feb	Tamaris	545	Fren	M	69/11/06	300	68
27-Feb	Chine et Havane	936	Fren	M	69/06/21	446	397
26-Mar	Italia	1086	Ital	M	69/08/02	520	360
13-Apr	Nelly	848	Fren	M	69/10/22	444	171
30-Apr	Macao	1076	Salv	A	69/11/04	436	400
2-May	Mongol	1006	Fren	M	69/10/09	496	339
24-Jun	Villa de Comillas	542	Span	A	69/11/17	290	267
14-Oct	Dos Hermanos	305	Span	M	70/03/03	251	245
10-Nov	Cataluna	1300	Span	M	70/03/15	524	449
1870							
6-Jan	Neva	1142	Rus	M	70/05/07	537	534
19-Mar	Italia / Esperance	1086	Ital	M	71/02/20	527	159
1871							
16-Jan	Altagracia	618	Span	M	71/05/26	361	343
25-Jan	Lucie	615	Fren	M	71/05/17	360	332
3-Feb	Cataluna	1300	Span	M	71/05/13	531	505
9-Mar	Encarnacion	567	Span	M	71/07/12	327	310
6-Oct	Blanche	533	Fren	M	72/02/16	332	321
11-Oct	Naples	927	Rus	M	72/02/11	511	427
11-Oct	Rene	393	Fren	M	72/02/11	274	270
27-Oct	Concepcion	1228	Span	M	72/03/08	495	481
28-Oct	Univers	387	Fren	M	72/02/29	291	266
31-Oct	Silence	419	Fren	M	72/03/15	217	197
9-Nov	Donna Maria Pia	671	Port	M	72/03/07	329	304
24-Nov	Jules Dufaure	483	Fren	M	72/03/15	311	306
5-Dec	Papillon	496	Fren	M	72/03/22	345	342

	Ship	Tons	Flag	From	Arr	On	Off
17-Dec	Linga	444	Fren	M	72/04/25	260	246
31-Dec	China	1652	Span	M	72/05/07	762	748
1872							
20-Jan	Alexandre Lavalley	1517	Fren	M	72/04/06	621	603
27-Jan	Salvadora	1880	Span	W	72/05/13	510	499
12-Mar	Bengali	432	Fren	M	72/07/18	287	214
15-Mar	Altagracia	618	Span	M	72/07/18	361	258
27-Mar	Rosa del Turia	654	Span	M	72/08/10	387	277
28-Mar	Maria	725	Span	M	72/08/07	413	342
7-Apr	Jacques Sevrin	496	Fren	M	72/09/03	300	235
26-Aug	Fatchoy	1081	Span	M	72/12/12	1005	931
14-Sep	Yrurac Bat	1494	Span	M	72/12/27	906	879
17-Oct	Amboto	1168	Span	M	73/01/10	786	780
30-Oct	Buenaventura	1479	Span	M	73/01/17	864	843
6-Dec	Alavesa	689	Span	M	73/03/21	418	414
21-Dec	Veloce	425	Fren	M	73/05/05	265	243
1873							
14-Jan	Anduizas	636	Span	M	73/05/06	367	350
16-Feb	Alexandre Lavalley	1517	Fren	M	73/06/14	630	474
18-Apr	Rosita y Nene	1268	Span	M	74/03/04	851	725
4-Jun	Charles Albert	1206	Fren	M	73/10/22	602	545
20-Jul	Juan	1228	Span	M	73/11/18	663	602
19-Aug	Amboto	1168	Span	M	73/11/19	905	843
24-Sep	Glensannox	1251	Ital	M	74/01/06	730	712
21-Oct	Nelusko	1776	Belg	M	74/01/17	1099	1055

	Ship	Tons	Flag	From	To	Arrive	On	Off
1868								
30-Apr	Marie Therese	502	Fren	HK	Suri	68/08/20	252	246?
1869								
6-Feb	Veritas	632	Brit	HK	Suri	69/05/29	202	180?
28-Apr	Ferdinand Brumm	830	Rus	HK	Suri	69/08/18	298	225?
1873								
23-Dec	Corona	1199	Brit	W	BG	74/02/23	388	388
1878								
24-Dec	Dartmouth	915	Brit	HK	BG	79/03/17	516	515
1881								
3-Nov	Clara	939	Brit	HK	Ant	82/02/01	322	
1884								
7-May	Prinz Alexander	1911	Ger	HK	Jam	84/07/12	694	680

Appendix VI
Departures for Australia

Key: Departure Ports
A: Amoy   HK: Hong Kong   S: Swatow

Table A6.1 Departures for Australia

	Ship	Tons	Flag	From	Arr	On	Off
1848							
5-Jul	Nimrod	234	Brit	A	48/10/02	120	120
25-Nov	London	388	Brit	HK	49/02/22	149	149
1849							
4-Nov	Cadet	465	Brit	A	50/04/23	150	138
1850							
22-Feb	Gazelle	241	Brit	A	50/05/14	134	131
8-Nov	Duke of Roxburgh	498	Brit	A	51/02/06	258	242
1851							
16-Aug	Duke of Roxburgh	498	Brit	A	51/11/09	240	227
14-Sep	Ganges	430	Brit	A	52/01/26	224	213
1-Oct	Arabia	387	Brit	A	51/12/21	196	179
15-Oct	General Palmer	571	Brit	A	52/02/16	335	264
22-Nov	Statesman	345	Brit	A	52/02/20	180	180
12-Dec	Amazon	370	Brit	A	52/03/17	303	290
1852							
1-Jan	Eleanor Lancaster	480	Brit	A	52/03/10	240	240
21-Jan	Spartan	364	Brit	A	52/04/29	250	210
11-Nov	Eleanor Lancaster	480	Brit	S	53/02/08	255	255
25-Nov	Royal Saxon	518	Brit	A	53/02/05	327	304
1853							
8-Jan	Spartan	364	Brit	A	53/04/07	254	180

Appendix VII
Departures for other Destinations

Key: Departure Ports
A: Amoy M: Macao W: Whampoa
HK: Hong Kong S: Swatow

Table A7.1 Departures for other destinations

	Ship	Tons	Flag	From	To	On
1846						
6-Jul	Joseph et Claire	304	Fren	A	Bourbon	90
1-Dec	l'Avenir	290	Fren	A	Bourbon	200
1851						
13-Nov	Thetis	460	Brit	A	Honolulu	200
1852						
5-Jun	Thetis	460	Brit	A	Honolulu	101
1853						
27-Jan	Sea Witch	1600	Amer	S	Panama	719
10-Feb	Bella Vascongada	480	Span	S	Panama	325
16-Sep	What Cheer	334	Amer	S	Honolulu	190
1855						
27-Dec	Sarah	455	Amer	W	Rio de Janeiro	
1864						
7-Dec	Ferdinand Brumm	830	Rus	HK	Tahiti	337
1865						
22-Jul	Alberto	653	Chil	HK	Honolulu	250
14-Aug	Roscoe	586	Brit	HK	Honolulu	276
20-Sep	Spray of the Ocean	845	Brit	HK	Tahiti	351
20-Oct	Albertine	1209	Ger	HK	Tahiti	347
1866						
11-Jul	Mary Frances	769	Brit	HK	Honolulu	62
3-Oct	Antonia Petronella / Eastfield	670	Dut	HK	Honolulu	200
1870						
9-Feb	Ville de St Lo	374	Fren	HK	New Orleans	195
2-Apr	Charles Auguste	740	Fren	HK	New Orleans	213
16-Jun	R W Wood	377	Haw	HK	Honolulu	61
18-Jun	Solo	1021	Haw	HK	Honolulu	188
21-Dec	Violette	381	Brit	HK	Honolulu	112
1872						
17-Nov	Glensannox	1251	Ital	M	Costa Rica	685

Glossary

Barracoon	Originally a sparse building or enclosure for the temporary confinement of slaves. A securely guarded shed was initially used in the context of the coolie trade. In latter years permanent premises were still called barracoons.
Bill of lading	A legal document of two or more copies used in the transportation of goods describing what is being shipped and where to.
Blackbirding	The practice of deceiving and kidnapping of South Sea Islanders to work in countries bordering the South Pacific.
Bumboat	A small boat used to take goods and passengers to ships at anchor in a harbour.
Caput	head (person).
Carlines	Pieces of timber, about five inches square, placed between beams upon which deck planking can be nailed.
Charter party	A shipping contract between a shipowner or his representative and a charterer for the use of the ship.
Charterer	A person or company who enters into an agreement with a shipowner.
Coamings	A raised frame around an opening in the deck to keep water out.
Crimp	Agent whose business it is to entrap
Death recorded	Term used by judges to record a death sentence as legally required, but considered to be successfully appealed, and therefore not carried out.
Debility	An enfeebled physical state
Donkey-boiler	An auxiliary boiler.
Dropsy	An old medical term for the abnormal swelling of tissues from a buildup of fluid.
Flush-decked	With a continuous main deck from stern to stern with no structures on it.
Hatch	An opening in the deck of a ship.

Jury rudder	A hastily made device to replace, temporarily, a damaged or lost rudder.
Kanakas	A Pacific islander worker.
Lascars	A sailor from the Indian sub continent.
Lay-days	The days specified in a charter party during which the vessel is to be available for the working of cargo.
Manilaman	A sailor from the Philippines.
Mizzen sail	A sail on the mizzen (aftermost) mast.
Nanyang	Term meaning "southern ocean" commonly referring to the littoral states of the South China Sea—particularly the Straits Settlements, Singapore, Indonesia and Thailand.
Orlop deck	The lowest deck of a ship
Positive inanition	A state of suffering from either a literal emptiness (of sustenance) or a metaphorical emptiness (of interest or energy).
Pratique	Free pratique is granted to ships entering port on proof the vessel is disease free.
Pro bono	Without payment
Ratlines	Thin ropes tied between the heavy ropes used to support a tall mast The ratlines are spaced so as to serve as a ladder for the crew to go aloft to stow the sails.
Royal sail	A small sail flown from the highest point of a mast.
Spar deck	The upper deck of a sailing ship.
Topgallant	A sail between a topsail and a royal sail.
Vomitire	An old fashioned mixture used to induce vomiting.
Weather shore	When the wind blows away from the shore to seaward.

Abbreviations

BPP	British Parliamentary Papers.
CLEC	Colonial Land and Emigration Commission.
CO	Colonial Office
GB	Great Britain
hp	horsepower
RCS	Royal College of Surgeons
WIC	West India Committee

National flags

Am	American	Ha	Hawaiian
Au	Austrian	It	Italian
Be	Belgian	Me	Mexican
Br	British	No	Norwegian
Ch	Chilean	Pe	Peruvian
Co	Colombian	Po	Portuguese
Da	Danish	Ru	Russian
Du	Dutch	Sa	Salvadorian
Fr	French	Sp	Spanish
Ge	German	Sw	Swedish

Editorial Practices

Shipping Sources Data

Where tables are stated to be, "Author's Compilation", the data have been gathered from a variety of sources, of varying degrees of accuracy and reliability. Where possible, figures have been cross-checked from two or more sources, but this sometimes produced conflicting results. In such circumstances, the more logical figure has been used with some trepidation.

Of the six departure ports covered in this study, the most authoritative figures for the whole period have been those published by the Harbour Master of Hong Kong. Information on vessels from the Chinese ports has generally been ascertained from British and American Consular officials in their various despatches. The quality of such reports varied considerably, with dates associated with ship departures seldom confirmed by newspaper reports on vessel movements in Chinese waters.

The detail of newspaper listings changed over time, even for the same newspaper. Similarly, numbers shipped were seldom accurate, with approximations the general rule. Newspapers were not generally privy to such numbers either. The weekly Portuguese Government publication *O Boletim*, in its various guises, provided the most useful data, with the consistency and accuracy of information steadily improving from 1862.

Shipping statistics on the Chinese emigration to the British West Indies is comprehensively reported in the Annual Reports of the Colonial Land and Emigration Commission along with some information on emigration to Surinam. The best source for information about Chinese immigrants to Cuba has been found in the Boletin de Colonizacion published by the Cuban Colonisation Commission, with only a few shipments not covered. Nevertheless, this is sometimes a little confusing especially when figures from the British Consul General in Cuba provide almost identical numbers but list more ship arrivals.

As with Cuba, the British Consul in Peru reported regularly to the British Foreign Secretary on the state of Chinese arrivals in that country. However, the periods covered have not always been continuous, so that the most authoritative means of comparison is J.B.H. Martinet.[185]

Where contradictory data has been sourced, the more pertinent figure is used. Where no data has come to hand, an entry may remain blank. Mortality rates quoted are generally based on the numbers embarked on all vessels for that destination irrespective of whether the vessel arrived at its destination or not and the numbers that actually disembarked. Different mortality rates will result from using figures based on ship arrivals only.

Mutinies versus insurrections

Mutinies are insurrections against authorities. At sea they would be by the crew against the Master or Captain. (There are at least two instances in this study). Passengers do not mutiny, but in the context of the time, newspapers invariably referred to the insurrections by the coolies as mutinies. In latter years officials began to realize that some insurrections were in fact planned acts of piracy. Newspapers however, preferred to continue referring to them as mutinies. In this study, 21 were classified as successful mutinies in that they resulted in the vessel not arriving at its destination. The other 47 were tabled as unsuccessful insurrections, purely to distinguish them from the first group.

Bibliography

Government Archives and Publications
GB CO 129, Hong Kong Original Correspondence, 1842-1951.
GB CO 132, Hong Kong Government Gazette, 1846-1853; 1890.
GB CO 133, Hong Kong Miscellaneous, 1844-1871.
GB CO 349/1-36, Hong Kong Register: Correspondence, 1849-1875, 1878.
GB CO 403, Hong Kong Entry Books, 1843-1871.
GB CO 489/1-15, Hong Kong Register: Out letters, 1872-1926.

GB Colonial Land and Emigration Commission Annual Reports.
GB FO Confidential Prints – Index (microform).
GB British Parliamentary Papers: Command Papers: 1852-53.
GB House of Commons Parliamentary Papers (BPP).

BPP 1844 [530] Emigration West Indies and Mauritius.
BPP 1847 [794] [812] Returns of the trade of the various ports of China, 1846.
BPP 1849 (593) (593-II) Papers relative to Emigration Part 1.
BPP 1849 [1119] Returns of the trade of the various ports of China, 1847 and 1848.
BPP 1852-53 (205) Reports from the Colony of Victoria and Report by Colonial Land and Emigration Coms., on Mortality on Emigrant Ships.
BPP 1852-53 (914) A Bill to amend the Passengers' Act .
BPP 1852-53 (986) Despatches relating to Chinese immigrants recently introduced into British Guiana and Trinidad.
BPP 1852-53 [1686] Correspondence with the Superintendent of British Trade on Emigration.
BPP 1854 (0.6) Correspondence relating to the Slave Trade.
BPP 1854-55 (0.7) Correspondence on Emigration from China.
BPP 1854-55 (0.4) Correspondence with British Ministers and Agents in Foreign Countries ... Slave Trade April 1854-March 1855.
BPP 1854-55 (0.7) China, Correspondence upon the subject of Emigration from China.
BPP 1856 (0.2)) Correspondence with British Ministers and Agents in Foreign Countries . Slave Trade April 1855-March 1856.
BPP 1857 Session 1 (147) Communications on Mortality on board British Ships carrying emigrants from China.
BPP 1857-58 (481) Correpondence on Emigration from Hong Kong and Chinese Empire to W Indies and to Foreign Countries.
BPP 1857-58 (521) Correspondence on Mortality on board British ships from China or India.
BPP 1860 [2714] China Correspondence respecting emigration from Canton.
BPP 1861 [2823.1] Correspondence with British Ministers relating to the Slave Trade.
BPP 1861 (2831) Cuban Slave Trade.

BPP 1865 [3489] Commercial Reports from HM Consuls in China 1862-64.
BPP 1865 [3576] Commercial Reports from HM Consuls in China 1864.
BPP 1866 [3707] Commercial Reports from HM Consuls in China 1865.
BPP 1867 [3940] Commercial Reports from HM Consuls in China 1865-66.
BPP 1867-68 (4000) Correspondence with British Commissioners relating to the Slave Trade.
BPP 1870 [C217] Board of Trade returns of wrecks 1869.
BPP 1871 [C403] Correspondence on Emigration of Chinese Coolies from Macao.
BPP 1872 [C504] Correspondence respecting Emigration of Chinese coolies from Macao.
BPP 1873 [C797] Correspondence respecting the Macao coolie trade and the steamer *Fatchoy*.
BPP 1873 [C829] Measures to prevent the fitting out of ships in the Coolie Trade.
BPP 1873 [C908] Correspondence respecting the Macao Coolie Trade.
BPP 1875 [C1212] Correspondence respecting the Macao Coolie Trade, 1874-75.
BPP 1875 [C1215] Correspondence respecting slavery in Cuba.
BPP 1878 [C2051] Report on the labour question in Cuba.

China. *Chinese emigration: Report of the Commission sent by China to Ascertain the Condition of Chinese coolies in Cuba, 1874*. Shanghai: Imperial Maritime Customs Press, 1876. Reprint ed. Taipei: Ch'eng Wen Publishing, 1970.

Great Britain, Parliament, House of Commons. Correspondence and returns respecting the emigration of Chinese coolies 1858-92. Shannon: Irish University Press,1971.
Great Britain, Parliament, House of Commons. Correspondence, ordinances, orders in council, reports and other papers respecting consular establishments in China 1833-81. Shannon: Irish University Press,1971.
Great Britain, Parliament, House of Commons. Correspondence, dispatches and other communications respecting emigration of Chinese Coolies, 1852-58. Shannon: Irish University Press,1971.
Great Britain, Parliament, House of Commons. Checklist 1000 Vol. series 1801-1899. Shannon: Irish University Press,1972.

Hong Kong. *Hong Kong Government Gazette*

Macao. *O Boletim do governo de Macao* (various titles), 1850-74.

Spain. Ministerio de Ultramar, Archivo Historico Nacional, Madrid.

US Executive Documents – House of Representatives, 1st session 33rd Congress.

US Executive Documents – Senate 1st and 2nd Sessions 34th Congress 1855-56.
US Executive Documents – Senate 2nd session 35th Congress 1858-59
US Executive Documents – Senate 1st Session 36th Congress 1859-60 No. 30.

Private Archive
Jardine, Matheson & Co. Archive (Cambridge University Library).

Journals and Newspapers

Adelaide, Australia
Adelaide Times, 14 July 1856.
South Australian Register, 25 July 1863.

Brussels, Belgium
Bureau Veritas Registre de Renseignements sur Navires,1852-72.

Havana, Cuba
Boletin de Colonizacion. Havana: Comision Central de Colonizacion, 1873.
Diario de la Marina, 1852–74.

Canton, China
Canton Register (microform), Canton: James Matheson, 1827–1843.
Chinese Repository, 1842-51.

Chicago, USA
Chicago Press and Tribune, 22 October 1859.

Hong Kong
China Mail (various, 1866-68)
Chinese Serial, Vol. II No. 12, 1854.
Daily Advertiser & Shipping Gazette, 2 January1872–30 April 1873.
Daily Advertiser and Shipping Gazette, 1871-78.
Friend of China and Hong Kong Gazette, 1842–59.
Hong Kong Daily Press (various, 1864-72).
Hong Kong Register & Government Gazette, 1844-58.
Hong Kong Mercury and Shipping Gazette, 1866.
Hong Kong Times, Daily Advertiser and Shipping Gazette, 1873-76.
Overland China Mail, 1853.
Overland Friend of China, 1876-79.
South China Morning Post, 1904.
The China Review, 1872

Honolulu
Hawaiian Gazette, 1865-70.
Pacific Commercial Advertiser, 1868-69.
Polynesian, 12 October 1861.

Transactions of the Royal Hawaiian Agricultural Society. Vol 1, Royal Hawaiian Agricultural Society, 1850.

London, UK
Lloyds Register of Shipping, London, 1852-74.
Nautical Magazine and Naval Chronicle. London: Simpkin Marshall & Co., for 1847. Reprint. Cambridge University Press, 2013.
Shipping and Mercantile Gazette, London, 1853.

Melbourne, Australia
Argus, 8 March 1855.

New York, USA
American Lloyds Register of American and Foreign Shipping, 1852-72.
New York Times (various 1852-56).

San Francisco, USA
Daily Alta, California (various, 1849–67).
San Francisco Call, 1897.
Weekly Alta, California 1849.

Shanghai, China
North China Herald, Shanghai, 1859.

Singapore
Singapore Free Press and Mercantile Advertiser, 1853.
Straits Times, 1846.

Sydney, Australia
Shipping Gazette and Sydney General Trade List.
Sydney Morning Herald (various, 1852-55)

Washington, USA
De Bow's Review, Vol. 23 Washington 1857.

Wellington, New Zealand
West Coast Times, 1866.

Yokohama, Japan
Japan Times' Overland Mail, 5 September 1868.

Books and Articles

Abend, Hallett. *Treaty Ports.* New York: Doubleday, Doran and Company, Inc, 1944.

Aldus, Don. *Coolie traffic and Kidnapping.* London: McCorquodale and Co., 1876.

Ankum-Houwink, J. 'Chinese contract migrants in Surinam between 1853 and 1870.' *Boletin de Estudios Latinoamericanos y del Caribe*, No. 17 (December 1974), pp. 42-69.

Atteck, Helen and Philip. *Stress of Weather.* St Catharines, Ont: Wanata Enterprises, 2000.

Ball, Benjamin Lincoln. *Rambles in Eastern Asia: Including China and Manila, During Several Years Residence.* Boston: James French and Co., 1856.

Ball, J. Dyer. 'The Hong Shan or Macao Dialect.' *The China Review*, Vol. 22, No. 2 (1896).

Bell, Georges. *Voyage en Chine du capitaine Montfort.* Paris, Libraire Nouvelle, 1860.

Blanchard, Peter. 'The "Transitional Man" in 19th C Latin America: The Case of Domingo Elias of Peru.' *Bulletin of Latin American Research*, Vol. 15, Issue 2, May 1996.

Blue, A.D. 'Chinese Emigration and the Deck Passenger Trade.' *Journal of the Hong Kong Royal Asiatic Society*, Vol. 10, 1970.

— 'Early Steamships in China.' *Journal of the Hong Kong Royal Asiatic Society*, Vol. 13, 1973.

Boulger, Demetrius Charles de. *The History of China.* W. Thacker & Co., London,1898.

Bourne, Kenneth & D. Cameron Watt (eds). *British Documents on Foreign Affairs – reports & papers from the FO Confidential print.* Frederick, Maryland: University Publications of America, 1989.

Bowring, John. *Autobiographical Recollections of Sir John Bowring*, London: Henry S. King & Co., 1877.

Briot, Claude and Jacqueline Briot. *Les Clippers Francais.* Douarnenez, Brittany: éditions Chasse-Marée/Armen, 1993.

Bryan, Patrick. 'The Settlement of the Chinese in Jamaica: 1854-c1970.'

Cardin, Jean-Luc. *L'immigration chinoise a la Martinique.* [Paris:] Editions l'Harmattan, 1991.

Caribbean Quarterly, Vol. 50, No. 2, 2004.

Cameron, Nigel. *Illustrated History of Hong Kong.* Hong Kong: Oxford University Press, 1971.

Campbell, Persia Crawford. *Chinese coolie emigration to countries within the British Empire.* London: F. Cass, 1971.

Canton Advertising & Commission Agency. *Canton: Its ports, industries & trade.* Reprint, Ch'eng Wen Publishing Company, 1971.

Chang-Rodriguez, Eugenio. 'Chinese Labor Migration into Latin America in the Nineteenth Century.' *Revista de Historia de America*, No. 46, December 1958.

Chen Yu. 'The Making of a Bund in China: The British Concession in Xiamen (1852-1930).' *Journal of Asian Architecture and Building Engineering*, Vol. 7, No. 1 May 2008/38.

Cheong W. E. *Mandarins and Merchants; Jardine Matheson & Co., a China agency of the early nineteenth century.* London: Curzon Press, 1979.

Clayton, Lawrence A. 'Chinese Indentured Labour in Peru.' *History Today*, Vol. 30, Issue 6, 1980.

Clementi, Sir Cecil. *The Chinese in British Guiana*, 1915. Guyana: Caribbean Press (reprint for the Guyana Classics Library), 2010.

Cohen, Lucy M. *Chinese in the Post Civil War South.* Baton Rouge, USA: Louisiana State University Press, 1984.

— 'The Chinese of the Panama Railroad: Preliminary Notes on the Migrants of 1854 who "Failed ".' *Ethnohistory*, Vol. 18, No. 4 (Autumn), 1971.

— 'Immigration of Chinese from Macao to Costa Rica 1872-1873.' *Revista de Ciebcias Sociales*, Vol. 119 (1), 2008, pp. 39-53.

Costin, W. C. *Great Britain and China, 1833-1860.* Oxford: The Clarendon Press, 1937.

Cox, Thomas R. 'Harbingers of Change: American Merchants and the Formosa Annexation Scheme.' *Pacific Historical Review*, Vol. 42, No. 2, May 1973, University of California Press.

Cracroft, P. 'Notes on a Voyage to China.' *Nautical Magazine and Naval Chronicle*, Vol. 21. London: Simpkin Marshall & Co., 1852.

Dana, William Buck (ed). *The Merchants' Magazine and Commercial Review*, Vol. 52 (from January to June inclusive), 1865. Classic Reprint, 2019.

Davids, Jules. *American Diplomatic & Public Papers: the US & China.* Wilmington Del: Scholarly Resources, 1973. Vol. 17 Coolie Trade. Vol. 20 Consular reports.

Duffield, A. J. *Peru in the guano age.* London: Richard Bentley and Son, 1877.

Dye, Bob. *Merchant Prince of the Sandalwood Mountains.* University of Hawaii Press, 1997.

Fairbank, John King. *Trade and Diplomacy on the China Coast: The Opening of the Treaty Ports, 1842-1854.* Cambridge MA: Harvard University Press, 1953.

Fairburn, William Armstrong and Ethel M. Ritchie. *Merchant Sail.* Center Lovell, Maine: Fairburn Marine Educational Foundation Inc., [1945-55].

Ferenczi, Imre. 'International Migration Statistics.' In *International Migrations, Volume I: Statistics*, ed. Walter F. Willcox. New York: National Bureau of Economic Research, 1929, pp. 47 - 76.

Friedland, Klaus (ed). *Maritime Aspects of Migration India-Surinam.* Koln: Bohlau, 1989.

Gonzales, Michael J. 'Chinese Plantation Workers and Social Conflict in Peru.' *Journal of Latin American Studies*, Vol. 21 No. 3 October 1989, pp. 385-424.

Griffin, Eldon. *Clippers and Consuls: American Consular and Commercial Relations in Eastern Asia, 1845-1860.* Ann Arbor, Mich: Edwards Bros, 1938.

Guterl, Matthew Pratt. *American Mediterranean: Southern Slaveholders in the Age of Emancipation.* Harvard University Press, 2008.

Hertslet, Edward. *Recollections of the Old Foreign Office.* London: John Murray, 1901.

Hitchens, Fred H. *Colonial Land and Emigration Commission.* London, 1913.

Holdsworth, May and Christopher Munn (eds), *Dictionary of Hong Kong Biography,* Hong Kong University Press, 2012.

Hollett, David. *Passage from India to El Dorado: Guyana and the great migration.* Cranbury New Jersey: Associated University Presses, 1999.

—*More Precious than Gold.* Cranbury New Jersey: Associated Universities Presses, 2008.

Howe, Octavius T. and Frederick C. Matthew. *American Clipper Ships, 1833-1858.* New York: Argosy Antiquarian, 1967.

Hu-Dehart, Evelyn. 'Chinese Coolie Labour in Cuba in the Nineteenth Century: Free Labor of Neoslavery.' *Contributions in Black Studies*: Vol. 12, Article 5. (1994), pp. 38-54.

—'Opium and Social Control: Coolies on the Plantations of Cuba and Peru.' *Journal of Chinese Overseas*, Vol. 1, No. 2, November 2004, pp. 169-183.

— 'La trata amarilla: "The Yellow Trade" and the Middle Passage 1847-1884.' In Emma Christopher, Cassandra Pybus, Marcus Rediker, Marcus Rediker (eds). *Many Middle Passages: Forced Migrations & the Making of the Modern World.* Berkeley: University of California Press, 2007.

— and Kathleen López. 'Asian Diasporas in Latin America and the Caribbean: An Historical Overview.' *Afro-Hispanic Review*, Vol. 27, No. 1, (Spring 2008), pp. 9-21.

Hutchinson, Thomas Joseph. *Two Years in Peru with Exploration of its Antiquities.* London: Sampson Low, Marston, Low, & Searle,1873.

Irick, Robert L. *Ch'ing policy towards the coolie trade 1847-1878.* (Asian Library Series, number 18.) San Francisco: Chinese Materials Center, 1982.

Jesus, C. A. Montalto de. *Historic Macao.* Hong Kong: Kelly & Walsh, 1902.

Jones, Clement Wakefield. *Chief Officer in China.* Liverpool: Charles Birchall & Sons, 1956.

King, Frank H.H. & Prescott Clarke. *Research Guide to China coast Newspapers, 1822-1911.* East Asian Research Center, Harvard University, 1965.

Labrosse, F. *Navigation of the Pacific Ocean, China Seas etc.* Washington, DC: Government Printing Office, 1875.

Look Lai, Walton. 'Chinese Indentured Labor: Migrations to the British West Indies in the Nineteenth Century.' *Amerasia Journal*, Vol. 15, No. 2 (1989), pp. 117-128.

—*Indentured Labor, Caribbean Sugar: Chinese and Indian Migrants to the British West Indies, 1838-1918.* [John Hopkins studies in Atlantic History and Culture.] Baltimore: John Hopkins University Press, 1993.

—*The Chinese in the West Indies 1806-1995.* Jamaica: UWI Press, 1998.

—'Coolie Trade.' In David Pong (ed). *Gale's Encyclopedia of Modern China.* Detroit: Charles Scribner's Sons/Gale, Cengage Learning, 2009.

— 'Images of the Chinese in West Indian History.' *Anthurium: A Caribbean Studies Journal,* Vol. 7 (1) The Asian Experience in the Caribbean, 2009.

— and Tan Chee-Beng (Eds). *The Chinese in Latin America and the Caribbean.* Brill, 2010.

Lane-Poole, Stanley. *The Life of Sir Harry Parkes.* London: Macmillan and Co., 1894.

Lawrence, K.O. *Question of Labour: Indentured Immigration into Trinidad and British Guiana, 1875-1917.* New York: St Martin's Press, 1994.

Leibo, Steven A. 'Not So Calm an Administration: The Anglo-French Occupation of Canton, 1858-61.' *Journal of the Royal Asiatic Society Hong Kong Branch,* Vol. 28 (1988), pp. 16-33.

López, Kathleen. *Chinese Cubans: a Transnational History.* Chapel Hill: University of North Carolina Press, 2013.

Lubbock, Basil. *The Opium Clippers.* Glasgow: James Brown and Son, 1933.

—*Coolie ships and Oil Sailers.* Glasgow: Brown, Son & Ferguson, 1935.

Luzón, José Luis. 'El Mar en el tráfico Chinero. Naufragios y amotinamientos.' In *Conquista y Resistencia en la Historia de America,* edited by Pilar Gracía Jordán. Spain: Universitat Barcelona, 1992.

Mathew, William M. *House of Gibbs and the Peruvian guano monopoly.* London: Royal Historical Society, 1981.

Maude, H.E. *Slavers in Paradise.* Stanford: Stanford University Press, 1981.

Mayers, Wm. Fred, N.B. Dennys, and Chas King. *The Treaty Ports of China and Japan.* London: Trübner & Company, 1867.

McDonald, John and Ralph Shlomowitz. 'Mortality on Chinese and Indian Voyages to the West Indies and South America, 1847-1874.' *Social and Economic Studies,* Vol. 41, No. 2 (June 1992), pp. 203-240.

Meadows, Thomas Taylor. *Desultory Notes on the Government and people of China.* London: Wm H. Allen, 1847.

Meagher, Arnold J. *The Coolie Trade: The Traffic in Chinese Laborers to Latin America 1847-1874.* [Philadelphia, Pa.]: Xlibris Corporation, 2008.

Mendoza, Mario Castro de. *El Transporte Maritimo en la Inmigración China, 1849-1874.* Lima: CONCYTEC, 1989.

Munn, Christopher. *Anglo-China: Chinese People and British Rule in Hong Kong, 1841-1880.* Richmond, Surrey: Curzon Press, 2001.

Narvaez, Benjamin Nicolas. *Chinese Coolies in Cuba and Peru: Race, Labor, and Immigration 1839-1886.* University of Texas, PhD Dissertation, 2010.

Northrup, David. *Indentured Labor in the Age of Imperialism, 1834-1922.* New York: Cambridge University Press, 1995.

O'Neill, Mark. 'Humans as Commodity – Macao centre of "coolie trade" in 19th century'. *Macao Magazine*, Issue 6, 1 January 2011.

Orovio, Consuelo Naranjo and Imilcy Balboa Navarro. 'Colonos asiáticos para una economía en expansión, Cuba: 1847-1880.' ['Asian Labourers for an Expanding Economy: Cuba 1847-1880.'] In *Revista Mexicana del Caribe*, No. 8 (1999), pp. 32-65.

Pan, Lynn (ed). *Encyclopaedia of Chinese Overseas*. Singapore: Chinese Heritage Centre, 2006.

—*Sons of the Yellow Emperor: the Story of the Overseas Chinese*. London: Secker & Warburg, 1990.

Pastor, Humberto Rodríguez. 'Trata de culíes chinos y barcos clíppers.' In *Nueva corónica 3* (Enero, 2014). Peru: Escuela de Historia, Universidad Nacional Mayor de San Marcos de Lima, pp. 435-454.

Pelcovits, Nathan A. *Old China Hands and the Foreign Office*. New York: King's Crown Press, 1948.

Pitcher, Rev. Philip Wilson. *In and about Amoy,* Shanghai: Methodist Publishing House in China, 1912.

Plowman, Robert J. 'The Voyage of the "Coolie" ship *Kate Hooper*, October 3, 1857 - March 26, 1858.' In *Prologue Magazine* Summer 2001, Vol. 33, No. 2. Seen at https://www.archives.gov/publications/prologue/2001/summer/coolie-ship-kate-hooper-1.html

Redman, Renee. 'From Importation of Slaves to Migration of Laborers: The Struggle to Outlaw American Participation in the Chinese Coolie Trade and the Seeds of United States Immigration Law.' (30 January 2010). *Albany Government Law Review*, Vol. 3, No. 1, 2010. Available at SSRN: https://ssrn.com/abstract=1658571.

Riva, Juan Perez de la. *La demographía de los culíes Chinois, 1803-1874*. Cuba: La Havana, 1967. Separata de la *Revista de la Biblioteca Nacional José Martí*. año 57, número 4. 1966. ALSO Riva, Juan Perez de la. 'La demographía de los culíes Chinois, 1803-1874.' In *Revista de la Biblioteca Nacional José Marti*, ano 57, num 4, 1966.

—'Los culíes chinos en Cuba 1847-1880: contribución al estudio de la inmigración contratada en el Caribe'. *La Habana Editorial de Ciencias Sociales*, 2000. [pp. 75-122]

Saunders, Kay. *Indentured Labour in the British Empire 1834-1920*. London: Croom Helm, 1984.

Scott, Rebecca J. *Slave Emancipation in Cuba: The Transition to Free Labour, 1860-1899*. Princeton, NJ: Princeton University Press, 1985.

Sherwood, Marika. 'Perfidious Albion: Britain, the USA, and Slavery in the 1840s and 1860s.' *Contributions in Black Studies*: Vol. 13, Article 6, 1995.

Sinn, Elizabeth. *Pacific Crossing: California Gold, Chinese Migration, and the Making of Hong Kong*. Hong Kong: Hong Kong University Press, 2013.

Stewart, Watt. *Chinese Bondage in Peru; a history of the Chinese coolie in Peru 1849-74*. Westport Ct: Greenwood Press, 1951.

Sue-A-Quan, Trevelyan A. *Cane Reapers: Chinese Indentured Immigrants in Guyana.* Vancouver: Riftswood Publishing, 1999.
Thomson, J. *Illustrations of China and its people: a series of two hundred photographs.* Vol. 4. London: Sampson Low, Marston, Low and Searle, 1873-74.
Tikhvinskii, S.L. (General Editor). Translated from Russian by Vic. Schneierson. *Chapters from the History of Russo-Chinese relations, 17th-19th centuries.* Moscow: Progress Publishers, 1985.
Toman, Rene de La Pedraja. *Oil and Coffee: Latin American merchant shipping from the imperial era to the 1950s.* Westport, CT: Greenwood Press, 1998.
Tsai, Shih-Shan Henry. 'American Involvement in the Coolie Trade.' *American Studies* (Taiwan). (Academia Sinica Publication), 6 (1976): pp. 49-66.
Turner, Mary. 'Chinese Contract Labour in Cuba, 1847-1874.' *Caribbean Studies*, Vol. 14, No. 2 (July 1974), pp. 66-81.
Wang Sing-wu. *Organization of Chinese emigration, 1848-88: with special reference to Chinese emigration to Australia.* San Francisco: Chinese Materials Center, c. 1978. Occasional series (Chinese Materials and Research Aids Service Center (Taipei)); No. 25.
Welsh, Frank. *A History of Hong Kong.* London: Harper Collins, 1993.
Wesley-Smith, Peter. 'Kwok A-Sing, Sir John Smale, and the Macao Coolie Trade.' In Shane Nozzal (ed). *Law Lectures for Practitioners.* Hong Kong Law Journal Ltd., Vol. 1993 (1993).
Wickberg, Edgar. *The Chinese in Philippine Life, 1850-1898.* New Haven Ct: Yale University Press, 1965.
Williams, S. Wells. *The Chinese commercial guide.* Hong Kong: A. Shortrede & Co., 1863.
Yen Ching-Hwang. *Coolies and Mandarins: China's protection of overseas Chinese during the late Ch'ing period (1851-1911).* Singapore: Singapore University Press, 1985.
Yun, Lisa. *The Coolie Speaks: Chinese Indentured Laborers and African Slaves in Cuba.* Philadelphia: Temple University Press, 2008.
—and Ricardo René Laremont. 'Chinese Coolies and African Slaves in Cuba.' *Journal of Asian American Studies.* John Hopkins University Press. Vol. 4 (No. 2), June 2001, pp. 99-122.
Yung Wing. *My Life in China and America.* New York: Henry Holt Company, 1909.

Website

Chinese to Cuba. www.cubagenweb.org/ships/chinese.htm
Graces Guide to British Industrial History, 1932. 'A Shipbuilding History, 1750-1932 (Alexander Stephen & Sons).' www.Gracesguide.co.uk.
'The 149 year illustrated log of the Edwin Fox', The New Zealand Maritime Record. http://www.nzmaritime.co.nz/edwinfox.htm

Unpublished Theses

Mahood, Geraldine. "British policy towards the Chinese coolie trade 1850-1860." University of Melbourne, Department of History MA Thesis, 1971.

Stasko, Thomas McTernan. "Moving through the Gate of Venus: The History of Cumsingmoon and the Coolie Trade: 1849-54." MA Thesis, Department of Social Sciences and Humanities, University of Macau, 2013.

Suggested Additional Reading

Confiant, Raphaël. *Case à Chine*. Mercure de France, 2007. (Novel)

Spar plan of screw steamers, *Glendarroch* and *Glensannox*. *Glensannox* left Macau, 17 November 1872 with 685 coolies for Costa Rica.

Notes

[1] For a useful description of currencies used in Hong Kong in C19th, see Elizabeth Sinn, *Pacific Crossing: California Gold, Chinese Migration, and the Making of Hong Kong*, Hong Kong: Hong Kong University Press, 2013, p. xvii.
[2] BPP 1852-53 [1686].
[3] Wm. Mayers, *et al.*, *The Treaty Ports of China and Japan*, 1867, p. 127.
[4] Prince Kung (1833-18988) was the sixth son of the Chinese Emperor Daoguang. As head of China's Foreign Ministry, known as the Zhongli Yamen, he negotiated a set of regulations with Rutherford Alock of Britain and Henry de Bellonnet of France to ensure the safety of Chinese emigrants. Dated 5 March 1866, this has become known as the Kung Convention.
[5] Don Aldus, *Coolie traffic and Kidnapping*, 1876, p. 31.
[6] Eldon Griffin, *Clippers and Consuls*, 1938, p. 29.
[7] John King Fairbank, *Trade and Diplomacy on the China Coast*, 1953, p. 217.
[8] The *Straits Times*, 12 December 1846.
[9] In 1803, aged twenty, John Crawfurd had joined the East India Company as a qualified medical doctor, working first in Penang and then Java. There he was entrusted with the administration of the ports of Semarang and Sourabaya where many Chinese resided. Very keen on languages and history, he soon became an expert on the region. He became the second British Resident of Singapore in 1823, on the recommendation of his friend Stamford Raffles, the first British Resident. Despite being an efficient and conscientious administrator, he was not a popular man, and he returned to Scotland in 1826 where he made several unsuccessful attempts to enter Parliament.
[10] BPP 1844 [530], 260.
[11] BPP 1844 [530] Emigration West Indies and Mauritius.
[12] https://www.temoignages.re/culture/culture-et-identite/2006-placee-sous-le-signe-du-chien-de-feu,13139
[13] See Georges Bell, *Voyage en Chine du capitaine Montfort*, 1860, p. 8.
[14] Juan Perez de la Riva, *La demographía de los culíes Chinois, 1803-1874*. 1966, p. 76.
[15] This is an example of conflicting information. The *Boletin de Colonizacion* gives an arrival date of 3 Jun 1847, the same date as recorded by the *Diario de la Marina*. Perez de la Riva however says the *Oquendo* arrived on 29 July.
[16] Juan Perez de la Riva, *op. cit.*, p. 77.
[17] Captain J. Thomas Larkins, formerly in the East India Company's maritime service, was then a merchant in Hong Kong.
[18] Sic (as spelt by Consul Layton. There ae numerous cases of this spelling in BPP. More often, we find the spelling, "taotai".
[19] Passengers purchased the ticket on credit to be paid back out of their wages on arrival.
[20] The first Peruvian Law to encourage the importation of overseas labour. It was intended for Europeans but it did not specifically ban Chinese and many more Chinese than Europeans were brought in. See Watt Stewart, *Chinese Bondage in Peru; a history of the Chinese coolie in Peru 1849-74*, Westport, Conn: Greenwood Press, 1951, p. 13.
[21] See Christopher Munn, *Anglo-China: Chinese People and British Rule in Hong Kong, 1841-1880*, Richmond, Surrey: Curzon Press, 2001, p. 269.

[22] *The Transactions of the Royal Historical Society*, Vol. 1. No. 1, p. 171.
[23] The details given in the contract are as follows:
Contract between So or Su, aged 25, from Nanhai County Guangdong Province, and the company "Lombillo, Montalvo y Ca." based in Havana, whose agent, Tanco Armero, is based in Macau. The contract is dated "29th Day of the 12th Month of the 7th Year of the Tongzhi Era" and registered at the Macau Procurator's Office for Chinese Affairs, 2 January 1869. So or Su agreed to board a ship in Macau, bound for Havana, as arranged by Tanco Armero, to work there for eight years. -- Many thanks to Mr Tony Yip for his advice on these details. Mr Yip gives these comments, "The Chinese in the contract is hard to understand and appears to be written by a non-native speaker. The first name of the future worker is illegible and the name of the signatory cannot be read. The handwriting at the top right hand corner of the contract is in Portuguese. It is difficult to convert the Chinese date into the Gregorian calendar, but it is useful to note that Tongzhi Emperor reigned from 11 November 1861 to 12 January 1875 (using the Gregorian calendar)."
[24] Captain Thomas George Beazley was born in 1811 and obtained his Masters Class 2 Certificate in 1847. The following month, on 20 September 1847 he obtained his Class 1 Certificate. He was awarded a Medal from the Hon. East India Company in 1843 for his exertions in the battles of Meanee and Hydrabad, whilst in command of the Company's steam vessel *Nimrod*.
[25] *South Australian Register*, 25 July 1863.
[26] *China Mail*, 29 April 1852.
[27] *Singapore Free Press*, 13 May 1853.
[28] Eldon Griffin, 1938, p. 413.
[29] *Ibid*.
[30] Mario Castro de Mendoza,. *El Transporte Maritimo en la Inmigración China, 1849-1874*. Lima: CONCYTEC, 1989.
[31] The *Argus*, 8 March 1855.
[32] *Sydney Morning Herald*, 16 March 1855.
[33] Watt Stewart, *Chinese Bondage in Peru*, 1951, p. 22.
[34] The *New York Times*, 10 January 1856.
[35] *San Francisco Call*, 11 April 1897.
[36] Watt Stewart, *Chinese Bondage in Peru*, 1951, p. 22.
[37] Humberto Rodríguez Pastor, 'Trata de culíes chinos y barcos clíppers,' in *Nueva corónica 3* (Enero, 2014). Peru: Escuela de Historia, Universidad Nacional Mayor de San Marcos de Lima, pp. 435-454, p. 422.
[38] BPP 1852-53 (986), p. 72.
[39] George Booker and his brothers initially managed cotton and sugar plantations in British Guiana. They then branched out into retailing, shipping and publishing. The Booker Prize was established by the family.
[40] BPP 1852-53 (1686), p. 1
[41] BPP 1852-53 (1686), p. 26.
[42] BPP 1852-53 (1686), p. 10.
[43] An Extract of Dr Ely's Diary can be found in Walton Look Lai, *The Chinese in the West Indies 1806-1995*. Jamaica: UWI Press, 1998, p. 10.
[44] Jules Davids, *American Diplomatic & Public Papers: the US & China*. Wilmington Del: Scholarly Resources, 1973. Vol. 17 Coolie Trade, p. 6.

[45] The *Chinese Serial*, 1 December 1854 (Vol. II, No. 12).
[46] The *China Mail*, 9 November 1854, quoting the *Morning Herald*, Jamaica, of 30 August 1854.
[47] Extract from, 'The 149 year illustrated log of the *Edwin Fox*', *The New Zealand Maritime Record*. http://www.nzmaritime.co.nz/edwinfox.htm
[48] "Death recorded" means that a convict was pardoned for his crimes rather than given the death sentence.
[49] The role of the *refaccionista* seems to have been that of middleman or dealer.
[50] Charles Batten Hillier (1820-1856) was Assistant Chief Magistrate of Hong Kong between 1843 and 1847 when he succeeded William Caine as Chief Magistrate. A merchant mariner he was appointed Emigration Officer under the Chinese Passengers' Act of 1855. He died shortly after arriving in Bangkok as the British Consul to Siam.
[51] BPP 1857-58 (521), p. 5.
[52] These figures appear to be rounded figures and differ from those supplied by the Harbour Master in Hong Kong and by the *Boletin de Colonization* in Cuba.
[53] James Nourse bought his first ship in 1861 and then formed his own company in 1864. He then won a contract with the British Crown Agents for the Colonies to transport coolies from India to the West Indies, Fiji and Mauritius.
[54] See Appendix II.
[55] *Adelaide Times*, 14 July 1856.
[56] Translated by the *The Friend of China*, 7 May 1856.
[57] Robert J. Plowman, 'The Voyage of the "Coolie" ship Kate Hooper, October 3, 1857 - March 26, 1858.' In *Prologue Magazine* Summer 2001, Vol. 33, No. 2. Seen at https://www.archives.gov/publications/prologue/2001/summer/coolie-ship-kate-hooper-1.html2001.
[58] "Report on the State of Disease on board the Ship Kitty Simpson" (i.e. on her recent voyage from Swatow to Havana).—How did this report come about? The British authorities were investigating the cause of high mortality on British coolie ships. British Havana consul-general Crawford made enquiries of the two British ships in port at the time, and also called on Dr Somerville, of this American ship, for similar information, which he generously supplied.
[59] BPP 1860 (2714), p. 60.
[60] Bazin & Leon Gay was founded in January 1846 through a merger between Bazin & Perier and the Compagnie Générale de Navigation à Hélice. The company was sold to Fraissinet in 1865.
[61] See Appendix I.
[62] The Chinese Passengers' Act stipulates three quarts per person per day. It is unclear for what purpose this 6 gallons per day is intended.
[63] See Jardine Matheson Archive MS JM F7/32.
[64] See also Chapter 6 in the present work.
[65] Usually the crew handled the ropes from the deck when making and furling sail. Because the deck was completely taken up by the passengers, the crew had to handle the ropes standing on the side rails: a dangerous practice.
[66] US Exec Doc16 HR 37th Congress 2nd Session.
[67] BPP 1861 (2831), p. 3.

[68] Contract in Spanish between Nong Sing of Namoi and Lombillo [*sic*, not "Lombrillo"], Montalvo y Ca." [i.e. Lombillo, Montalvo & Co.]
Mr Tony Yip makes the following comment about the place name, "Namoi". "I assume 'Namoi' is the same as 'Nanhai'. The place 'Nanhai' is sometimes transliterated into English as 'Namhoi'. In Spanish, the 'h' sound is always silent, it's probably why 'Namoi' is used in the Spanish version of the contract."
Tony Yip makes the following interesting contrasts between the Chinese-language and Spanish-language contracts which are both shown in this book: "The same agent and same company are mentioned in both versions. In the Chinese version, it's mentioned that Tanco Armero is based in Macau, I don't see the same mention in the Spanish version. In the Chinese version, it says the labourer agrees to board a ship arranged by Tanco Armero to leave Macau for Havana. In the Spanish version, it's just saying that the labourer agrees to work in Havana." Tony Yip also points out as follows: "The agent is called 'N. Tanco Armero' (I can't say for sure that 'N' stands for 'Nicolas' by reading either the Spanish or the Chinese version)."

[69] Steven A. Leibo, 'Not So Calm an Administration: The Anglo-French Occupation of Canton, 1858-61.' *Journal of the Royal Asiatic Society Hong Kong Branch*, Vol. 28 (1988), pp. 16-33, p. 19.

[70] Rutherford Alcock (1809-1897) served as British Consul in Foochow, Shanghai, Canton. He was the Consul-General in Tokyo and headed the British legation in Peking between 1865 and 1869.

[71] See BPP 1860 (2714), p. 1.

[72] *Ibid.*

[73] William S. Frederick Mayers (1831-1878) was a British student interpreter recruited to serve in China. He was appointed an interpreter to the Allied Comission in Canton until it ceased operations. He then stayed on in Canton as interpreter to the British Consulate there.

[74] Even neighbouring villages had different dialects. This is one of the reasons why so many crimps had to be employed to canvas relatively small areas.

[75] Inglis first entered Hong Kong Government service on 15 March 1844 as a police clerk. Caught in the fever of the California gold rush, Inglis tendered his resignation in May 1849, but returned to Hong Kong and rejoined government service on 4 May 1857 as Clerk and Interpreter to the Marine Magistrate. He became Acting Harbour Master on 30 April 1858 and assumed the position permanently on 25 August when the previous Harbour Master Watkins resigned on medical advice that the climate was unsuitable. In May 1859, Inglis was granted 12 months leave following a diagnosis of Bright's disease of the kidney, a fatal illness.

[76] Sir Cecil Clementi, *The Chinese in British Guiana*, *op. cit.*, p. 43.

[77] John Gardiner Austin (1812-1900) was born at Lowlands Plantation in Demerara in 1812. He was sent to school in England, before returning to manage the family estates. He married and raised a family in Georgetown but then determined to settle in England. With the sugar slump of 1844, the Austins returned to Demerara, and John Gardiner had to seek Government employment, first as Stipendiary Magistrate, then Assistant Government Secretary. He became Immigration Agent in 1853.

[78] See Austin to Merivale, 8 September 1858. ('Requests a passage at the Government rate.' CO 129/072, pp. 46-47.)
[79] BPP 1860 (714), p. 19.
[80] More specifically the Superintendent of Customs (Hoppo) of the Imperial Maritime Service. A copy of the "Emigration Regulations made by the Governor General of the Liang Kuang Provinces in November 1861" is available in Sir Cecil Clementi, *The Chinese in British Guiana*, Guyana: Caribbean Press (reprint of the 1915 edition for the Guyana classics Library), 2010, pp. 269-273.
[81] The website http://www.touscreoles.fr/2009/07/28/l-immigration-chinoise-en-martinique-ou-ceux-qu-on-appelle-chin/ claims that three ships transported in total 987 Chinese labourers to Martinique.
[82] Jean-Luc Cardin. *L'immigration chinoise a la Martinique*. [Paris:] Editions l'Harmattan, 1991.
[83] *Chicago Press and Tribune*, 22 October 1859.
[84] See FO 228-286, p. 77.
[85] Rev. William Lobschied (1822-1893) was sent to China in 1848 by the Rhenish Missionary Society. Under the guidance of Karl Gutzlaff another missionary now in Government service, he quickly learned the Chinese language, and travelled about Kwangtung Province. After a short return to his homeland, he returned to Hong Kong in 1853. His active involvement in education there earned him a position as Inspector of Chinese Schools with the Hong Kong Government from 1855 to 1859, during which time he joined Gutzlaff in the establishment of the Chinese Evangelization Society.
[86] See Extract of Letters from J.G. Austin (Hong Kong) to Mr Walcott (Trinidad) dated 13 December 1861, CO 318/236/559-560, as quoted by Helen and Philip Atteck, *Stress of Weather*, 2000, p. 70.
[87] Jardine Matheson Archive JM 7/15 6986, as quoted by Helen and Philip Atteck, *Stress of Weather*, 2000, p. 71.
[88] See Extract of Letters from J.G Austin (Hong Kong) to Rev. Mr Lobscheid (Hong Kong) 19 December 1861. CO 318/236/560a-561, as quoted by Helen and Philip Atteck, *Stress of Weather*, 2000, p. 70.
[89] Sir Cecil Clementi, *The Chinese in British Guyana, op. cit.*, p. 95.
[90] The full text of the Kung Convention is transcribed in Walton Look Lai, *The Chinese in the West Indies 1806-1995*, 1998, p. 194.
[91] Captain Henry George Thomsett (1825-1892) was the Master Commanding of the station ship HMS *Princess Charlotte* and was appointed temporary Harbour Master in 1861, and made the permanent officer in April 1864. Permanent he was, as he occupied the position until the end of 1873 when he retired to join the Hong Kong and Shanghai Bank, and being appointed to the Legislative Council in 1884.
[92] In *The Chinese in the West Indies 1806-1995*, 1998, Walton Look Lai lists 286 as having landed, including 120 women and 17 children. Ankum-Houwink agrees with him that 485 had embarked, but differs in claiming 197 (rather than 199) had died. Ankum-Houwink's calculation of the voyage time of 115 days does not match the departure date recorded by the Harbour Master in Hong Kong, nor the arrival date as stated by Walton Look Lai.
[93] The *Daily Press*, 6 November 1867.

[94] See The *Daily Press*, 30 November 1868.
[95] Sir Cecil Clementi, *The Chinese in British Guiana*, op. cit., p. 79.
[96] T. Thornton Warner, *Report on Chinese Emigration*, Calcutta: printed at the "Englishman" Press, 1868. Enclosure in 'Emigration Abuses at Hong Kong', Despatch from Emigration Board to Sir F. Rogers, Under-secretary of State for the Colonies, dated 19 September 1868. (CO129/134, pp. 684-719, pp. 695ff., HKU Microform 2507143.) Many thanks to the University of Hong Kong Library for providing advice during the editing process.
[97] 30th General Report of the Emigration Commissioners, p. 31.
[98] Walton Look Lai shows that in 1884 the *Diamond/Prince Alexander* (*sic* for 'Prinz Alexander") loaded at Macao and Hong Kong for Jamaica. (Table 1: 'List of vessels travelling to the British, French and Dutch West Indies from China between 1853 and 1884', *The Chinese in the West Indies 1806-1995*, 1998, p. 278.) However, the Hong Kong Harbour Master's Returns for the period do not include the *Diamond*. There were no reports of any ship named *Diamond* in Chinese waters at that time, and no news of any ships being dismasted. It would also be unlikely that emigrants would be leaving from Macao at that time rather than from Hong Kong.
[99] Watt Stewart, *Chinese Bondage in Peru*, 1951, p. 23.
[100] See *O Boletim*, 12 February 1859.
[101] The Californian *Daily Alta*, 12 December 1859 and 25 December 1859.
[102] See Appendix II.
[103] See Appendix II.
[104] See Appendix II.
[105] See Appendix II.
[106] See Appendix II.
[107] The *Hong Kong Register*, 24 October 1860.
[108] "The cabin" on a sailing ship usually referred to the accommodation at the after end of the upper deck. It housed the Captain who had his own cabin at the stern, usually lavishly furnished. On smaller ships the officers shared a cabin on one side, and passengers usually in one or two (not many) on the other side around a central area where the passengers ate and could relax.
[109] *West Coast Times*, 4 July 1866.
[110] The *Japan Times' Overland Mail*, 5 September 1868.
[111] See *Pacific Commercial Advertiser*, 10 September 1869.
[112] The *Polynesian*, 12 October 1861.
[113] In 1865 the British Government objected to Juan Pastor Sevilla being nominated as Peruvian Consul-General in Hong Kong. See, 'Unfitness of Don Juan Pastor Sevilla ...', 18 November 1865. (CO 129/107 pp. 337-341.)
[114] BPP 1871 (C403), p. 2.
[115] BPP 1871 (C403), p. 7.
[116] HR Exec. Doc. 16, 37th Congress 2nd Session.
[117] No first name for this gentleman has been found.
[118] Consuelo Naranjo Orovio and Imilcy Balboa Navarro. 'Colonos asiáticos para una economía en expansión, Cuba: 1847-1880.' ['Asian Labourers for an Expanding Economy: Cuba 1847-1880.'] In *Revista Mexicana del Caribe*, No. 8 (1999), pp. 32-65, p. 58.
[119] *London and China Telegraph*, 27 July 1869.

[120] José Luis Luzón, 'El Mar en el tráfico Chinero. Naufragios y amotinamientos,' In *Conquista y Resistencia en la Historia de America*, edited by Pilar Gracía Jordán (Spain: Universitat Barcelona), 1992, pp. 247-272.
[121] *China Mail*, 7 January 1868.
[122] Mary Turner, 'Chinese Contract Labour in Cuba, 1847-1874,' *Caribbean Studies*, Vol. 14, No. 2 (July 1974), pp. 66-81, p. 75.
[123] British consuls in China no longer reported to Hong Kong, but to the British representative in Beijing.
[124] My understanding is that it was local (Chinese) brokers who did this work. These brokers would have an "understanding" with the foreign Emigration Agents, whereby they would send out their crimps on an order from the foreigner. The brokers took the gamble on whether to recruit, regardless of orders or wait for an order. If a broker waited too long to fulfil an order he could find that other brokers had taken his place. European Emigration Agents did not have to take any risks. They had ample notice of requirements from Cuba and Peru. It was only a matter of availability of shipping for them, and then bribing the Portuguese officials to have their ships given priority.
[125] Vice-consul Mayers to Sir R. Alcock, dated Canton, 1 November 1866. Enclosure No. I in Despatch No. 44. FO 881-1738.
[126] Enclosure No. 4 in Despatch No. 144. FO 881-1738.
[127] Don Aldus, *Coolie traffic and Kidnapping*. London: McCorquodale and Co., 1876, p. 41.
[128] *O Boletim*, 23 September 1867.
[129] No details of the circumstances for this shooting are known.
[130] *Daily Alta*, 21 August 1867.
[131] S.L. Tikhvinskii, (General Editor). Translated from Russian by Vic. Schneierson. *Chapters from the History of Russo-Chinese relations, 17th-19th centuries*. Moscow: Progress Publishers, 1985, p. 266.
[132] Mary Turner, 'Chinese Contract Labour in Cuba, 1847-1874,' p. 75.
[133] *New Batavia Handelsblad*, 8 May 1872, as reprinted by the *Straits Times*, 23 May 1872 and *Hong Kong Daily Press*, 31 May 1872.
[134] *Graces Guide to British Industrial History*, 1932. 'A Shipbuilding History, 1750-1932 (Alexander Stephen & Sons).' www.Gracesguide.co.uk.
[135] Peter Wesley-Smith, 'Kwok A-Sing, Sir John Smale, and the Macao Coolie Trade,' in Shane Nozzal (ed). *Law Lectures for Practitioners*. Hong Kong Law Journal Ltd., Vol. 1993 (1993), p. 124.
[136] Elizabeth Sinn, *Pacific Crossing: California Gold, Chinese Migration, and the Making of Hong Kong* (Hong Kong: Hong Kong University Press), 2013, p. 87.
[137] Not the same as the formerly Brtish-flagged *Emigrant*, later *Emigrante*, referred to above.
[138] Lucy M. Cohen,'Immigration of Chinese from Macao to Costa Rica 1872-1873,' *Revista de Ciebcias Sociales*, Vol. 119 (1), 2008, pp. 39-53, p. 41.
[139] See Appendix II.
[140] C. A. Montalto de Jesus, *Historic* Macao, Hong Kong: Kelly & Walsh, 1902, p. 333.
[141] Imperial Maritime Customs Press, 1876. Reprint ed. Taipei: Ch'eng Wen Publishing, 1970.

[142] The rebellion referred to was the Cuban rebellion. Many Chinese supported the rebellion and this was one factor in closing down the Chinese coolie trade to Cuba.
[143] Yen Ching-Hwang, *Coolies and Mandarins: China's protection of overseas Chinese during the late Ch'ing period (1851-1911)*. Singapore: Singapore University Press, 1985, p. 121.
[144] BPP 1873 (C829), p. 1.
[145] BPP 1873 (C829), p. 19.
[146] BPP 1873 (C908), p. 11.
[147] Yen Ching-Hwang, *Coolies and Mandarins*, 1985, pp. 133-4.
[148] Eugenio Chang-Rodriguez, 'Chinese Labor Migration into Latin America in the Nineteenth Century.' *Revista de Historia de America*, No. 46, December 1958, p. 391.
[149] BPP 1857-58 (491), p. 71.
[150] BPP 1875 (C1212), p. 8.
[151] My reading of it is that Portugal wanted to enter into an agreement with China over the question of emigration through the port of Macao. Purely as a gateway. Macao was a convenient scapegoat for recruitment atrocities which China took no measures to stop themselves. The focus was on Macao, not China and the Chinese authorities were quite happy with that. I think it was C.A. Montalto de Jesus who recounts that the Portuguese sent returnees back across the border to the authorities each week, only to have them sold back to the crimps for "recycling".
[152] The reason why this table title refers to, "Indentured coolie shipments", whereas the tables relating to other ports simply refer to "Shipments" is because Hong Kong was the only port from which both indentured and free labour were shipped and it is important to indicate which is referred to in this table.
[153] The second largest was on the *Norway*, with 1,038; next, the *Fatchoy* with 1,005, and then the *Francois I* with 1,000.
[154] *Boletin de Colonizacion* Ano 1 Num 20 15 Nov 1873.
[155] www.cubagenweb.org/ships/chinese.htm.
[156] Peruvians seem to have frequently used the term, "colonos", even though the "colonos" were expected to leave when their term expired.
[157] *South China Morning Post* 13 January 1904
[158] Emigration Commission. Twenty-ninth general report of the Emigration Commissioners. p. 90.
[159] Emigration Commission. Twenty-ninth general report of the Emigration Commissioners. p. 20.
[160] Emigration Commission. Thirty-third general report of the Emigration Commissioners. Appendix 16, p. 77.
[161] Emigration Commission. Twenty-ninth general report of the Emigration Commissioners, p. 22.
[162] Emigration Commission. Thirty-first general report of the Emigration Commissioners, p. 10.
[163] Emigration Commission. Thirty-third general report of the Emigration Commissioners. Appendix 16, p. 77.

[164] Emigration Commission. Thirty-second general report of the Emigration Commissioners, p. 11.
[165] Emigration Commission. Thirty-third general report of the Emigration Commissioners, p. 22.
[166] Walton Look Lai, *The Chinese in the West Indies 1806-1995*, 1998.
[167] Walton Look Lai, 1998, p. 283.
[168] Some of the flags were of entities that were later absorbed into others and the number "twenty" refers to the number of present-day countries involved. For example, Oldenburg and Sardinia were later absorbed into Germany and Italy respectively and are not counted separately.
[169] John McDonald, and Ralph Shlomowitz. 'Mortality on Chinese and Indian Voyages to the West Indies and South America, 1847-1874.' *Social and Economic Studies*, Vol. 41, No. 2 (June 1992), pp. 203-240, p. 204. These statisticians conducted a quantitative analysis on the mortality on Chinese and Indian coolie voyages.
[170] Sir Cecil Clementi, *The Chinese in British Guiana*, op. cit., p. 128.
[171] John McDonald, and Ralph Shlomowitz. 'Mortality on Chinese and Indian Voyages', *Social and Economic Studies*, Vol. 41, No. 2 (June 1992), pp. 203-240, p. 219.
[172] This illustration from *Harper's New Monthly Magazine*, v. 29 (June-Nov 1864, pp. 1-10) relates to the following text from 'A chapter on the Coolie Trade' by Edgar Holden, telling the story of a mutiny that took place on the American ship, *Norway*, which sailed for Cuba from Macao in the late 1850s: "The coolies mounted the side one after the other, most of them naked to the waist, wearing only the loose coolie trousers, and broad-brimmed straw hat. Slung at the belt were a pouch and purse and a little case for the chop-sticks. A few were in good humour but most were sullen and desponding. They were tallied over the gangway like so many bales of cotton..." (p. 4).
[173] Reproduced, courtesy of the Penobscot Marine Museum.
[174] *China Mail*, 19 April 1866.
[175] *China Mail*, 19 April 1866.
[176] *China Mail*, 19 April 1866.
[177] *China Mail*, 19 April 1866.
[178] *China Mail*, 19 April 1866.
[179] *China Mail*, 19 April 1866.
[180] *China Mail*, 19 April 1866.
[181] *China Mail*, 19 April 1866.
[182] *China Mail*, 4 September 1868.
[183] Author's translation from the Portuguese version as found in, *Boletim da Provincia de Macau e Timor*, 1 June 1872.
[184] Source mislaid. This 1874 Regulation is a good summary of previous regulations.
[185] J.B.H. Martinet, *L'agriculture au Pérou, Résumé du mémoire présenté au Congrés International de l'agriculture* (Paris: Au Siège de la Société, 1878), as quoted by Michael J. Gonzales, 'Chinese Plantation Workers and Social Conflict in Peru,' *Journal of Latin American Studies*, Vol. 21, No. 3 (October 1989), pp. 385-424.

INDEX

A. P. Christina, 337
Abella, Francisco, Emigration Agent, 171, 275, 278, 293
Abissinian, 266
Achenbach, CaptainA.P., 152
Adamastor, 116
Admiraal Van Heemskerk, 147
Admiral, 133
Admiral Baudin, 193
Agra, 200
Agustina, 227, 311
Alavesa, 117, 342
Albert, 52, 53, 64, 322, 346
Albertine, 216
Alberto, 216
Alcantara, Captain E., 278
Alcock, Rutherford: British Consul, Canton, 174; British Minister Plenipotentiary, 263, 265
Aldama, Domingo, Cuban planter, 256
Alexander Stephen & Sons, British shipbuilders, 277
Alexandre Delphine, 162
Alexandre Lavalley, 276
Alexandre Ralli, 160
Alfonso d'Albuquerque, 258
Alianza (brig), 134
Alice Thorndike, 148
Allied Commissioners, 174, 176, 179, 190, 191, 222
Almeida, Captain F.D.P., 259
Almeida, Januario Correia de, Governor of Macao, 300, 310, 311
Alson, Macao Emigration Agent, 71
Altagracia, 167, 168, 276, 282
Amadeo, King of Spain, 273
Amalia (Italian), 229
Amalia (Peruvian), 71
Amaral, Jose do, Governor of Macao, 225
Amazon, 56
Amboto, 276
Ambrogue, Captain, 231
America, (ship), 247, 264, 345
Amiral Trehouart, 254
Ammerland, 162
Amoy, 31, 32, 33, 35, 36, 37, 38, 39, 40, 41, 42, 43, 44, 45, 46, 48, 51, 57, 62, 63, 64, 65, 70, 75, 79, 80, 85, 86, 88, 89, 90, 91, 92, 93, 94, 95, 96, 97, 98, 102, 103, 109, 110, 111, 113,
114, 115, 117, 118, 120, 125, 133, 134, 146, 149, 152, 158, 162, 174, 178, 185, 204, 205, 207, 208, 209, 217, 222, 253, 255, 258, 305, 320, 321, 326, 347, 353, 355
Anais, 137
Anduizas, 276
Ango, 251
Ansuatique, Captain L., 277
Antares, 261, 298
Anthon, Henry, American Vice-Consul, Jakarta, 139, 161
Antigua, 22, 219, 257, 339
Antonia Petronella, 216
Antonia Terry, 76
Aramburn, Emigration Agent, 241
Araucoa, Captain Antonio de, 151, 179, 222, 237, 238, 244, 350
Architect, 117
Argo, 242
Arieta, Ignacio de, Cuban planter, 40
Arima, 207
Arizona, 167, 254
Armero, Nicolas Tanco, Emigration Agent, 120, 158, 170, 171, 275, 300
Arrow, 173
Arue, Captain Nissour, 221
Asia, 230, 248
Astorquia, Captain Antonio, 230, 281, 282, 345, 350
Aubril, Captain Auguste, 163
Aucan, Captain Alexandre, 280
Augustin, Cuban importer, 254
Aurora, 243, 249
Austin, J Gardiner:Colonial Secretary, 217; Emigration Agent, 187, 188, 189, 195, 197, 198, 199, 200, 201, 202, 204, 205, 206, 207, 217, 224; Government Secretary, British Guiana, 82
Australia, 69, 95, 124
Avon, 257, 270, 271
Ayala, Lopez de, Spanish Minister of the Colonies, 273

B

Baak, Emigration Agent, 214
Bacalan, 228
Backhouse, George, British Commissary Judge Cuba, 115
Backhouse: John:British Acting Consul, Amoy: 91, 93, 114, 115

455

Bailey, D.H., American Consul, Hong Kong, 288
Bakker, Captain, 123
Bald Eagle, 75
Balligui, Captain M., 276
Banca, 136
Bangkok, 255, 266
Barkly, Henry: Governor of British Guiana, 79, 80, 82, 95, 101; Governor of Jamaica, 106, 107
Barone Kellner, 157
Basseterre, Captain J. Luis, 227
Bate, Captain, 219
Baud, Dutch merchant, 280
Bauran, Emigration Agent, 161
Bazin & Léon Gay, French shipowners, 153, 160
Beatrice, 68
Beazley, Captain Thomas, 60, 61, 62
Beckwith, Captain N.W., 269
Bell, Captain John, 158
Bella Gallega, 117, 256
Bella Vascongada, 106, 116
Bellona, 133
Benavides, Captain E., 117
Bengale, 167
Bengali, 282
Bernice, 284
Berry, Captain J.C., 178
Bianchi y Profumo, Peruvian importer, 242
Bidau, R., Emigration Agent, 180, 181, 195
Bilbaina, 168, 170, 261
Bilton, Captain George, 96
Blair, Dr Daniel, British Guiana, 88
Blanchard, American Vice Consul, Canton, 180
Blanche, Captain Charles la, 259
Blenheim, 110
Bluck, Captain, 180
Bogue, Adam, Australian merchant, 41
Bois-Agett, Richard di, Chief Mate, 92
Boju, Captain E., 267, 274
Boletin de Colonizacion, 110, 120, 152
Bollo, Captain A., 247
Bollo, Captain Joao B., 229, 241, 352
Bollo, Captain Sebastian, 233, 241, 242

Bonham, Sir George, Governor of Hong Kong, 41, 42, 79, 80
Borainca, Captain Domingos, 164
Borel, Foochow Sub-Agent, 152
Borneo, Dutch warship, 268
Botelho, Captain F., 240
Bowen y Yngram, Emigration Agents, 269
Bowring, John: Acting Superintendent of Trade, 83, 85, 91, 93, 101, 102; British Consul, Canton, 56, 62, 73, 74, 80, 81; Governor of Hong Kong, 89, 91, 104, 122, 126, 132, 152, 154, 173, 185, 186
Boye, L, Emigration Agent, 155, 169
Brave Lourmel, 154
Brechin Castle, 206
Bristow, Captain Frank, 40
British Sovereign, 109
Broadbent, Captain, 133
Brown, Captain T., 60
Brown, H.O., Acting Commissioner, Imperial Maritime Customs, 310
Bryson, Captain Leslie, 62
Bucton Castle, 207
Buenaventura (steamer), 277
Buis, Captain F., 125
Burrill, Charles, American merchant, 254
Bustamente, Antonio G., 166, 167
Butts, R.G., British Guiana merchant, 88
Byrne, D.J.L., Peruvian importer, 226

C

Cadet, 42, 43
Cailes, 278
Caillet, Captain, 37
Calderon, B., Emigration Agent, 169, 260
Calderon, Captain B., 248
Caldwell, Daniel, Superintendent of Police, Hong Kong, 99, 100
Callao, 48, 49, 50, 51, 53, 54, 57, 60, 61, 62, 64, 65, 67, 68, 70, 71, 72, 75, 76, 77, 78, 85, 164, 170, 179, 218, 221, 222, 226, 227, 228, 229, 230, 232, 233, 234, 235, 236, 237, 238, 239, 240, 241, 242, 243, 244, 245, 246, 247, 248, 249, 251, 255, 259, 270, 271, 280, 281, 283, 284, 287, 288, 298, 299, 300, 302, 311,

448   Coolie Ships of the Chinese Diaspora

312, 322, 326, 333, 334, 335, 336, 337, 342, 343, 344, 345, 348, 350, 351, 352
Callao (ship), 237, 249, 313, 343
Camillo Cavour, 230, 234, 249, 281, 311, 337, 345, 350, 351
Camino y Cia, 169, 191, 239
Camoes, 258, 261, 271
Campbell, Captain John, 111, 112, 113
Campbell, Cuban planter, 152, 153, 154, 254, 332
Campbell, Robert, Chief Mate, 113
Candamo, Peruvian importer, 284
Canet & Gavalena, Cuban merchants, 253
Canevaro, Peruvian importer, 169, 170, 232, 240, 243, 245
Cano, Munoz del, Spanish Consul Macao, 170, 171
Canton, 35, 38, 47, 48, 49, 52, 55, 56, 62, 65, 71, 73, 80, 83, 84, 86, 89, 97, 148, 156, 157, 163, 173, 174, 176, 177, 178, 179, 180, 181, 182, 185, 188, 189, 190, 191, 195, 196, 197, 198, 199, 200, 204, 205, 206, 207, 217, 218, 222, 223, 224, 253, 258, 263, 271, 285, 286, 305, 308, 310, 311, 317, 323, 338, 340, 341, 349, 431
Capello, Captain Domenico, 301
Caravagno, Captain Stefano, 230, 281
Carbaga, Jose, Cuban merchants, 253
Cardona, Captain, 124
Cardonnet, Captain M., 158
Carignac, Captain J., 137
Carlowitz, Richard von, Spanish Consul, Canton, 181
Carlton, Captain G.H., 118
Carmeline, 261
Carmen, 67
Carmencita, 166
Caro, Charles, Cuban trader, 152, 153, 156, 157, 158, 162, 163, 169, 261
Caroline, 163
Carpentaria, 117
Carrington, 258
Cass, Captain John, 57
Cass, Lewis, American Secretary of State, 253
Cassiterides, 70

Castaynhola, Captain J.B., 247
Castilla, Ramon, President of Peru, 74, 225
Castillo, Captain, 162
Castro, Henrique, Secretary-General, Macao, 289, 300
Castro, Ignacio F., de, Emigration Agent, 115, 119, 166, 167, 168, 169, 191, 227, 240, 254
Catalina, 60
Cataluna, 260, 275, 332, 343
Catherine Glen, 133
Cavassa, Captain D.A., 246
Cayalti, 234, 236, 249
Cecilia, 342
Cercal, Barao, Italian Consul Macao, 236, 300
Cervantes, 158
Chabert, E., Emigration Agent, 161
Chaldecott, Dr J.A, 196
Challenge, 122, 229
Challenger, 229
Chansel, Captain M., 298
Chapman, Dr Clarence, 204
Chappot, Captain E., 255
Charles Albert, 293
Charles Auguste, 217
Charles Martell, 153, 154
Chen Lanpin, Commissioner, Chinese Educational Commission, 304, 314
Chesnez, Martineau de, French Army, 174
Childs, Dr A.P., 141, 142
Chile, 71
Chili, 53, 62
China, 275
Chinchas, 50, 57, 60, 62, 72, 73, 74, 335
Chinese Law, 49, 72, 77, 221, 225, 226, 238, 333
Claire, 240, 342
Clara, 219
Clarence, 341
Clarendon, 96
Clarendon, Earl of, British Foreign Minister, 73, 74, 131, 132, 248, 249
Cleopatra, 158
Cleverly, British Consular Agent, Macao, 142, 143
Closmadeau, Captain H., 153; Emigration Agent, 154, 155, 169
Clothilde (barque), 242

Codina, John C., Peruvian shipowner, 234, 235
Coeur de Lion, 123
Colombia, 311
Colome, Juan A., Cuban planter, 124, 151
Colonial Land and Emigration Commission, 34, 82, 102, 132, 355
Colonizadora, Cuban consortium, 151, 166, 256
Columbia, 310
Columbus, 114
Compania Maritima del Peru, 255, 289, 336
Compania Maritima del Peru 1, 244
Compania Maritima del Peru 2, 230, 244, 245, 255
Competitor, 159
Compodonico, Captain Felipe, 238
Comstock, Samuel W., 105
Comus, HMS, 76
Concepcion, 119, 275
Concha, Jose, Capitan-General, Cuba, 151
Condray, Captain L. de, 266
Conil, Captain, 153
Connolly, John, Amoy merchant, 92
Conroy, Thomas, Peruvian shipowner, 238
Cooper, Captain, 258
Cora, 71, 133
Corich, Captain J.M., 157
Cornabe, William, Amoy merchant, 90, 92, 93
Coromandel, 60
Corona, 218
Corsair (brig), 56
Cortina, Captain, 151
Corvo, Joao de, 316
Cote d'Or, 163
Cotte, Captain P., 254
Courbe, Captain L., 262
Crawford, Captain, 123
Crawford, Jos T: British Commissary Judge Cuba, 165; British Consul-General, Havana, 132, 153
Crawfurd, John, British Consultant, 34, 35, 36, 83
Cruikshank, Captain D., 158
Cuba, 20, 21, 22, 39, 89, 109, 110, 115, 118, 119, 120, 121, 124, 138, 144, 148, 149, 150, 151, 161, 164, 165, 166, 167, 168, 169, 170, 174, 178, 190, 191, 193, 217, 218, 224, 228, 253, 254, 256, 257, 262, 263, 265, 266, 270, 271, 273, 275, 276, 278, 280, 300, 302, 303, 304, 305, 306, 307, 311, 314, 320, 321, 324, 326, 328, 330, 331, 332, 333, 340, 342, 351, 352, 374
Cumsingmoon, 48, 49, 50, 51, 52, 53, 54, 60, 61, 62, 64, 68, 71, 83, 134, 322, 326, 347, 348
Cunha, A.F. da, Port Captain, Macao, 221
Curtis, Thomas, American shipowner, 65, 67, 237
Cutler, Captain A.S, 219
Cyclone, 270

D

d'Abouville, M., 173
d'Assas, French warship, 280
Dabry, M., French Consul, Canton, 285
Daguerre, 154
Dalmatia, 70
Dartmouth, 219
David, Captain A., 154
David, Captain G., 162
Davis, Sir John, Governor of Hong Kong, 40
de Haai, Dutch warship, 123
de Surinaamsche Immigratie-Maatschappij, 211, 215
Dea del Mare, 229, 231
Delfshaven, 75
Dent & Co., Hong Kong, 80
Diago, Pedro, Cuban planter, 40
Diana, 159
Diario de la Marina, 110, 162
Dias, Captain E., 335
Dick, Captain David, 200
Dobaran, Captain M., 118
Doggersbank, 152
Dolores Ugarte, 230, 236, 249, 262, 287, 288, 289, 342
Dom Pedro II, 245
Don Fernando, 258
Don Jose, 228
Don Juan, 289, 290, 296
Don Julian, 151, 167
Donna Maria de Gloria, 257, 261
Donna Maria Pia, 240, 241, 251, 256, 344, 351
Doty, Rev. Elihu, 89, 119
Drain, F.D, Cuban importer, 269
Drake y Cia, Cuban importer, 158

458

Dream, 154
Duble, Captain Francisco, 76
Dubois, Captain F., 157, 351
Ducit, Captain, 256
Duck, James A., British shipowner, 271
Dudbrook, 208
Duke of Argyll, 40
Duke of Portland, 129
Duke of Roxburgh, 43
Dunlop, Graham, British Consul, Havana, 293
Dupierris, Marcial, Cuban planter, 151, 254
Durand, Emigration Agent, 59
E
Earl of Eglinton, 134
Earl of Windsor, 200, 201
Eastfield, 216
Echevarria, Captain Juan B., 222, 227, 277
Eckert, Captain R, 219
Edwin Fox, 121, 146
Ehlers, Paul & Co., Hong Kong merchants, 293, 295, 296
Elder, Captain James, 99
Elias, Domingo, Peruvian planter, 48, 49, 51, 52, 53, 59, 60, 61, 64, 68, 72, 73, 242, 335
Elias, Jesus, son of Domingo, 51, 53
Elias, John, son of Domingo, 53
Eliza, 60, 69, 240
Eliza Morrison, 60
Elizabeth Jane, 42
Ellen Oliver, 145
Elliot, Charles, Governor of Trinidad, 184
Elmslie, Adam W., British Consul Canton, 83
Elorrieta, Captain Pio de, 312
Elvina Dovale, 338
Ely, Dr Edward, 94, 95,155
Emigrant (barque), 92
Emigrant (ship), 98
Emigrante (753 tons) 116, 167, 254
Emigrante (962 tons), 298, 311
Emile Pereire, 154
Emma, 43
Emmanuel, 266
Empresa, 51, 222, 240
Encarnacion, 168, 231, 254, 345
Epsom, 103
Ernani, 71
Escajadillo, Captain V., 260

Espantoso, A., Emigration Agent, 284
Esperance, 267, 274
Espinasse, Captain, 41
Etoile, 152
Eugene et Adele, 267
Eva, 245
Evans, Captain E., 261
Evans, Captain H., 208
Everett, Edward, American Secretary of State, 97
F
Falcon, 270
Falconer, Jamaican doctor, 107
Fanny Fern, 258
Fanny Kirchner, 180
Fatchoy, 278, 293, 294, 295, 296, 346
Felix, 125
Ferdinand Brumm, 215
Fernandes, B.S., Peruvian Charge d'Affairs, 289
Fernandez, 137, 160
Ferran, Antonio, Emigration Agent, 124, 125, 129, 134, 138, 145, 146, 147, 149, 151, 169, 190, 254
Ferras, Captain J., 160
Figari and sons, 337
Fishbourne, Commander, RN, 91
Flavin, Captain, 75
Flora Temple, 140
Flore, 164, 228
Florence Nightingale, 221
Florencia, 247, 312
Florida, 117
Flotard, Carlo, Emigration Agents, 152
Flying Childers, 139
Forest Eagle, 154
Formose, 161
Forth, Frederick, Hong Kong Acting Colonial Secretary, 186
Fourrau, Captain de, 239
Francis A. Palmer, 271
Francis P Sage, 148
Francisco, 71
Francisco Calderon, 311, 312
Francois 1, 153, 154, 168, 169
Franklyn, Captain, 65
Fray Bentos, 247, 311
Frederic, 279, 280, 284, 325, 348
Frederick Wilhelm, 49
Freeman, Alfred, American Acting Consul Shanghai, 118

French Maritime Agency, 156, 163, 191
French, Acting Captain, *Waverly*, 52, 65, 66, 67
Freya, 146
Fulle, Captain Angelo, 244
Fulton, 194
G
Galdiz y Nenninger, Cuban importers, 162
Galdiz, Captain J. de, 162
Galilee, 194
Galileo, 230, 245
Gallet, Captain C., 261
Gandia, Captain, 231
Ganges, 206, 341
Garay, Captain D. Cecilio, 288
Garcia y Garcia, Captain Guillermo, 312
Garcia y Garcia, Captain Manuel A., Peruvian Special Envoy, 313
Garcia y Garcia, Captain Narciciso, 243
Garcia, Filomena M. de, Portuguese shipowner, 258
Garcia, Joao, Emigration Agent, 167
Garcia, Virana, Emigration Agent, 167, 254
Gardoqui, Captain J.A., 167
Garibaldi, Guiseppe, Italian patriot, 48
Gastel, Malavois, & Assier, French merchants, 193
Gaulois, 157
*Gazelle (*brig*)*, 43
Gazelle (ship), 71
General Prim, 226, 227
General Wyndham, 186, 187
Genghis Khan, 206
Gerard, Thomas, Emigration Agent, 185
Gertrude, 111, 194
Geycour, Captain, 76
Giacomo, Captain Ansaido, 229
Giraud, Captain J., 267
Gironde French warship, 141
Giscours, 147
Glendarroch, 277
Glenlee, 271
Glensannox, 277, 310
Glentanner, 89
Golden Eagle, 117
Golden Horn, 212

Gon Netscher, Adriian van der, British Guiana merchant, 88
Gonzales, Captain B., 48
Gorman, Captain, 67, 335
Goss, Captain Fred A., 239
Governor Morton, 148, 178
Grace Brothers, American steamship company, 315
Granville, Earl, British Foreign Secretary, 293
Gravina, 162
Grey, Earl, British Colonial Secretary, 79, 82, 106, 107, 184
Greyhound, 144
Grimaneza, 68, 69
Guadaloupe, 194, 328
Guadaloupe (ship), 166, 167, 168, 254
Guardia, Tomas, President of Costa Rica, 300
Guillon, Emigration Agent, 59
Guiraud, Captain A., 267
Guiseppe Rocca, 221
Gulnare, 121
Guterres, Captain, 116
Gwynne, Dr Thomas, 146
H
Haas, Captain, 71
Hacendados, Cuban importer, 275, 276, 278, 302
Haldane, Captain Augustus M., 283
Hale, Frederick, British Vice Consul, Foochow, 147, 152
Hamen, Captain, 242
Hamilton, Captain James A., 235
Hamilton-Gordon, Governor of Trinidad, 217
Hankow, 283
Harland, Captain, 60
Harris, Governor of Trinidad, 95, 96
Harry Brigham, 243
Hartwell, Hawaiian Judge, 301
Harvey, Frederick, Secretary to Superintendency of Trade, 91
Hasselhoff, Captain, 116
Havana, 40, 79, 109, 110, 111, 113, 114, 115, 116, 117, 118, 119, 120, 121, 122, 123, 124, 125, 127, 128, 130, 131, 132, 134, 135, 136, 137, 139, 140, 142, 143, 144, 145, 146, 147, 148, 149, 151, 152, 153, 154, 155, 157, 158, 159, 160, 161, 162, 163, 164, 165, 166, 167, 169, 170, 171, 178, 180, 231, 232, 241, 243,

246, 247, 249, 254, 255, 256, 258, 259, 260, 261, 262, 263, 266, 267, 268, 269, 270, 271, 273, 274, 276, 278, 279, 282, 293, 295, 302, 305, 306, 311, 312, 326, 329, 330, 332, 337, 342, 343, 344, 345, 348, 350, 351, 429
Heaton, G.H, Hong Kong Surveyor, 186
Helguero, Hong Kong merchant, 239
Henley, Captain, 221
Henri IV, 230
Henrietta Maria, 123
Henry Miller, 120
Henry, Captain John, 203
Hermes HMS, 91
Herrera, Captain R., 299
Heu, Captain Achilles, 293
Heyden, Captain F. van der, 277
Heymans, Captain, 136
Hill, Captain George, 243
Holloway Colonel, British Army, 174
Holmes, Coolie Master, 148
Holmes,, Captain E.W., 222
Homachea, Captain D. de, 276
Hong Kong, 16, 40, 41, 42, 47, 49, 51, 52, 53, 55, 56, 57, 59, 60, 61, 70, 73, 75, 76, 79, 80, 82, 83, 86, 89, 92, 96, 98, 101, 102, 103, 104, 105, 107, 114, 120, 121, 124, 125, 126, 127, 129, 130, 131, 132, 133, 135, 138, 145, 146, 148, 152, 154, 160, 163, 168, 170, 173, 178, 180, 182, 186, 188, 191, 195, 196, 197, 198, 199, 200, 202, 204, 206, 207, 208, 211, 212, 213, 214, 215, 216, 217, 218, 219, 230, 231, 232, 239, 240, 244, 245, 246, 248, 249, 258, 259, 260, 261, 269, 270, 271, 278, 279, 280, 281, 282, 285, 286, 287, 288, 289, 291, 292, 293, 296, 300, 301, 302, 309, 310, 312, 316, 317, 318, 324, 328, 337, 338, 340, 347, 348
Hong Kong (opium ship), 185
Hong Kong (ship), 345, 351
Honolulu, 56, 57, 58, 62, 216, 221, 230, 236, 238, 242, 244, 246, 251, 288, 301, 335
Hope, 121
Horta, Joao do, Governor of Macao, 271
Hound, 116

Hubbe, Otto, Costa Rican Agent, 300, 301
Huber, Commissioner of Customs, Tientsin, 304
Hubertson, Captain George F., 56
Hughes, Captain R., 197
Hunter, Captain, 70
Hurst, Captain John, 94
Hussey, Captain Samuel B., 75, 161
Hyde, Hodge & Co., British shipowners, 82, 88, 89

I

Ibanez, Francisco, Cuban importer, 275, 277, 278, 293
Inchiman, 114
Independence, 148, 258
Independencia, 313
Indiaman, 72, 75
Indien, 194
Ingersoll, Captain Thos R., 148
Inglis, Andrew L., Emigration Officer, 186
Ingram, Captain, 215
Iron Duke HMS, 299
Isabel, 312
Isabel Quintana, 61, 62
Italia, 170, 261, 274

J

J Wakefield, 148
J. Prats y Cia, Cuban importer, 278
Jackson, Captain John J., 138, 139
Jackson, Robert, Emigration Agent, 46, 89, 92
Jacques Sevrin, 293, 346
JAU, 261, 332
JCU, 72
Jeddo, 209, 347
Jefferson, Captain E.M., 76
Jenkins, Captain RN, 76
Jerningham, Wm Stafford, British Charge d'Affairs, Lima, 248
Jewett, James C., American merchant, 254
Johanna, 248
John Bright, 278
John Calvin, 127
Johnson, Captain Charles R., 140
Johnstone, Dr John M., 95
Jong, Captain W.P. de, 274
Jonquer, Captain W.J., 228
Jordan, Captain, 258
Jorge, Jose Vicente, Emigration Agent, 48, 115
Josefita y Almira, 266, 267

Joseph et Claire, 37, 38
Jourdain, 251
Juan, 278, 279, 289
Juanpore, 283
Jui-lin, Governor-General of Kwangtung and Kwangsi, 308, 310, 311
Julia G. Tyler, 258
Julian de Unzueta, 146
Juliao, 228
K
Kate Hooper, 137
Keate, Robert W., Governor of Trinidad, 203
Keene, Captain James, 143
Kellogg, Dr E.W., 314
Kennedy, Arthur, Governor of Hong Kong, 309
Kepler, 116
Kimberley, Earl, Colonial Secretary, 309
Kirsopp, Captain, 43
Kitty Simpson, 145, 148, 159, 181
Koens, Captain N., 151
Kwok A Sing, mutineer, 285
L
l'Avenir, 38
l'Olivier, 280, 284
La Alianza y Cia, Cuban importers, 169, 260, 261, 266, 267, 268, 270, 271, 274, 275, 276, 278
LaBelle, Captain, 194
Labouchere, Henry, British Colonial Secretary, 122, 126, 132, 154, 184
Lady Amherst, 113
Lady Elma Bruce, 205
Lady Flora Hastings, 98
Lady Montague, 49, 50, 51, 52, 53, 322, 354
LaFontaine, Captain, 164, 228
Lambayeque, 47
Lamsa, 67
Landa, Captain N., 167
Landabaso, Francisco de Captain, 230, 281, 345
Emigration Agent, 170
Landstein, William R., Hong Kong merchant, 269
Lang, Dr, 209
Laou, 175, 179, 182, 189
Larco, N., American ship broker, 243
Larkins, Captain J. Thomas, 41
Las Casas, Captain, 53

Lavagna, Captain, 221
Lavalley, Alexandre, French Engineer, 276
Lavarello, Captain Luiz, 236, 237, 244
Lavignac, Captain, 157
Layton, Temple, British Consul, Amoy, 40, 41, 42, 86, 125
Le Shaw, Captain, 51
Leal, Mendes, Portuguese Foreign Minister, 249
Lecoeur, Chief Mate, 268
Lee, Captain Richard, 266
Leonidas, 155, 156, 157
Leopold Cateaux, 167, 279
Leswick, 34
Leung Ashew, emigrant survivor, 291
Li Huang-chang, Viceroy, 313, 314
Light Brigade, 208
Light of the Age, 207
Liguria, 229, 231
Lin Hwan, broker, 90, 92
Linscott, Captain W.C., 243
Live Yankee, 147, 148
Livingston, Dr John, 99
Loa, 227, 231
Lobschied, Rev. William, 195, 199, 200, 201, 212, 213, 215, 216
Lola, 312, 342
Lombard, 332
Lombillo, Gabriel, Cuban planter, 170, 259, 260, 261, 262, 266, 332
Lomer & Co. Peru, 72, 75
London, 42
Lord Elgin, 86
Lothair, 338
Louis, 163
Louise, 67
Louisiana, 217
Lucie, 268
Luisa Canevaro, 162, 298, 312
Luisita, 258, 261
Lukey, Captain, 60, 70
Lyall, Still & Co. Hong Kong, 124, 138, 148, 178
M
M'Clelland, Captain, 86
M'Leod, Captain, 46
Macao, 38, 53, 59, 71, 72, 76, 83, 101, 115, 116, 119, 123, 127, 129, 134, 135, 136, 137, 138, 139, 140, 142, 143, 144, 147, 148, 149, 151, 152, 153, 154, 155, 156, 157, 158,

159, 160, 161, 162, 164, 166, 167,
168, 169, 170, 177, 178, 179, 180,
182, 183, 184, 185, 186, 187, 190,
191, 193, 211, 215, 217, 221, 222,
223, 224, 225, 227, 228, 229, 230,
231, 232, 233, 234, 235, 236, 237,
238, 240, 241, 242, 243, 244, 245,
246, 247, 248, 249, 253, 254, 255,
256, 257, 258, 259, 260, 261, 262,
263, 264, 265, 266, 267, 268, 269,
270, 271, 273, 274, 275, 278, 279,
280, 281, 282, 283, 284, 285, 286,
287, 288, 293, 294, 296, 297, 298,
299, 300, 301, 302, 303, 305, 307,
308, 309, 310, 311, 312, 313, 314,
315, 316, 317, 318, 326, 328, 330,
332, 333, 335, 336, 337, 338, 343,
347, 350, 352, *354*, 355
Macao fort, 156
Macao (ship), 249, 255, 311, 342
MacDonnell, Richard, Governor of Hong Kong, 212, 213, 217, 218
Mackay, Aeneas, Amoy merchant, 90, 110
Macpherson, Commissioner of Customs, Hankow, 304
Maggie Lauder, 241
Maggie Miller, 200, 262
Major, Captain Hugo B., 142
Malabar, 147
Malcolm, Captain J., 206
Malmesbury, Earl, Foreign Secretary, 83
Mandarina, 242
Manila (ship), 282
Manio, Captain J., 231
Manton, Captain Ben, 178
Manuelita, 53, 322
Maria Clotilde, 167, 227
Maria Luz, 299, 313, 333
Maria Morton, 262
Maria Natividad, 75, 221
Maria (brig), 228
Maria (ship), 276
Maria (barque), 240
Marie Laure, 229
Marie Therese, 214
Mariner, 60
Marion, 238, 240, 257
Maristoni, Captain J., 227
Marques, British Consular Agent, Macao, 267
Marques, Captain J.V., 258
Marshall, Captain Thomas, 46

Marshall, Humphry, American Commissioner, Canton, 97
Martin L. White, 77
Martin Luther, 117
Martinique, 193, 194, 328
Mary Frances, 216
Mary Whitridge, 159
Mauritius, 158
May Queen, 148
Mayers, William, British Interpreter, Canton, 180, 181
Mayers, William, British Vice Consul, Canton, 263, 265
McCaslin, Captain A.A., 261
McKellar, Captain Duncan, 31
Medina, 114
Meiggs, Keith, American railroad builder, 300
Menard, Captain, 228
Menchacatore, Matia, Spanish merchants, 39
Menser, C.R., Hong Kong merchant, 295
Menzies, 117
Mercer, William T., Hong Kong Colonial Secretary, 186
Merino Gilledo, Cuban importers, 254, 255
Messenger, 143, 148, 178, 180, 181, 182, 257
Miceno, 48
Mille Tonnes, 281
Minandes, Captain, 137
Minister Pahud, 211
Minister Van Staat Rochussen, 283
Mitchell & Co., Hong Kong, 92
Mitchell, E.R. Hong Kong Emigration Officer, 154
Mongol, 262
Monillot, Captain J., 230
Montalvo, Cuban importer, 259, 260
Montfort, Captain, 37
Montgomery, 178
Montrose, 206
Morales, Jose M., Cuban planter, 120, 123, 158, 159, 170, 180, 195, 331
Morayshire, 341
Moreley, Captain David, 227
Moro, Captain Rafael de, 232, 246, 350
Morrison, M.C., British Consul, Amoy, 158, 207
Morton, Captain J.H., 147

Mota, Captain Ramon, 247, 283, 350
Moulen, Captain Van der, 178
Muir, James D., Hong Kong merchant, 79
Mullens, Captain William L., 54
Murray, Sir Charles, British Ambassador, Lisbon, 249
Mysore, 255
Mystery, 199

N

Namoa, 46, 67, 68, 91, 95, 96, 98, 102, 103, 104, 105, 114, 320, 321
Naples, 271, 275
Napoleon, 221
Napoleon Canevaro, 232, 246, 350
Natoma, 222
Nattini, Captain Alberto, 234, 236
Nelly, 262, 266, 287
Nelusko, 277, 311, 330
Nepaul, 60
Neptuno, 222
Neva (1142 tons), 271, 274
Neva (1626 tons), 271, 275
New Orleans, 76, 217, 333, 351
Newcastle, Duke of, Colonial Secretary, 95, 107, 186, 203, 204
Nicaise, Captain A., 167, 279, 280, 284
Nichols, Doctor G.W., 98
Niemen, 269
Nimrod, 41
Nina, 259
Nolte, Captain G., 298
Nordberg, Captain C.V., 270
Norma, 146
Normann, Captain Johan, 146
Noronha, F.P., Emigration Agent, 170
North America, 245
Norway, 142
Nouveau Tropique, 37
Nouvelle Penelope, 256, 284, 285, 286, 287, 296
Nuevo Providencia, 312
Nunez, Captain Joao A., 258
Nunez, Captain, Ramon, 166
Nye, Gideon, American Vice Consul, Macao, 143

O

O'Lanyer, Louis, French shipowner, 161, 193
Ocean Telegraph, 208
Odin HMS, 161

Ohio, 71
Olano, Aureliano, Emigration Agent, 278, 279
Olano, Captain Aureliano, 227
Olivaud, Captain J., 164
Olyphant and Co., American steamship company, 315
Omba, 214
Omega, 338
Onate, Captain J.D., 271, 274
Onrust, 228, 342
Opossum HMS, 270
Oquendo, 40
Oracle, 311
Ordano, Captain Tomaz, 284
Orixa, 53
Orixa (937 tons), 267
Osollo, Captain, 39
Our Union, 242

P

Pactole, 164
Padang Panjang, 255
Paine, Captain Jean, 52
Palladium, 37
Palmerston, Lord, British Foreign Secretary, 40, 80
Panama, 105, 106, 107, 110, 338, 342
Panama (barque), 110
Papillon, 275
Paquita, 119
Paraja, Captain, 296
Paria, 207
Parker, Peter, American Acting Commissioner, 116
Parkes, Harry S., British Interpreter, Canton, 83; British Consul, Canton, 173, 174
Parliament, 261
Passos, Captain Francisco, 115
Pastor, Juan, Peruvian Vice Consul, 239
Paulsen, Captain N., 49
Pauncefote, Julian, Attorney General, Hong Kong, 286
Pax, Paul, Australian journalist, 44
Pearce, Henrique W., Emigration Agent, 170
Peck, Captain Amos, 116
Pedder, William, Harbour Master, Hong Kong, 98
Pedro 1, 236, 248
Pedroso, Martin, Cuban planter, 40, 151, 170

464

Peerless, 243
Pellew, Dr E.B., 146
Penny, Captain M.H., 68
Pereda, Machado y Cia, Cuban importers, 109, 115, 116, 117, 119, 151, 153, 166, 178, 331
Peregrine, Captain, 159
Pereira, A. Marques, Superintendent of Chinese Emigration, 223
Perks, Captain Eduardo, 247, 312
Perry, Oliver H., American Consul, Canton, 179, 190
Perseverancia, 228, 240, 259
Perseverant, 256
Persia, 202, 204
Peru, 47, 48, 49, 51, 52, 53, 59, 60, 62, 70, 73, 74, 75, 76, 81, 83, 163, 168, 169, 171, 191, 221, 222, 225, 226, 228, 230, 231, 233, 237, 238, 239, 240, 241, 243, 245, 246, 247, 248, 249, 250, 256, 257, 262, 265, 270, 271, 273, 278, 280, 287, 289, 298, 299, 300, 302, 303, 307, 308, 309, 311, 313, 314, 315, 322, 323, 324, 326, 328, 333, 335, 336, 337, 342, 345, 346, 350, 351, 352, 355
Peru (ship), 311
Perusia, 338
Petronila, 238, 335
Pezzolo, Captain A., 229
Pielago, Mariano del, Emigration Agent, 255
Pieter Cornelis zn Hooft, 151
Pih Kwei, Governor of Canton, 173
Pillsbury, Captain Thomas, 154
Pineyro, F., Peruvian Consul, Canton, 222
Pioneer, 148, 178
Poilbout, Captain J., 262, 266
Pollock, Captain, 232
Ponte, Manuel A., Macao merchant, 240
Port de Bordeaux, 137
Port Durand, 351
Poszetto, Captain L., 147
Potts, Dr Gerald, 147, 148
Pouyallet, Captain, 146
Pratolongo, Peruvian importer, 242
Price, Captain James G., 211
Pride of the Ganges, 208
Primera de Espana, 147
Prinz Alexander, 219
Providencia, 311

Providenza, 234
Q
Queen of England, 162
Queen of the East, 206
R B Forbes, 240
R
R Pratolongo, 228, 342
R W Wood, 216
Ramsay, Captain, 43
Raunie, Captain Phillipe, 268
Raupach, Captain, 71
Ravult, Captain, 162
Red Riding Hood, 208
Red Rose, 246, 345
Reid, Captain David, 113
Reina del Oceano, 168
Remedios, Captain Valerio A., 266
Resolucao, 135
Ribeiro, Captain Antonio, 267
Richon, St. Ange, French shipowner, 162
Ritchie, A.A. & Co., 52
Robert Bowne, 62, 63, 64, 346, 347
Robert Small, 117
Robert, Captain J., 164
Robert, Captain L., 351
Robertson, Sir D. Brooke, British Consul, Shanghai, 118, 310
Robinet, William M., Hong Kong merchant, 47, 48, 57, 60, 65, 67, 68, 71, 73, 133
Robinson, Captain C., 45
Robinson, Hercules, Governor of Hong Kong, 215
Rodovalho, Captain E.A., 240
Rodrigues, Hermenegildo, Emigration Superintendent, Macao, 286
Rodriguez, Juan, Peruvian planter, 49, 138
Rohilla, 341
Rosa del Turia, 276
Rosa Elias, 64, 65
Rosa y Carmen, 227
Rosalia, 335
Rosciano, Captain Jose, 282, 284
Roscoe, 216
Rosina, 229
Rosita y Nene, 294
Rossi, Captain Francisco X., 242
Rousseau, Captain C., 160
Roxburgh Castle, 117
Royal George, 185, 186, 187
Royal Saxon, 45

Rozario, Captain, 115
Russell & Co., Hong Kong, 80
Russell, Lord John, British Foreign Minister, 165
S
Sagittaire, 158
Sagues, G., Emigration Agent, 169, 256
Salamander, HMS, 55, 90
Salamis, HMS, 270
Salvadora, 276
Sama, Sotolongo y Cia, Cuban importer, 162
Sampson, Boarding Officer, Hong Kong, 296
Sampson, British Vice Consul, Canton, 76
Sampson, Theophilus, Emigration Agent, 163, 189, 195, 206, 207, 209, 210, 211, 217, 218, 219, 263
Samuel Boddington, 93, 155, 208
Samuel Enderby, 134
San Francisco, 51, 56, 57, 62, 71, 76, 77, 105, 216, 217, 222, 230, 243, 244, 245, 271, 301, 315, 316, 341
San Juan, 311
San Juan, Captain J.F., 117, 337
Sanchez, Gomez. Peruvian Foreign Minister, 74
Sandford, Captain Joshua, 114
Santa Lucia, 179
Santos, Captain J.F. dos, 241
Sappho, 117
Saracen, 233
Sarah, 64
Sarah Chase, 261
Saul, Captain Jose Peres, 236, 262, 287, 288
Savage, Thomas, American Vice Consul, Havana, 253
Scarnichia, J.E., Port Captain Macao, 300
Schimper, Fernandez, Cuban importer, 160
Scindian, 341
Scotia, 69, 158
Sea Witch, 105, 106, 120
*Sebastopo*l, 157, 198, 208
Sellier, French shipowner, 160, 161
Sequeira, Captain C.J., 259
Serafina, 162
Serrano, Francisco, Captain-General Cuba, 164
Sevilla, 207

Sevilla, Jose, Peruvian merchant, 59, 60, 61, 64, 68, 326, 335
Sevinton, Captain, 70
Shanghai, 56, 76, 118, 193, 283, 305, 428, 430, 435
Shier, Dr David, 82
Shinkwin Lieutenant, British Army, 204
Shotwell, Captain J.M., 76, 77
Sicard, Captain Miguel, 241
Sigisbert Cezard, 154
Silva, Captain Jose da, 261
Sir George Seymour, 206
Sir Thomas Gresham, 114
Sky Lark, 117
Smale, Sir John, Chief Justice, Hong Kong, 286
Smith, Captain J.H., 204
Smith, Captain James R., 49
Solares, Bernado, Emigration Agent, 162, 164, 169
Solide, 162
Solo, 216
Somerville, Dr Thomas H., 145
Soolo, 116, 178
Sophia, 115
Sorenson, Captain J.P., 146
Sotomayor, Fevjo, Cuban planter, 40
Souza, Antonio Sergio de, Governor of Macao, 249, 296, 297
Souza, Captain E.A. da, 116, 241, 256, 351
Sovinto, 269
Spanish Royal Decree, 119, 164, 224, 253
Spartan, 46
Spartan HMS, 123
Spirit of the Times, 259
Splivalo, Captain Stephano, 230, 244
Spray of the Ocean, 216
St Croix, Captain Philip de, 200
St Iver, 287
Staghound, 160, 161
Stanley, Lord, Secretary of State for War and the Colonies, 36
Starlight, 228
Ste. Croix, 164
Steggman, Captain, 248
Straubenzee, Sir Charles, British Army, 173
Strickland, Captain Thomas, 69, 70
Succes, 147
Suffren, 37

Sulivan, British Consul, Lima, 73, 74
Sullivan, Captain Mortimer O., 75, 159, 270
Sullivan, George, British Consul Amoy, 92
Suomi, 269
Surinam, 193, 197, 208, 211, 212, 213, 214, 215, 325, 327, 328, 338, 348
Susannah, 60
Swallow, 147, 178
Swatow, 31, 46, 57, 60, 65, 66, 67, 71, 72, 75, 89, 95, 96, 98, 106, 116, 117, 119, 120, 121, 122, 124, 133, 134, 137, 145, 146, 149, 159, 160, 164, 174, 185, 198, 202, 204, 206, 217, 221, 253, 305, 320, 321, 322, 347, 353, 354
Swordfish, 125
Syme, Francis D., Emigration Agent, 33, 38, 79, 80, 89, 90, 92, 93, 109

T

Tahiti, 195, 215, 216, 229
Tait, James, Emigration Agent, 39, 65, 67, 87, 89, 109, 255
Tamaris, 268
Tampico, 229
Tarolinta, 227
Tasmania, 133, 146
Telegraph, 243
Tentam, Captain, 133
Teresita, 124
Terry, John, Peruvian shipowner, 76
Theresa (brig), 241
Theresa (Italian), 233
Theresa (Peruvian), 241
Theresa Jane, 107
Theresa Terry, 76, 77
Thetis, 57
Thomsett, H.G., Harbour Master Hong Kong, 211, 212, 214, 215, 217
Thorndike, Captain Eben A., 148; Emigration Agent, 144, 148, 190
Tinita Torices, 147
Tonnochy, Registrar General, Hong Kong, 213
Topaz, 70, 324
Torices, Rafael, Cuban importer, 120, 124, 134, 135, 138, 143, 147, 148, 149, 151, 169, 190, 331
Tramoja, Captain D., 167
Treadwell, Captain, 75

Tricolor, 211, 212
Troncoso, Narciso, Cuban importer, 163, 166, 167, 168, 169, 170, 261, 269
Turner & Co., Canton merchants, 89
Tuskina, 133
Tuton, Captain Juan A., 119
Tuton, Captain Modesto, 275
Tuton, Jose A., Emigration Agent, 170, 260, 275, 286
Twee Guzusters, 211
Twichell, Rev. J.H., 314
Twilight, 243

U

Ugarte, J.M. Emigration Agent, 168, 169 Peruvian importer, 78, 227, 238, 240
Uncowah, 170, 251, 298
Union, 313

V

Vaello, Captain M.L., 260
Vallancey, Richard, mate, *Australia*, 90, 93
Valparda, Captain A. de, 167
Vampire, 107
Van Calcar, Captain P., 75
Vargas, S.R., Emigration Agent, 134, 147, 148, 169, 178, 181, 190
Vasco de Gama, 257, 261
Vaucher Freres & Co., Hong Kong Sub-Agent, 152
Vaucher, French Vice Consul, 239
Vaux, John, British shipowner, 49
Velarde, Narciso, Portuguese Consul-General, Lima, 248, 288
Venus, 278
Veritas, 213, 214
Vermial, Captain J., 53
Versailles, 259
Viajante, 115
Victoria (barque), 115
Victoria (ship), 221
Victory, 54, 55, 64, 322
Vidaurrazaga, Captain A.V., 274
Vigoureux, Captain le, 284
Vildosola, Captain E. de, 271
Villa de Comillas, 255
Ville d'Agen, 239
Ville de Dieppe, 160
Ville de Grenade, 298
Ville de Lima, 161, 179
Ville de St Lo, 157, 217
Ville, A.G. de, Emigration Agent, 157, 160, 239, 255

Villeta, Captain J., 166
Villoldo, Wardrop y Cia, Cuban importers, 109, 110, 111, 114, 115, 124, 330, 331
Vincent, Captain E., 56, 57, 71
Vines, Captain D.F., 276
Violette, 217
Vistula, 271, 282, 287
Vixen, 293
Voss, Captain A.F., 215
Vriendschap, 125

W

Walcott, Stephen, CLEC Secretary, 96, 204
Wanata, 203
Wandering Jew, 118, 354
Wang, Sub-Prefect of Amoy, 90
Wang-te-Chang, Jamaican interpreter, 107
War Hawk, 117
Ward, John E., American Envoy Extraordinary, 182, 183
Warner, Thornton, Emigration Agent, 217
Warwick, Captain, 270
Waverly, 65, 66, 67, 117
Weasel , HMS, 156
Wellesley, 341
Wellman, Captain, 65
Wells, Captain, 49
West India Committee, 34, 36, 37, 79, 102, 185, 187
West, Captain Joseph, 209
Westward Ho, 75, 78, 151, 178, 222, 240, 343, 345, 350
Whampoa, 48, 49, 71, 75, 76, 78, 83, 96, 97, 98, 99, 134, 143, 147, 148, 149, 157, 160, 163, 164, 168, 175, 176, 178, 179, 180, 182, 184, 189, 190, 191, 193, 194, 197, 198, 206, 207, 208, 215, 219, 223, 231, 276, 281, 310, 323, 338, 349
Whirlwind, 195, 208, 212
White Cloud, 290
White Falcon, 232
White, Captain (American), 159
White, Captain Thomas B., 51, 60
White, James T., Emigration Agent, 79, 96, 98, 103, 104, 187, 206
Wild, Captain W., 98
Wiles, Captain Lewin, 69, 70
Williams, Samuel Wells, American Chargé d'Affaires, 183, 304
Williamsburgh, 105

Williamson, Captain, 42
Wilson, Captain Alexander, 134, 154
Wilson, Captain C.J.H., 60
Winchester, Charles A.: Acting British Consul Foochow, 147; Acting British Consul, Canton, 197; British Doctor, Amoy, 85, 86, 101, 104
Winged Racer, 67, 75, 335
Witch of the Waves, 47
Wodehouse, P.E., Governor of British Guiana, 184
Wohang, Hong Kong agent, 216
Wood, Captain John, 155
Wooldridge, Chief Mate E. Gurney, 61, 62
Worth, Captain, 216
Wortley, Samuel S., Jamaican merchant, 107

Y

Ybanes, Cuban importer, 171
Ye Ming Chen, Governor of Canton, 173
Yriberri, Captain Ignacio, 163, 282, 346, 351
Yrurac Bat, 276
Yturraide, C.J., Emigration Agent, 144
Yung Wing, Commissioner Chinese Educational Commission, 307, 313
Zangronis, Y.M. Cuban importer, 161, 162, 163, 164, 169
Zetland, 75
Zouave, 206
Zulueta, Captain Raymundo de, 261
Zulueta, Julian, Cuban planter, 39, 40, 119, 151, 155

Royal Asiatic Society Hong Kong Studies Series

The Royal Asiatic Society Hong Kong Studies series is designed to make widely available important contributions on the local history, culture and society of Hong Kong and the surrounding region. Generous support from the Sir Lindsay and Lady May Ride Memorial Fund makes it possible to publish a series of high-quality works that will be of lasting appeal and value to all, both scholars and informed general readers, who share a deeper interest in and enthusiasm for the area.

Titles in the RAS Hong Kong Studies Series

A Faithful Record of the Lisbon Maru *Incident* Brian Finch

Ancestral Images: A Hong Kong Collection Hugh Baker

Cantonese Society in Hong Kong and Singapore Marjorie Topley, Jean De Bernardi (ed.)

Custom, Land and Livelihood in Rural South China 1750-1950 Patrick Hase

Dragon and the Crown. Hong Kong Memoirs Stanley Kwan with Nicole Kwan

Early China Coast Meteorology. The Role of HK 1882-1912 Kevin MacKeown

East River Column. Hong Kong Guerrillas in the Second World War and After Chan Sui Jeung

Escape from Hong Kong: Admiral Chan Chak's Christmas Day Dash, 1941 Tim Luard

For Gods, Ghosts and Ancestors Janet Scott

Forgotten Souls: The Social History of Hong Kong Cemetery 1845-1918 Patricia Lim

Governors, Politics and the Colonial Office Gavin Ure

Hong Kong Internment 1942-45. Life in the Japanese Civilian Camp at Stanley Geoffrey Emerson

Ireland's Imperial Mandarin. Sir Robert Hart. Mark O'Neill

Policing Hong Kong – An Irish History Patricia O'Sullivan

Portugal, China and the Macau Negotiations 1986-1999 Carmen Mendes

Public Success, Private Sorrow. The Life and Times of Charles Henry Brewitt Taylor Cyril Cannon

Reluctant Heroes. Rickshaw Pullers in Hong Kong and Canton 1874-1954 Fung Chi Ming

Resist to the End. Hong Kong 1941-1945 Charles Barman, Ray Barman (ed.)

Scottish Mandarin. The Life and Times of Sir Reginald Johnston Shiona Airlie

Six Day War of 1899. Hong Kong in the Age of Imperialism Patrick Hase

Southern District Officer Reports. Islands and Villages in Rural Hong Kong John Strickland (ed.)

The Lone Flag. Memoir of the British Consul in Macau during World War II John Reeves

Watching Over Hong Kong. Private Policing 1841-1941 Sheila Hamilton

Select Titles From Proverse Hong Kong

Jean Berlie, *The Chinese of Macau a Decade after the Handover.*

Gillian Bickley, Ed., *The Complete Court Cases of Magistrate Frederick Stewart.*

—*The Development of Education in Hong Kong, 1841-1898.*

—*A Magistrate's Court in Nineteenth Century Hong Kong,* 1st ed. 2005, 2nd ed. 2009.

—*Through American Eyes: The Journals (18 May 1859 - 1 September 1860) Of George Washington (Farley) Heard (1837-1875).*

—*Journeys with a Mission: Travel Journals of The Right Revd George Smith (1815-1871) first Bishop of Victoria (Hong Kong) (1849-1865).*

— *The Golden Needle: the Biography of Frederick Stewart (1836-1889)*

Richard Collingwood-Selby and Gillian Bickley, Eds, *In Time of War* (Diary entries and letters by Lt. Cmdr. Henry C.S. Collingwood-Selby, R.N. (1898-1992)).

Jun Fang and Lifang He, *The Romance Of A Literatus And His Concubine In Seventeenth-Century China.* Annotated translation into English of "Reminiscences Of The Plum-shaded Convent" (Yingmeian Yiyu 影梅庵憶語) by Mao Xiang (1611-1693) with the original Chinese text.

Brian Finch, *A Faithful Record Of The "Lisbon Maru" Incident.* (Translation from Chinese with additional material.)

James McCarthy, *The Diplomat of Kashgar: A Very Special Agent. The Life of Sir George Macartney, 18 January 1867 to 19 May 1945.*

Find Out More About Proverse Authors, Books, International Prizes, And Events

Visit our website:
http://www.proversepublishing.com
Visit our distributor's website: www.cup.cuhk.edu.hk

<www.twitter.com/ProverseBooks>

"Like" us on www.facebook.com/ProversePress
Request our free E-Newsletter
Send your request to info@proversepublishing.com.

Availability
Most books are available in Hong Kong and world-wide
from our Hong Kong based Distributor,
The Chinese University Press of Hong Kong,
The Chinese University of Hong Kong, Shatin, NT,
Hong Kong SAR, China.
Website: Web: www.cup.cuhk.edu.hk

All titles are available from Proverse Hong Kong
http://www.proversepublishing.com
and the Proverse Hong Kong UK-based Distributor.
We have stock-holding retailers in Hong Kong,
Canada (Elizabeth Campbell Books),
Andorra (Llibreria La Puça, La Llibreria).
Orders can be made from bookshops
in the UK and elsewhere.

Ebooks
Most Proverse titles are available also as Ebooks.

www.ingramcontent.com/pod-product-compliance
Lightning Source LLC
Chambersburg PA
CBHW051347290426
44108CB00015B/1911